RESISTING THE EUROPEAN COURT OF JUSTICE

The European Union's (EU's) powerful legal framework drives the process of European integration. The European Court of Justice (ECJ) has established a uniquely effective supranational legal order, beyond the original wording of the Treaties of Rome and transforming our traditional understanding of international law. This work investigates how these fundamental transformations in the European legal system were received in one of the most important member states, Germany. On the one hand, Germany has been highly supportive of political and economic integration; yet, on the other, a fundamental pillar of the postwar German identity was the integrity of its constitutional order. How did a state whose constitution was so essential to its self-understanding subscribe to the constitutional practice of EU law, which challenged precisely this aspect of its identity? How did a country that could not say "no" to Europe become the member state most reluctant to accept the new power of the ECJ?

Bill Davies is a legal historian focusing on the development of a constitutional practice of law in the European Union. He holds a PhD from King's College London and currently works as an Assistant Professor in Justice, Law, and Society in the School of Public Affairs at American University in Washington, DC. He has published on the German role in the formation of the European legal system in the *Journal of European Integration History* and the *Contemporary European History Journal*.

Resisting the European Court of Justice

WEST GERMANY'S CONFRONTATION WITH
EUROPEAN LAW, 1949–1979

BILL DAVIES

American University

CAMBRIDGE
UNIVERSITY PRESS

CAMBRIDGE
UNIVERSITY PRESS

32 Avenue of the Americas, New York NY 10013-2473, USA

Cambridge University Press is part of the University of Cambridge.

It furthers the University's mission by disseminating knowledge in the pursuit of education, learning and research at the highest international levels of excellence.

www.cambridge.org
Information on this title: www.cambridge.org/9781107685352

First published 2012
First paperback edition 2013

A catalogue record for this publication is available from the British Library

Library of Congress Cataloguing in Publication data
Davies, Bill, 1979–
  Resisting the European Court of Justice : West Germany's confrontation with European law, 1949–1979 / Bill Davies.
    p.   cm.
  Includes bibliographical references and index.
  ISBN 978-1-107-02453-3 (hardback : alk. paper)
  1. Conflict of laws – Jurisdiction – Germany (West) – History.   2. Court of Justice of the European Communities.   3. Constitutional law – Germany (West) – History.   4. International and municipal law – European Union countries.   5. Law – European Union countries – International unification.   6. Jurisdiction – European Union countries.   I. Title.
  KK961.7.D38   2012
  341.242'22840943–dc23   2012012068

ISBN 978-1-107-02453-3 Hardback
ISBN 978-1-107-68535-2 Paperback

For Eunice and Amelie

Contents

Preface

The European Union's (EU's) powerful legal framework has proven to be the vanguard moment in the process of European integration. Through the doctrines of direct effect (1963) and primacy (1964), the European Court of Justice (ECJ) sought to establish an effective and powerful supranational legal order, far beyond the original wording of the Treaties of Rome. Whereas scholars have analyzed the evolution of EU law and built models to explain the ECJ's success, none has examined how the member states received this process at a time when the then–European Community was undergoing a number of difficult political and economic crises through the historian's lens.

This book investigates how these fundamental transformations in the European legal system were received at the national level, specifically, in one of the European Union's most important member states, the Federal Republic of Germany. This case provides the opportunity to examine a fascinating paradox: On the one hand, Germany has been regarded as highly supportive of political and economic integration; yet, on the other, a fundamental pillar of the postwar German identity was the integrity of its national constitutional order. How did a state whose constitution was so essential to its political and cultural self-understanding subscribe to the constitutionalization of European Community law, which challenged precisely this aspect of its identity?

Through close documentation of the reception process in West Germany, this book shows for the first time how the resistance offered by the highest echelons of the German judiciary had its origins in broader social discourse, with academic and public opinion in particular opposed to the constitutional practice. It demonstrates that, while supportive of other aspects of integration, West Germans were highly critical of the apparent danger posed by the ECJ's doctrines to the national constitution. As government policy toward the ECJ remained unchanged, the Federal Constitutional Court became the only means of articulating dissent to legal integration. Most important, this resistance mattered far beyond expectations, affecting several critically important changes in European governance at the end of the 1970s.

Acknowledgments

This book could not have been completed without the financial and academic support of the Departments of German and of European Studies and the School of Humanities at King's College London, the School of Public Affairs at American University, and the American Consortium on European Studies (ACES) in Washington, DC. I hope that this work provides you with some reward for the assistance and encouragement you have so generously given. I would like specifically to thank Chris Thornhill, Robert Weninger, Michelle Egan, Josh Barkan, Fernanda Nicola, Jon Gould, and Mana Zarinejad for their effort in providing advice, commentaries, and encouragement over the past years. Chana Barron is, in addition, a truly remarkable colleague and friend, who has been tireless in her support of this work.

I thank Karen Alter and Piers Ludlow for working hard to read and improve this manuscript. You gave me one of the most terrifying and most fulfilling experiences one might ask for as a scholar during my defense of the groundwork for this book. Thank you to my other colleagues, most especially Morten Rasmussen, Peter Lindseth, and Anne Boerger, for the opportunity to discuss much of this work with you.

I owe a huge debt of gratitude to the Studienstiftung des Berliner Abgeordnetenhauses for the generous scholarship and housing they provided, making the time spent in German archives so much easier and more pleasant. In particular, I would like to thank Petra Fritsche, Manuela Ebel, and Professors Ingolf Pernice and Gert-Joachim Glaeßner for their invaluable assistance during my time in Berlin. The Walter-Hallstein-Institut in Berlin provided much help and support during my frequent trips to the German capital.

Many thanks for the invaluable work of the many archivists and numerous support staff at the Politisches Archiv des Auswärtiges Amt, Bundesarchiv, Historical Archives of the European Commission, Konrad-Adenauer-Stiftung, Friedrich-Ebert-Stiftung, and the Press and Information Office of the German Federal Government.

Thank you to my friends, who have listened and read beyond the call of duty and encouraged and strengthened me constantly. Numbered in that group is my doctoral supervisor, Dr Jan Palmowski. His patience, support, and belief in my work have been beyond value. I will genuinely be eternally thankful.

Finally to my family: Nothing would be possible without you.

Abbreviations

AG	Advocate General
ASEL	Academic Society for European Law
BL	Basic Law (Grundgesetz)
CDU	Christian Democratic Union of Germany
DGB	The Confederation of German Trade Unions (Deutscher Gewerkschaftsbund)
EC	European Community
ECJ	European Court of Justice
ECSC	European Coal and Steel Community
EDC	European Defence Community
EPC	European Political Community
FAC	Frankfurt Administrative Court
FAZ	Frankfurter Allgemeine Zeitung
FCC	Federal Constitutional Court of West Germany (Bundesverfassungsgericht)
FPD	Free Democratic Party of Germany
FRG	Federal Republic of Germany (Bundesrepublik Deutschland)
ITL	Integration through Law
MEP	Member of the European Parliament
RTC	Rhineland Tax Court
SPD	Social Democratic Party of Germany
VVDStRL	Publication of the Association of German Public Law Teachers

Archives Consulted

AdsD   Archive of Social Democracy – Friedrich-Ebert-Stiftung
BA   German Federal Archive in Koblenz
BPA   Press and Information Office of the Federal Government
ECH   European Commission Historical Archive
FES   Friedrich Ebert Foundation
KAS   Archive of Christian Democratic Politics of the Konrad Adenauer
        Foundation
PAA   Political Archive of the German Foreign Ministry

Cases

FEDERAL CONSTITUTIONAL COURT DECISIONS

2 BvE 4/52 – *EDC Treaty*, 7 March 1953 – BVerfGE 2, 143
2 BvL 29/63 – *Tax on Malt Barley*, 5 July 1967 – BVerfGE 22, 134
1 BvR 248/63 & 216/6 – *European Regulations*, 18 October 1967 – BVerfGE 22, 293
2 BvR 225/69 – *Milk powder*, 9 June 1971 – BVerfGE 31, 145
2 BvF 1/73 – *Basic Treaty*, 31 July 1973 – BVerfGE 36, 1
2 BvL 52/71 – *Solange I*, 29 May 1974 – BVerfGE 37, 271
2 BvL 6/77 – *Perhaps*, 25 July 1979 – BVerfGE 52, 187
2 BvR 197/83 – *Solange II*, 22 October 1986 – BVerfGE 73, 339
2 BvR 2134, 2159/92 – *Maastricht*, 12 October 1993 – BVerfGE 89, 155
2 BvE 2/08, 2 BvE 5/08, 2 BvR 1010/08, 2 BvR 1022/08, 2 BvR 1259/08, 2 BvR 182/09 – *Lisbon*, 30 June 2009 – BVerfGE 123, 267
2 BvR 987/10, 2 BvR 1485/10, 2 BvR 1099/10 – *Euro Bailout*, 7 September 2011

OTHER DECISIONS:

Decisions of the Italian Constitutional Court:

7 March 1964, n. 14, *Costa/ENEL, in Giur. Cost.*, 129
27 December 1973, n. 183, *Frontini e a., in Giur. Cost.*, 2401
30 October 1975, n. 232, *Società industrie chimiche Italia centrale (I.C.I.C.), in Giur. Cost.* 2211

Decisions of the United States Supreme Court:

Marbury v. Madison, 5 U.S. (Cranch 1) 137 (1803)
Dred Scott v. Sandford, 60 U.S. 393 (1857)
Brown v. Board of Education of Topeka, 347 U.S. 483 (1954)

Decisions of the Berlin State Court:

Ruckerstattungssache Krüger u.a/Deutsches Reich – 151/155/157/142 WGK 69/57 und 161/57 (Landgericht Berlin)

Texts of Often Mentioned Constitutional Articles

ARTICLE 24: TRANSFER OF SOVEREIGNTY
(IN PREAMENDMENT FORM)

(i) The Federation may by a law transfer sovereign powers to international organizations.

(ii) With a view to maintaining peace, the Federation may enter into a system of mutual collective security; in doing so it shall consent to such limitations upon its sovereign powers as will bring about and secure a lasting peace in Europe and among the nations of the world.

(iii) For the settlement of disputes between states, the Federation shall accede to agreements providing for general, comprehensive and compulsory international arbitration.

ARTICLE 25: INTERNATIONAL LAW AND FEDERAL LAW

The general rules of international law shall be an integral part of federal law. They shall take precedence over the laws and directly create rights and duties for the inhabitants of the federal territory.

ARTICLE 79 (III): AMENDMENT OF THE BASIC LAW

Amendments to this Basic Law affecting the division of the Federation into *Länder*, their participation on principle in the legislative process, or the principles laid down in Articles 1 and 20 shall be inadmissible.

Adapted from official English translation: https://www.btg-bestellservice.de/pdf/80201000.pdf.

1

Between Sovereignty and Integration

West Germany, European Integration, and the Constitutionalization of European Law

The European Economic Community is a remarkable legal phenomenon. It is a creation of law; it is a source of law; and it is a legal system.... Previous attempts to unify Europe depended on force or conquest.... The majesty of the law is to achieve what centuries of "blood and iron" could not.

Walter Hallstein, 1972[1]

The establishment of the primacy and direct effectiveness of the law of the European Communities in the early 1960s over and against the law of the Member States is the most radical moment in the European integration project. The European Court of Justice's (ECJ's) now-famous *Van Gend*[2] and *Costa v. E.N.E.L.*[3] decisions laid the foundations for the effective legal framework of the contemporary European Union. At the same time, they represented a massive inroad into the sovereign legal independence of the Member States and boldly positioned the Court as Europe's supreme judicial voice. In fact, in its *Internationale Handelsgesellschaft* ruling in the early 1970s, the ECJ went further still, declaring the primacy of European law unbound even by national constitutions.[4] This "foundational" phase of integration ushered in the "constitutionalization" of European law,[5] and for some contemporaries it seemed as if the ECJ had become Europe's "Super Constitutional Court."[6] These developments are especially intriguing to the historian of European integration because it was in this very same era that

---

[1] Walter Hallstein, *Europe in the Making* (London: Allen and Unwin, 1972), p 30.
[2] Case 26/62 *Van Gend vs. Nederlandse Administratie der Belastingen* [1963] European Court Report 1.
[3] Case 06/64 *Costa vs. ENEL* [1964] European Court Report 585.
[4] Case 11/70 *Internationale Handelsgesellschaft vs. Einfuhr- und Vorratsstelle für Getriede und Futtermittel* [1970] European Court Report 1125.
[5] Joseph Weiler, *The Constitution of Europe: "Do the New Clothes Have an Emperor?" and Other Essays on European Integration* (Cambridge; New York: Cambridge University Press, 1999).
[6] This description ("*Superverfassungsgericht*") appeared in an article of the *Frankfurter Allgemeine Zeitung*, a leading German broadsheet, on 8 October 1968.

the political atmosphere in the then-Communities became particularly sour and hostile. With the veto of British accession and the Gaullist boycott of the Council of Ministers institutions in the "Empty Chair Crisis," the goal of uniting the states of Western Europe seemed to be under an existential threat. Moreover, if we consider the profound difficulties in agreeing to a constitutional document experienced by the contemporary European Union, we must ask ourselves, How then did the ECJ make this happen? Why, if the Member States of the period were prepared to go to the brink politically and to square up so resolutely against the supranational ambitions of the European Commission, was so little resistance manifest in reining in the ECJ's expansive, constitutional interpretation of the Communities' foundational documents?

The question as to why the ECJ appeared so successful in driving a federalizing agenda in the legal realm despite the seemingly recalcitrant political atmosphere of the mid-1960s and since, has become recurrent in political and legal sciences ever since. Legal theorists, particularly in the early analyses of the Court's work, propagated the idea that the expansion of the ECJ's power represented a wholly natural legal interpretation of the Treaties of Rome. Its articulation in the ECJ's jurisprudence had saved the process of integration from its political opponents and the vagaries of economic cycles.[7] Others highlighted how the ECJ's activism had led the court too far astray from its original purpose, imagining a role for itself beyond any legal or political mandate.[8] Merging the lines between legal theory and political science, scholars during the 1980s and 1990s frequently made mention of a "constitutionalization" paradigm,[9] describing the functioning of EU and national law as akin to that of a federal constitutional order and explainable only through an understanding of the broader political context. Such models – usually grouped together under the heading of "Integration through Law" (ITL) theories[10] – made assertions about the strategic nature of the ECJ's choices,[11] or the influence of empowered

---

[7] Eric Stein, "Lawyers, Judges and the Making of a Transnational Constitution," *American Journal of International Law* 75.1 (1981); Pierre Pescatore, "Aspects of the the Court of Justice of the European Communities of Interest from the Point of View of International Law," *Zeitschrift fur auslandisches offentliches Recht un Volkerrecht* (1972).

[8] Hjalte Rasmussen, *On Law and Policy in the European Court of Justice: A Comparative Study in Judicial Policymaking* (Dordrecht; Boston; Lancaster: Martinus Nijhoff Publishers, 1986).

[9] JHH Weiler, *The Constitution of Europe – "Do the New Clothes Have an Emperor?" and Other Essays on European Integration* (Cambridge: Cambridge University Press, 1999).

[10] Mauro Cappelletti, Monica Seccombe and Joseph Weiler, *Integration through Law: Europe and the American Federal Experience*, Series a, Law/European University Institute = Series a, Droit/Institut Universitaire Européen (Berlin; New York: W de Gruyter, 1985).

[11] Geoffrey Garrett, "The Politics of Legal Integration in the European Union," *International Organisation* 49.1995 (1995); Geoffrey Garrett, Daniel R Keleman and Heiner Schulz, "The European Court of Justice, National Governments and Legal Integration in the European Union," *International Organisation* 52.1 (1998); Andrew Moravcsik, *The Choice for Europe: Social Purpose and the State Power from Messina to Maastricht* (London: UCL Press, 1998).

subnational actors,[12] or the willingness on the part of Member States to accept less escape from their legal obligations in exchange for greater voice in the formation of those laws.[13] Most scholars have seen legal integration as a self-propelled process, continually augmented by the compounding influence of the European judicial system.[14] Others have viewed the Court's development as a necessary prerequisite for successful intergovernmental bargaining.[15] While these models have provoked a huge amount of debate among scholars of the European Union, and indeed inspired this particular study, their insights have never been put under empirically grounded historical scrutiny. In other words, no matter how insightful and influential these models have been, until they stand against what really went on during the 1960s and 1970s in terms of legal integration, they will always remain at a level of unsatisfying abstraction.

Recently, there has been a turning point in how we study the European Court of Justice and the development of the European legal system. Not only has the concept of a constitutionalization paradigm come under question,[16] but the ongoing release of primary sources from national archives has allowed for the initial testing of the Integration through Law theories.[17] Historians are now beginning to come to grips

---

[12] Anne Marie Burley and Walter Mattli, "Europe before the Court: A Political Theory of Legal Integration," *International Organisation* 47 (1993); Walter Mattli and Anne-Marie Slaughter, "Revisiting the European Court of Justice," *International Organisation* 52.1 (1998); Walter Mattli and Anne-Marie Slaughter, "Law and Politics in the European Union: A Reply to Garrett," *International Organisation* 49.1 (1995); Walter Mattli and Anne-Marie Slaughter, "The Role of National Courts in the Process of European Integration: Accounting for Judicial Preferences and Constraints," *The European Courts and the National Courts – Doctrine and Jurisprudence: Legal Change in Its Social Context*, ed. Anne-Marie Slaughter, Alex Stone-Sweet and JHH Weiler (Oxford: Hart Publishing, 1998).

[13] Weiler, *The Constitution of Europe: "Do the New Clothes Have an Emperor?" And Other Essays on European Integration.*

[14] Alec Stone-Sweet, *Governing with Judges: Constitutional Politics in Europe* (Oxford: Oxford University Press, 2000); Alec Stone-Sweet, "Path Dependence, Precedent and Judicial Power," *On Law, Politics, and Judicialization*, ed. Martin Shapiro and Alex Stone-Sweet (Oxford: Oxford University Press, 2002); Burley and Mattli, "Europe before the Court: A Political Theory of Legal Integration"; Garrett, Keleman and Schulz, "The European Court of Justice, National Governments and Legal Integration in the European Union."

[15] Moravcsik, *The Choice for Europe: Social Purpose and the State Power from Messina to Maastricht*; Garrett, "The Politics of Legal Integration in the European Union"; Garrett, Keleman and Schulz, "The European Court of Justice, National Governments and Legal Integration in the European Union."

[16] Morten Rasmussen, "Constructing and Deconstructing European 'Constitutional' European Law: Some Reflections on How to Study the History of European Law," *Europe: The New Legal Realism*, ed. Karsten Hagel-Sørensen, Henning Koch, Ulrich Haltern and Joseph Weiler (Aarhus: DJØF Publishing, 2010); Antoine Vauchez, "The Transnational Politics of Judicialization: Van Gend En Loos and the Making of EU Polity," *European Law Journal* 16.1 (2010).

[17] See, for instance, the special edition of the *Journal of European Integration* 2008, vol. 14, number 2; some of the contributions to Wolfram Kaiser, Brigitte Leucht and Morten Rasmussen, *The History of the European Union: Origins of a Trans- and Supranational Polity 1950–72*, Routledge/Uaces

with the origins of the ECJ in the Rome Treaties[18] and how its early personnel[19] and interinstitutional and transnational relationships[20] were instrumental in prompting the Court's activism. These historical accounts, as well as this one, refer to the "constitutional practice of European law,"[21] rather than the "constitutionalization," to reflect the complicated and ongoing dispute about the nature of European law. Peter Lindseth has recently completed a provocative cross-disciplinary work with strong historical foundations, which locates the European integration in longer-term trends of delegation of authority,[22] which ultimately is at the expense of parliamentary control.[23] Contemporary complaints about the lack of democratic control over the institutions of the European Union have their origin in this movement away from the locus of popular sovereignty, and the ECJ's massive expansionism serves to exacerbate and be symptomatic of this problem still further. Ultimately, however, the enigma of the ECJ's expansion can only be explained by looking at how the Member States "received" the ECJ's decisions, not only within the courtroom, but, much more crucially, among the public and academia and within the government machinery itself. Such "reception studies" are now beginning to be undertaken.[24] It is in these three interconnected realms of public life that the debates that would make or break the ECJ took place.

At the center of the concept of a reception study is the idea that each Member State represents a distinctive set of contextual, cultural, and legal circumstances that

---

Contemporary European Studies Series 7 (New York: Routledge, 2009); and a new edition of the *Contemporary European History* journal, forthcoming in 2012.

[18] Anne Boerger, "La Cour de Justice dans les Négociations du Traité de Paris Instituant La Ceca," *Journal of European Integration History* 14.2 (2008).

[19] Cohen and Antonin, *Scarlet Robes, Dark Suits: The Social Recruitment of the European Court of Justice* (Florence: European University Institute [EUI], Robert Schuman Centre of Advanced Studies [RSCAS], 2008).

[20] Rasmussen, "Constructing and Deconstructing European 'Constitutional' European Law: Some Reflections on How to Study the History of European Law"; Morten Rasmussen, "Exploring the Secret History of the Legal Service of the European Executives, 1952–1967," *Contemporary European History*, forthcoming in 2011.

[21] *Contemporary European History Journal*, forthcoming in 2012.

[22] Peter L Lindseth, *Power and Legitimacy: Reconciling Europe and the Nation-State* (Oxford; New York: Oxford University Press, 2010).

[23] For an account of the deliberate sidelining of the West German Bundestag by the executive branch, see Deniz Alkan, "Der Duldsame Souverän: Zur Haltung des Deutschen Bundestags Gegenüber der Rechtlichen Integration Europas durch die Rechtsprechungdes Europäischen Gerichtshofs 1963–1978," dissertation, Heinrich-Heine-Universität 2011.

[24] Bill Davies, "Constitutionalising the European Community: West Germany between Legal Sovereignty and European Integration, 1949–1975," dissertation, King's College London, 2007; Bill Davies, "Meek Acceptance? The West German Ministeries' Reaction to the *Van Gend En Loos* and *Costa* Decisions," *Journal of European Integration History* 14.2 (2008). See also "Reception Studies" on France by Julie Bailleux (University of Panthéon Sorbonne, forthcoming), on the Netherlands by Jieskje Hollander (University of Groningen), and on the United Kingdom by this author.

determine the willingness and the conditions under which a particular Member State's government and judiciary will submit to the primacy of European law. These factors include elite perceptions of national interest, varying domestic institutional constellations, and oscillating streams of public and intellectual opinion toward the ECJ and European integration. This latter point – the importance of public and intellectual discourse beyond the courtroom – is of particular importance. Even when there have been explicit calls to look "beyond the law" when examining the ECJ and its reception, these have been limited to examining "social and economic data," such as trade figures, preliminary ruling references to the ECJ, and Member State population size.[25] There is, however, a rich vein of media and academic material that not only relates specifically to the attempt to constitutionalize European law, but also was instrumental in determining the judicial reception in the Member States.[26] Indeed, this reception study historiography reveals a more nuanced reality than can be readily incorporated into any generalizing model and, most decisively, that the reception process has mattered in the formation of the European legal system. Indeed, this book will chart an important change in the judicial governance of the European Union as a direct and immediate response to concerns expressed in Member States beyond the simple intracourt dialogue highlighted elsewhere.[27]

It is the aim of this book to engage with and supplement the preexisting models that have explained European legal integration. To do so, it will incorporate an unseen and comprehensive set of new materials documenting government archives,

---

[25] Alec Stone-Sweet and Thomas L Brunell, "The European Court and the National Courts: A Statistical Analysis of Preliminary References 1961–1995," *Journal of European Public Policy* 5 (1998); Alec Stone-Sweet and Thomas L Brunell, "The European Court, National Judges, and Legal Integration: A Researcher's Guide to the Data Set on Preliminary References in Ec Law 1958–98," *European Law Journal* 6.2 (2000).

[26] This approach to the formation of the European legal arena works on the presumption that judicial decision making stands in dialectical correlation with broader social discourse, simultaneously mirroring and informing debates in wider society, and that legitimate judgment requires a delicate reconciliation of legal rationale with the reason of popular will. Paul W Kahn, *The Cultural Study of Law: Reconstructing Legal Scholarship* (Chicago: University of Chicago Press, 1999). In essence, neither the judge nor the courtroom, be it national or supranational, exists in a vacuum, immune to broader historic and political forces and public and intellectual opinion. This is not to make the questionable assertion that judges of the highest courts across Europe pander to public opinion in their decision making, but rather that as participants in as well as keen, well-educated observers of public and academic discourse on legal matters, judges are fully aware of varying trends and groundswells of support or resistance to certain ideas and standards. If there are long-standing and well-articulated concerns in society about a certain legal issue, it is hardly realistic to think that judges neither are aware of them nor include them in some way in that decision-making rationale.

[27] Alec Stone-Sweet, "Constitutional Dialogue in the European Community," *The European Courts and National Courts – Doctrine and Jurisprudence: Legal Change in Its Social Context*, ed. Anne-Marie Slaughter, Alex Stone-Sweet and JHH Weiler (Oxford: Hart Publishing, 1998); Karen Alter, *Establishing the Supremacy of European Law: The Making of an International Rule of Law in Europe*, Oxford Studies in European Law (Oxford; New York: Oxford University Press, 2001).

public opinion, academic discourse, and courtroom argument surrounding the reception of European legal primacy in the Federal Republic of Germany (FRG). This is a particularly interesting choice of study as the courts in the FRG were both the first to accept the doctrine of primacy and to place conditions on it and thereby question the legitimacy of the ECJ, all in the space of seven years (1967–74). This conditional acceptance offered by the West German judiciary on the issue of European legal primacy was not just a grab for power, a question of who was to have the final say on the law, as has been suggested elsewhere.[28] Instead, it was reflective of a broader unease with the path taken toward a European constitutional system in West German society, which could not, nor wanted to, be articulated by the FRG's political elites. As such, the judiciary, and particularly its highest echelons, became the means of expressing resistance to the process. Because of the claims to objective legal interpretation, the judiciary was less open to criticisms of being nationalist or anti-European.

This book will argue two points, namely, that broader social discourse beyond the courtroom was crucial in framing West German judicial resistance to the ECJ and that this resistance truly mattered and was instrumental in reshaping governance by the European institutions. To be more precise, the first contention will demonstrate that the debates in legal academia from the 1950s onward were crucial in defining the intellectual parameters and terminology for the resistance to the constitutional practice. Second, the articulated public grievances with the same process provided West German judges with the mandate to try to impose their will on the European system. The specific characteristics of the FCC's adjudication – a heavy reliance on legal academic opinion, a well-identified "delay tactic" used to allow legal academic debates to reach an equilibrium, and the unusual predominance of academics as judges – as well as awareness and even participation in public media debates on the issue of European law by the FCC judges suggest strongly that these broader discourses beyond the law played some role in the deliberations of the Court – even if the justices would never admit to this. Moreover, in the face of a passive and broadly prointegration government, the FCC knew that it was the one institution capable of articulating the broadly held concerns in the academy and the media. It chose to pick a fight with the government and with Europe despite the difficulties this would raise. In this, they were successful. Concerns resulting from the acceptance of European legal primacy, particularly about fundamental rights protection, were institutionalized not just legally, but *politically* too,

---

[28]   JHH Weiler and Ulrich Haltern, "Constitutional or International? The Foundations of the Community Legal Order and the Question of Judicial Kompetenz-Kompetenz," *The European Courts and National Courts – Doctrine and Jurisprudence: Legal Change in Its Social Context*, ed. Anne-Marie Slaughter, Alex Stone-Sweet and JHH Weiler (Oxford: Hart Publishing, 1998).

into a new mode of European governance.[29] This resulted not only in the modification of ECJ jurisprudence in the *Hauer* decision of 1979,[30] but most importantly in the binding of the Community's political institutions to the European Convention of Human Rights (ECHR) in 1977.[31] The documentation of resistance and "push back" at the national level and a clear and direct response by the European institutions in reaching a workable compromise recasts our understanding of the dynamics of European legal integration. Resistance and response to legal integration have therefore led to a nonlinear acceptance of the ECJ's jurisprudence by national actors across time and across geography.[32] What exists across Europe is a patchwork, contingent judicial settlement, in which different Member States impose differing conditions on the acceptance of legal primacy, dependent on the broader reception of the ECJ, European integration, and European law at that given time. Legal integration is only partially self-propelling, and what the historical approach reveals is a much more timid set of European institutions than we have come to expect, afraid of, in this particular case, West German recalcitrance and willing to reach important compromises in order to save face and garner support. Here for the first time was a national judiciary "pushing back" against the ECJ – and making a real, institutionalized difference in doing so. We can no longer think of the European legal order as a creation of the ECJ. We now have documented evidence to show the judicial and political impact made by the resistance of national judiciaries to the constitutional practice.

BETWEEN SOVEREIGNTY AND INTEGRATION: WEST GERMANY AND EUROPE

As the most populous and economically muscular Member State, the FRG is essential to the functioning and financing of the European integration project. In reverse, European integration has been of equal necessity to the Federal Republic. Emerging from the horrors of the 1940s, the battered, occupied, and divided German state was

---

[29] This offers a differing account from standard narrative, in which the *Solange* decision is responded to by the ECJ only through its *Hauer* decision. Frank Schimmelfennig, "Competition and Community: Constitutional Courts, Rhetorical Action, and the Institutionalization of Human Rights in the European Union," *Journal of European Public Policy* 13.8 (2006).

[30] Case 44/79 *Hauer vs. Land Rheinland Pfalz* [1979] European Court Report 321.

[31] *Joint Declaration by the European Parliament, the Council and the Commission*, in *Official Journal of the European Communities* (OJEC). 27 April 1977, No C 103, p 1.

[32] For a review of the judicial reception of the primacy doctrine, see among others Stephen Weatherill, *Law and Integration in the European Union*, Clarendon Law Series (Oxford; New York: Clarendon Press; Oxford University Press, 1995); Stephen Weatherill and PR Beaumont, *EU Law*, 3rd ed. (London: Penguin, 1999); Paul Craig and Grainne De Burca, *EU Law: Text, Cases and Materials*, 4th ed. (Oxford: Oxford University Press, 2007).

neither existentially nor economically secure. Two increasingly hostile blocs divided
and occupied the territory of the former Third Reich, leaving the idea of a single,
unified postwar German state uncertain. As the cold war developed, the division
of the country between the two camps consolidated as Germany became an early
battleground between the cold war antagonists. The solidification of the country's
division, particularly during the Berlin blockade in 1948, saw the merging of the
areas under Western occupation into a new state, which mirrored the political and
economic preferences of the Allies. Yet what to do with this new Federal Republic –
the German Question – remained the most pressing matter of the late 1940s. The
new political elite of the western half was forced into a balancing act between the
desire for a return to sovereignty and stable government and the need to reassure
Germany's neighbors of its peaceful intentions. Economically, the industrial and
social displacement caused by the war left a longing for increased economic stability
and prosperity, made all the more urgent by the need to accommodate and integrate
the millions of Germans expelled from Eastern Europe. There were a number of
possible solutions to the German Question, not least likely of which was the prospect
of a nonaligned, disarmed German state in central Europe. European integration,
as another option, held the promise of access to markets for West German industry, in turn bolstering economic prosperity and thus allaying the perceived threat
of the Communist movement. It would also reassure West Germany's neighbors of
its reliability and ideally provide West Germany with an equal footing with those
countries who shared its desire for integration. Through peaceful and cosmopolitan
cooperation, the West Germans could also seek to reassimilate themselves into the
international community and secure for themselves a "position of strength"[33] vis-à-
vis their eastern counterparts.

As such, for the incumbent political leadership, European integration provided
a means to achieve both its economic and its political goals. Although contended
strongly by some, including the Social Democrats, that the policy of *Westbindung*
made reunification less likely, the FRG had found a means of both developing its
war-ravaged industrial base and restoring its credibility with the occupying Allied
powers.[34] Under the strong direction of the first chancellor, Konrad Adenauer, the
FRG sought to bind itself to its Western neighbors, particularly as tensions between
the occupying powers continued to rise in Korea and beyond. The division of

[33] Lothar Kettenacker, *Germany since 1945* (Oxford: Oxford University Press, 1997), p 60.
[34] The differing political concepts for the postwar period between (and within) the governing Christian
Democratic Union (CDU) and the opposition parties, the Social Democratic Party (SPD) and Free
Democratic Party (FDP), are discussed at length in Chapter 4. An excellent resource for this is found
in Wolfram Kaiser, "Institutionelle Ordnung und Strategische Interessen: Die Christdemokraten
und 'Europa' Nach 1945," *Das Europaische Projekt zu Beginn des 21. Jahrhunderts*, ed. Wilfried Loth
(Opladen: Leske & Budrich, 2001).

Europe and Konrad Adenauer's long tenure as chancellor ensured that this process was oriented decidedly toward the West,[35] with the FRG's ties to the United States of America, the North Atlantic Treaty Organization (NATO), and its most important western neighbor, France, becoming ever closer as the 1950s progressed. Locked into this western orientation by the overwhelming and continued domestic success of Adenauer and the predilections of the Allies, the FRG was inherently willing to consider forms of integrated European governance. Creating a united Europe through a surrendering of sovereignty that it did not yet fully exercise anyway, and picking up some of the bills for integration thereafter would be a small "sacrifice" in redeeming itself for its historical indiscretions.[36]

The newly minted Basic Law, the FRG's provisional[37] constitution ratified in May 1949, contained clauses that left the state intrinsically open to modes of international cooperation (Article 25) and transference of sovereignty (Article 24), which, of course, as an occupied state, the FRG did not yet fully enjoy. It was therefore no surprise that Adenauer, who listed European integration as one of the key goals of the new state, jumped at the chance of cooperation with the French through the Schuman Declaration of 1950. By pooling sovereignty over its war-enabling coal and steel industries, and subsequently its entire economy through the Treaties of Rome, Germany through European integration began the process of reconciliation with its immediate neighbors and became an integral part of the Western alliance. Of course, this process was not without setbacks. A long struggle in the Bundestag to pass a West German contribution to the suggested Pleven Plan, which would have created a European Defence Community,[38] failed when the French rejected the plan in 1954. This served

[35] Among others: Adrian Hyde-Price, *Germany and European Order: Enlarging Nato and the EU* (Manchester: Manchester University Press, 2000), pp 78–9; Peter Pulzer, *German Politics 1945–1995* (Oxford: Oxford University Press, 1995), pp 14–17; Kurt Sontheimer and Wilhelm Bleek, *Grundzüge des Politischen Systems der Bundesrepublik Deutschland* (Bonn: Bundeszentrale für politische Bildung, 2000), p 44; Dennis L Bark and David R Gress, *West Germany: From Shadow to Substance 1945–1963* (London: Blackwell Publishing, 1989), pp 274–7; AJ Nicholls, *The Bonn Republic: West Germany Democracy 1945–1990* (London: Longman, 1995), p 117; Wolfram F Hanrieder, *Germany, America, Europe: Forty Years of German Foreign Policy* (New Haven, Conn.; London: Yale University Press, 1989), pp 2243–6.

[36] This idea of "sacrifice" will become a leitmotif throughout West German society's dealings with the European legal system – until a certain point. For analysis of the idea of "sacrifice" in postwar West Germany, see Robert G Moeller, *War Stories: The Search for a Usable Past in the Federal Republic of Germany* (London: University of California Press, 2003).

[37] The Basic Law was meant to be a temporary document, governing the western half of Germany until unification could be achieved. See, among others, Dieter Hesselberger, *Das Grundgesetz: Kommentar für die Politische Bildung* (Bonn: Bundeszentrale für Politische Bildung, 2001), pp 28–9.

[38] For an excellent discussion of the creation, specifics, and ultimate failure of the European Defence and Political Communities, see Richard T Griffiths, *Europe's First Constitution: The European Political Community 1952–1954* (London: Federal Trust, 2000).

only to dampen, not quell West German ambitions for an ever closer European union. More importantly, the FRG, as Europe's biggest export economy, had been instinctively supportive of economic and political integration, because the increased economic exchange that integration undoubtedly furthered fueled its prosperity and underlined its postwar identity as Europe's "Economic Wonder."[39] Germany has been the biggest contributor to the European purse from the outset and one of the most open supporters of a federal European government, which it was felt would help secure the new democratic order in the FRG.[40] Politically, too, Adenauer's formula of regaining sovereignty, rearmament, and regaining control of West German industry through closer integration in the West was unarguably successful. The promise of a pacified and united Europe, as a precursor for the reunification of Germany, proved a remarkably popular idea among the West German populace.[41]

Yet at the same time, there was a constitutional paradox in the policy of western integration. Submission to European legal primacy, vital as it was according to the ECJ to the functioning of the European integration project, threatened another crucial aspect of the FRG's self-definition, namely, the rigorous constancy of its new democratic constitutional system. The Basic Law was designed to provide the western half of Germany with a new progressive and peaceful identity and not only contained clauses allowing integration, but also rejected militaristic modes of diplomacy (Article 26) and contained a preamble espousing the virtues of world peace. Most importantly of all, though, the "spectre"[42] of the Weimar Republic led many to reflect continually on whether long-standing trends in German culture were compatible with democracy at all.[43] In response, essential parts of the document

---

[39] Germany's role as the so-called *Wirtschaftswunder* in postwar Europe is a central narrative in most of the most influential histories of the period. Werner Abelshauser, *Deutsche Wirtschaftsgeschichte seit 1945* (Munich: CH Beck Verlag, 2004), pp 15–19; Nicholls, *The Bonn Republic: West Germany Democracy 1945–1990*, pp 95–8; Pulzer, *German Politics 1945–1995*, pp 62–5; Manfred Gortemaker, *Kleine Geschichte der Bundesrepublik Deutschland* (Munich: CH Beck Verlag, 2005), pp 45–61; Kettenacker, *Germany since 1945*, pp 80–105.

[40] Simon Bulmer and Paterson William, *The Federal Republic of Germany and the European Community* (London: Allen and Unwin, 1987).

[41] For extensive opinion poll data expressing the general support of European integration in West Germany throughout the selected period of research, see Chapter 3.

[42] Peter Merkl, "The German Response to the Challenge of Extremist Parties 1949–1994," *The Postwar Transformation of Germany: Democracy, Prosperity and Nationhood*, ed. John S Brady, Beverly Crawford and Sarah Elise Wiliarty (Ann Arbor: University of Michigan Press, 1999).

[43] Friedrich Meinecke, *Die Deutsche Katastrophe; Betrachtungen und Erinnerungen* (Zürich: Aero-verlag, 1946); Gerhard Ritter, *Europa und die Deutsche Frage; Betrachtungen über die Geschichtliche Eigenart des Deutschen Staatsdenkens* (München: Münchner Verlag, 1948); Fritz Fischer, *Griff Nach der Weltmacht; Die Kriegszielpolitik des Kaiserlichen Deutschland 1914/18* (Düsseldorf: Droste, 1961); Fritz Fischer, *Bündnis der Eliten: Zur Kontinuität Der Machtstrukturen in Deutschland 1871–1945* (Düsseldorf: Droste, 1979).

were made inviolable by constitutional dictum.[44] A German Constitutional Court judge, Brun-Otto Bryde, once compared the West German constitution to a car, in both of which "the brakes are the part that function best."[45] Above all else, this included an unequivocal adherence to a progressive set of basic rights enshrined in its first twenty articles. Most famously and indicatively, the first of these read, "Human dignity shall be inviolable."[46] Combined with a clear separation of powers and incorporation of checks and balances, foremost of which were powerful judicial controls over the executive through the Federal Constitutional Court (FCC), the new national constitutional order sought to define and demarcate the essence of the new democratic and liberal "Germany," different essentially from its authoritarian predecessors and contemporary counterpart under Soviet occupation. This was, as Karl Arnold famously put it, the framework for the new "good house for all Germans."[47]

It was the role of the FCC, founded in 1951, two years after the creation of the republic, to be the final "guardian" of this constitutional and constitutive document. The court's function is entirely dedicated to the task of constitutional review, and it is therefore not part of the regular judicial system, as, for instance, the Supreme Court is in the United States. It is located in Karlsruhe, separate and apart from the other government institutions that were formerly in Bonn and now in Berlin. It is composed of two Senates of eight judges, which are divided into three member chambers for certain hearings. Both Senates have a chairperson, one of whom serves as the president of the Court, the other as vice president. The presidency alternates between Senates. A Senate may only overturn a standing judgment of the other after discussion and vote in a full plenary session of all members of both sides of the Court. Half of the judges on the Court are selected by the Bundestag and the other half by the Bundesrat. A judge must be at least forty years old when selected for the twelve-year term, and no judge may serve beyond the age of sixty-eight. Unlike most other German courts, the FCC allows and publishes the dissenting opinions of its judges. The FCC has been consistently the German public institution with the most legitimacy and support,[48] starting from a strong position but enforcing a strict denazification of its personnel, unlike some of the other branches of the FRG government.[49] The Court quickly established fundamental rights as one of its core

---

44 Hesselberger, *Das Grundgesetz: Kommentar fur die Politische Bildung*, pp 56, 202–9.

45 Brun-Otto Bryde, "Fundamental Rights as Guidelines and Inspiration," *Wisconsin International Law Journal* 25.2 (2006).

46 German Basic Law, Article 1, sentence 1.

47 See "International: Berlin to Bonn" in *Time* magazine, 13 Sept., 1948 in http://www.time.com/time/magazine/article/0,9171,888465,00.html.

48 Donald P Kommers, "The Federal Constitutional Court in the German Political System," *Comparative Political Studies* 26.4 (1994).

49 Bryde, "Fundamental Rights as Guidelines and Inspiration."

areas to be protected, expanding from enforcing a typical "defensive" jurisprudence of rights protection (where it is sufficient that they are not violated) to their active promotion (where there is a duty to protect rights).[50]

It is hard to imagine a particular national historiography where the role (or perhaps the failure) of law, justice, and the constitution has had such a sustained and prominent position as in Germany. In imperial Germany, for instance, legal debates were closely related to questions about the social and political identity of the newly unified country.[51] In the Weimar Republic, too, the constitution was central to the aspirations of the state in theory and its failure in practice.[52] In the post-1945 period, the absolute rule of law – the democratic *Rechtstaat* – was central to the self-understanding of the West German state and was to be protected against any possible threat. The banning of the Communist Party and the right-wing Socialist Reichs Party in the early 1950s was seen as symptomatic of the new robustness of the "militant democracy" that West Germany represented.[53] The creation of a legitimate and democratic constitutional order was a highly successful replacement for the varieties of imperialist or national-socialist bonds espoused in previous incarnations of the German state.[54] It served equally well as an antithetical demarcation from the Soviet-style "dictatorship of the proletariat" found in the other half of the country, the German Democratic Republic.[55] The rule of law, and also, in particular, the immense emphasis placed on the guarantee of basic fundamental human rights in the immutable first twenty articles of the Basic Law therefore became one of the pillars of the West German political system in the postwar period.[56]

This centrality of law, the constitution, and the judiciary has been increasingly recognized by German historians. Perhaps the most prominent of any of these

---

[50] Bryde, "Fundamental Rights as Guidelines and Inspiration."

[51] Michael John, *Politics and the Law in Late Nineteenth-Century Germany: The Origins of the Civil Code* (Oxford: Oxford Historical Monographs, 1989).

[52] Hesselberger, *Das Grundgesetz: Kommentar Fur Die Politische Bildung*, pp 17–20; Christoph Gusy, *Die Weimarer Reichsverfassung* (Tübingen: Mohr Siebeck, 1997).

[53] On the banning of the parties, see Merkl, "German Response to the Challenge of Extremist Parties 1949–1994." For a discussion (and critique) of the concept of "militant democracy" in Germany see Otto Kirchheimer, *Political Justice: The Use of Legal Procedure for Political Ends* (Princeton, N.J.: Princeton University Press, 1961).

[54] The ways in which constitutionalism formed part of the Germany identity and conception of citizenship was the focus of a research project based at King's College London, entitled "Constituting the German Nation: The Construction of National Identity through Constitutional Theory and Practice 1898–1998."

[55] Pulzer, *German Politics 1945–1995*, pp 170–1; David P Conradt, *The German Polity*, Comparative Studies of Political Life (New York: Longman, 1978), pp 44–55; Hermann Avenarius, *Die Rechtsordnung der Bundesrepublik Deutschland* (Bonn: Bundeszentrale für Bildung, 2002), pp 13–14.

[56] See, for instance, Sontheimer and Bleek, *Grundzüge des Politischen Systems der Bundesrepublik Deutschland*, chapter 10.

particular debates occurred in the Historikerstreit of the 1980s.[57] German historians and philosophers from a Left-liberal perspective have argued at length in favor of the idea of a postnational conception of citizenship based on the universality of a constitutional document. The concept of "constitutional patriotism" was championed by Jürgen Habermas[58] but conceived originally in radically different terms by Dolf Sternberger.[59] The Historikerstreit predominately dealt with the place of the Third Reich in German and wider European history, but the "constitutional patriotism" argument was a further important dimension to the debate. Historians from the liberal Left[60] and conservative Right[61] set out to convince each other that their particular interpretation of history since the Third Reich was the best for understanding the current nature of West German citizenship.[62] Scholars around Habermas argued that a sense of identity could be rationalized through the discussion and creation of common values, potentially within a constitutional document. Those opposed to this view argued that rationalized identity could never be as powerful or as binding for true social cohesion, and identities forged on common history, symbols, and myths could not be entirely replaced. This highly contentious debate has left an indelible mark on discussions of citizenship in the FRG and revealed just how important the national constitutional order is to the self-understanding of the West German state. Indeed, similar debates have also occurred between Habermas and other protagonists in regard to constitutional patriotism at the EU level as well.[63]

Less abstractly, law and justice have garnered increasing attention in historiographical surveys that focus on the Nuremburg, Auschwitz, and RAF trials as key

[57] For an excellent recollection of the texts involved in the Historikerstreit, see Jürgen Peter, *Der Historikerstriet und die Suche nach Einer Nationalen Identität der Achtziger Jahre* (Frankfurt am Main; Berlin; Bern; New York; Paris; Vienna: Peter Lang, 1995).

[58] See Jürgen Habermas, "Staatsburgerschaft und Nationale Identitat," *Faktizitat und Geltung*, ed. Jürgen Habermas (Frankfurt: Suhrkamp, 1992); or Jurgen Habermas, "Remarks on Dieter Grimm's 'Does Europe Need a Constitution?'" *European Law Journal* 1 (1995).

[59] Sternberger's "constitutional patriotism" was above all else centered on the state and the freedoms that the state guaranteed as a result of its construction through the constitution. The constitution served as an ersatz to the nation, which was, at that time, irreconcilably divided. See Dolf Sternberger, "Verfassungspatriotismus, Aus: Frankfurter Allgemeine Zeitung Vom 23.5.1979," *Verfassungspatriotismus Als Ziel Politischer Bildung?*, ed. Günter C Behrmann and Siegfried Schiele (Schwalbach: Wochenschau Verlag, 1979).

[60] Supporting Habermas's view were historians such as Wolfgang Mommsen, Hans Mommsen, Heinrich August Winkler, Kurt Sontheimer, and Eberhard Jäckel.

[61] Opposed to Habermas's views were predominantly Ernst Nolte, Joachim Fest, Karl Dietrich Bracher, Hagen Schulze, and Andreas Hillgruber.

[62] Scholars around Habermas argued that a sense of identity could be rationalized through the discussion and codification of common values, potentially within a constitutional document. Scholars opposed to this view argued that rationalized identity could never be as powerful or as binding as identities forged on common history, symbols, and myths.

[63] See Habermas, "Remarks on Dieter Grimm's 'Does Europe Need a Constitution?'" and Dieter Grimm, "Does Europe Need a Constitution?" *European Law Journal* 1 (1995).

moments in the German transition to democracy.[64] Of course, the notion of justice has always been particularly important for the West German state in a number of ways, whether in regard to the denazification process, reparation payments to war affected states, or the return of POWs from the Soviet Union. Nevertheless, the important role played by law in the framing of the new state has become increasingly salient in recent works.[65] Prominent among these works is Ulrich Herbert's examination of the liberalization and modernization of the West German state.[66] Herbert argues convincingly that the FRG underwent a "breathtaking" political and economic modernization, as well as a fundamental legal and constitutional liberalization that allowed it to distance itself and attempt to overcome its horrific near-history.[67] Notwithstanding the economic and political progress made by the FRG in its first twenty-five years, Herbert also stresses the impact made on the "way of life" by legal reforms in the familial, cultural, and criminal spheres.[68] Through legal reforms promoting female equality and sexual liberty and liberalizing marriage and abortion, the FRG was able to reorient itself to a general Western/American way of life, thus normalizing itself and overcoming the idea of a German *Sonderweg* (special path).[69] This liberalization Herbert describes as a "learning process," as Germans through legal reform also learned what it meant to live in a normalized, democratic state.[70] Herbert's thesis is not without its critics, but the point here is not to assess the virtues of the idea, but rather to show the increasing centrality of law and justice to notions of (West) German postwar identity and its historiography.

Finally, the judiciary, and most particularly the FCC itself, has featured in many works of contemporary German history. Of particular relevance to our discussion is the role played by the courts in the political life of the FRG. The court has also frequently and consistently served as a final arbiter in the major contentious foreign policy decisions taken by the FRG. This trend began soon after the court's creation in the early 1950s. The most controversial of these early cases was related to the European Defence Community (EDC), mentioned earlier, and whether the FRG could legally rearm and contribute to the proposed European army. A prolonged and controversial argument broke out not just between the Court and the government,

---

[64] See Anthony Kauders, "Democratisation as Cultural History, or: When Is (West) German Democracy Fulfilled?" *German History* 25.2 (2007), pp 252–7.

[65] Devin O Pendas, *The Frankfurt Auschwitz Trial, 1963–1965: Genocide, History, and the Limits of the Law* (Cambridge: Cambridge University Press, 2006); Rebecca Wittmann, *Beyond Justice: The Auschwitz Trial* (Cambridge, Mass.: Harvard University Press, 2005).

[66] Ulrich Herbert, "Liberalisierung als Lemprozeß: Die Bundesrepublik in der Deutschen Geschichte – Eine Skizze," *Wandlungsprozesse in Westdeutschland: Belastung, Integration, Liberalisierung, 1945 bis 1980*, ed. Ulrich Herbert (Gottingen: Wallstein, 2002).

[67] Herbert, "Liberalisierung als Lemprozeß," p 7.

[68] Herbert, "Liberalisierung als Lemprozeß," pp 26–8.

[69] Herbert, "Liberalisierung als Lemprozeß," pp 33–4.

[70] Herbert, "Liberalisierung als Lemprozeß," p 49.

but between the two Senates of the FCC itself. That the two Senates could disagree with each other on these issues will become important to the story being told here much later, in that the FRG's government hoped that the First Senate could be used to bring about a reversal of the Second Senate's Solange decision. Ultimately this idea failed to bear fruit. While Kommers argues that the dispute ultimately strengthened the court institutionally,[71] the EDC controversy set a precedent for foreign affairs, particularly European ones, being acutely thorny ones for the court to arbitrate. In fact, as Chapter 2 will show, the contributions made to the EDC debate, particularly from legal academia, were absolutely essential in framing the FCC's subsequent jurisprudence on the validity of European law.[72] Most famous perhaps was the decision made by the FCC's Second Senate on the Basic Treaty between East and West Germany in 1973, just a year before the court's major decision on European legal primacy. While clearly on different topics, the judges of the Second Senate were clearly accustomed at this point to making decisions with profound domestic and international implications. The FCC had developed a role as the guardian of the constitution in the face of both internal and external dynamics. It was in this particular way that the FCC has come to find itself in open judicial conflict with the ECJ on numerous occasions.

Unfortunately, we cannot find equivalent emphasis on the law or judiciary in the existing historiography of European integration.[73] This is above all else due to a preoccupation with political and economic aspects of integration and the role of leading individuals in shaping this development. The first comprehensive account to historicize the integration process was the mammoth documentation of the postwar European movement by Walter Lipgens and Wilfried Loth. Published collectively during the mid-1980s,[74] these represented the work of twenty years collating the ideas and designs of federalist and idealist conceptions for a united Europe. However, lacking the disclosure of national archives, due to the widespread time delay on releasing government documents, these publications represent little more than a collection of, albeit extremely important, documents. Lipgens saw the genesis of integration formed predominantly in the war experience and Europeans'

---

[71] Donald P Kommers, *Judicial Politics in West Germany: A Study of the Federal Constitutional Court* (Beverly Hills, Calif.; London: Sage Publishing, 1976).

[72] Most especially, Herbert Kraus's submission to the court in 1952, which basically framed the terminology of the "structural congruence" that came to determine the FCC's response to the ECJ. See Institut für Staatslehre und Politik (Mainz Germany), *Der Kampf um den Wehrbeitrag*, Veröffentlichungen des Instituts für Staatslehre und Politik in Mainz, 2 vols. (München: Isar Verlag, 1952), band II.

[73] See in particular the analysis of integration historiography by Piers Ludlow in Michelle P Egan, Neill Nugent and William E Paterson, *Research Agendas in EU Studies: Stalking the Elephant*, Palgrave Studies in European Union Politics (Basingstoke; New York: Palgrave Macmillan, 2010).

[74] See the four volumes of *Documents on the History of European Integration*, published from 1982 until 1990.

attempts to match the larger and more influential superpower rivals.[75] This argument was based on the nature of the documents collected by the authors and has had a fundamental impact on subsequent historiography of the immediate postwar period.[76]

With the opening of ever more archival material by the early 1990s, many scholars attempted to historicize the integration process. Prompted by the pragmatic focus of the political scientist Ernst Haas on the effects of successful integration "spilling over" into other jurisdictions, these attempts have, above all else, been fixated on the politics and economics of integration, going against the earlier focus on the role of ideology.[77] Regarding the latter, undoubtedly the most influential text has been Alan Milward's interpretation of integration as a means of "rescuing" the European nation state from physical and financial ruin.[78] Standing in direct contrast to the idealist interpretation of Lipgens, as well as the pronouncements of the leading political figures at the time, Milward argues that the impetus provided by the Common Market was exploited by national leaders to strengthen and bolster national welfare and economic systems, and thus the states themselves, and was not meant to be a replacement of the nation state by a federal Europe.[79] More recently, John Gillingham has also argued that economic considerations have indeed been the driving force behind integration, but it is more economic theory, particularly of a liberal nature, that has shaped the path of integration and not merely the perceived practical gains for the nation state from the Common Market.[80]

Similarly to Milward in the economic sphere, Andrew Moravcsik has sought to debunk Lipgen's idealist prescription within the political context.[81] Arguing that the

---

[75] Walter Lipgens, A History of European Integration: vol. 1, The Formation of the European Unity Movement 1945–50 (Oxford: Clarendon Press, 1982), pp 44–52.

[76] See, for instance, the emphasis placed by Paul W Kaelble, "Europabewusstsein, Gesellschaft und Geschichte: Forschungsstand und Forschungschancen," Europa im Blick der Historiker: Europaische Integration im 20. Jahrhundert: Bewusstsein und Institutionen, ed. Rainer Hundemann, Hartmut Kaelble and Klaus Schwabe (Munich: R Piper & Co Verlag, 1995) on a European "consciousness." Boris Schilmar, Der Europadiskurs im Deutschen Exil 1933–1945 (Munich: Oldenbourg Wissenschaftsverlag, 2004), gives a thorough and specific account of the European "idea" in the German speaking world during the exile period 1933–45.

[77] "Intensities of ideological convictions associated with each of these types of expectations [toward integration] vary distinctly. We are here concerned not with the committed 'European,' be he liberal, conservative, or socialist, but with permanently functioning elites for whom 'Europe' is one of several important symbols, but not necessarily the dominant one"; Ernst Haas, The Uniting of Europe: Political, Social and Economic Forces 1950–1957 (Stanford, Calif.: Stanford University Press, 1968), pp 286–9.

[78] Alan S Milward, The Reconstruction of Western Europe, 1945–51 (London: Methuen, 1984).

[79] Milward, Reconstruction of Western Europe, pp 491–8.

[80] John Gillingham, European Integration, 1950–2003: Superstate or New Market Economy? (Cambridge: Cambridge University Press, 2003).

[81] Moravcsik, The Choice for Europe: Social Purpose and the State Power from Messina to Maastricht.

"supranational" concept developed by Haas in the 1950s and 1960s merely represented a pooling of national sovereignty, and thus simply a mode of "conventional statecraft,"[82] Moravcsik went on to question the value and role of the supranational institutions themselves. Moravcsik's understanding of the ECJ is that merely of a delegated authority, serving the interests of the Member States and always working within their limits of tolerance. Moreover, as with Milward, Moravcsik's conception that national interest is served through integration is underdeveloped. Room for dissenting visions of the national interest within the nation state are duly underplayed. State preferences are, of course, complex negotiated compromises of a multitude of conflicting voices and positions. For every interest satisfied, it is likely that another preference remains unfulfilled. The ECJ, or any other institution or government, would find it impossible to satisfy everyone's interests. Clearly, through the process of integration there are voices that will advocate and resist, win and lose. A dominant policy may win out, but rarely is it without modification and adjustment to accommodate a multitude of views inherent in all democratic states. While the politics and economics of this spectrum have received extensive focus, legal integration has thus far been widely ignored. Even in the newest trends in historiography, methods such as Europeanized and transnational history,[83] Transfergeschichte[84] and Histoire Croisée,[85] the law and the development of constitutionalism have received negligible

[82] Andrew Moravcsik, "Negotiating the Single European Act: National Interests and Conventional Statecrafft in the European Community," *International Organisation* 45 (1991).

[83] See the arguments in favor of understanding German history in a Europeanized context in Ute Frevert, "Europeanizing Germany's Twentieth Century," *History and Memory* 17.1/2 (2005). For the complexities of Europeanizing national histories, see the seminal text by Michael Geyer, "Historical Fictions of Autonomy and the Europeanization of National History," *Central European History* 22.3 (1989).

[84] *Transfergeschichte* (entangled history) can be understood as a method within the framework of cross-national history; maintaining its original German as the focus of its inquiry has been the particularly close postwar relationship between France and Germany. Born out of the work of Michel Espagne, Michael Werner Michel Espagne, and Michael Werner, *Les Relations Interculturelles dans L'espace Franco-Allemand (Xviiie et Xixe Siècle)*, Transferts (Paris: Editions Recherche sur les civilisations, 1988), it seeks to explain the process through which concepts, ideas, and norms are transferred from one culture to another. Because of this, transfer historians direct their attention to the "meeting points" of cultures: migration, tourism, translation, and cultural exchange. As such, the Franco-German cooperation has provided a rich source of analysis, particularly, but not limited to, of the contemporary period. Not constrained in terms of national boundaries, *Transfergeschichte* looks at cultural flows from multiple origins and to multiple destinations with often little need for an understanding of the overall national historical experience: Regions and localities are often as, if not more, important as nation states. Nation states, they argue, are merely the amalgamation of a number of cultural transfers in the regional and global context.

[85] *Histoire Croisée* (entangled history) originates from Bénédicte Zimmerman and Michael Werner, and like *Transfergeschichte* focuses on the cultural and social connectivity between nation states, differing not in content analysis, but rather in the historical reflective process itself. It is a discipline in which it is not the historical narrative that lies at the center, but the terminology of history itself that must be reflected upon and reconfigured. The traditional conceptions of "nation," "state," and "society"

attention. Notable exceptions are the remarkable piece by Paul Betts (2005), which attempts to place Germany in the development of international systems and understandings of justice through the progression of the twentieth century[86] and the joint article by Jan Palmowski and Franz Mayer, which discusses the potential for encounters with European law to create a sense of European identity.[87]

Because of the massively influential and polarizing works of Lipgens, Haas, Moravcsik, Gillingham, and Milward, almost all integration historiography has centered on the ideological, political, and economic factors highlighted in those texts. This is clearly understandable, as these works are the cornerstones of integration historical analysis, but it also unfortunately shifts focus away from the legal and judicial history of European integration. It seems as if Hallstein's quote that opens this book has continually flown under the radar. A typical example of this is a recently published volume on the FRG's role in the integration process from 1949 till 2000.[88] In this substantial volume of six hundred pages and nearly thirty individual contributions, the overwhelming emphasis falls on the "political" and "social and economic" aspects of Germany's membership in the EU. Legal-constitutional aspects of European integration historiography are deeply neglected,[89] even if there

are only relevant in the extent to which this terminology was understood by the historical actor at the time. Without historicization of these terms, genuine analysis cannot take place. Much more important are the regional and transnational cultural influences acting on individuals and historical processes at one given time. Accordingly, *Histoire Croisée* represents the meeting point of the longue durée narrative and immediate historical condition of the subject of analysis. Importantly, *Histoire Croisée* demands that historians themselves become "entangled" in the history that they are writing, achievable through the constant refocusing of the *Fragestellung* and their own reflective subjectivity through interaction with the historian's own historical constructions. By seeking to redefine, or better historicize, much of the terminology surrounding the nation state (as a historical construction), *Histoire Croisée* seems particularly suited to the rigors of historicizing the European integration project and its attempts to overcome these traditional structures. See Benedict Zimmerman and Michael Werner, "Beyond Comparison: *Histoire Croisee and the Challenge of Reflexivity*," *History and Theory* 45 (2006).

[86] Paul Betts, "Germany, International Justice and the Twentieth Century" *History and Memory* 17.1/2 (2005).

[87] Franz C Mayer and Jan Palmowski, "European Identities and the EU – the Ties That Bind the Peoples of Europe," *JCMS: Journal of Common Market Studies* 42.3 (2004).

[88] Mareike König and Matthias Schulz (eds.), Die Bundesrepublik Deutschland und die europäische Einigung 1949–2000: Politische Akteure, gesellschaftliche Kräfte und internationale Erfahrungen. Festschrift für Wolf D. Gruner zum 60. (Munich: Franz Steiner Verlag, 2004).

[89] Griffiths, *Europe's First Constitution*, provides an account of the constitutional discussion surrounding the negotiations of the European Defence Community and the European Political Community bound in with that. These discussions, however, proved fruitless and were not linked to the later developments in the Community. Anke John, "Konzeptionen fur Eine Eg-Reform: Der Europaische Verfassungsdiskurs in der Bundesrepublik 1981–1986," *Die Bundesrepublik Deutschland und die Europaische Einigung 1949–2000: Politische Akteure, Gesellschaftliche Krafte und Internationale Erfahrungen: Festschrift fur Wolf D Gruner zum 60. Geburstag*, ed. Marieke König and Matthias Schulz (Stuttgart: Franz Steiner Verlag, 2004), in the König and Schulz edition, provides an account

is a burgeoning literature on the topic in political science and the court cases at the FCC continually garner good press and legal-academic coverage. Yet it is clear that through their integration into modes of European cooperation, the Member States have at best weakened and at worst endangered the integrity and immutability of their constitutional and legal orders. By agreeing to hand over huge portions of sovereignty to the European institutions, supranational public authorities not bound by national constitutions, the Member States, and most particularly West Germany consented to the fact that citizens may be subject to laws contrary to their guaranteed basic rights. As such, this crucial paradox of West German history has never been the subject of attention, particularly within the more influential surveys of postwar history. In none of the established "classics" of post-1945 West German historiography is the relationship between European integration and the establishment of constitutional practice even alluded to.[90] Yet clearly legal integration was one of the most important forces impacting the European nation state in the twentieth century, if not since the consolidation of the state system after the 1648 Peace of Westphalia.

EXPLAINING THE ECJ'S SUCCESS?
THE INTEGRATION THROUGH LAW PARADIGM

How then do we explain why the Member States were seemingly so passive toward this "revolution" emanating from Luxembourg? Could it be, as one writer famously stated, that no one was paying attention to what was happening in the small, sleepy duchy?[91] Or should we believe that it was perceived to be in the Member States' interest to allow the ECJ such wide scope?[92] Named after an early and famous attempt[93] to explain the ECJ's perceived success in creating a constitution-like legal system for Europe, Integration through Law has been interpreted by scholars who have developed a number of approaches and theories to explain how the ECJ was able to consolidate its most important doctrines without provoking a destructive

of the constitutional discourse in the FRG but chooses a far too late date to incorporate or even include the crucial period of constitutionalization during the 1960s.
[90] There are no mentions of this relationship, for example, in Gortemaker, *Kleine Geschichte der Bundesrepublik Deutschland*; Golo Mann, *Deutsche Geschichte des 19, und 20, Jahrhunderts* (Frankfurt am Main: Fischer Verlag, 2004); Kettenacker, *Germany since 1945*; Dietrich Thränhardt, *Geschichte der Bundesrepublik Deutschland* (Frankfurt am Main: Suhrkamp Verlag, 1996); Nicholls, *The Bonn Republic: West German Democracy 1945–1990*; Pulzer, *German Politics 1945–1995*; Christoph Kleßmann, *Die Doppelte Staatsgrundung: Deutsche Geschichte 1945–1955*, 5th ed. (Gottingen: Vandenhoek & Roprecht, 1991). This is, of course, not an exhaustive list of histories of post-1945 Germany, but the trend is evident.
[91] Stein, "Lawyers, Judges and the Making of a Transnational Constitution."
[92] Moravcsik, *The Choice for Europe: Social Purpose and the State Power from Messina to Maastricht*.
[93] Cappelletti, Seccombe and Weiler, *Integration through Law: Europe and the American Federal Experience*.

response from the Member States. ITL theories draw particularly on the methodologies of social and political science, as well as, in large part, on legal theory and analysis of court decision making. There is some disagreement about how best to define what constitutes an ITL theory. Ulrich Haltern's simple definition of an ITL theory as any that considers the role of law or the ECJ as an institution in the process of integration is straightforward, but not entirely instructive in this case.[94] Indeed, more useful are the models proposed by Karen Alter[95] and JHH Weiler,[96] who look at a small number of crucial cases from the ECJ of "constitutional" importance – namely, the doctrines of direct effect and primacy and their consolidation in subsequent ECJ case law.[97]

However, it is not the intention of this book to recount once again at length this amply covered case law narrative.[98] This type of formal legal "history" can never reveal the full spectrum of understanding and notions that underlie the law and judicial decision making in the period. If we are to discover, or at least begin to explore, what Duncan Kennedy might refer to as the "legal consciousness" of the period, we must recognize that while the case law narrative has a certain amount of "autonomy," this is contextual and "intelligible only in terms of the larger structures of social thought and action."[99] It is, then, one of the book's central contentions that it is more revealing and important to examine the decisions in the context of the debates, discourse, and institutional constellations in which they happened. As Robert Gordon has noted, "the aim of sound intellectual historiography should be the reconstruction of past reasoning modes as they were understood by the lawyers who used them."[100] The legal systems that appear to us to possess a sense of

---

[94] "Die einigdene Erkenntnisinteresse von ITL (Integration through Law) ist die Untersuchung der Rolle des Rechts und der Rechtsinstitutionen im Prozess der europäischen Integration," Ulrich Haltern, "Integration Durch Recht," *Theorien der Europaischen Integration*, ed. Hans Jurgen Bieling and Marika Lerch (Wiesbaden: VS Verlag fur Sozialwissenschaften, 2005), p 399.

[95] Alter, *Establishing the Supremacy of European Law*.

[96] Weiler, *The Constitution of Europe – "Do the New Clothes Have an Emperor?" and Other Essays on European Integration*.

[97] This study chooses also to focus on the standard signpost cases of the "constitutionalization" narrative, with the addition of some ECJ case law of the late 1970s and the political declaration of the European institutions of the 1977.

[98] Ingolf Pernice, director of the Walter Hallstein Institute for European Law in Berlin, Germany, has been a leading jurist on the relationship between European and German law for many years, and his many works on the subject provide an outstanding overview of the case law dialog. The institute's Web site is a veritable mine of information and scholarship on the case law of the German and European courts. See http://www.whi-berlin.eu. The classic "textbooks" of European Union case law are Craig and De Burca, *EU Law: Text, Cases and Materials*; PP Craig and G De Búrca, *The Evolution of EU Law*, 2nd ed. (Oxford; New York: Oxford University Press, 2011); and Weatherill and Beaumont, *EU Law*.

[99] Duncan Kennedy, "Toward an Historical Understanding of Legal Consciousness: The Case of Classical Legal Thought in America, 1850–1940," *Research in Law and Society* 3 (1980).

[100] Robert W Gordon, "Recent Trends in Legal Historiography," *Law Library Journal* 69 (1976).

permanence and the decisions that emerge from it seem inevitable. But these struc-tures are "frail and collapsible" and historically contingent.[101] The broader context adds a texture to courtroom dialogue that is both exciting and necessary. However, this courtroom dialogue forms the skeleton around which the flesh of this book sits, and so it seems to be common sense to outline it, at least in brief, at this point.

THE CONSTITUTIONAL NARRATIVE:
THE ECJ AND FCC IN JUDICIAL DIALOGUE

This story began in earnest in 1963, five years after the Treaties of Rome added the European Economic Community and European Atomic Community to the already existing European Coal and Steel Community. The Treaties famously required the institutions of the Communities continually to lay "the foundations for an ever closer union among the European peoples."[102] The Court of Justice, housed in Luxembourg, was to be the final arbiter in disputes among legal personalities in the Community system and in the interpretation of European law. In order to do so, the institutions were equipped with a number of legislative tools, most notable of which were regulations that were directly applicable within the Member States without any kind of national transposition. The Treaties, however, did not include an explicit primacy clause to deal with cases of when said regulations conflicted with preexisting or subsequent national legislation. This appeared to be a rather important oversight. Speculation as to the original intentions of Europe's "Founding Fathers" in not dealing with the relationship between European and national law in the Treaty ranges from the mundane[103] to the conspiratorial.[104]

A crucial aspect of the European legal system was the inception of the Preliminary Ruling Mechanism (ex-Article 267 TEC, ex-Article 267 TEU, currently Article 267 TEC). This mechanism enabled national courts to refer cases involving an aspect of European law to the ECJ for an early advisory ruling before the national court's decision fell. While lower national courts were not required to use the mechanism, national courts of final instance were. However, lower national courts took up the opportunity to refer to Luxembourg with some relish. Multiple studies have dem-onstrated the exponential growth in Art. 267 rulings as the Community grew in importance and size.[105] For sake of comparison, by the end of the 1970s, the ECJ

---

[101] Robert W Gordon, "Critical Legal Studies," *Legal Studies Forum* 10.3 (1986).

[102] Preamble, Treaty Establishing the European Economic Community, 1957.

[103] Vauchez, "The Transnational Politics of Judicialization: Van Gend En Loos and the Making of EU Polity."

[104] Rasmussen, "Exploring the Secret History of the Legal Service of the European Executives, 1952–1967."

[105] Stone-Sweet and Brunell, "European Court and the National Courts: A Statistical Analysis of Preliminary References 1961–1995"; Stone-Sweet and Brunell, "European Court, National Judges,

had ruled on ninety-nine infringement proceedings – cases where noncompliance with European law was suspected – yet had made almost eight hundred preliminary rulings.[106] As such, national judiciaries, litigants, and legal professionals have in part offered a huge amount of cooperation in the enforcement and application of European law. New historical findings indicate that while some of this "cooperation" was unconscious – cases unintentionally involved European law – there were also deliberate attempts to bring cases before certain judges in certain countries, predominately the Netherlands, to ensure that the ECJ would be able to rule on the matter.[107] Indeed, figures inside the Community institutions, most notably Michel Gaudet,[108] director general of the Commission's Legal Service, always deemed the Mechanism to be the most promising means of spreading the influence of European law across the Member States. Gaudet was massively influential in the creation of national associations of European law used to coordinate litigious action and promote the use of European law. From 1961 on, these groups were aided by a pan-European umbrella organization, the Fédération Internationale pour le Droit Européen (FIDE), which helped select and push cases that the ECJ could use to reinforce its own position and power.[109] Ultimately, as will be shown later, this group, however, failed to convince German academia of its constitutional interpretation of the Treaties.

And so it came to be through cases referred through Article 267 under the guidance of FIDE that the ECJ was able to transform the nature of European law.[110] First among these was a referral from the Netherlands in 1962, involving a Dutch importer and a trade tribunal. In this case, *Van Gend v. Nederlandse Administratie der Belastingen*, the ECJ was able to rule that under certain conditions – clarity and unconditionality – European law was directly effective not just horizontally between Member States, but also vertically for citizens as individual legal subjects within Member States.[111] Drawing on the general "scheme and

and Legal Integration: A Researcher's Guide to the Data Set on Preliminary References in Ec Law 1958–98"; Jonathan Golub, "The Politics of Judicial Discretion: Rethinking the Interaction between National Courts and the European Court of Justice," *West European Politics* (19 April 1996); Alter, *Establishing the Supremacy of European Law*.

[106] Adapted from Alter, *Establishing the Supremacy of European Law*, p 15.

[107] Rasmussen, "Exploring the Secret History of the Legal Service of the European Executives, 1952–1967."

[108] Rasmussen, "Exploring the Secret History."

[109] See especially the section on FIDE in Karen Alter, *The European Court's Political Power: Selected Essays* (Oxford; New York: Oxford University Press, 2009); and Vauchez, "The Transnational Politics of Judicialization: Van Gend En Loos and the Making of EU Polity."

[110] Rasmussen, "Exploring the Secret History."

[111] This marks a fundamental departure from the standard understanding of international law, which applies only to states. A fascinating exploration of the ECJ's understanding of international law and supranational law is found in Ole Spiermann, "The Other Side of the Story: An Unpopular Essay on

spirit" of the Treaty, the ECJ found original and new grounds to grant individuals within the Member States rights and duties that moved European law away from a standard version of international law, which generally applies to states only. The Court wrote:

> We must conclude ... that the Community constitutes a new legal order in international law, for whose benefit the States have limited their sovereign rights, albeit within limited fields, and the subjects of which comprise not only the member-States but also their nationals. Community law, therefore, apart from legislation by the member-States, not only imposes obligations on individuals but also confers on them legal rights. The latter arise not only when an explicit grant is made by the Treaty, but also through obligations imposed, in a clearly defined manner, by the Treaty on individuals as well as on member-States and the Community institutions.[112]

In this way, the ECJ guaranteed a huge rise in the number of Article 267 references as individuals sought to use national court systems to enforce their newly gained rights. Through *Van Gend* and the Preliminary Ruling Mechanism, European law became the "law of the land for national citizens."[113]

The immediate and obvious question to arise from this is, if Community law and national law both imposed duties and rights on citizens, what was to happen in cases where these conflicted?[114] The ECJ answered this question shortly after *Van Gend*, establishing the doctrine of European legal primacy in the *Costa v. E.N.E.L.* case in 1964. Reinforcing the "originality" of the Community as a distinct and new legal order, the ECJ stated:

> By contrast with ordinary international treaties, the Community treaty has created its own legal system which, on the entry into force of the treaty, became an integral part of the legal systems of the member states and which their courts are bound to apply. By creating a Community of unlimited duration, having its own institutions, its own personality, its own legal capacity and capacity of representation on the international plane and, more particularly, real powers stemming from a limitation of sovereignty or a transfer of powers from the states to the community, the Member States have limited their sovereign rights and have thus created a body of law which binds both their nationals and themselves.... The law stemming from the treaty, an independent source of law, could not because of its special and original nature, be overridden by domestic legal provisions, however framed, without being deprived

the Making of the European Community Legal Order," *European Journal of International Law* 10.4 (1999).

[112] Case 26/62 *Van Gend vs. Nederlandse Administratie der Belastingen* [1963] European Court Report 1.

[113] Simon Hix, *The Political System of the European Union* (London: Macmillan Palgrave, 1999), p 108.

[114] For an interesting take on the noninevitability of *Costa* and *Van Gend*, see Vauchez, "The Transnational Politics of Judicialization: Van Gend En Loos and the Making of EU Polity."

of its character as community law and without the legal basis of the community itself being called into question.[115]

If the *Van Gend* decision made the Rome Treaties the "law of the land," then the doctrine of primacy made European law the "higher Law of the land."[116] The result of this judgment was that the Community legislation took another step away from being a standard system of international norms and moved one step closer to being the "constitutional" system described by Weiler and other scholars. Not only did European law have direct applicability within national states, but European legal norms also took precedence over conflicting national legislation in any fields of Community competence. Essentially, Member State governments – if they wanted the integration project to work – had forsaken the right to legislate in areas that the European institutions now controlled. The irony should not be unstated that this revolutionary moment in European legal history was brought about by a small claims court case involving an unpaid electricity bill amounting to just a few U.S. dollars.

Rather obviously, though, these decisions only mattered if the Member States – governments, judiciaries, and citizenry – took them seriously. However careful the ECJ had been in the wording of its decisions to ensure at least some receptiveness by the judges and legal experts of the Member States,[117] if they refused to swallow the massively expansionist interpretation of the Treaties, the ECJ would be left out on a limb. As Lisa Conant's theory of contained justice suggests, the ECJ only matters when people are motivated to use it.[118] In fact, at the start, all did not bode well. The Netherlands, Belgium, and the FRG had submitted opinions to the ECJ in the *Van Gend* case that denied the principle of direct effect.[119] The Court had simply ignored them in its reasoning but now waited on tenterhooks for the national responses.

Broadly, the judicial reception in the FRG to the events of 1962 and 1963 was mixed. The first challenge was from the Tax Court of Rhineland-Palatinate (RTC), which stopped a hearing on the applicability of a European regulation to refer the case to the Federal Constitutional Court.[120] In its referral to the FCC, the RTC challenged the constitutionality of transferring sovereignty to European institutions to a great extent, likening the surrendering of control over the democratic constitution to

---

[115] Case 06/64 *Costa vs. ENEL* [1964] European Court Report 585.
[116] Hix, *Political System of the European Union*, p 109.
[117] Francesca Bignami, "Comparative Law and the Rise of the European Court of Justice," (Boston: European Union Studies Association, 2011).
[118] Lisa J Conant, *Justice Contained: Law and Politics in the European Union* (Ithaca, N.Y.: Cornell University Press, 2002).
[119] Case 26/62 *Van Gend vs. Nederlandse Administratie der Belastingen* [1963] European Court Report 1.
[120] 2 BvL 29/63 – *Tax on Malt Barley*, 5 July 1967 – BVerfGE 22, 134.

what had happened in Germany in the 1930s.[121] Indeed the RTC questioned whether the ratification of the Treaties of Rome was constitutional at all. By asking the FCC to rule on the issue, the RTC sought a definitive national reaction to the ECJ's doctrines from the most respected and popular of all the German institutions.[122] The RTC neither obtained an affirmation of its position, nor prompted a warm response by the FCC in favor of primacy. After delaying to monitor the evolution of academic and public debates on the issue carefully, a standard tactic used by the court,[123] the Second Senate ruled in July 1967 that the submission of the RTC was invalid on technical grounds.[124] Moreover, it argued, even if it had found the particular directive in question unconstitutional, that would not mean that membership of the Community was also in doubt. This was an acquiescence to the existence of an independent, separate European legal order, but it certainly was not a warm welcome.

Indeed, the FCC rounded off its rather subdued acceptance of the ECJ's jurisprudence later in October of the same year. This time, the First Senate ruled that it was empowered to rule only on acts of German public authority, not on European regulations.[125] As such, European public authority, being "separate and independent" from that of the Member States, could not be tried in a German court. Somewhat unenthusiastically, the FCC had de facto accepted the ECJ's doctrines, and at this time in the mid-1960s had become the first supreme court in Europe to do so. In the subsequent *Milk Powder* ruling, the FCC even ordered its lower courts to apply legal rules stemming from the ECJ, which because of the transfer of authorities through Article 24 should "be recognized by the originally exclusive bearer of sovereignty."[126]

It is worth mentioning at this point that by the end of the 1960s, both Senates of the FCC had ruled in favor of European legal primacy, albeit in a relatively tepid manner. The senate system in the FCC works to divide decision making between panels of judges. The First and Second Senate both hear cases of constitutional complaint (*Verfassungsbeschwerde*) and regulation control (*Normenkontrolle*), whereas the Second Senate has the remit to respond to all over cases. These might include interinstitutional or federal-state disputes, as well as impeachment hearings, electoral scrutiny, or the banning of anticonstitutional parties, such as the Communist

---

[121] "The most important aim of the Constitution is to avoid a repetition of the developments which, in the Weimar Republic, led to the abolition of the separation of powers and thus to the collapse of the rule of law." 2 BvL 29/63 – *Tax on Malt Barley*, 5 July 1967 – BVerfGE 22, 134.

[122] Kommers, "Federal Constitutional Court in the German Political System."

[123] Clarence J Mann, *The Function of Judicial Decision in European Economic Integration* (The Hague: Martinus Nijhoff Publishers, 1972); Kommers, *Judicial Politics in West Germany: A Study of the Federal Constitutional Court*; Kommers, "Federal Constitutional Court in the German Political System."

[124] 2 BvL 29/63 – *Tax on Malt Barley*, 5 July 1967 – BVerfGE 22, 134.

[125] 1 BvR 248/63 & 216/6 – *European Regulations*, 18 October 1967 – BVerfGE 22, 293.

[126] 2 BvR 225/69 – *Milk powder*, 9 June 1971 – BVerfGE 31, 145.

and neo-Nazi parties mentioned earlier. Neither Senate is considered more senior than the other. A Senate may not, according to Article 16 (1) of the law establishing the FCC,[127] rule against the opinion of the other Senate. If conflicts arise, the sixteen judges must sit together in a plenary session to decide the issue. This particular point will become important much later on in our discussion as the Commission and West German government consider using the First Senate against the Second to reverse the *Solange* decision. Just seven short years later, the FCC had radically changed its mind. Undoubtedly a key moment in this rapid change of opinion was the continuing expansion of the ECJ's interpretation of the power of European law. In its *Internationale Handelsgesellschaft* ruling of 1970, the ECJ refused to be bound in its interpretation of European law by national constitutional traditions, which continued a line of jurisprudential thinking from the late 1950s.[128] It argued that being so limited would threaten the very existence of a functioning legal system and hence the European project altogether:

> Recourse to the legal rules or concepts of national law in order to judge the validity of measures adopted by the institutions of the community would have an adverse effect on the uniformity and efficacy of community law. The validity of such measures can only be judged in the light of community law. In fact, the law stemming from the treaty, an independent source of law, cannot because of its very nature be overridden by rules of national law, however framed, without being deprived of its character as community law and without the legal basis of the community itself being called in question. Therefore the validity of a community measure or its effect within a member state cannot be affected by allegations that it runs counter to either fundamental rights as formulated by the constitution of that state or the principles of a national constitutional structure.[129]

The ruling in this case came about as a result of a preliminary ruling request by the Administrative Court in Frankfurt. Unhappy with the ECJ's advice, the Administrative Court somewhat mischievously rereferred the case – this time to the FCC. It was the FCC's version of this very same case that became known as the first *Solange* – or "as long as" – decision. The ECJ was aware that change was afoot in the FRG, having monitored the debates in West German legal academica on the question of the validity of European law, and just two weeks before the FCC made its ruling, the ECJ tried some preemptive reconciliation. In its *Nold* ruling of May 1974, the ECJ stated:

---

[127] See http://bundesrecht.juris.de/bverfgg/index.html (last accessed 31 May 2011).

[128] See Case 1/58 *Stork vs. High Authority* [1959] European Court Report 17 and Case 36–38 and 40/59 *Ruhrkohlenverkaufsgesellschaften vs. High Authority* [1960] European Court Report 423.

[129] Case 11/70, *Internationale Handelsgesellschaft GmbH vs. Einfuhr- und Vorratsstelle für Getreide und Futtermittel* [1970] European Court Report 1125.

Fundamental rights are an integral part of the general principles of law the observance of which the Court ensures. In safeguarding these rights the Court is bound to draw inspiration from the constitutional traditions common to the Member States and cannot uphold measures which are incompatible with the fundamental rights established and guaranteed by the Constitutions of these States.[130]

This built on a mention of the "fundamental human rights enshrined in the general principles of community law and protected by the court" in the ECJ's *Stauder v. Ulm* decision from five years earlier.[131] This still proved insufficient for the FCC. It had, in its decisions in the domestic arena, developed a proactive, protectionist jurisprudence of the Basic Law's fundamental rights.[132] It was now prepared to apply this to European law too. Shortly after the *Nold* ruling, the FCC placed restrictions on its future acceptance of European law, dependent on its own judgment as to whether national fundamental rights provisions were under threat. It said:

As long as the integration process has not progressed so far that Community law receives a catalog of fundamental rights decided on by a parliament and of settled validity, which is adequate in comparison with the catalog of fundamental rights contained in the Basic Law, a reference by a court of the Federal Republic of Germany to the Federal Constitutional Court in judicial review proceedings, following the obtaining of a ruling of the European Court under Article 267 of the Treaty, is admissible and necessary if the German court regards the rule of Community law which is relevant to its decision as inapplicable in the interpretation given by the European Court, because and in so far as it conflicts with one of the fundamental rights of the Basic Law.[133]

Two outcomes of great importance immediately emerged from this. The more obvious was that the FCC saw comparative shortcomings in basic rights protection at the European level and was going to withhold final say on such issues until that point that the European institutions had remedied this particular deficiency. In essence, this was a high-level judicial carrot and stick approach – if Europe did as the FCC wished, West Germany would accept constitutionalization; as long as it failed to do so, the FCC would flex its quite considerable muscles. Second, and this is a fact most often neglected in analyses of the *Solange* decision, there was a prerequisite established that the catalog be "decided on by a parliament." In the context, this seemed a difficult proposition – the European Parliament was not yet selected by direct elections and its powers were massively inadequate compared to those of the other European institutions or its national counterparts. So while

---

[130] Case 04/73 *Nold vs. Commission* [1974] European Court Report 491.
[131] Case 29/69 *Stauder vs. Ulm* [1969] European Court Report 419.
[132] Bryde, "Fundamental Rights as Guidelines and Inspiration."
[133] 2 BvL 52/71 – *Solange I*, 29 May 1974 – BVerfGE 37, 271.

criticizing European governance for its lack of rights protection, the FCC was also bemoaning its lack of democratic and parliamentary accountability. This is a crucial point for understanding why the FCC has continually played a gadfly to the ECJ and European integration in general. Hefty conditions were placed on the eventual acceptance of European legal primacy and this judicial dialog continues to the present day. Decisions on the Maastricht[134] and Lisbon Treaties,[135] as well as the Euro Bailout Mechanism,[136] with their focus on the democratic nature of European governance, have proven central in directing the path of integration. Moreover, the political conditions incorporated into the *Solange* language are crucial for understanding why the European response was both judicial and political in nature.

Faced with the growing threat to the coherence of the European legal order that *Solange* posed, the European institutions were forced to respond. The 1970s was a particularly difficult decade for Europe, with the entrance of reluctant Member States like Britain and Denmark, the repeated failure of attempts to create a common currency, and now rebellion not just by the German judiciary, but also the Italian,[137] albeit in somewhat milder terms. As a result, the Commission had no other realistic option but to compromise. Fending off calls from the European Parliament to bring the FRG under treaty infringement proceedings, the Commission and the West German government worked together behind the scenes to ameliorate the situation. The details of this compromise will be revealed in Chapter 5, but it ultimately produced a number of actions. In 1977, seemingly at the behest of the European Parliament (note again the conditions in *Solange*), the political institutions of the Community issued a Joint Declaration stating their respect for the European Convention of Human Rights. Moreover, by 1979, direct elections to the European Parliament had been instigated. In addition, the ECJ modified its *Nold* ruling in the *Hauer* decision of 1979, finding inspiration in both national and international (ECHR) rights standards. It stated:

> Fundamental rights form an integral part of the general principles of the law, the observance of which is ensured by the Court. In safeguarding those rights, the latter is bound to draw inspiration from constitutional traditions common to the Member States, so that measures which are incompatible with the fundamental rights recognized by the constitutions of those States are unacceptable in the Community. International treaties for the protection of human rights on which the Member

[134] 2 BvR 2134, 2159/92 – *Maastricht*, 12 October 1993 – BVerfGE 89, 155.
[135] 2 BvE 2/08, 2 BvE 5/08, 2 BvR 1010/08, 2 BvR 1022/08, 2 BvR 1259/08, 2 BvR 182/09 – *Lisbon*, 30 June 2009 – BVerfGE 123, 267.
[136] 2 BvR 987/10, 2 BvR 1485/10, 2 BvR 1099/10 – *Euro Bailout*, 7 September 2011. For more on the very recent bailout decision, see http://www.spiegel.de/international/germany/0,1518,784859,00.html.
[137] 27 December 1973, n. 183, Frontini e a, in Giur. Cost., 2401.

States have collaborated or of which they are signatories, can also supply guidelines which should be followed within the framework of Community law.[138]

All of these changes proved ultimately sufficient for the FCC, at least in terms of fundamental rights provisions, if not completely in terms of the accountability of the European institutions to the European electorate. The FCC rescinded its 1974 decision in the subsequent 1986 ruling, *Solange II*,[139] but the German judiciary remains massively skeptical about the democratic nature of European governance. The question posed by the ITL theories is only sharpened by this. If the ECJ is so radically changing the nature of the European legal system and the national judiciaries were reluctant to accept this without some conditions, why did the Member State governments remain so inert?

Early examinations of the ECJ's jurisprudence were undertaken by jurists and lawyers, with American scholars, in particular, comparing the ECJ with a young U.S. Supreme Court.[140] Legalists' theories had two basic positions, focused on either the dynamism of the Court itself or the nature of its interpretation of the Treaty. For the former, the ECJ's powerful codified position in the Community's institutional framework and the many legal tools at its disposal made it an inherently strong voice, able to foster supranationality in a legally rationalized way.[141] This powerful position was given purpose through a literal interpretation of the constitutive goals given to the European's institutions through Article 4 of the EEC Treaty, that is, further and deeper integration and the creation of a liberalized Common Market.[142] From this perspective, the ECJ has merely adhered to the letter of the law in its decision making in implementing the task originally given to it by the Member States. Direct effect and primacy in particular were doctrines established not because the Court has followed its own political agenda, but simply because litigants asked the ECJ to rule on these issues.[143] Backing up its case law with justifiable legal reasoning, the Court never left the Member States in a position to challenge or curtail the Court or its jurisprudence. The second position moved beyond this quasi-positivist view of the Court and placed more emphasis on the ECJ's own agenda in its interpretation

---

[138] Case 44/79 *Hauer vs. Land Rheinland Pfalz* [1979] European Court Report 321.

[139] 2 BvR 197/83 – *Solange II decision*, 22 October 1986 – BVerfGE 73, 339.

[140] For instance, Eric Stein, "Toward Supremacy of Treaty – Constitution by Judicial Fiat: On the Margin of the Costa Case," *Michigan Law Review* 63 (1964); Stuart Scheingold, *The Rule of Law in European Integration: The Path of the Schuman Plan* (New Haven and London: Yale University Press, 1965); Andrew Wilson Green, *Political Integration by Jurisprudence: The Work of the Court of Justice of the European Communities in European Political Integration* (Amsterdam: AW Sijthoff-Leyden, 1969).

[141] Pescatore, "Aspects of the the Court of Justice of the European Communities of Interest from the Point of View of International Law," pp 240–2.

[142] Pescatore, "Aspects of the the Court of Justice," pp 240.

[143] Pescatore, "Aspects of the the Court of Justice," pp 251–2; Stein, "Toward Supremacy of Treaty," p 492.

of the Treaty. Accordingly, again on the basis of Article 4, the ECJ sought to constitutionalize the Treaties of Rome because of its interpretation of the "spirit" and
intention of the document's writers. In this linear model of legal development, the
initial desire for greater economic and political integration is seen as a starting point,
from which the Court has laid out, in a legally rationalized manner, the jurisprudence constitutionalizing the Treaty. Arguing that a legitimate legal system must
have some kind of justifiable "coherence," this school of thought demonstrates that
the ECJ chose to advocate a teleological interpretation of the Treaty to preserve the
"integrity" of the Community and to fulfill the values found in the preamble of
the Rome Treaty.[144] The Court's own published reasoning, particularly in the *Costa*
case, strengthens this argument where the ECJ referred to the original aims of the
Member States.[145] This is a narrative of a "heroic" court, holding its ground against
wavering Member States and rescuing the project

Jurists have centered on the autonomy of legal reasoning and the ECJ's expertise in interpreting the Treaty to explain the Court's successful pursuance of an
expansive reading of European law. In a sense, they have viewed the establishment
of constitutional practice in a form of specialist vacuum, which is not surprising as
most proponents of this viewpoint were lawyers or legal scholars. The overwhelming majority of early scholarship on the Community's nascent legal system took
this form. The most obvious reason is that the extralegal impact of the ECJ's jurisprudence was not always immediately relevant and the Court often developed its
doctrines over an extended period, resulting in a delay in the actual effects of the
decision on the political system. The legalist perspective remains a useful argument, highlighting both the strength of legal rationale and the influence of the
Court as an institution. In our analysis, we should not forget that the separation of
powers doctrine precludes, in theory, the intervention of political voices in the judicial process. This serves to insulate the court system to a large degree and makes
politicians wary of the fallout involved in seeming to be meddling in judges' affairs.
This was, for obvious reasons, especially true for post-1945 West Germany. Of
course, ECJ judges are appointed by Member State governments, and so there is
inherently political influence in the court's composition, but the secrecy involved
in court voting and the lengthy terms served by judicial personnel help to ameliorate,
if not totally remove, this problem.

---

[144] Joxerramon Bengoetxea, Neil MacCormick and Leonor Moral Soriano, "Integration and Integrity in
the Legal Reasoning of the European Court of Justice," in De Burca, Grainne & Jhh Weiler (eds.),
European Court of Justice (2001), pp 47–8.
[145] The Court stated in its reasoning, "By creating a Community of unlimited duration, having its own
institutions, its own personality, its own legal capacity ... and real powers stemming from a limitation
of sovereignty or a transfer of powers from the States to the Community, the Member States have
limited their sovereign rights"; Case 06/64 *Costa vs. ENEL* [1964] European Court Report 585.

However, legalism failed to provide a full explanation of the legal integration process. Early works underplayed the role of the ECJ's own strategic interpretation, as nowhere in the Treaty was it clearly worded that European legislation was supreme or directly effective; these doctrines were merely the ECJ's expansive interpretation of the Treaty's intentions. Therefore, in a sense, the legalist argument was open to the same criticism leveled at legal positivists from the late nineteenth into the mid-twentieth century: Simply applying the letter of the law is impossible without some form of contextual or, in this case, political interpretation.[46] In response, later legalist works attempted to factor in the issue of interpretation. Yet these also focused too narrowly on the legal teleology of the Court, ignoring the vitally important, extra-legal factors that the Court had to reckon with when issuing its decisions. Its relations with the other European institutions and the Member States determined these factors. The ECJ was entirely reliant on its dialog with the Member States and their judiciaries, for both their referrals to and compliance with the Court's decisions. By issuing a judgment that would have found no resonance within either the Member State governments or judiciaries, the ECJ would have seriously undermined its own legitimacy. Paul Kahn's examination of modern legal legitimacy sees a profound need for courts to reconcile legal reason with the reason of popular will.[47] This is particularly true for figurehead supreme courts, the role the ECJ sought to play in the Community and especially so in its early years, when it could not count on automatic acceptance. With such a high profile, it would be hard to imagine that the ECJ did not take into account the preference and reticence of other European institutions and Member State actors before issuing its judgments.

By the early 1980s, the failure of legal scholars to explain entirely the success of the ECJ prompted many political scientists to move away from broader grand theories of integration and into concentrating on the ECJ's role in the European institutional framework, which shadowed developments in integration scholarship more generally.[48] This began in earnest in 1981 through two now classic works: first, Stein's account of the creation of a "transnational constitution," based on the legal reasoning of partisan lawyers and litigants and the failure of Member States to check this process;[49] second, through Weiler's juxtaposition of concurrent legal integration

---

[46] In the German case, some have argued that the adherence to the principles of positivism led, in part, to the legal takeover of power by the Nazis. See, most famously, Gustav Radbruch, "Gesetzliches Unrecht und Übergesetzliches Recht," *Süddeutschen Juristenzeitung* (1946), or Ernst-Wolfgang Bockenforde, *Recht, Staat, Freiheit: Studien zur Rechtsphilosophie, Staatstheorie und Verfassungsgeschichte* (Frankfurt am Main: Suhrkamp, 1991).

[47] "Reason and will work together to create an almost impregnable redoubt for the rule of law as our deepest cultural commitment"; Kahn, *Cultural Study of Law: Reconstructing Legal Scholarship*, p 13.

[48] Markus Jachtenfuchs, "The Governance Approach to European Integration," *Journal of Common Market Studies* 39 (2001).

[49] Stein, "Lawyers, Judges and the Making of a Transnational Constitution."

and political disintegration in the mid-1960s.[150] Weiler, in particular, called for a reassessment of the Court's role and status in the integration process, contradicting the "technical-serviant"[151] role commonly ascribed to the ECJ and courts in general. Fueled further by the impetus of the Single European Act and then Maastricht, by the early 1990s political scientists began in earnest to question the hierarchy and nature of the European legal system, asking who really was the Master of the Treaty: the ECJ or the Member States?[152]

One of the first of these attempts understood the ECJ as merely one among many strategic political actors in European governance, fulfilling as far as possible the agendas of the Member States while also pursuing its own interest. This realist rational-choice model approximated the intergovernmental theory of integration by denying the importance of supranational governance to the integration project, seeing sovereignty merely "delegated"[153] to autonomous supranational actors to undertake specialist roles that the Member States do not wish to undertake themselves. Member States have in various forms retained oversight over the actions of these institutions, through unilateral veto, heavy influence in policy formation, or, in the case of the ECJ, reliance on the national judiciaries to refer to and enforce supranational jurisprudence.[154] Realist theories understood the jurisprudence of the ECJ exclusively as a fulfillment of the preferences of the Member States. The constitutionalization of European law was therefore a direct intention of the Member States, who sought an effective, efficient Community system and actively chose not to rein in the court, at least at this point.

The main protagonist of the realist argument was Geoffrey Garrett,[155] who viewed both the Member States and the ECJ as strategic rational actors with their own set of independent interests, intent on maximizing their own benefits and minimizing costs. Through the Member States' contracting out of the actual arbitration and monitoring of integration to the ECJ, the Court gained significant leeway for pushing its own agenda in the pursuance of the Member States' general goals.[156] The ECJ's agenda consisted of extending "the ambit of European law and [its] authority to interpret it," while winning the "acquiescence" of Member States' governments

[150] Cappelletti, Seccombe and Weiler, *Integration through Law: Europe and the American Federal Experience*.

[151] JHH Weiler, "Community, Member States and European Integration: Is the Law Relevant?" *The European Community: Past, Present and Future*, ed. Loukas Tsoukalis (Oxford: Blackwell, 1983), p 39.

[152] Karen Alter, "Who Are the 'Masters of the Treaty'? European Governments and the European Court of Justice," *International Organisation* 52.1 (1998).

[153] Moravcsik, *Choice for Europe*, p 67.

[154] Moravcsik, *Choice for Europe*, p 68.

[155] Garrett, "Politics of Legal Integration"; Garrett, Keleman and Schulz, "European Court of Justice, National Governments and Legal Integration in the European Union."

[156] Garrett, "Politics of Legal Integration," p 179.

for [its] declarations.[157] The Court could not afford to provoke the Member States into "collective responses [that] circumscribe the Court's authority."[158] In this way, Garrett argued that while the Court did have ways and means of acting in its own interests, it could not have acted in a way outside the interest of the Member States. Garrett described the ECJ as "manifestly neither master nor servant,"[159] merely an actor in a complicated, nuanced relationship.

When providing evidence for his argument, Garrett (and Moravcsik) has called heavily upon the ECJ's 1979 decision known generally after the French liqueuer involved, *Cassis de Dijon*. In this case, the ECJ established the doctrine of "Mutual Recognition," whereby products available for sale in one Member State should be able to be sold in all other Member States. In this case, the product was the named liqueur, which did not correspond to German brewing standards. The ECJ ruled the German regulation to be an illegal restriction on intra-European trade.[160] This he argues is a prime example of why the ECJ has been allowed to further the power of the European legal system. He contends that the West German government fought its case during the hearing but did not dispute the case after the pronouncement because actually losing the case suited its strategic rationalized goals. Germany is the largest exporter in the EU and thus gains the most when trade in Europe is free. The *Cassis* decision was a huge marker in trade liberalization. When balanced against the tiny impact of the French liqueur on the German alcohol market, already dominated by powerful beer and wine industries, it actually made sense, according to the theory, for the German government to let the decision stand. Garrett writes, "the government's strategy of fighting hard in the court but then accepting the ultimate decision sent two desirable signals. Domestically, the government indicated its willingness to support sheltered sectors that would be harmed by freer trade. Internationally, the German government underlined its commitment to reciprocal trade liberalization ... by accepting a decision that apparently hurt it."[161]

The realist approach has been criticized on many grounds and Garrett was involved in especially intense dialog with the neofunctionalists.[162] First, by going to the other extreme from legalism, realists appeared to forget the extremely powerful logic of legal rationale. If legal legitimacy, as Kahn argues, lies in the synthesis of

---

[157] Garrett, "Politics of Legal Integration," p 173.
[158] Garrett, Keleman and Schulz, "European Court of Justice, National Governments and Legal Integration in the European Union," p 174.
[159] Garrett, Keleman and Schulz, "European Court of Justice, National Governments and Legal Integration in the European Union," p 175.
[160] Case 120/78 *Rewe-Zentral AG vs. Bundesmonopolverwaltung für Branntwein*, [1979] European Court Report 649.
[161] Garrett, Keleman and Schulz, "European Court of Justice, National Governments and Legal Integration in the European Union," p 176.
[162] See Mattli and Slaughter, "Law and Politics in the European Union."

legal reason and popular will, then realists appeared to go too far along the scale toward fulfilling the (popular) will of the Member States. Second, even if Garrett argued that the doctrines were in the Member States' interests, subsequent political developments demonstrated that the incursion on national legal sovereignty by the ECJ was indeed resented.[163] If the Member States were entirely rational in their decision making and had mechanisms for consistently determining what was in a particular "national interest," a prerequisite for the realist model, they would have acted earlier on this resentment; the implication is either that they were unable to or that the information concerning the implications of the jurisprudence was incomplete. Both responses fundamentally weakened the rational-choice model. Finally, the Member States themselves are not monolithic entities with a single, easily identifiable "interest." Indeed, as this book will demonstrate, the reception of the ECJ varied greatly both between and within different societal groupings, various epistemic communities, and even the ministries and institutions of the West German government itself. Pleasing all the subnational, regional, and national interests in Europe would be far beyond the ECJ. Ultimately, what amounted to West German "national interest" in regard to Europe was the default, prointegration position of the leading European administrations – the foreign and economics ministries. The problems began in the 1970s because the position of these two was not shared by either its justice counterpart or the FCC and a large swath of the West German legal academy and media. The FCC's *Solange* decision is a clear reflection of this, in which the FCC felt compelled and legitimated in acting against the ECJ in the face of a passive government response.

Garrett's main critics in the early 1990s were the neofunctionalists, whose accounts were based loosely on Haas's grand integration theory.[164] This explained a dynamic of integration beyond the control of the Member States, driven by nonstate actors with a particular self-interest in the promotion of functional forms of integration. This process eventually gathered its own momentum (the "spillover effect") as further actors saw their interests reflected in the pursuit of deeper integration. Even in Stein's original account, legal integration was seen to have been furthered by "lawyer-bureaucrats," whose real interest in the applicability of European law was that "a lawyer must press any available legal argument that may 'win the case.'"[165] Using this as a basis, scholars such as Mattli and Slaughter[166]

---

[163] It is argued that the pillar system incorporated in the Maastricht Treaty was designed specifically to keep the ECJ out of affairs over which the Member States wanted to retain control. In Renaud Dehousse, *The European Court of Justice* (London: Macmillan Palgrave, 1998), pp 162–72; Alter, *Establishing the Supremacy of European Law*, pp 205–6.

[164] Haas, *Uniting of Europe: Political, Social and Economic Forces 1950–1957*.

[165] Stein, "Lawyers, Judges and the Making of a Transnational Constitution," p 27.

[166] Mattli and Slaughter, "Law and Politics in the European Union," Mattli and Slaughter, "The Role of National Courts in the Process of European Integration: Accounting for Judicial Preferences and Constraints."

described a constellation of subnational and supranational actors, who by pursuing self-interest could circumvent obstructionist Member States and promote further integration.[167] Interaction between the two levels bypassed the national level using the Preliminary Ruling Mechanism. Using this, judges on lower national courts could circumvent higher national courts and appeal directly to the ECJ for advice on matters concerning Community law. Mattli and Slaughter cited the exponential growth in Article 267 (ex. 267) references over the last thirty years[168] as proof of not just how the system worked efficiently, but also how the momentum of successful Article 267 cases promoted its ever wider use by national courts.[169] In this way, direct effect and primacy were welcomed and accepted by national judiciaries as a major empowerment of national courts vis-à-vis other branches of national government.[170]

Seeking to overcome Garrett's oversimplification of interests, Mattli and Slaughter's work was both nuanced and sophisticated. It respected the autonomy of legal argument as well as explained how the judiciary accepted integration and circumvented Member States' governments unwilling to countenance such a big loss in legal sovereignty. However, several weaknesses remained. First, the empirical use of the frequency of the number of Article 267 referrals was open to major doubt.[171] Far more importantly, however, it appeared utopian to envision national judiciaries

[167] The sub-national actors are in this case lawyers, judges and litigants, who believe they might use the EU legal system for various personal benefits. Also taking from Weiler's earlier account, they described the empowerment of national courts through enhanced career opportunities and increased influence vis-à-vis other higher national courts. Litigants might simply call on EU law to win a case in point in court whereas lawyers can also further their career opportunities by specialising in EU law or by moving into the European legal system. The supranational actor is primarily the ECJ, which seeks to expand its power and influence as far as possible and thereby furthering integration as a whole.

[168] See Stone-Sweet and Brunell, "The European Court and the National Courts: A Statistical Analysis of Preliminary References 1961–1995." and Stone-Sweet and Brunell, "The European Court, National Judges, and Legal Integration: A Researcher's Guide to the Data Set on Preliminary References in Ec Law 1958–98"; Golub, "The Politics of Judicial Discretion: Rethinking the Interaction between National Courts and the European Court of Justice"; Alter, *Establishing the Supremacy of European Law*.

[169] Mattli and Slaughter, "Law and Politics in the European Union."

[170] Mattli and Slaughter, "Law and Politics in the European Union," pp 65–7.

[171] The growth in referrals is better explained by the growth in technical regulation as the Common Market was completed. Moreover, Article 267 references are somewhat unreliable in nature, as anomalies, such as the United Kingdom's low referral rate or the fact that the advice issued by the ECJ need not be heeded by the referring court undermine the potential significance of the data. Much deeper empirical analysis of the Preliminary Ruling Mechanism is needed before it can be reliably used as evidence of this sort. For facts and figures concerning Art. 267 reference rates, see Stone-Sweet and Brunell, "The European Court and the National Courts: A Statistical Analysis of Preliminary References 1961–1995," and Stone-Sweet and Brunell, "The European Court, National Judges, and Legal Integration: A Researcher's Guide to the Data Set on Preliminary References in Ec Law 1958–98"; Golub, "The Politics of Judicial Discretion: Rethinking the Interaction between National Courts and the European Court of Justice"; Alter, *Establishing the Supremacy of European Law*.

and litigants all sharing a remarkably prointegration agenda. The possibility of a critical national judicial reception seemed to be ruled out. We know that a critical reception has occurred, and not just at the higher levels of national judiciaries. We have seen how, in the West German case, the FCC's major opinions on the doctrines of direct effect and primacy occurred after references to it by lower courts critical of the ECJ and concerned by the penetration of potentially unconstitutional European law into the national constitutional order.[172]

As a result, the issue of national reception of ECJ jurisprudence has become an essential point in political science research since the late 1990s.[173] Stone Sweet was one of the first to highlight the constitutional "dialog" that occurred between the ECJ and national judiciaries and most importantly the need for greater research into and a reassessment of national judicial interests.[174] Thus, understanding the establishment of the constitutional practice within the "context" of the national political atmosphere or as "dialogue" between the national and supranational levels has provided a fourth, and more successful school of thought within ITL. A leading light in this area, Karen Alter, has examined the national judicial reception of the primacy doctrine in both France and Germany.[175] Her account is at heart a synthesis of neofunctionalism, setting up a constellation of sub- and supranational actors connected by Article 267, and the realist model of defining Member State interests. She shows how the development of the European legal system represented a "negotiated compromise"[176] between the ECJ, unwilling to undermine its legitimacy by incurring the wrath of the Member States through an overly radical jurisprudence, and lower national courts (LNCs), working in their own self-interest vis-à-vis higher national courts (HNCs). Alter demonstrates that LNCs had most to gain in this configuration and have therefore been the most prolific partners of the ECJ in terms of Article 267 references.[177] HNCs were much more reticent with their referrals as they viewed the ECJ as a rival court, promoting subversion in LNCs and disrupting autonomous national legal traditions. As a result, the ECJ was careful to

---

[172] See cases: 2 BvL 29/63 – *Tax on Malt Barley decision*, 5 July 1967 – BVerfGE 22, 134 and 2 BvL 52/71 – *Solange* I decision, 29 May 1974 – BVerfGE 37, 271.

[173] For instance, the influential collected work *The European Court and National Courts – Doctrine and Jurisprudence*, edited by Slaughter, Stone-Sweet and Weiler in 1998, carried for the first time "national reports" about the historical judicial reception of European law in the main Member States.

[174] "National courts did not just receive this message [constitutionalization] passively, but talked back, fully conscious that their response would be registered by the European Court"; Stone-Sweet, "Constitutional Dialogue in the European Community," p 312.

[175] Alter, *Establishing the Supremacy of European Law*.

[176] Alter, *Establishing the Supremacy of European Law*, p 38.

[177] Stone-Sweet and Brunell offer a similar argument, showing that national courts with most expertise and experience of European legislation are the most prolific users of Art. 267. Stone-Sweet and Brunell, "The European Court and the National Courts: A Statistical Analysis of Preliminary References 1961–1995."

avoid any kind of "backlash"[178] from Member State governments and "rival" HNCs, as well as skeptical public opinion.

However, the "backlash" concept in Alter's work remains crucially underdocumented, as she provides little evidence of any skeptical academic or public discourse to be feared by the ECJ. Indeed, while the concept of a dialog or "compromise" between national and supranational judiciaries is extremely compelling, it is not a step too far to assume that the ECJ was also in a dialog with national bureaucracies and academics and fully aware of the media and public opinion context within the Member States. So, while arguing successfully that the FCC conditioned the ECJ's jurisprudence through the *Solange* decision, Alter provides only bare details of the national discourse, legal or extrajudicial, that may have shaped or influenced the decisions made by either the ECJ or the FCC. Indeed, if the concept of dialog and compromise holds true, then this raises the question as to whether the ECJ was aware of other forms of opinion. Why should the ECJ stop at the judicial and high political environments, without also considering the impact of its verdicts on public opinion, on national administrations, and among legal experts? It is one of the main aims of this book to supplement Alter's conception of this dialog by documenting the causes and origins of the much feared "backlash," since the FCC did react and it did have a real effect on European governance.

One scholar who has focused attention on the historical and political context of the judicial dialog more than any other has been JHH Weiler. Weiler's work has long been central in the field of European law and has provocatively inspired many studies since the 1980s, this one included. Building on his huge body of work dating back to the early 1980s, Weiler argues that the "very dichotomy of law and politics is questionable"[179] and thus presents a system in which the ECJ was only able to issue such radical jurisprudence as a result of the political environment in which it occurred. His "fundamental explanation is that the Member States, severally and jointly, balanced the material and political costs and benefits of the Community" at a time "characterized by legal scholars as a heroic epoch in constitution building in Europe … [and] … by political scientists as a nadir in the history of European integration."[180] His model of how the ECJ successfully issued such radical jurisprudence is only comprehensible if one also understands the political environment in which the ECJ was acting. He argues that the installation of De Gaulle in France was the catalyst for an extended

---

[178] For HNC, this might be in the form of a rejection of ECJ argumentation. For Member State governments, action is more limited, but more powerful. The "Nuclear Option" – treaty amendment to limit the ECJ – is the ultimate sanction, yet nigh on impossible to achieve. Alter, *Establishing the Supremacy of European Law*, p 119.

[179] Weiler, *The Constitution of Europe – "Do the New Clothes Have an Emperor?"* p 15.

[180] Weiler, *The Constitution of Europe: "Do the New Clothes Have an Emperor?"* p 30.

period of lost desire for integration across the Community, with the French position deeply affecting the idealism found in the approaches toward integration in other Member States.[181] This context was crucial for the court. Adapting a practice established by the German-American sociologist Albert Hirschman,[182] Weiler posits two variables, "selective exit"[183] and "voice,"[184] and explains that by issuing its famous decisions in 1963 and 1964, the ECJ signified that "Community obligations, Community law and Community policies were 'for real.'" The court had "closed" selective exit. This prompted the "cataclysmic event" of 1965, when the Empty Chair Crisis, prompted by a French withdrawal from the council of ministers, led to the Luxembourg Accord, which provided each Member State with a veto over European legislation.[185] This in turn brought to an end many other features of supranational governance in favor of a "burdened" Community, controlled and driven by the Member States.[186] In essence, in the face of the new binding obligations of the "hard law" of the Community, the Member States had as a "natural reaction" demanded, and received, more "voice" in Community decision making.[187] This was not to suggest, according to Weiler, direct and empirical correlations among *Van Gend en Loos*, *Costa*, and the Empty Chair Crisis, but rather that "the constitutionalization process created a normative construct in which such a precipitous political development becomes understandable."[188]

Thus, the legal and political realms overlapped and the balance between exit and voice equalized. As Weiler writes, "crudely put, a stronger 'outlet' for [v]oice reduces pressure on the [e]xit option and can lead to more sophisticated processes of self-correction. By contrast, the closure of [exit] leads to demands for enhanced [v]oice."[189] Weiler writes that we might understand the Court in this context as acting unilaterally, stepping in "to hold the [Community] construct together," and that

---

[181] In particular, this book will show that the French position had a major impact on public and ministerial opinions toward integration in general and the ECJ specifically.

[182] Albert Hirschman developed exit and voice in the context of consumer behavior in the 1970s and then later applied the concepts to political events. See, for instance, his analysis of the collapse of East Germany in Albert Hirschman, "Exit, Voice, and the Fate of the German Democratic Republic: An Essay in Conceptual History," *World Politics* 45.2 (1993).

[183] This represents, in its extreme form – exit – the ability of a Member State to leave the EU. In its moderate form, selective exit, it denotes the ability of a Member State to escape the obligations placed on it by membership of the EU. Weiler, *Constitution of Europe – "Do the New Clothes Have an Emperor?"* p 18.

[184] This is the ability of the Member States to amend, correct, and lessen the obligations involved in EU membership. Weiler, *Constitution of Europe – "Do the New Clothes Have an Emperor?"* p 30.

[185] Weiler, *Constitution of Europe: "Do the New Clothes Have an Emperor?"* p 30.

[186] Weiler, *Constitution of Europe: "Do the New Clothes Have an Emperor?"* p 31.

[187] Weiler, *Constitution of Europe: "Do the New Clothes Have an Emperor?"* p 34.

[188] Weiler, *Constitution of Europe: "Do the New Clothes Have an Emperor?"* p 35.

[189] Weiler, *Constitution of Europe: "Do the New Clothes Have an Emperor?"* p 17.

"the integrating federal legal development was a response and reaction to a disintegrating confederal political development."[190] More interesting, though, is the question as to why then Member State judiciaries seemingly responded so well to the ECJ's actions. Here, by synthesizing the strengths of the other three schools of ITL thought, Weiler's answer is comprehensive. First, Member State governments could not argue with the judicial legitimacy, legal rationale, and "undeniable coherence"[191] of the ECJ's jurisprudence, which "seemed truly to reflect the purposes of the Treaty to which the Member States had solemnly adhered."[192] Second, once agreed to by one Member State judiciary, this triggered a "domino effect" – "transnational incrementalism"[193] – of acceptance among other national judiciaries. Additionally, Weiler argues that the "wide and enthusiastic use of the Article [267] procedure" revealed a "heady" story of "plain and simple judicial empowerment"[194] for LNC vis-à-vis other branches of government that LNC judges found irresistible. Finally, to complete the circle, the greater say in the "hard lawmaking" for the Member State governments (and here, Weiler means the executive branches, which gain vis-à-vis the legislative, compounding the "democratic deficit"[195]), essentially the growth of intergovernmentalism, laid the ground for the continuing acceptance of the ECJ's jurisprudence. As Weiler tells us, "had no veto power existed ... it is not clear to my mind that the Member States would have accepted with such equanimity what the European Court was doing."[196]

Weiler's account has a pleasing and compelling aesthetic to it. The circular equilibrium established between exit and voice seems to work – closure of selective exit led to demands for more voice, and the institutionalization of more voice led to the willingness to accept less selective exit. Exit and voice appear to be good tools for explaining the context in which the constitutional practice occurred. However, one fundamental problem remains in Weiler's work. He claims that the political-historical context is the key to understanding how constitutionalization occurred, yet, as is also the case with Alter's study, the actual amount of historical analysis of public and elite opinion, supposed national interests, or legal-academic discourse is truly minimal. Far too often, Weiler dismisses the need to explain historical events or leaves questions to "remain speculative."[197] This is an attempt to write a history of European "law in context,"[198] but Weiler does not and, in all fairness, should not be expected

---

[190] Weiler, *Constitution of Europe – "Do the New Clothes Have an Emperor?"* p 32.
[191] Weiler, *Constitution of Europe – "Do the New Clothes Have an Emperor?"* p 33.
[192] Weiler, *Constitution of Europe – "Do the New Clothes Have an Emperor?"* p 33.
[193] Weiler, *Constitution of Europe – "Do the New Clothes Have an Emperor?"* p 33.
[194] Weiler, *Constitution of Europe – "Do the New Clothes Have an Emperor?"* p 33.
[195] Weiler, *Constitution of Europe – "Do the New Clothes Have an Emperor?"* pp 37–8.
[196] Weiler, *Constitution of Europe – "Do the New Clothes Have an Emperor?"* pp 37–8.
[197] Weiler, *Constitution of Europe – "Do the New Clothes Have an Emperor?"* p 32.
[198] Weiler, *Constitution of Europe – "Do the New Clothes Have an Emperor?"* p 15.

to approach this subject as a historian, with the historian's emphasis on sources and empirical methodology. Unfortunately, this means his theory, however compelling, rests on certain assumptions that must be tested against historical sources. As always, the subsequent chapters of this book will reveal that the reality of the situation was much more complex and nuanced than might be simply guessed. As a result, Weiler's theory shares with the realist argument the simplicity of an easily definable national interest, which allowed the ECJ to interpret an acceptable level of exit and voice for all Member States successfully. Like the neofunctionalist argument, Weiler also talks about a general desire for integration, without providing any evidence about from whom, in what form, and how much integration actually was desired. Consequently, we find the two most sophisticated and influential moments in ITL theory, those of Weiler and of Alter, have reached the same impasse, where theoretical progress is only possible through withstanding real historical testing, in particular in regard to the Member States' reception of the ECJ's jurisprudence. Only through a closer understanding of the judicial, public, political, and academic discourses within the Member States, which led to their acceptance and conditioning of the constitutional practice can the theoretical models so far proposed be fully scrutinized. At this juncture, it seems as if current scholarship has reached an impasse: On the one hand, political scientific and legal models explaining the constitutional practice are in desperate need of historical scrutiny in order to test their legitimacy, while, on the other hand, integration historians have been increasingly fixated on all aspects of the integration process except the legal one. National histories seem happy to incorporate legal narratives into their analysis but either are unaware of or underestimate the European dimension. Bridges have to be built. This book offers just that.

RESISTING THE ECJ: THE PLAN OF THE BOOK

- What were the defining features of the West German reception of the ECJ's constitutional understanding?
- In what way did reactions differ in various societal groupings? How did these reactions interact?
- What conclusions can be drawn from this reception about the nature of the nascent constitutional order of the Federal Republic?
- Did the West German reception have an effect at the European level at all? Did national resistance to legal integration matter?
- Do the ITL theories stand up to historical scrutiny? What have we learned from this case about the formative period of the European legal system?

Through analysis of archived governmental material, political party publications, personal memoirs and papers, public opinion polls, mass media, academic texts, and judicial decision making, the book will attempt to answer all of these questions. It examines the reception of the ECJ's major "constitutional" decisions, highlighting the interplay and interlinkages in reactions among various social groupings, specifically among legal academia, public opinion, and bureaucratic and government officials. Drawing conclusions with implications for both German and integration historiography, as well as for political science models explaining the success of the ECJ in establishing its doctrines, it will show that the reception of the constitutional practice beyond the courtroom in the FRG was multifaceted and, most surprisingly, not positive at all. Reactions were tempered with a good deal of skepticism toward the European institutions, which reflected both the perceived failings of the integration project in democratic and judicial terms, and the growing self-confidence of West Germans in the FRG's constitutional order. Finally, it will highlight the significance of this first real attempt to historicize the reception of European law in its Member States for our understanding of European legal integration theory more generally.

This book draws together the common lacunae of political science, legal theory, and historiographical scholarship to provide an account of how the constitutional practice was received in West Germany during the period from the start of integration in the early 1950s until the late 1970s. To do this, the analysis is divided into four chapters, the first three of which focus on how, in each case, one particular, important group in West German society dealt with and responded to the ECJ's jurisprudence. These groups are:

1. Legal academia, represented in the publications of law journals, books, and conference papers, and in speeches given at academic gatherings
2. The public, represented in opinion poll data, newspaper reporting and editorials, and radio and television broadcasts
3. The Civil Service, represented in the archived government documents of the Foreign, Economics, Justice, and Interior Ministries

While in part each grouping is distinct from the others in this analysis, separated by the types of media used, the close interrelatedness of all three groupings is given special emphasis in the discussion.[199] In summarizing the research on the three groupings, it is crucial to emphasize the artificiality of the divisions imposed by necessity on the historical material. One of the greatest difficulties encountered during the process of writing this book has been to prize apart the material into such neatly ordered subheadings as "legal academia," "public opinion," and

---

[199] To be able to demarcate clearly which source belongs in which chapter, the importance of the medium is highlighted. If, for instance, a ministerial official publishes an article in an academic journal, then this forms part of the legal academic debate. If an academic publishes in a newspaper, then this is part of the public and media debate.

"government." While at times this was relatively easy if we simply look at the media used, at other times, the role played by extremely active advocates of the "constitutional view" of European law highlights the interdependency and interlinkages of the three "groups." This highly vocal, incredibly productive group of "supranationalists" included people with real impact on policy decisions (Walter Hallstein, Wilhelm Grewe, Carl Friedrich Ophüls, Karl Carstens, Ulrich Everling), influence in academia (Professors Hans-Peter Ipsen, Gert Nicolaysen, Ernst Steindorff, Bodo Börner), and impact on the media (the Frankfurter Allgemeine Zeitung journalist Hans Herbert Götz) and in the European institutions (ECJ Justice Hans Kutcher, Commissioner Hans von der Groeben, Legal Service Director General Claus-Dieter Ehlermann).[200]

To counter this, it was decided that the medium in which the entry to the debate occurred would determine in which group it would fall. For instance, Bucher's article in the Stuttgarter Nachrichten[201] falls under Chapter 3 even though the article he published at the same time in the Neue Juristische Wochenschrift[202] appears in the academic discussion. Bucher was also, of course, a key figure in the ministerial debate, being a controversial, anti-European justice minister.[203] However, most crucially for the story being told here, it is those times when the concerns of public and intellectual discourse are not received by actors in the government – when the interlinkages essential to the democratic order fail – that our story becomes especially relevant. It is *exactly* the unresponsiveness of the German ministries to public and intellectual unease that forced the FCC to articulate those opinions. The West German government was so tied into a prointegration policy by the governing elite around Adenauer that voices of dissent and disquiet were effectively ignored (public opinion), shunned (academia), or procedurally sidelined (civil servants). Given this situation, the FCC was compelled to act.

Chapter 2 focuses on the reception and debate of the ECJ's jurisprudence among the grouping in the best position to understand the implications of the Court's action: West German legal academia. The survey will demonstrate that in the early period up until 1963, legal academic discussion attended to questions about the openness of the national constitution to international norms and under what conditions membership of international organizations was to be permitted. Importantly, the idea of a necessary "structural congruence" between equivalent domestic and

[200] This does not pretend to be an exhaustive list of people active in the supranationalist camp over the thirty years that this study encompasses. It does give a sense of the breadth and importance of the personalities involved.

[201] "Ist es wirklich Europa?" *Stuttgarter Nachrichten*, 8 March 1957.

[202] Ewald Bucher, "Verfassungsrechtliche Probleme des Gemeinsamen Marktes," *Neue Juristische Wochenschrift* 10 (1957), pp 850–2.

[203] Letter, 29 September 1967, in PAA-B20–200–1662 Allgemeine Rechtsfragen nicht Institutionelle Art (4 Nov 1966–30 Juni 1970).

international institutions moved to the fore. The issues surrounding the use of Article 24 of the Basic Law (BL) to transfer sovereignty and the extent to which sovereignty could be transferred to supranational organizations dissimilar to the FRG's own constitutional order were debated at length by scholars. Once the ECJ's case law became reality post 1963, attention shifted to whether direct effect and primacy should be accepted. This discourse forged a massive rift between two opposing epistemic communities:[204] On the one side, traditionalist scholars, who understood the Community to be merely a standard international organization, saw European law as no different from traditional international law, and therefore ultimately subject to domestic control. On the opposing side was a smaller, elite group of "supranationalist" scholars, who were based around and believed in the independence and primacy of the European legal system. Bolstered by the FCC's acceptance of primacy and direct effect in 1967, the supranationalist view gradually replaced the traditionalist as mainstream, only for the challenge to the ECJ to be renewed by growing concerns about the protection of the basic rights and a lack of democratic structural congruence at the turn of the 1970s. The chapter concludes that the FCC played a careful, calculated game, monitoring the intense academic debate through the early 1970s, and that its *Solange* decision in 1974 represented a middle path in an increasingly entrenched and embittered argument. As such, the legal academic discourse is best understood as forming the intellectual and terminological framework for the FCC's resistance to the ECJ.

Similarly, Chapter 3 on public opinion reveals a division caused by the ECJ's decision making. While early public and media opinion toward integration is shown to be highly idealistic, the subsequent failure of the EDC during the mid-1950s, the perceived anti-German bias in many ECJ decisions, as well as the impact of Gaullism increased the disillusionment of the public with the European project. The ECJ, seen by some newspapers as a remedy to the impasse created by Gaullist policies, was, during the mid-1960s, called upon to make ever more strides toward a federal legal order and to improve the democratic and judicial controls over the executive. However, by highlighting the ECJ's failure to make more progress in these areas, public and media opinion turned against the Court. In essence, it was not the radical nature of the ECJ's jurisprudence that soured public opinion, but rather that the Court had not gone *far enough*! Clearly, the idealistic tone of West German popular discourse had set high standards for the ECJ, which, when compared to the judicial protection of the individual in the national realm, it had not reached. In particular, the so-called postmodern generational shift around 1968 moved attention to issues of democratic participation and basic rights protection. By the mid-1970s, public and

---

[204] Peter M Haas, "Introduction: Epistemic Communities and International Policy Coordination," *International Organization* 46.1 (1992).

media opinion arrived at much the same place as academic opinion, asking how the national constitutional order could be protected from the democratic and judicial deficiencies at the Community level. The FCC judges were aware of this, even contributing to media debates in the 1970s to inform the listening and reading public about why and how they were addressing widely articulated concerns in the media. If the legal academic discourse set the terms of the FCC's resistance, then public discontent gave the Court the popular mandate for its actions of the 1970s.

Chapter 4 builds on the results of the previous two, posing the question as to why, if the ECJ was making such substantial inroads into national legal sovereignty and if public and academic opinion was increasingly opposed to the ECJ's jurisprudence, the national government did not act to amend or rein in the court. The chapter demonstrates the causes of this lie in three main factors. First, the ministerial constellation and policy blockages in terms of authority and leadership were crucial in understanding why there was no forceful response to the ECJ. Above all else, the unwavering support of the governing leadership (as opposed to early opposition from the nongoverning Social Democrats and Liberals) for European integration really locked in the FRG to a policy of political acceptance. Frequently, this was phrased in terms of a "sacrifice" that West Germany had to make to make amends for the past.[205] As such, the default position for the government – especially the economics and foreign ministries – was prointegration and pro-ECJ. Key to this "locking in" was the dominance of pro-European personalities such as Konrad Adenauer, Walter Hallstein, and Karl Carstens. Second, at key moments in the constitutional practice when resistance might have been offered, the political leadership was "distracted" by other, more urgent concerns. In each of the relevant periods, 1963–4, 1967, and May 1974, there was a change in government or political leadership. In part, European law slipped under the radar. Third, this meant the ministries had a large amount of independence in shaping West German European policy. The authority to decide on action in the European context was divided between the Economics and Foreign Ministries, which prompted a competition for leadership between the two. As a result, the growing concerns of the ministries with the responsibility to monitor issues of constitutional development – the so-called *Verfassungsressorts* of the Interior and Justice Ministries – were increasingly

---

[205] A good example of the West German willingness to underplay their role in European integration is in the awarding of national orders to personnel at the European Court of Justice. The first German judge, Otto Riese, frequently complained that he, out of all the judges of the Court, was the only one not to receive some kind of national commendation for his service. The Foreign Ministry thought that such an award would imply that Riese was "serving the German cause" and so delayed for more than three years while deliberating the pros and cons of the process. Riese was finally awarded a national order at the very end of 1961. The Commission president Hallstein received a national medal a month before Riese, while Advocate General Karl Roemer and Commissioner Hans Von Der Groeben had to wait till 1963 and 1967, respectively. See PAA B8 675 and PAA B8 348.

sidelined from European policy formation. Therefore, the prointegration attitudes of both the Economics and Foreign Ministries overwhelmed the voices of dissent in the *Verfassungsressorts*. The culmination of all of these factors was that little action was taken by the West German government against the ECJ.

Chapter 5 draws the public, academic, and ministerial debates together around the Constitutional Court's *Solange* decision in 1974. It will show that the Court's candidly expressed purpose in the case was to prompt the ECJ into moving on the issue of fundamental rights protection at the level of European governance and that it was responding to concerns in the public and academic spheres. The decision left the government between a rock and a hard place. Put under intense pressure by its own Constitutional Court, which claimed to be articulating discomfort that it had consciously avoided, the government also faced the threat of an infringement proceeding by the European Commission, with Members of the European Parliament positively baying for such an action. The government's assessment of the situation was serious, with the idea that the process of European integration, already stalled during the 1970s anyway, was under existential threat. Conversely, the Commission found itself in the unenviable position of squaring up against the largest, richest Member State on an issue as contentious as the Community's lack of basic rights protection. Faced with this crisis, both sides backed down and simply had to compromise. Aided by an adept suggestion of the then–German advocate general, Gerhard Reischl, the results of this were the Joint Declaration of the political institutions about the European Convention on Human Rights (ECHR) in 1977 and the modification of ECJ jurisprudence in the *Hauer* case of 1979. The ongoing debates instigated by the 1977 Joint Declaration and whether the Community could formally accede to the ECHR were only finally resolved in 2010.[206] Clearly, the resistance or the "push back" offered by the Constitutional Court had its desired impact. We can see for the first time how national judicial resistance has had real and important consequences for the nature of European governance right through to the current day.

---

[206] Modifications introduced by the Lisbon Treaty and Protocol 14 to the ECHR allow for European Union accession. The latter of these changes came about in June 2010. For analysis of the EU and ECHR in context, see, among others, Helen Keller and Alec Stone-Sweet, *A Europe of Rights: The Impact of the Echr on National Legal Systems* (Oxford; New York: Oxford University Press, 2008).

2

Conditional Acceptance or Accepted Condition?

West German Legal Academia and the Constitutionalization of European Law, 1949–1979

INTRODUCTION

Our analysis begins with the reception of the ECJ's doctrines in West Germany's legal academy. This is an important and appropriate starting point for a number of reasons. In the FRG, the legal academics were not the detached, quasi-Olympian community that we might usually associate with members of the ivory tower. This was instead a population with an inordinate amount of influence over political and judicial proceedings throughout the entire period. Real world events were shaped by academic opinion and it is eminently clear from the writings analyzed in this chapter that legal academics stayed abreast of the latest developments emanating from the courtroom and the political arena. The incorporation of academic discourse into this particular reception study is massively important. The FCC has developed a useful tool in its decision-making process – a "delay tactic"[1] – which has allowed it to wait and to follow how academic debates on a particular issue were resolved before issuing its judgment. FCC justices have taken part in the debate through publications and occasional media contributions, through which it is obvious to see that they are aware of, shaped by and directly address the most contentious moments in the discourse. As such, the highest institution in the West German judiciary relied profoundly on the theoretical legal approaches debated by constitutional scholars. It would seem reasonable to assume, given the findings of other similar studies, that legal academic discourse has been as equally important in determining the reception of the constitutional practice in other Member States.[2]

Incorporating analysis of legal academic discourse in West Germany into this study is even more important than in most other cases. There are three grounds for

---

[1] Mann, *The Function of Judicial Decision in European Economic Integration*, pp 184, 420–1.
[2] See especially Julie Bailleux's doctoral thesis work at the University of Panthéon Sorbonne on the French reception and the importance of academic discourse in that study.

this. First, legal academics are a disproportionately influential community within the Federal Republic's political and social system and were described famously in Dahrendorf's work as the FRG's "general estate."[3] As such, they were massively influential in the development of the early FRG and the recasting of its self-understanding. This is equally so on the modern reunited incarnation of the state – Blankenburg points out that during reunification, the transposition of the FRG's *Rechtsstaat* tradition onto the eastern half of the country was "officially emphasized,"[4] and that the West German legal profession simply "took over the judiciary in East Germany in the hope of demonstrating the superior traditions of their rule of law."[5] From a sociological perspective, legal-academia also has a powerful structural presence on both political leadership and the bureaucracy. First, the German legal profession and court systems are notable for their size, being twice as many attorneys and judges per 100,000 inhabitants in Germany than in neighboring France.[6] Dahrendorf claimed that in 1962, about the midpoint in our narrative, one half of the most powerful people in the Federal Republic were trained lawyers and that admission to higher civil service was controlled by a "lawyer's monopoly," with 85 percent of higher bureaucrats having a legal education.[7] As he also points out, "the law faculties of German universities are the only institution in which a considerable part of the German political class spends a part of its path through life together."[8] Within this powerful elite, it should also be noted that academic relationships – which professors' classes you attended, who your classmates were – is all the more significant. Because of the idiosyncrasies of German legal education, it is university professors who are the decisive influence on whether a student will graduate from his or her legal studies or not, regardless of whether they plan to follow a career in law or in public service.[9] Of the four incumbent Chancellors in the period under analysis, two were trained lawyers: Konrad Adenauer and Kurt-Georg Kiesinger. We might imagine the power and influence that legal academics held over the opinions of personnel in important political and civil service positions. The interrelatedness of political and legal professions is of course tempered by the strong constitutional provisions for an

---

[3] Ralf Dahrendorf, *Gesellschaft and Freiheit*, 2nd ed. (Munich: R Piper Verlag & Co, 1963), p 232.

[4] Ethard Blankenburg, "Changes in Political Regimes and Continuity of the Rule of Law in Germany," *Courts, Law and Politics in Comparative Perspective*, ed. H Jacob, E Blankenburg, H Kirtzer, DM Provine and J Sanders (New Haven, Conn: Yale University Press, 1996), p 249.

[5] Blankenburg, "Changes in Political Regimes," p 249.

[6] Germany (1992): 94 attorneys/100,000 people, 28 judges/100,000 people; France (1992): 41 Attorneys, 10 Judges. Blankenburg, "Changes in Political Regimes," p 271.

[7] Dahrendorf, *Gesellschaft and Freiheit*, pp 267–75.

[8] Ralf Dahrendorf, *Society and Democracy in Germany* (London,: Weidenfeld & Nicolson, 1967), p 248.

[9] Blankenburg, "Changes in Political Regimes," p 267.

independent judiciary. Yet as Blankenburg points out, there was a distinct reluctance in the German legal profession to return to "several periods in German history when politics manipulated law."[10] Indeed, as he continues, "the scales have turned to the language of law dominating the discourse of politics."[11] The debates outlined in this chapter really matter in understanding the FRG's reception of European law.

It is also absolutely central to the story to be told here that the leading voices in accepting the ECJ's vision were also political actors of some significance. We might call this group the "supranationalists," as they agreed with the ECJ that European law was an independent system with precedence over West German law as a result of the FRG's free choice to be a member of the Community. It was in essence caused by the fact that this small community of pro-European scholars had direct access to the levers of power that they were able to steady the ship to some extent during the initial release of the ECJ constitutionalization doctrines. In the first half of the period under investigation, these actors included such luminaries as Walter Hallstein, but also other scholars such as Carl-Friedrich Ophüls, who was a lead delegate on West Germany's negotiating team in Rome, and Wilhelm Grewe, one of the FRG's most important diplomats in the 1950s and 1960s and part of Hallstein's team framing the Hallstein Doctrine.[12] In the second half of the period, this grouping was augmented by figures such as Karl Carstens,[13] a top political official at the Foreign Ministry throughout the period and later federal president, Ulrich Everling, Kai Bahlmann and Manfred Zuleeg, all subsequently justices at the ECJ after serving in prominent positions in the West German government machinery. If we take Hallstein alone, we see just how powerful and influential this group actually was. Before and during the war, Hallstein was a professor of law at universities in Berlin, Rostock and Frankfurt and spent time in a American prisoner camp after being captured while serving in the army in France. On his return to Germany, he was elected Rector at Frankfurt University and after a short stay in the US to teach at Georgetown University, he headed the foreign policy section of Adenauer's Chancellor's Office and then the Foreign Ministry itself. In this role, he led the negotiations of the Schuman Plan, which created the European Coal and Steel Community, as well

---

[10]   Blankenburg, "Changes in Political Regimes," p 314.

[11]   Blankenburg, "Changes in Political Regimes," p 314.

[12]   Wilhelm G Grewe (1911–2000) worked during the Third Reich in the Deutsches Institut für Außenpolitische Forschung. After the war Grewe held positions as head of the Foreign Ministry Legal and then Political Department; ambassador to the United States, Japan, and NATO; and as a member of the Permanent Court of Arbitration in the Peace Palace in The Hague. He was a key legal adviser to Adenauer and a delegate to the negotiations ending the Allied occupation of Germany.

[13]   Karl Carstens served in the Foreign Ministry as state secretary (1960–6), state secretary of the Defence Ministry (1966–8), head of the Chancellor's Office (1968–9), and federal president (1979–84), as well as actively publishing on European law during this period.

as framed the eponymous Hallstein Doctrine, which set West Germany's relations with the Eastern Bloc well into the 1970s. After playing a crucial role in the negotiations around the Treaties of Rome itself, Hallstein was appointed in 1958 as the first president of the subsequent European Commission, where he remained until 1967. He was a figure of genuine importance in domestic and European politics, as well as being a heavyweight legal academic, crucial in early debates on the nature of European integration.

There was, of course, much resistance to the ECJ too. Academic opinion did not at first divide itself along the lines of who accepted the constitutional practice and who rejected it. The debate was not really about the ECJ's reasoning in *Van Gend* or *Costa*, but rather on the nature of the transfer of sovereignty to third parties and about the characteristics of Community governance. The majority of opinion – the "mainstream" so to speak – was represented by pillars of the West German legal academic community like Herman Mosler, Director of the Max Planck Institute for International Law in Heidelberg, West Germany's most prestigious legal university. This "traditionalist" view held that the Community was clearly a complex international organization, but still ultimately only an international organization. As such, they rejected the view of the supranationalists, who saw the European legal system as something new and external to the West German constitutional order. European law was, according to the traditionalists, qualitatively identical to standard international law. West German membership of the Community was therefore subject to the stipulations of Article 24 of the Basic Law and the restrictions placed on that by other constitutional clauses, not least, ones stipulating the need for the democratic nature of the constitution to be safeguarded. Out of these discussions in the 1950s, a position emerged that called for a necessary amount of "structural congruence" between the domestic and international institutions of governance for the transfer of sovereignty to be legitimate and just. After the reality of *Van Gend* and *Costa* hit home, the debate from the mid-1960s evolved away from these initial questions and instead focused on how much "congruence" was necessary and whether it existed between the Community and the FRG. By the 1970s, vociferous debate between the supranationalists, who believed congruence was evident, and traditionalists, who denied this, fed indelibly into the FCC's *Solange* decision. The arguments about "congruence" are reminiscent of the later theories of Bulmer, Jeffrey and Padgett[14] and Katzenstein[15] that seek to explain Germany's on-going engagement with and empowerment through Europe by highlighting the structural similarities between

[14] Simon Bulmer, Charlie Jeffery and Stephen Padgett, *Rethinking Germany and Europe: Democracy and Diplomacy in a Semi-Sovereign State* (Houndmills, Basingstoke, United Kingdom; New York: Palgrave Macmillan, 2010).

[15] Peter J Katzenstein, *Tamed Power: Germany in Europe* (Ithaca, N.Y.: Cornell University Press, 1997).

the respective institutional frameworks. As will be shown here, at least in the minds of the German legal academy (and later German media), that congruence was much less than has been supposed.

Third, this constant and strident juxtaposition of opposing views created the conditions for a discourse in West German academia, which stands out for its quality, quantity and prescience. While the question of European legal primacy and applicability is still being debated in countries like the UK,[16] the West German legal academic community was grappling with, and in part, answering this question decades ago. The community played a crucial role in analyzing and contesting the developments emanating from Luxembourg, informing and influencing both public opinion and the governing elite. The impact of the arguments among the legal and constitutional experts on the subsequent public and bureaucratic debates will be clearly demonstrated. After all, "experts," Giandomenico Majone argues, "play an important role in setting standards for public policy even when they appear to be dealing with purely factual questions."[17] In an area as specialized and as new as the constitutional practice, the influence of "experts" – those able to best closely follow and understand the expansion of the European legal system – was all the greater. This is a fact forgotten in most legal or judicial recountings of the relationship between European and national law.[18] Indeed, as will be shown, many constitutional justices themselves were actively involved in the debates and that *Solange* represented an attempt by the FCC to find a middle ground between two increasingly entrenched academic camps. For this reason, the lack of thorough analysis of the legal-academic reception represents a fundamental lacuna in the historiography of European legal integration. In this specific case, the pivotal role played by the legal academia within West German political and judicial life only underlines the necessity of examining legal-academic opinion further. By highlighting the full scale of arguments, this chapter contends that despite the heavy criticism levied against the FCC in 1974,[19] the *Solange* decision represented a middle path in this

---

[16] See the ongoing parliamentary committee discussions on these issues: http://www.publications.parliament.uk/pa/cm200607/cmselect/cmhaff/76/7602.htm (last accessed 30 May 2011).

[17] Giandomenico Majone, *Evidence, Argument and the Persuasion in the Policy Process* (New Haven and London: Yale University Press, 1989), p 26.

[18] This is indeed one of our main criticisms of the legalists' and contextualists' perspective of ITL, seeing the judicial dialog occurring within a specialist vacuum between courts.

[19] See, for instance, Hans Peter Ipsen, "Bverfg versus Eugh Re "Grundrechte"; Zum Beschuß des Zweiten Senats des Bundesverfassungsgerichts vom 29 Mai 1974 (Bverfge Bd, 37 S, 271)," *Europarecht* 14.3 (1975); Reinhard Riegel, "Zum Problem der Allgemeinem Rechtsgrundsätze und Grundrechte im Gemeinschaftsrecht," *Neue Juristische Wochenschrift* 36 (1974b); Meinhard Hilf, "Sekundares Gemeinschaftsrecht und Deutsche Grundrechte: Zum Beschluss des Bundesverfassungsgericht vom 29. Mai 1974," *Zeitschrift für ausländisches offentliches Recht und Volkerrecht* (1975); Eckart Klein, "Stellungnahme aus der Sicht des Deutschen Verfassungsrechts," *Zeitschrift fur auslandisches offentliches Recht un Volkerrecht.*1975 (1975).

spectrum of opinions and related directly to an earlier line of argument in academic discourse relating to the need for a certain level of similarity between the institutions of governance in Europe and in the Member State. Furthermore, it will also argue that far from being a power grab on the part of the FCC or an example of growing national retrenchment typical of the early 1970s period in European integration,[20] the *Solange* decision was a genuine attempt by the FCC to engage with the problems of European governance at that time. At the top of this agenda were fundamental rights protection and parliamentary democracy. As such, the FCC's prompting of the European institutions was in part successful, as action was taken almost immediately on both of these issues by the European institutions.

This chapter, with its focus on the academic discourse throughout the period, offers something substantially new and different to existing analyzes of the legal academic debate in West Germany. Previous studies have either underplayed the importance of this particular discourse or placed emphasis on the wrong period in trying to explain why the FCC has remained seemingly belligerent in its decision-making on European law right through to the contemporary period. Of the first group who underplay or underdocument the academic reception, Mann looks predominately at the case law dialogue between the ECJ and German courts with minimal wider social or political contextualization,[21] setting a trend for the majority of later works looking at this exclusively judicial discourse.[22] While noting that the Frankfurt Administrative Court (FAC) was "sharply attacked in the [legal-academic] literature"[23] in 1963 and that a "dramatic change ... in the thinking of German public lawyers"[24] occurred at the Kiel Conference in 1964, Mann's account of these deliberations go without further elaboration. Green also focuses exclusively on the case law affecting European and national courts, leaving the

---

[20] For differing views on the perceived stagnation in European integration during the 1970s, see Peter MR Stirk, *A History of European Integration since 1914* (New York: Pinter, 1996); Desmond Dinan, *Europe Recast: A History of European Union* (Basingstoke and New York: Palgrave Macmillan, 2004); Desmond Dinan, *Origins and Evolution of the European Union*, New European Union Series (Oxford; New York: Oxford University Press, 2006); Desmond Dinan, *Ever Closer Union: An Introduction to European Integration*, 4th ed. (Boulder, Colo.: Lynne Rienner Publishers, 2010); Jonas Christoffersen, *The European Court of Human Rights between Law and Politics*, New Book ed. (New York: Oxford University Press, 2011); and Ed Bates, *The Evolution of the European Convention on Human Rights: From Its Inception to the Creation of a Permanent Court of Human Rights* (Oxford; New York: Oxford University Press, 2010).

[21] Mann, *Function of Judicial Decision in European Economic Integration*.

[22] See, for instance, Dieter H Scheuring, "The Approach to European Law in German Jurisprudence," *German Law Journal* 5.6 (2004); Christian Tomuschat, "Alle Guten Dinge Sind Iii? Zur Diskussion um die Solange-Rechtsprechung des Bverfg," *Europarecht* 25.4 (1990); Gunnar Folke Schuppert, "Public Law: Towards a Post-National Model," *Germany, Europe and the Politics of Constraint*, ed. K Dyson and KH Goetz (Oxford: Published for the British Academy by Oxford University Press, 2003).

[23] Mann, *Function of Judicial Decision in European Economic Integration*, p 419.

[24] Mann, *Function of Judicial Decision in European Economic Integration*, p 419.

reader with the impression that court decisions are made in an intellectual vacuum, under little influence from constitutional arguments occurring within academia.[25] Both surveys place the FCC as the hub around which the whole question of the applicability of European law in West Germany revolved. While this chapter would not seek to contend that the FCC was an essential player in events, it will contest that the real epicenter of debate was within the legal-academic discussion itself, not the courtroom. Karen Alter, unlike Green or Mann, has the advantage of writing long after the events, but her account of the "negotiated compromise" between the FCC and ECJ still relies heavily on the case law dialogue rather than the wider intellectual or political debates. Alter does not entirely ignore the academic debate underlying this discourse. For instance, her reference to Hans Heinrich Rupp's polemic criticism of the ECJ in 1970[26] at least does not overlook academic discourse entirely, but her admission that "it is hard to gauge the impact of Rupp's speech and article"[27] accepts that further analysis of this event is needed. In fact, this chapter will show that Rupp had a massively powerful influence on the FCC's decision-making and demonstrates that by focusing more at the intellectual context, hidden factors of real importance to understanding the historical events can be revealed.

The second body of literature that tries to deal with the academic debates on European law has generally focused on the wrong period of analysis. This chapter will show that the important moments in the debate leading up to *Solange* happened in the 1950s, and that *Solange* itself set the tone and terminology for subsequent FCC decisions on the validity of European law in the FRG. Juliane Kokott's hugely influential and important two-part survey of the German judicial reception of European law focuses on the influences and considerations placed on the FCC and its decision-making by the process of European integration.[28] However, her documentation of the early period – the constitutionalization period – provides merely background information to the main focus of her analysis, namely the post-Maastricht period. It therefore remains succinct on the explanation of legal-academic opinion prior to the *Solange* decision, whereas we will see here that the origin of the FCC's more recent Europe-related jurisprudence is in fact in the pre-1974 period. Armin Von Bogdany does recognize the contentious nature of debates ("initial hesitation") on European law prior to 1964, but then makes the generalization that thereafter, legal academics

---

[25] Green, *Political Integration by Jurisprudence*.

[26] Hans Heinrich Rupp, "Die Grundrechte und das Europäische Gemeinschaftsrecht," *Neue Juristische Wochenschrift* 9 (1970).

[27] Alter, *Establishing the Supremacy of European Law*, p 88.

[28] Julianne Kokott, "German Constitutional Jurisprudence and European Legal Integration: Part I," *European Public Law* 2.2 (1996a); Julianne Kokott, "German Constitutional Jurisprudence and European Legal Integration: Part II," *European Public Law* 2.3 (1996b).

have "tacitly assented" to European legal primacy.[29] Finally, Kai Bahlmann's 1982 article "Der Grundrechtsschutz in der Europäischen Gemeinschaft" looks at the relationship between European integration and the integrity of West German constitutional basic rights. While Bahlmann makes a promising start by looking at the highly influential Congresses of German Public Law Teachers in 1959 and 1964, he then proceeds to skip ten years in his discussion, ignoring the period immediately after *Van Gend* and *Costa,* moving directly to the *Solange* decision in 1974. This decision, in his own words, represented a "radical reversal of position"[30] from that formed in 1964, but he fails to explain why this happened or elaborate on any of the legal academic debate in the intermittent decade. This is very unusual considering that Bahlmann was employed in the Justice Ministry at the time and was heavily involved in the government's response to the FCC.[31] Perhaps Bahlmann, who was a judge at the ECJ during the writing his article, wanted to downplay or rewrite the history of the academic debates in West Germany. This seems problematic because this chapter demonstrates that it was exactly in these years that the debate entered its most heated and prolific phase.

THE ERLANGEN ERA, 1949–1963:
HOW AND WHEN TO TRANSFER SOVEREIGNTY?
THE ORIGINS OF STRUCTURAL CONGRUENCE

In this phase of analysis, we focus on the earliest debates in West German academia, before the *Van Gend* decision, about the ability of the government to transfer sovereign authorities to international organizations. As we have already seen, the Basic Law was inherently open to forms of international cooperation, with constitutional provisions, in particular Articles 24 and 25 explicit in this purpose. European integration, though, was not the only point in which these articles were discussed in this period. West Germany's entry into NATO (1955) was the final moment in a long discussion during the late 1940s and early 1950s about West German rearmament and contribution to international armies. This question also ended up in front of the FCC[32] and actually provided the origins for the "structural congruence" argument that would become so predominant in the debates

---

[29] Armin Von Bogdany, "A Bird's Eye View on the Science of European Law: Structures, Debates and Development Prospects of Basic Research on the Law of the European Union in a German Perspective," *European Law Journal* 6.3 (2000).

[30] Kai Bahlmann, "Der Grundrechtsschutz in der Europäischen Gemeinschaft – Wege der Verwirklichung," *Europarecht* 17.1 (1982), p 4.

[31] See especially Chapter 5 for Bahlmann's role in trying to sideline the vice president of the FCC during the government's response to the European Commission's letter about the *Solange* decision in 1974–5.

[32] 2 BvE 4/52 – EDC Treaty decision, 7 March 1953 – BVerfGE 2, 143.

about European law. Accordingly, this period of academic discourse deals with three questions:

1. Can sovereignty be transferred to international organizations?
2. Under what conditions is this transfer valid, legitimate, and just?
3. What is the nature and status of the organization that accepts the transfer of authorities?

Held toward the end of the period, the German Public Law Teacher's Association meeting in Erlangen in 1959 really sets the tone for the debate in this first phase. By dealing with these three questions, the discussion at the meeting was indicative of the concerns and divided opinion about the Community and the future course of integration.

The implications of Articles 24 and 25 BL caused an immediate controversy for legal experts, even as early as in the proceedings of the Constituent Assembly drawing up the Basic Law in the late 1940s. In relation to Article 25 BL, a heated debate took place in the Assembly over whether the Social Democrat's (SPD) desire to see the "general rules of international law" applied in West Germany was to be granted, or whether the rules had to be first clearly defined, as members of the conservative Christian Democratic Union (CDU) requested.[33] The Main Committee of the Assembly chose the SPD's version of the article but raised the question about the weighting of international law in comparison to constitutional law. As Walter Pigorsch argued, opinion during the 1950s differed widely from those who subsumed international law to the Basic Law to those who placed it equal to or above the constitution.[34] In relation to Article 24 BL, attempts were first made by members of the conservative right to amend Article 24 (i) BL to ensure a constitutional amendment was required to affect a transfer of national sovereignty.[35] This proposal was however rejected by several members of the Social Democrats, who claimed that merely a simple law should be required to facilitate the "internationalization" of the West

---

[33] Klaus-Berto von Doemming, Rudolf Werner Füsslein and Werner Matz, "Entstehungsgeschichte der Artikel des Grundgesetzes im Auftrage der Abwicklungsstelle des Parlamentarischen Rates und des Bundesministers des Innerns auf Grund der Verhandlungen des Parlamentarischen Rates," *Jahrbuch des Öffentlichen Rechts der Gegenwart* 1.1 (1951), pp 229–35.

[34] Wolfgang Pigorsch, *Die Einordnung Völkerrechtlicher Normen in das Recht der Bundesrepublik Deutschland: Eine Studie Ze Den Artikeln 25, 59 und 79 des Grundgesetzes für die Bundesrepublik vom 23. Mai 1949* (Hamburg: Hansischer Gildenverlag, 1959), pp 32–75.

[35] The suggestion of Abg. Dr. Seebohm was to amend 24 (i) BL to the following: "Der Bund kann mit verfassungsändernder Mehrheit Hoheitsrechte auf zwischenstaatliche Einrichtungen übertragen," in von Doemming, Füsslein and Matz, "Entstehungsgeschichte der Artikel des Grundgesetzes im Auftrage der Abwicklungsstelle des Parlamentarischen Rates und des Bundesministers des Innerns auf Grund der Verhandlungen des Parlamentarischen Rates," p 226.

German political system.[36] The Main Committee of the Assembly again sided with the Social Democrats and rejected the need for a constitutional amendment. This would have important implications for the later debate. Second, the question was raised about the applicability of decisions made by international courts within the national legal system. The Social Democrats requested that the decisions of international courts be directly effective on the national system.[37] This idea was rejected in the final editing because, it was argued, any binding legal obligation beyond that agreed in specific international legal treaties would not be congruent with the nature of the constitution.[38]

The Constitutional Assembly established within the Basic Law an intrinsic openness to modes of international cooperation, which removed many of the formal legal obstacles to membership of the European Coal and Steel Community (ECSC), even if, in the political arena, opposition remained strong.[39] Despite the political uncertainty, West Germany became a founding member of the organization in 1951. This radical form of supranational organization integrated areas of profound national importance and marked a revolutionary shift in European relations. The High Authority was granted extensive legal powers to administer the heavy industries of the Member States,[40] initiating a debate in West German legal-academia concerning the nature of the transference of national sovereignty to a supranational community.

As the ECSC was so innovative, it fell at first to one of the lead members of the West German delegation on the negotiations of the treaty, Carl Friedrich Ophüls,[41] to open the debate on the new supranational order. In an article published a few days before the ECSC Treaty came into force,[42] Ophüls highlighted the innovative

[36] "einfaches Gesetz"; von Doemming, Füsslein and Matz, "Entstehungsgeschichte der Artikel des Grundgesetzes im Auftrage der Abwicklungsstelle des Parlamentarischen Rates und des Bundesministers des Innern auf Grund der Verhandlungen des Parlamentarischen Rates," p 226.
[37] The suggestion of Abg Dr. Schmidt was to amend 24 (iii) BL to the following: "Die in der Schiedsgerichtsbarkeit gefällten Entscheidungen binden unmittelbar," in von Doemming, Füsslein and Matz, "Entstehungsgeschichte der Artikel des Grundgesetzes im Auftrage der Abwicklungsstelle des Parlamentarischen Rates und des Bundesministers des Innern auf Grund der Verhandlungen des Parlamentarischen Rates," p 225.
[38] von Doemming, Füsslein and Matz, "Entstehungsgeschichte der Artikel des Grundgesetzes im Auftrage der Abwicklungsstelle des Parlamentarischen Rates und des Bundesministers des Innern auf Grund der Verhandlungen des Parlamentarischen Rates," p 229.
[39] See Chapter 4 for the political opposition to integration both from within the CDU and from the SPD and FPD.
[40] Alter, *Establishing the Supremacy of European Law*, pp 5–15; Dehousse, *The European Court of Justice*, pp 5–35.
[41] Carl Friedrich Ophüls (1895–1970) was a jurist and politician of some note, holding positions in the Federal Ministry of Justice and Foreign Ministry, then as ambassador in Brussels and permanent representative to the Community.
[42] The ECSC Treaty went into force on 23 April 1951.

nature of the community, which held its own sovereignty independently and auton-omously from its constituent Member States.[43] He stressed that the new community was much more than the result of a simple international agreement, and instead fused certain national sovereign rights into a new form of supranational governance, which represented the most practical means of fulfilling the goal of a politically united Europe.[44] The supranational element, Ophüls demonstrated, was most obvi-ous in the legal framework of the community. The Treaty writers, most notably the German delegation,[45] had sought to overcome the general "weakness of continental constitutionalism" by giving the rule of law particular emphasis in the ECSC,[46] so that, according to Ophüls, individual legal rights were better protected in the community than in many of its Member States![47] It was the role of the Court of the ECSC, he continued, to maintain an objective balance against excesses from the High Authority on the one hand and against the prejudices of national states against the supranational on the other.[48] Disputes heard by the Court in relation to com-munity law, Ophüls contended, were not questions of international law, rather an issue of administrative or constitutional jurisdiction.[49] In this, Ophüls made a highly controversial claim, in that he went against the overwhelming majority opinion of West German public lawyers in the 1950s.

In contrast to this view, the majority of scholars held the view that the ECSC was very little more than an intense and complex form of international organization, and that legal issues arising out of community legislation remained firmly within the realm of international public law. The sovereign supranationality of the ECSC was completely denied. This opinion was most evident during the early fifties at the 1953 Congress of German Public Law Teachers held in Bonn.[50] This Congress, the most

[43] Ophüls, 1951 Carl Friedrich Ophüls, "Juristische Grundgedanken des Schumanplans," *Neue Juristische Wochenschrift* 4.8 (1951b), p 289.

[44] Ophüls, "Juristische Grundgedanken des Schumanplans," p 289.

[45] Ophüls, "Juristische Grundgedanken des Schumanplans," p 291.

[46] "Wenn es bisher eine Schwäche des kontinentalen Verfassungslebens gegenüber dem angelsächsis-chen war, daß die rule of law, die richterliche Gewalt, in ihr zu geringe Ausprägung fand, so hat die Verfassung der Gemeinschaft dies zu vermeiden versucht"; Ophüls, "Juristische Grundgedanken des Schumanplans," p 291.

[47] "Insgesamt geht hiernach der von der Gemeinschaft gewährte Rechtsschutz weiter als der Rechtschutz in irgendeinem der beteiligten Länder"; Ophüls, "Juristische Grundgedanken des Schumanplans," p 291.

[48] Carl Friedrich Ophüls, "Gerichtsbarkeit und Rechtsprechung im Schumanplan," *Neue Juristische Wochenschrift* 4.8 (1951a), p 694.

[49] Ophüls, "Gerichtsbarkeit und Rechtsprechung im Schumanplan," p 694.

[50] This Congress began its meetings in 1922, continued until 1932, and was then reinitiated in 1949. Protocols of presentations and subsequent discussions can be found in Veröffentlichungen der Vereinigung der Deutschen Staatsrechtslehrer (VVDStRL). Further information about the Congress itself can be found in Archiv des öffentlichen Rechts 97 (1972) and its Web site: http://www.jura.uni-freiburg.de/institute/ioeffr4/staatsrechtslehrer/index.html (last accessed: 31 May 2011).

prestigious and established in the German public law circles, represented the central formative point for mainstream academic opinion.[51] At the meeting, Wilhelm Grewe spoke on the foreign policy authorities of the Federal Republic, in which he proposed, like Ophüls, that the tendency toward deeper forms of international integration demanded new ways of understanding international public law. Integration and supranational law stood next to, but separate from standard international public law.[52] Moreover, Grewe advocated the straightforward adoption of international public norms into the West German legal framework under the remit of Article 25 BL. The audience's response to Grewe's progressive understanding of international relations was unmistakably critical. His copresenter, Eberhard Menzel,[53] denied the ECSC Treaty was anything but a standard international treaty,[54] while others declared that Grewe had read too much into Article 24 (i) BL[55] and that there should be no reason why the FRG had to adopt the rules of the international community unconditionally into the national legal framework.[56] These criticisms notwithstanding, the vast bulk of opinion went against Grewe simply because nobody was willing to recognize the ECSC as a new form of international public law, a supranational recipient of national sovereignty, with its own law making functions.

The recognition of supranational sovereignty per se and that European institutions, with their own legal personality, had the right to issue binding decisions within the FRG national legal system was indeed radical for the 1950s and only a small group of scholars, particularly around Hallstein and Ophüls readily committed to this opinion. The most noted of these scholars formed an "Academic Society for European Law" under the organization of the Hamburg Professor Hans Peter Ipsen[57] in 1961.[58] Members included Hallstein, Ophüls, ECJ judge Otto Riese,[59]

[51] For a survey of the Congress's importance to German public law culture, see Daniel Thym, "The European Constitution: Notes on the National Meeting of German Public Law Assistants," *German Law Journal* 6.4 (2005).
[52] Wilhelm Grewe, "Die Auswärtige Gewalt der Bundesrepublik," *Veröffentlichungen der Vereinigung der Deutschen Staatsrechtslehrer* 12 (1954), pp 129–75.
[53] Eberhard Menzel (1904–73) was professor of international law and director of the Institut für Internationales Recht an der Universität Kiel
[54] Eberhard Menzel, "Die Auswärtige Gewalt der Bundesrepublik," *Veröffentlichungen der Vereinigung der Deutschen Staatsrechtslehrer* 12 (1954), p 212.
[55] Menzel, "Die Auswärtige Gewalt der Bundesrepublik," pp 227 and 229.
[56] Menzel, "Die Auswärtige Gewalt der Bundesrepublik," p 230.
[57] Hans Peter Ipsen (1907–98) was professor of law at the University of Hamburg and a leading voice of the supranationalists, publishing several highly influential tracts on European law in this period
[58] Details of the highly influential Bensheim Colloquium held by the society in 1964 are discussed in Chapter 3 and can be found in BA N1266 1156 Nachlaß: Walter Hallstein: Wissenschaftliche Gesellschaft für Europarecht.
[59] Otto Riese (1894–1974) was a law professor at the University of Lausanne in 1950 and became chief justice on the Federal Court of Justice in Karlsruhe in 1951, before moving to the ECJ in 1952, serving twelve years in Luxembourg as a judge.

the FRG's ECJ lawyer Arved Deringer,[60] the Advocate General at the ECJ, Karl Roemer,[61] and many other senior ministerial jurists.

Mainstream legal-academia remained deeply convinced throughout the mid-1950s that the Treaty establishing the ECSC could not be separated from standard conceptions of international public law. Important figures, such as Hermann Mosler, refused to acknowledge that the new ECSC institutions contained any element of supranationality at all, continuing to refer to them instead as a *Staatengemeinschaft* (community of states)[62] or *Staatenverein* (association of states).[63] Neither of these terms carry a connotation of a supranational entity, independent of the states on which it is based. Mosler contended that the legal order deriving from the transference of national authorities to the ECSC was based somewhere between the international and national legal frameworks,[64] thereby insinuating that the ECSC was neither an independent autonomous legal entity nor did it define a new international legal position, as Grewe and Ophüls disputed. While not opposed to European integration, which he describes as a "creative idea,"[65] Mosler could not afford the ECSC any specific or special relevance other than it represented a first step on the integration process.[66] Mosler emphasized the lack of clarity of exactly what the ECSC was meant to represent: a truly supranational order, or an international public regulator. The blame for this ambiguity lay firmly with the Member States, although it was understandable because of the unique nature of the new institutions.[67] The CDU MP and jurist Fritz Münch[68] concurred with Mosler's view, seeing no clear difference between the ECSC and a standard international treaty.[69]

[60] Arved Deringer (1913) was a member of Federal Parliament (CDU) from 1957 to 1969 and the European Parliament from 1958 to 1970; he was head of the EP Legal Committee from 1966 to 1970. His legal firm represented the federal government in numerous cases at the ECJ.

[61] Karl Roemer (1899–1984) served twenty years in this period (1953–73) as advocate general at the ECJ

[62] Hermann Mosler, "Internationale Organisation und Staatsverfassung," *Rechtsfragen der Internationalen Organisation, Festschrift für Hans Wehberg zu Seinem 70. Geburtstag*, ed. Walter Schätzel and Hans-Jürgen Schlochauer (Frankfurt am Main: Vittorio Klostermann, 1956), p 273.

[63] Mosler, "Internationale Organisation und Staatsverfassung," p 284.

[64] Mosler, "Internationale Organisation und Staatsverfassung," p 276.

[65] Mosler, "Internationale Organisation und Staatsverfassung," p 299.

[66] Mosler, "Internationale Organisation und Staatsverfassung," p 299.

[67] "Die Verwirklichung der Vertragzwecke bedarf entwicklungsfähiger Grundsätze, die in der Auslegung und Anwendung durch die Gemeinschaftsorgane ihr Profil erhalten müssen. Die Gründer konnten es ihnen noch nicht schaffen, weil die neuartige Institution, die ihnen vorschwebte, noch niemals rechtlich gestaltet worden war"; Hermann Mosler, "Zur Anwendung der Grundsatzartikel des Vertrages über die Europäische Gemeinschaft für Kohle und Stahl," *Zeitschrift für ausländisches öffentliches Recht und Völkerrecht* (1957), p 427.

[68] Fritz Münch (1906–95) was professor of law at the Max Planck Institute in Berlin from 1955. He was an MP for the CDU from 1952 to 1972 and then later stood as a candidate for the NPD in the 1970s.

[69] Fritz Münch, "Internationale Organisationen mit Hoheitsrechten," *Rechtsfragen der Internationel Organisation: Festschrift für Hans Wehberg zu Seinem 70, Geburtstag*, ed. Walter Schätzel and Hans-Jürgen Schlochauer (Frankfurt am Main: Vittorio Klostermann, 1956), p 311.

Münch even went so far as to question whether a transference of sovereignty to an international organization could even take place, as each national state utilizes its own sovereignty so differently.[70] Münch also recognized the democratic failings of the ECSC, in particular the weakness of the legislature, but welcomed this in an article published in "die dritte Gewalt" in 1953 by commenting that the High Authority had no need to "solve problems by compromising to so many [parliamentary] interests."[71] His was perhaps the only voice at the time to welcome the dirigiste nature of the system at this time.

By the late 1950s, a growing differentiation in mainstream opinion is discernible regarding the "supranationality" of the European legal order. If the University of Frankfurt academic, Hans Jürgen Schlochauer[72] had written earlier in the 1950s with enthusiasm for the integration project,[73] by 1956, his argument had become more complex and multifaceted. He too, like Mosler, still regarded the European institutions as a form of "Staatenverbindung"[74] (combination of states), an understanding of the ECSC's legal framework as somewhere between the fields of international and national public law. However, Schlochauer attributed the ECSC with a supranational legal power autonomous and directly effective in the Member States. He argued that if Article 24 (i) BL allowed national authorities to be transferred, and if Article 79 (iii) BL afforded protection of the core of the Basic Law, then the ECSC should have full legal discretion within these areas of competence for two reasons. First, the transference of powers under Article 24 (i) BL required that the body receiving such powers had to hold a "structural congruence"[75] with the Federal Republic – a democratic-like division of powers and a rule of law – and only organizations with a degree of internal homogeneity could achieve this.

This argument has its basis in the earlier writings of the Vienna-based Professor, Alfred Verdroß,[76] whose writings were required reading in the Foreign Ministry's

---

[70] Münch, "Internationale Organisationen mit Hoheitsrechten," p 310.

[71] "[die Hohe Behörde] hat es gar nicht nötig, Ihre Probleme durch ein Kompromiß der widerstreitenden Interessen zu lösen," in "Die Montanunion als Staatsmodell," die dritte Gewalt, 21 December 1953.

[72] Hans Jürgen Schlochauer (1916–90) was a professor of international law at the University of Frankfurt from 1951. He was a cofounder, along with Walter Hallstein, of the Finance and Law School at this university (1953).

[73] Hans Jürgen Schlochauer, "Der Übernationale Charakter der Europäischen Gemeinschaft für Kohle und Stahl," *Juristen-Zeitung*.10 (1951).

[74] Hans Jürgen Schlochauer, "Rechtsformen der Europäischen Ordnung," *Archiv des Völkerrechts* 5 (1955), p 42.

[75] Hans Jürgen Schlochauer, "Zur Frage der Rechtsnatur der Europäischen Gemeinschaft für Kohle und Stahle," *Rechtsfragen der Internationalem Organisation, Festschrift für Hans Wehberg zum Seinem 70. Geburtstag,* ed. Walter Schätzel and Hans-Jürgen Schlochauer (Frankfurt am Main: Vittorio Klostermann, 1956), p 367.

[76] Alfred Verdroß (1890–1990) was a professor of international law at the University of Vienna, as well as justice on the European Court of Human Rights until 1977.

Legal Section,[77] and Göttingen Professor Herbert Kraus.[78] Verdroß contended that any *Staatengemeinschaft* straying too far from the basic legal principles of its constituent parts would dissolve in a flurry of diplomatic notes, treaties, and court cases.[79] Kraus had been heavily involved in the debates and FCC court case around the legality of the West German contribution to the European Army proposed in the failed European Defence Community Treaty in 1954. In his submission to the FCC at that time, he had argued that a necessary "structural congruence" was required between the FRG and any international organization that it chose to transfer areas of sovereignty to.[80] Indeed, he argued that the most important consideration of this transfer was that the international organization should not be given the power to alter, block or override the Basic Law through a simple piece of secondary legislation. Technically, Article 79 BL placed strict limits on the use of Article 24 BL. In a remarkable piece of foresight, Kraus continued to highlight the basic rights as the most important area to be guarded during any transfer of sovereignty. Here was a preshadowing of the FCC's *Solange* decision twenty years in advance and before the Rome Treaties had even been written.

Schlochauer, obviously aware of the arguments of Verdroß and Kraus, thought that the ECSC did hold a sufficient level of homogeneity, but only when given full autonomy in the areas of its competence. Second and most importantly, Schlochauer regarded the ECSC as a functional body with a responsibility to efficiently coordinate its tasks in the coal and steel markets.[81] It could only do this with a fully sovereign legal structure.[82] He continued to argue that any further integration,

---

[77] See PAA B80–22. Verdroß also held a speech at the Foreign Ministry in March 1954, which officials were actively encouraged to attend. The Legal Section at the Foreign Ministry held joint responsibility with its equivalent in the Economics Ministry for monitoring European legal developments and therefore was extremely influential in shaping overall government opinion about the ECJ. See Chapter 4 for more detail on this role, especially in relation to the submission to the ECJ in the *Van Gend* decision.

[78] Herbert Kraus (1884–1965) was a professor of international public law at the University of Göttingen. Kraus served as a defense counsel for Hjalmar Schacht at the Nuremberg Trials.

[79] "Diese Formulierung ist aber nur ein abgekürzter Ausdruck dafür, daß das positive Völkerrecht von bestimmten, von ihm bereits vorausgesetzten Rechtsgrundsätzen abhängig ist. Ohne sie würde such die Staatengemeinschaft in verschiedene, sich gegenseitig bekämpfende Machtkomplexe auflösen....Ohne diese Grundlage würde sich das positive Völkerrecht in eine unendliche Mannigfaltigkeit von diplomatischen Noten, Verträgen und Schiedssprüchen auflösen"; Alfred Verdroß, "Zum Problem der Völkerrechtlichen Grundnorm," *Rechtsfragen der Internationalen Organisation, Festschrift für Hans Wehberg zu Seinem 70. Geburtstag,* ed. Walter Schätzel and Hans-Jürgen Schlochauer (Frankfurt am Main: Vittorio Klostermann, 1956), p 394.

[80] Institut für Staatslehre und Politik (Mainz Germany). *Der Kampf um den Wehrbeitrag.*

[81] Schlochauer calls the basis of the ECSC's competence as that of "völkerrechtlichen Koordinationsrecht"; Schlochauer, "Rechtsformen der Europäischen Ordnung," p 57.

[82] Schlochauer, "Rechtsformen der Europäischen Ordnung," p 60; Schlochauer, "Zur Frage der Rechtsnatur der Europäischen Gemeinschaft für Kohle und Stahle," p 373.

referring explicitly to the construction of a Common Market, should be based on a functional integration, rather than any political reasoning, as this was the only way for the process to succeed.[83] Schlochauer was clearly aware that the political failure of the European Defence Community (EDC) the previous year had rocked the integration process and he was therefore advocating a functional, pragmatic approach similar to the one taken by the heads of state at Messina in that same year this article was published. This pragmatism was understandable. Integration as a concept was threatened by the failure of the EDC and thus so were the benefits that integration was expected to bring West Germany. The elements in Schlochauer's argument – a definitively pragmatic approach – suggest that the reason for the growing willingness to view European integration as a process with its own autonomous identity, an independent legal power and a constitutional effectiveness, was born out of simply material reality. The fact was that the ECSC had proven a success for an extended period of time, thus becoming an issue that warranted greater consideration and a deeper analysis.

The negotiations around the Treaties of Rome brought about an intensification of the academic debate concerning the nature of the transfer of sovereignty and the supranational legal order, particularly as the proposed Community would be a great progression from the limited ECSC. The FDP jurist and later justice minister, Ewald Bucher,[84] published an article in the Neue Juristische Wochenschrift (NJW) in 1957, which attempted to excite a discussion on the question as to whether the Treaties of Rome was compatible with the Basic Law.[85] While Bucher conceded that the institutions of the Common Market were basically like those of the ECSC, he argued that the Common Market had much greater domestic political influence within the Member States, so the fact that parliamentary control of the executive powers was so limited, could no longer be ignored.[86] The structural congruence referred to by Schlochauer earlier no longer existed according to Bucher.[87] Bucher's argument would prove to cause him political difficulties in his later role as justice minister, which Chapter 4 will show.

Moreover, the ECJ's jurisprudence had begun to raise concerns about its ability and willingness to adhere to national constitutional standards and to enforce basic rights protection. To begin with, in the *Stork v. High Authority* decision of 1959,

[83] Schlochauer, "Rechtsformen der Europäischen Ordnung," pp 61–2.

[84] Ewald Bucher (1914–91) earned a doctorate in law from the University of Munich in 1941, serving as a lawyer until 1953. He was an FDP MP from 1953 until 1969, serving as justice minister from 1962 to 1965 and running for president in 1964. He switched allegiance to the CDU in 1984. Bucher, as a critical voice, played a crucial role in ministerial disputes regarding the reception of European law during the 1960s

[85] Bucher, "Verfassungsrechtliche Probleme des Gemeinsamen Marktes," pp 850–2.

[86] Bucher, "Verfassungsrechtliche Probleme des Gemeinsamen Marktes," p 851.

[87] Bucher, "Verfassungsrechtliche Probleme des Gemeinsamen Marktes," p 852.

the ECJ expressed its unwillingness to apply the legal standards set in Member States to European law[88] and then in 1960 in the *Ruhrkohlenverkaufsgesellschaften v. High Authority* case, the ECJ refused explicitly to even apply national constitutional norms to Community decisions.[89] Bucher's intention to provoke a debate on the issue worked: During the 1959 Congress of German Public Law Teachers held in Erlangen, heavy criticism was again rained down against the integration process. The Erlangen meeting was to prove extremely consequential for all subsequent debate on the acceptance of European legal primacy right through to the mid-1980s. The topic of the two presentations was whether it was possible for the Basic Law to be violated by the transference of powers under Article 24 (i) BL. Both speakers, Werner Thieme[90] and Georg Erler,[91] agreed that the Community represented an autonomous legal order, binding on Member States, and therefore constitutional violation was possible.[92] They then sought to set limits on the extent to which the Basic Law, and in particular the unalterable basic rights, should be guaranteed. Protection, they argued, against European law was only enforceable through Community courts; however the Community had no basic rights catalog comparable to the Basic Law. Yet as Erler describes, this was a "sacrifice" that the Federal Republic had to make in the name of integration.[93] The speakers arrived at the conclusion that Article 79 (iii) BL had to be the limit to protect the Basic Law, and if a legal norm established by the Community is declared unconstitutional by the FCC when transformed into West German law, then only the national law can be revoked. The question as to what became of the conflict between the judgment of the FCC and the standing European law, particularly if it is declared directly effective and supreme by the ECJ, was not answered at the Congress.

Many others spoke during the Congress of the need to use the European Convention of Human Rights as the standard for European law. This would prove to be remarkably prescient, as this was exactly the solution offered to deal with the fallout to the *Solange* decision fifteen years later. However, at this moment, it was pointed out that this was not possible because France had not yet ratified the

[88] Case 01/58 *Stork vs. High Authority* [1959] European Court Report 17.
[89] Case 36–38 and 40/59 *Ruhrkohlenverkaufsgesellschaften vs. High Authority* [1960] European Court Report 423.
[90] Werner Thieme (1923–) was a professor of public law at the University of Saarland from 1956 to 1962, later also working at the University of Hamburg and on the Constitutional Courts of the Saarland and of the state of Hamburg.
[91] Georg Erler (1905–81) was a professor of international law at the University of Göttingen until 1965.
[92] Georg Erler and Werner Theime, "Das Grundgesetz und die Öffentliches Gewalt Internationaler Staatengemeinschaften," *Veröffentlichungen der Vereinigung der Deutschen Staatsrechtslehrer* 18 (1959), pp 7–112.
[93] Erler and Theime, "Das Grundgesetz und die Öffentliches Gewalt Internationaler Staatengemeinschaften," pp 48, 110.

Convention.[94] Many voices at the conference argued that the situation was "absurd" for the protection of Basic Rights secured after years of totalitarian regime to be transferred to a system lacking sufficient democratic protection.[95] This again was remarkably similar to the reasoning submitted by the Rhineland Tax Court in its referral to the FCC in 1967. We can see that even as early in 1959, much of the subsequent debate and terminology of the West German struggle with European law is encapsulated in the discussions at the Erlangen conference.

However, the 1959 Congress was not totally one-sided. In particular, Hans-Peter Ipsen disputed the conclusion of the speakers. Ipsen argued that the nationally defined basic rights need not be the benchmark for the European law-making process, because the Community itself contained the same fundamental legal principles as its constituent Member States.[96] It was also, therefore, logical that the ECJ be the body that enforces fundamental rights protection in European law, even though no codified text of basic rights existed at the time.[97] Moreover, Ipsen argued that as the Community was basically a technical and economic entity and that the chances of basic rights provision being of any importance in European law was minimal. Of course, traditional supporters of the integration process also spoke out in favor of the Treaties of Rome. Ophüls, writing in 1961, declared that it was not the intention of the European treaties to remain static and to weakly fear impinging on national legal orders. Instead, the treaties were written, and signed, with the dynamic intention of building a new Europe.[98] Therefore, it was the responsibility on the one hand of the Member States not to impede this process, and on the other hand of the European institutions to foster and promote a growth of authority and effectiveness for the Communities. Ophüls argued that this made the Treaties of Rome qualitatively different from the standard treaties of international law referred to by other scholars in this period. States signing standard international treaties generally sought to avoid impingements on their sovereignty, usually at the cost of the effectiveness of the organization created. This was not the case for the Treaties of Rome, which enabled it to create institutions with the dynamism to pursue the goal of deeper integration. The ECJ was to prove Ophüls' observation correct in the very next year.

---

94   France, a signatory to the original Convention in 1950, did not ratify the document until May 1974.
95   Erler and Theime, "Das Grundgesetz und die Offentliches Gewalt Internationaler Staatengemein-schaften," p 111.
96   Erler and Theime, "Das Grundgesetz und die Offentliches Gewalt Internationaler Staatengemein-schaften," pp 86–8.
97   Erler and Theime, "Das Grundgesetz und die Offentliches Gewalt Internationaler Staatengemein-schaften," p 96.
98   Carl Friedrich Ophüls, "Über die Auslegung der Europäischen Gemeinschaftsverträge," *Wirtschaft, Gesellschaft und Kultur: Festgabe für Alfred Müller-Armack*, ed. Franz Greiß and Fritz W Meyer (Berlin: Duncker & Humblot, 1961), p 289.

THE BENSHEIM ERA, 1963–1969: COMPETING VISIONS –
SUPRANATIONALISTS VERSUS THE MAINSTREAM

This second period of analysis deals with the impact of the *Van Gend* and *Costa* decisions. These cases indubitably raised the profile of European law considerably among legal-academia, although the implications of European integration for the West German constitutional system was already being considered in broad terms by scholars involved in the debates during the 1950s. Whereas in the 1950s, the issue had been, in its purest sense, academic, from 1963 on, the debates were, in contrast, dealing with substantive changes in the European legal arena. The impact of the ECJ's decisions was to transform general intellectual concerns into more specific, concrete issues and to invite a much broader spectrum of opinion on the desirability of legal integration. As a result of the changed reality post-*Van Gend* and *Costa*, the sides of the debate sharpened considerably. Those in favor of the ECJ's reasoning – the supranationalists – found themselves competing with the bulk of international law scholars who either remained inert or became hostile toward the new ideas. We can imagine then the supranationalist group, led by scholars like Ophüls, Hallstein and Hans-Peter Ipsen and receiving financial and logistical backing from the Foreign Ministry[99] and from the European institutions, as a vanguard for the ECJ, pushed for ever greater acceptance of primacy and direct effect. In this, they were only partly successful. While change was evident and the supranationalist partly succeeded, particularly if we compare the discussions at the massively influential Public Law Teachers meetings in 1953, 1959 with the Bensheim meeting of 1964, doubts persisted among traditionalist scholars about the validity of the ECJ's jurisprudence that would feed into the decisive period at the turn of the 1970s.

One of the most important changes in this period was the consolidation of "European law" as an academic subject in itself. This represents at least in part a victory for the work of the supranationalists and their backing from the European level, particularly the FIDE organization.[100] Morten Rasmussen's seminal work on the Commission's Legal Service has demonstrated how its French Director General, Michel Gaudet, was instrumental in the creation of both the pan-European

---

[99] The West German Foreign Ministry sponsored, in part, the publication of the *Europarecht* (European law) journal. This was a preeminent vehicle for the publication of prointegration articles written by the supranationalist grouping. When the journal's existence was financially threatened in the late 1970s, the Foreign Ministry arranged for further funding to maintain it. See PAA 424.50 – 121873.

[100] See Alter, *European Court's Political Power: Selected Essays* and Vauchez, "The Transnational Politics of Judicialization: Van Gend En Loos and the Making of EU Polity," for overreaching claims on the success of FIDE in pushing its interpretation of EU law. Compare with Alexandre Bernier, "Constructing and Legitimating: Transnational Jurist Networks and the Making of a Constitutional Practice of European Law, 1950–1970," *Contemporary European History*, forthcoming.

umbrella organization, as well as its German association,[101] the Academic Society for European Law (*Wissenschaftliche Gesellschaft für Europarecht*) (ASEL) in 1961.[102] Whereas European law had previously been an issue specifically for specialists of international law, it now became established as a distinct subject for debate in itself. This was manifested in many ways. European law began to be taught at a growing number of German universities. Mosler reported that forty different lecture and seminar courses under the rubric of "European law" were held during the 1965–6 university semester.[103] At the same time, Mosler also stated that research groups and institutes dedicated to the study of European law were "shooting up from the ground like mushrooms," with at least thirty associated to German universities by 1967.[104] The literature stemming from this, he claimed, had become unmanageable. Official media for academic discussion were quick to pick up this growth in interest. For instance, the *Neue Juristische Wochenschrift* began to issue a quarterly survey of developments within European law for the "deepening" and "widening" of its reader's knowledge[105] and in 1966, *Europarecht*,[106] a journal specifically dealing with issues of European law was founded. Moreover, conferences and colloquia began to incorporate the theme too. The 1964 meeting of the premier public lawyers association, the Congress of German Public Law Teachers, was held under the title "The Preservation and Alteration of Democratic and Legal Constitutional Structures through International Communities," which, while not explicitly mentioning the Community in its title, was dominated by this issue. The ASEL also held a major meeting in 1964 at Bensheim examining "The Relationship of European to National Law." Both of these meetings were of fundamental importance in shaping broader academic opinion in favor of further integration.

The very first article to appear in the NJW's European survey was from Carl Friedrich Ophüls, who championed the acceptance of the *Van Gend* decision with his usual enthusiasm. He insisted that directly effective European norms were vital to the overall project of integrating Europe, and that the ECJ's decision was a logical progression from the fact that Member States had willingly signed up to the

---

[101] Interestingly, the Germans had been hesitant about joining the pan-European organization at first and failed to send representatives to the first two meetings designed to create it. See Bernier, "Constructing and Legitimating."

[102] Morten Rasmussen, "Exploring the Secret History of the Legal Service of the European Executives, 1952–1967," *Contemporary European History*, forthcoming.

[103] Hermann Mosler, "Begriff und Gegenstand des Europarechts," *Zeitschrift fur auslandisches offentliches Recht un Volkerrecht* (1968), p 482.

[104] Mosler, "Begriff und Gegenstand des Europarechts," p 482.

[105] Carl Friedrich Ophüls, "Quellen und Aufbau des Europäischen Gemeinschaftsrechts," *Neue Juristische Wochenschrift* 16 (1963), p 1697.

[106] On the first editorial board of Europarecht were, among others, Hans-Peter Ipsen and Gert Nicolaysen.

Treaties of Rome and could therefore expect the institutions to execute their tasks effectively.[107] In this, Ophüls sniped at the opinion developed through the 1950s in academic opinion that the supranational institutions did not hold their own legal autonomy and were dependent on national legal compliance. Ophüls recognized that the direct effect doctrine immediately raised the question as to whether a national law could be overruled by a European law. He contended that as European law could only be deemed directly effective in those areas where the Community held exclusive competence, only the ECJ had sufficient expertise to rule on the applicability of European norms.[108] The same procedural question was also recognized by the two Hamburg based scholars Hans Peter Ipsen and Gert Nicolaysen[109] and they feared that confusion might spread among national judges as to which law should be applied in cases of conflicting norms, preempting the ECJ's argument in the *Costa* decision.[110] While in principle agreeing with Ophüls position, which they claimed was logical and demonstrated the "Community Spirit,"[111] they realized that Ophüls' prointegration view was far from representative of the West German legal-academic community as a whole.

In their article, Ipsen and Nicolaysen grouped a long list of academics who opposed the views of Ophüls and the prointegration academics. One of the names they listed as in the opposition group was Hans Jürgen Schlochauer, who had earlier argued for a more pragmatic approach to integration after the crisis around the EDC in the 1950s. In this sense, Schlochauer's view did indeed differ from the supranationalists around Ophüls, but Schlochauer's argument is more complex than a direct rejection of this position. In 1963, Schlochauer asserted that European and national law actually stand equal with each other – affirming the supranationalist position on the independence of European law – but that in application in the FRG, European law was still subordinated to the Basic Law.[112] Moreover, he stated that if the principle of direct effect can not be assumed from the Treaty itself, it also can not be assumed that "federal" law – in this sense European law – should break "state" law automatically.[113] By rejecting direct effect, Schlochauer set out again

---

[107] Ophüls, "Quellen und Aufbau des Europäischen Gemeinschaftsrechts," p 1699.

[108] Ophüls, "Quellen und Aufbau des Europäischen Gemeinschaftsrechts," p 1701.

[109] Gert Nicolaysen (1931) is professor of public and economic law at the University of Hamburg, working closely alongside Ipsen. He retired from academic life in 1996.

[110] Hans Peter Ipsen and Gert Nicolaysen, "Haager Kongreß für Europarecht und Bericht über die Aktuelle Entwicklung des Gemeinschaftsrechts," *Neue Juristische Wochenschrift* 17.1964 (1964a), pp 340–1.

[111] "Der Gedankengang, den Ophüls … entwickelt hat…, zeugt von zwei Tugenden: von Logik und von europäischen Gemeinschaftsgeist"; Ipsen and Nicolaysen, "Haager Kongreß fur Europarecht und Bericht uber die Aktuelle Entwicklung des Gemeinschaftsrechts," pp 340.

[112] Hans Jürgen Schlochauer, "Das Verhältnis des Rechts der Europäischen Wirtschaftsgemeinschaft zu den Nationalen Rechtsordnung der Mitgliedstaaten," *Archiv des Völkerrechts* 11.1 (1963), p 18.

[113] Schlochauer, "Das Verhältnis des Rechts der Europäischen Wirtschaftsgemeinschaft zu den Nationalen Rechtsordnung der Mitgliedstaaten," pp 26–7.

what was intended to be a pragmatic formula for the integration process: Instead of a blanket doctrine of direct effect, he called for a case-by-case judgment on the applicability of the Community norm.[114] Preempting the ECJ's jurisprudence, he asserted that a primacy doctrine is also unnecessary for two reasons: first, that cooperation between national and European institutions would ensure that norms do not come into legal conflict; second, that sufficient enforcement mechanisms existed in the Treaty itself to ensure Member States comply with European law.[115] In other words, Schlochauer believed that cooperation at a political level would forestall the need for closer judicial integration and the compromising of the West German constitutional system.

Also in 1963, an article by Günther Jaenicke[116] took a similar approach to that of Schlochauer. First, Jaenicke also saw enough mechanisms and obligations already in the Treaty itself to ensure the compliance of Member States unwilling to or unknowingly not employing an applicable European norm.[117] Second, he felt that the overall question as to whether directly effective European norms were supreme to conflicting national regulations was overblown in importance.[118] Instead he suggested that a concrete case-by-case approach be adopted to see how conflicts could be solved would be the most effective way of dealing with the question. In other words, national courts should only be obliged to refer cases to the ECJ in which a real, actual conflict occurs between the two legal systems. It is then the exclusive responsibility of the ECJ to adjudicate on the conflict.[119] Like Schlochauer, Jaenicke also stressed the overwhelming importance of a political will for integration, without such a will, the Treaty mechanisms designed to ensure compliance would remain unused and useless, leaving the European legal framework unenforceable.[120] However, in contradistinction to Schlochauer, Jaenicke tended toward the supranational line, in which the Community held its own autonomous, sovereign legal framework, whereas Schlochauer, even in 1963, still defined the Treaties

---

[114] Schlochauer, "Das Verhältnis des Rechts der Europäischen Wirtschaftsgemeinschaft zu den Nationalen Rechtsordnung der Mitgliedstaaten," p 28.

[115] Schlochauer, "Das Verhältnis des Rechts der Europäischen Wirtschaftsgemeinschaft zu den Nationalen Rechtsordnung der Mitgliedstaaten," pp 28–9.

[116] Günther Jaenicke (1914) is a specialist in international and public law at the University of Frankfurt from 1959 till the current day (emeritus).

[117] Gunther Jaenicke, "Das Verhaltnis Zwischen Gemeinschaftsrecht und Nationalem Recht in der Agrarmarktorganisation der Europaischen Wirtschaftsgemeinschaft," *Zeitschrift fur auslandisches offentliches Recht und Volkerrecht*.1963 (1963), pp 525–7.

[118] Jaenicke, "Das Verhaltnis Zwischen Gemeinschaftsrecht und Nationalem Recht in der Agrarmarktorganisation der Europaischen Wirtschaftsgemeinschaft," pp 533–5.

[119] Jaenicke, "Das Verhaltnis Zwischen Gemeinschaftsrecht und Nationalem Recht in der Agrarmarktorganisation der Europaischen Wirtschaftsgemeinschaft," p 533.

[120] Jaenicke, "Das Verhaltnis Zwischen Gemeinschaftsrecht und Nationalem Recht in der Agrarmarktorganisation der Europaischen Wirtschaftsgemeinschaft," p 525.

of Rome as a treaty of international law.[121] This represented the fundamental schism in academic opinion: Was the Community an autonomous, independent and most importantly supranational legal order, or did it simply represent a complex, but conventional international institution?

Despite the number of prointegration, pragmatic, and skeptical opinions forming on the questions around the ECJ's doctrines, this basic problem of definition remained the clearest line of demarcation for many scholars. Alter's claim that "the German legal community has never accepted the 'special' nature of the Rome Treaty or that European is in some fundamental way different from international law"[122] misses this crucial point. While the majority, mainstream opinion was far from convinced at this point that the European law was anything other than standard international law, a small, but vocal minority were championing the supranationality of European law. This is the fundamental division in the legal academic reception. The Commissioner and legal scholar, Hans von der Groeben,[123] highlighted the division precisely during a speech held at the University of Marburg in June 1964.[124] Despite his pragmatic approach, Schlochauer was still an opponent to prointegration scholars for holding the view that the Community was a standard international organization. The supranationalists were now becoming more organized and more vocal. This activity reached its highpoint in 1964.

A crucially important moment in the development of the prointegration voice was the ASEL's Bensheim colloquium in 1964. The Bensheim meeting was undoubtedly the turning point in the legal-academic debate, from which point on the pro-supranational argument became increasingly popular and accepted. Alluding to the dividing line in scholarly opinion, the members of the European Commission's Legal Service reported in a memo to Walter Hallstein from July 1964, that the most

---

[121] Schlochauer, "Das Verhältnis des Rechts der Europäischen Wirtschaftsgemeinschaft zu den Nationalen Rechtsordnung der Mitgliedstaaten," p 3.

[122] Alter, *Establishing the Supremacy of European Law*, p 74.

[123] Hans von der Groeben (1907–2005) studied law and political economy before eventually working for Erhard and the Economics Ministry on the Schuman Plan. Afterward he represented West Germany at the ECSC, as a lead delegate at both the ESCS and Treaties of Rome negotiations. He was a commissioner on the Community Commission from 1958 to 1970 and afterward worked as adviser on the CDU's European policy.

[124] "Dabei ist der Ausgangspunkt immer wieder der dem klassischen Völkerrecht entnommene Satz gewesen, daß in zwischenstaatlichen Verträgen gesetzte, unmittelbar verbindliche Rechtsnormen durch die transformierende Kraft des Ratifikationsgesetze Bestandteil des nationalen Rechts werden und den gleichen Rang wie dieses haben. Ich glaube, daß die Anwendung solcher herkömmlichen Regeln des Völkerrechts der besonderen, neuartigen Natur der Gemeinschaft und des Gemeinschaftsrechts ebenso wenig gerecht wird wie Analogien mit staatsrechtlichen Begriffen und Vorstellungen," in "Ausführungen über das Verhältnis des Rechts der Gemeinschaft zu dem Recht der Mitgliedstaaten im Rahmen des Vertrages von Herrn von der Groeben vor der Universität Marburg am 22. Juni 1964," in KAS I-659–042/1 Nachlaß Hans von der Groeben.

prominent scholars of "classical international law"[125] had not taken part in the meeting.[126] Despite this, many of the important academics, lawyers, and government officials, so-called Spitzenbeamten,[127] who attended the conference, were in a position to shape West Germany's European policy.[128] Moreover, the high profile attendance of the ECJ's president and advocate general points to the conclusion that the ECJ was actively attempting to shape the outcome of the meeting. This agrees with findings in other studies that suggest almost simultaneous meetings across West Germany and France[129] at this time were part of a bigger strategy on the part of the European institutions, particularly the Commission's Legal Service, and FIDE to ensure a positive reception of the primacy doctrine.[130] The battle of ideas had begun, not just here, but across Europe.[131] While they did partially succeed in this goal, ensuring a large swing in favor of European legal primacy, this success would ultimately prove to be only temporary.[132] Ultimately, the group failed to win the battle overall.

The conference dealt with two issues, namely the relationship between national and European law, dealt with by Ipsen and Erich Bülow of the Justice Ministry,

---

[125] "Hauptvertreter des klassischen Völkerrechts" in Memorandum, 16 July 1964, in BA N1266 1156 Nachlaß Walter Hallstein: Wissenschaftliche Gesellschaft für Europarecht.

[126] Memorandum, 16 July 1964, in BA N1266 1156 Nachlaß Walter Hallstein: Wissenschaftliche Gesellschaft für Europarecht

[127] *Spitzenbeamten* translates as "top official" and refers to those in the higher echelons of the Civil Service; usually two or three levels down from the state secretary. Further information on the ranks and responsibilities of German civil servants can be found on the government Web site http://www.bundesregierung.de (last accessed 31 May 2011) and in Chapter 4.

[128] Attendees included, among many others, ECJ President Donner, ECJ Advocate General Karl Römer, the FRG's European lawyer, Arved Deringer; from the Federal Justice Ministry: MinDir Roemer, MR Dr. Arnold, ORR Bülow; from the Federal Interior Ministry: MR Dr Everling, MNDGT Dr Kölbe, MR Dr von Meibom; from the Foreign Ministry: Ophüls, VLRI von Puttkamer; Professors Fuß, Ipsen, Jaenicke, Kaiser, Nicolaysen, Von Simson, Zweigert.

[129] The French Association des Juristes Europeens held a similar discussion in December 1964 in Paris. See Council of Europe, Directorate of Human Rights, "Information Sheet" (Strasbourg: The Directorate, 1984), vol. 23. FIDE had organized conferences in the Hague in 1963 to deal with direct effect and Paris in 1965 on primacy.

[130] See Rasmussen, "Constructing and Deconstructing European 'Constitutional' European Law: Some Reflections on How to Study the History of European Law"; Rasmussen, "Exploring the Secret History of the Legal Service of the European Executives, 1952–1967," Alter, *European Court's Political Power: Selected Essays.*

[131] For a pioneering analysis of the role and contestation of ideas in the process of European integration, see Craig Parsons, "Showing Ideas as Causes: The Origins of the European Union," *International Organisation* 56.1 (2002). While Parsons analyzes the battle for ideas in the French case, much of what he writes is equally applicable here in the German case – a small minority of supranationalists, backed by the European institutions and with some access to power, sought to sway the opinions of a much larger indifferent or hostile body of mainstream opinion.

[132] For an account documenting the similar failure of FIDE-affiliated groups in France, see Bernier, "Constructing and Legitimating: Transnational Jurist Networks and the Making of a Constitutional Practice of European Law, 1950–1970."

and a technical issue on the right of establishment in the Community. Ipsen put forward the view that the effectiveness of the European institutions was paramount (mirroring the ECJ's argumentation in *Costa*). This meant that the laws issued by the Community had to be supreme and directly effective, in order to keep them "out of reach"[133] of meddling Member State governments issuing subsequent, conflicting legislation. Ipsen argued that European law superceded even national constitutional law, as that in the very few cases where a collision between the Basic Law and European legislation might occur, ultimately the choice to transfer sovereignty under Article 24 (i) BL meant that European law had to take precedence.

Bülow's view differed slightly from Ipsen, in that at no point did he deny the supranationality of the European institutions, but he did question the primacy of European law. Bülow argued that the ECJ's reasoning in the *Costa* decision was not convincing enough to establish a genuine primacy doctrine and that the onus was on the ECJ to provide a more persuasive argument. These counterpoints ignited a lively debate, led by Ophüls, among the audience. The report to Hallstein stated that the vast majority sided with Ipsen, with only Jaenicke supporting Bülow's argument about the lack of clarity in the ECJ's decision. Tellingly, in the final questions of the debate, the issue of a conflict between European law and the constitutional Basic Rights was raised, despite many arguing that the importance of this question had been overestimated.[134] The report stated that there was full agreement that fundamental rights were to be adhered to in European legislation, but not necessarily the Basic Rights guaranteed in the Basic Law or any other national constitution. While this conclusion suited the scholars at this fiercely prointegration colloquium, the question of Basic Rights proved much more problematic for other legal thinkers later on in the decade.

A further memo to Hallstein from the Community's Legal Service in 1965[135] reported on the Congress of German Public Law Teachers meeting of the previous year and highlighted, as Mann does,[136] that it marked a major break with the thinking of mainstream public law opinion toward the Community. The memo

---

[133] "Aus dem Grundsatz der Effektivität ergibt sich deshalb die 'mitgliedstaatliche Unantastbarkeit' der Gemeinschaftsregelungen: Diese Unantastbarkeit wird auch nicht etwa infolge des Grundsatzes "lex posterior derogt legi priori eingeschränkt oder aufgehoben," in Memorandum, 16 July 1964, in BA N1266 1156 Nachlaß Walter Hallstein: Wissenschaftliche Gesellschaft für Europarecht.

[134] "Man war sich im übrigen darüber einig, daß die Frage der Grundrechtskonformität der Gemeinschaftsakte, schon wegen des weiten Nachprüfungsspielraum des Gerichtshofs, in ihrer Bedeutung und auch ihrer Schwierigkeit im allgemeinen überschätzt werde," in Memorandum, 16 July 1964, in BA N1266 1156 Nachlaß Walter Hallstein: Wissenschaftliche Gesellschaft für Europarecht.

[135] "Vermerk an Herrn Präsident Hallstein, betr: Verhältnis von Gemeinschaftsrecht an nationalen Recht," 11 January 1965, in BA N1226 1796 Nachlaß Walter Hallstein: Verhältnis Gemeinschaftsrecht – Nationales Recht.

[136] Mann, *Function of Judicial Decision in European Economic Integration*, p 419.

stated in particular that the results of the meeting of the Bensheim Colloquium had proven influential in shaping this change in opinions.[137] In the Bonn 1953 and Erlangen 1959 meetings, the general opinion had been that the Communities were still merely complex international treaties and therefore their legal autonomy and effectiveness was regarded as the same as standard international organizations. Attention fell mostly on the Basic Law itself and the ways and extent to which it could afford authorities to international organizations. Now in Kiel 1964, this opposition to the independent dynamism of the integration process had been modified, so that Ipsen could cheerfully declare during the discussions that he felt part of a new "Kiel Wave."[138]

Two speakers, Joseph Kaiser[139] and Peter Badura,[140] focused on the legal identity of the Community itself, with much of the discussion losing the "Grundgesetzintrovertiertheit"[141] of the earlier discussions. This helped the members to reach a number of new positions: First, there appeared a growing acceptance that a total structural congruence between the Communities and the Federal Republic was impossible to achieve and no longer necessary. Enough of national legal standards existed in the Community legal framework for it to conform to the requirements of Article 24 (i) BL, and even if the democratic control was qualitatively weaker at the supranational level, this was a "sacrifice" the FRG had to make in the name of integration[142]; Second, it became clear that although the parliamentary control of executive power in the Communities was below the standards of the national level, it was not suitable for national practices simply to be transferred to the Community level – the European institutions could only form their own system of democratic controls suitable for the demands of supranational governance[143]; Third, it was accepted that the European legal framework was independent from national control, particularly national judicial control, but that the European law

---

[137] "Zusammenfassen kann, soweit auf Grund der bisherigen Berichte zu übersehen ist, gesagt werden, daß sich nach dem Erfolg der Bensheim Tagung der Gesellschaft für Europarecht nunmehr auch die Betrachtungsweise der deutschen Staatsrechtslehrer stärker im gemeinschaftsfreundlichen Sinne entwickelt hat," in "Vermerk an Herrn Präsident Hallstein, betr: Verhältnis von Gemeinschaftsrecht an nationalen Recht," 11 January 1965, in BA N1226 1796 Nachlaß Walter Hallstein: Verhältnis Gemeinschaftsrecht – Nationales Recht.

[138] Joseph Kaiser and Peter Badura, "Bewahrung and Veränderung Demokratischer und Rechstaatlicher Verfassungsstruktur in den Internationalen Gemeinschaften," *Veröffentlichungen der Vereinigung der Deutschen Staatsrechtslehrer* 23 (1964), p 128.

[139] Joseph Kaiser (1921–98) was a professor of international law at the University of Freiburg im Breisgau.

[140] Peter Badura (1934) is a professor of state and administrative law, based from 1964 to 1970 at the University of Göttingen and since 1970, at the University of Munich.

[141] Translated literally, "Basic Law introversion"; Kaiser and Badura, "Bewahrung and Veränderung Demokratischer," p 146.

[142] Kaiser and Badura, "Bewahrung and Veränderung Demokratischer," p 30.

[143] Kaiser and Badura, "Bewahrung and Veränderung Demokratischer," pp 97–8.

was still bound to the same principles as national law – freedom, basic rights, and democracy[144]; finally, European law was subject to national constitutional control, in that it was agreed that the FCC had the right to measure the national laws transforming Community norms into West German law against the constitution and to rule them unconstitutional if this were the case.[145] However the FCC did not have the competence to test the constitutionality of directly effective European law – this was the exclusive competence of the ECJ.[146]

Mann's revelation of a "dramatic change"[147] to an extent then holds true. From the findings of the earlier Congresses, the results of the Kiel meeting did represent a radical shift in position. It is now possible to understand that this "dramatic shift" did not take place in one revolutionary moment. Instead, it has been shown that the original tendency to regard the Community as standard international organizations had slowly evolved because of two factors: First, the radical jurisprudence of the ECJ establishing direct effect and primacy made it virtually impossible to continue regarding the Community as merely complex international bodies. The reality of the autonomy and sovereignty of the European legal framework was impossible to ignore or to deny. Second, the consistent logic of prointegration scholars, such as Ophüls and Ipsen, undermined the basis of the majority position. Nothing is more illustrative of the shift in mainstream opinion toward the nature of European law than an article published by Hermann Mosler in 1968. Mosler was at the time Director of the Max Planck Institute for International Law in Heidelberg, West Germany's most prestigious legal university, and later became a judge on the European Court of Human Rights (1959) and the International Court of Justice (1976). He was, undoubtedly, through his work and the positions held, one of the most influential voices in West German legal academia. Throughout the 1950s, Mosler had repeatedly denied the legal autonomy of the ECSC institutions, seeing integration as little more than the result of particularly complex international treaties. Yet by 1968, even Mosler felt the need to reconsider his view. He wrote that the existence of a separate and unique system of European law can no longer be denied,[148] and it was no longer possible to analyze this system through the terminology of standard international law.[149] Even the primacy of European law in areas of

[144] Kaiser and Badura, "Bewahrung and Veränderung Demokratischer," p 98.
[145] Kaiser and Badura, "Bewahrung and Veränderung Demokratischer," pp 100–1.
[146] Kaiser and Badura, "Bewahrung and Veränderung Demokratischer," pp 102–3.
[147] Mann, *Function of Judicial Decision in European Economic Integration*, p 419.
[148] "Die Tatsache, daß das neue Fach existiert und daß man es nicht mehr abschaffen könnte, selbst wenn man es wollte, ist sicherlich genügender Anlass, sich damit auseinanderzusetzen"; Mosler, "Begriff und Gegenstand des Europarechts," p 484.
[149] "Das Europarecht kann deshalb nicht unmittelbar an die Maximen und Völkerrechtssätze anknüpfen, die das alte öffentliche Recht Europas konstituiert haben," Mosler, "Begriff und Gegenstand des Europarechts," p 501.

Community competence had been intellectually established, if not widely agreed upon in detail.

By the mid-1960s, there did, however, remain one important question yet to be fully resolved, although it was frequently touched upon: basic rights. The following problem had not been solved: How could the primacy and direct effectiveness of European law be reconciled with the inviolability of the Basic Law's fundamental rights? There was also the question of authority to rule on issues involving conflicts between them and European law. The problem of structural congruence as a prerequisite for legitimate transfer of sovereignty remained. It was this problem then that legal-academia entered the period of the mid-1960s attempting to resolve.

Even as early as 1964, the question of comparable or congruent fundamental rights protection was being discussed in legal-academic circles. Klaus Vogel[150] wrote of his support for the integration project based on the fact that the fundamental decision made by the fathers of the Basic Law to make it an intrinsically international constitution bound the Federal Republic to the European project and its legal consequences.[151] Erich Bülow recognized the fact that the transference of sovereignty under Article 24 (i) BL meant that power could be exercised over the West German population that was no longer bound by the Basic Law.[152] The protection afforded by the fundamental rights by Article 79 (iii) BL no longer held any power. However, he also correctly pointed out that the Communities were obliged to adhere to the central constitutional principles found in its Member States.[153] This left the protection of fundamental rights in a precarious position, even more so as the authorities of the Communities grew and the lack of parliamentary control over executive power became ever wider.[154] Bülow's answer was to call for a powerful, directly elected parliament to control any excesses of executive power and maintain the Communities' structural congruence with the Federal Republic.[155] This, however, left much to be desired as a solution to the problem.

[150] Klaus Vogel (1930) is a professor of state and administrative law from Hamburg, who was based at the University of Munich from 1977 to 1996. At the time of writing the cited article, he was based at the University of Erlangen-Nuremburg.

[151] Klaus Vogel, *Die Verfassungsentscheidung des Grundgesetzes für Eine Internationale Zusammenarbeit: Ein Diskussionsbeitrag zu Einer Frage der Staatstheorie Sowie des Geltenden Deutschen Staatsrechts,* Recht und Staat in Geschichte und Gegenwart (Tübingen,: Mohr, 1964).

[152] Erich Bülow, "Das Verhaltnis des Rechts der Europaischen Gemeinschaften zum Nationalen Recht," *Aktuelle Fragen des europäischen Gemeinschaftsrechts, Gemeinschaftsrecht und nationales Rechts Niederlassungsfreiheit und Rechtsangleichung – Europarechtliches Kolloqium* (Bensheim: Ferdinand Enke Verlag, 1965), p 57.

[153] Bülow, "Das Verhaltnis des Rechts der Europaischen Gemeinschaften zum Nationalen Recht," p 58.

[154] Bülow, "Das Verhaltnis des Rechts der Europaischen Gemeinschaften zum Nationalen Recht," pp 58–9.

[155] Bülow, "Das Verhaltnis des Rechts der Europaischen Gemeinschaften zum Nationalen Recht," p 59.

Former ECJ Judge, Otto Riese, writing in 1966, agreed with Bülow that the protection of fundamental rights in the Communities was too weak in comparison to the Federal Republic's own safeguards.[156] Nevertheless, Riese remained convinced that basic rights could still be protected by the existing treaties, in that mechanisms already existed through which offending Community decisions could be brought to the ECJ for preliminary review, even by individuals, by means of Article 267.[157] For Riese, the failings of the Community's basic rights protection could be resolved not by national intervention by the Member States, in particular a revision of the founding Treaty, but rather by the tools already existing within the Community itself. In this sense, both Riese and Bülow adopted a proceduralist approach to the problem, seeing solutions to the issue in improving and increasing accessibility to preexisting Community mechanisms. Hanspeter von Meibom[158] blamed the lack of clarity of the authority to rule on fundamental rights protection at the European level on the practical necessity of reaching compromise during the initial Treaties of Rome negotiations.[159] Despite this, von Meibom supported the primacy doctrine, regarding it necessary for the Community to have an effective appearance in the eyes of economic leaders, who were ultimately the people who held the future success of economic integration in their hands.[160] Writing in response to an article in the same journal from the Cologne based lawyer, Dietrich Ehle,[161] von Meibom rejected Ehle's assumption that the authority authority to rule on European law remained a national constitutional prerogative. This, he claimed, ignored the fact that in the Treaties of Rome, the Member States had sacrificed knowingly and willingly areas of national sovereignty to the European institutions.[162] Ehle, who had earlier

---

[156] Otto Riese, "Über den Rechtsschutz von Privatpersonen und Unternehmen in der Europäischen Wirtschaftsgemeinschaft," *Probleme der Europäischen Rechts: Festschift für Walter Hallstein zu Seinem 65. Geburtstag*, ed. Ernst Caemmerer, Hans-Jürgen Schlochauer and Ernst Steindorff (Frankfurt am Main: Vittorio Klostermann, 1966), p 420.

[157] Riese, "Über den Rechtsschutz von Privatpersonen und Unternehmen in der Europäischen Wirtschaftsgemeinschaft," p 430.

[158] Von Meibom was a ministerial adviser (*Ministerialrat*) at the Federal Interior Ministry (BMI) and attendee of the 1964 Bensheim Colloquium. The Bensheim Colloquium was the key turning point in the shift of academic opinion toward the acceptance of the supranationality of European law.

[159] "Diese Auffassung übersieht, daß in den Vertragsverhandlungen die von Fachgruppen erarbeiteten Teile des Vertrages nur sehr notdürftig mit dem so genannten institutionellen Teil ... abgestimmt werden konnten.... Irgendwelche weiterreichende, generelle, d.h. das Rechtssystem der Gemeinschaften betreffende Bedeutung ist dieser Vorschrift dagegen nicht direkt zuzumessen"; Hans Peter von Meibom, "Beiträge zum Europarecht," *Neue Juristische Wochenschrift* 11 (1965), p 465.

[160] "Der Erfolg des Versuches einer Wirtschaftsintegration hängt letztlich davon ab, daß die Wirtschaft selbst ihn ernst nimmt, seine Konsequenzen in ihre wirtschaftliche Planungen einbezieht und Vertrauen in die Effektivität und Dauerhaftigkeit der in Gang gesetzten Entwicklungen gewinnt"; von Meibom, "Beiträge Zum Europarecht," p 466.

[161] Dietrich Ehle (1935) is a Cologne-based lawyer, specializing in European and customs law.

[162] "Es zeigt sich in dieser Vorschrift die Bereitschaft der Mitgliedstaaten des EWG-Rechtsordnung dort, wo Abgrenzungen zwischen dem EWG-Rechtssystem und dem nationalen Rechtssystem notwendig

confirmed the *Van Gend* decision,[163] cited Article 87 of the Treaties of Rome, which gave the Council the authority to decide on the relationship between European and national law, as proof that the final say belonged to the relevant national authority, that is, the highest national court.[164] Ehle felt however that the problem of protecting the Basic Rights was not truly an issue, writing that the Community had more to fear from Member States rejecting the ECJ's jurisprudence, than the Member States had of the Community overruling fundamental rights provisions.[165]

Hans von der Groeben went even further than Ehle in an article in 1966 concerning the protection of fundamental rights in the Community. Von der Groeben argued that as soon as it became possible for a Member State to ignore European law out of national constitutional considerations, even those concerning basic rights protection, then the Community would lose all effectiveness.[166] It was unthinkable that basic rights, which were cataloged in all six Member States, could be violated by the Community as the Treaty, the Community's constitution, was the sum of the work of the Member States and could not be altered without unanimous approval.[167] Even without its own catalog, the possibility that all six Member States would agree to an unconstitutional amendment to the Community Treaty was unimaginable.[168]

---

werden sollten, die Vorrangigkeit dem EWG-Rechts zuzuerkennen.... Hinzukommen muß immer noch die weitere Denkkategorie der Zielsetzung des Vertrages und der bekundeten Bereitschaft der Mitgliedstaaten, das hierzu Erforderliche zu tun"; von Meibom, "Beiträge zum Europarecht," p 465.

[163] "Aus den vorstehenden Erwägungen ergibt sich, daß nach dem Geist, der Systematik und dem Wortlaut des Vertrages, Art 12 dahin auszulegen ist, daß er unmittelbare Wirkungen erzeugt und individuelle Rechte begründet, welche die staatlichen Gerichte zu beachten haben"; Deitriche Ehle, "Commentary to European Court of the Justice Decision 26/62," *Neue Juristische Wochenschrift* 21 (1963), p 976.

[164] "Für den Bereich der integrierten Rechtsordnungen in jedem Mitgliedstaat bleibt das Verhältnis beider Rechtssysteme aber eine Frage des nationalen Verfassungsrechts und damit der Entscheidungskompetenz des innerstaatlichen Richters.... Für die Richtigkeit dieser Auffassung spricht vor allem Art 87, Abs. 2, Buchst. E EWGV. Danach kann der Rat das Verhältnis zwischen den innerstaatlichen Rechtsvorschriften einerseits und den in den Art 85ff EWGV enthaltenen Bestimmungen andererseits festlegen. Nur für diesen Einzelfall ist ein Gemeinschaftsorgan, das zudem am stärksten innerstaatlich verwurzelt ist, ermächtigt, eine Rangordnung mit allgemeiner Wirkung zu schaffen"; Dietrich Ehle, "Verhältnis des Europaischen Gemeinschaftsrechts zum Nationalen Recht," *Neue Juristische Wochenschrift* 50 (1964), p 2332.

[165] "Echte Gefahren hat die Gemeinschaftsordnung allenfalls durch innerstaatlichen Gesetze zu befürchten, die ihrer Kompetenzausweitung nicht nachgeben....Von den Verfassungsgarantien, deren Beachtung zudem in der Macht der Gemeinschaftsorgane liegt, sind ... keinerlei Hindernisse oder Nachteile zu befürchten"; Ehle, "Verhaltnis des Europaischen Gemeinschaftsrechts zum Nationalen Recht," p 2333.

[166] Hans von der Groeben, "Über das Problem der Grundrechte in der Europäischen Gemeinschaft," *Probleme der Europäischen Rechts: Festschrift für Walter Hallstein zu Seinem 65 Geburtstag*, ed. Ernst Caemmerer, Hans-Jürgen Schlochauer and Ernst Steindorff (Frankfurt am Main: Vittorio Klostermann, 1966), p 232.

[167] von der Groeben, "Über das Problem der Grundrechte in der Europäischen Gemeinschaft," pp 244–5.

[168] von der Groeben, "Über das Problem der Grundrechte in der Europäischen Gemeinschaft," p 245.

Moreover, von der Groeben posited that whereas in most constitutional states there exists a tension between the codified legal ideals and the political reality in which they are to be honored, in the Community, the single political reality was the fulfillment of its basic values – equality, freedom, and justice – in the form of an open and complete Common Market. As a result of these two factors, basic rights were in fact better guaranteed within the Community than they were in individual Member States![169]

Manfred Zuleeg[170] took a very similar line to von der Groeben's, disputing the possibility of a constitutional violation by the Community because the individual was so well protected by the Treaty and by the legal traditions of the Member States – with or without a catalog of rights to match the national documents.[171] He suggested that even if the FCC ruled a European law as unconstitutional, this would only be applicable by West German courts, which although a serious occurrence, would not render the Community norm itself invalid. The FCC lacked the competence to rule on the validity of European law.[172]

The supranationalists were heavily criticized by those who opposed the transference of West German sovereignty to institutions that did not explicitly protect fundamental rights. Again Hans Jürgen Schlochauer voiced his view in 1966 that the Community legal system was separate and distinct from the national structures (in traditional international law terms) and therefore had no competence to rule on issues of national constitutionality.[173] According to Schlochauer, this raised a problem that had been thoroughly discussed in legal-academic circles but was not yet satisfactorily answered: How can the FRG's commitment to fundamental rights be honored by a legal system whose powers are directly effective and supreme but does not have the competence to assess the value of national legal norms?[174] Like the pragmatic approaches of Riese, Bülow, and Jaenicke before him, Schlochauer saw the answer to this conundrum in the Treaties of Rome itself. Using Article 267, decision-making cooperation between Member States courts, which are the true guardians of national constitutions, and the ECJ

---

[169] von der Groeben, "Über das Problem der Grundrechte in der Europäischen Gemeinschaft," p 245.

[170] Manfred Zuleeg (1935) is a professor of international public law at the University of Frankfurt. In this period, he was employed by the Universities of Cologne (1962–71) and Bonn (1971–8). He was an ECJ justice from 1988 to 1994 and has represented the FRG on cases before the ECJ.

[171] Manfred Zuleeg, "Fundamental Rights and the Law of the European Communities," *Common Market Law Review* 8 (1971), pp 43–4.

[172] Zuleeg, "Fundamental Rights and the Law of the European Communities," pp 109–10.

[173] Hans Jürgen Schlochauer, "Der Gerichtshof der Europäischen Gemeinschaften als Integrationsfaktor," *Probleme der Europäischen Rechts: Festschrift für Walter Hallstein zu Seinem 65. Geburtstag*, ed. Ernst Caemmerer, Hans-Jürgen Schlochauer and Ernst Steindorff (Frankfurt am Main: Vittorio Klostermann, 1966), pp 434–5.

[174] Schlochauer, "Der Gerichtshof der Europäischen Gemeinschaften als Integrationsfaktor," pp 435–6.

could be fostered so that both goals of integration and of fundamental rights protection can be achieved.[175]

However, other opponents did not take Schlochauer's procedural compromise to heart. Wilhelm Wengler[176] insisted the transference of authorities to the Community was only valid if the Community held a similar set of fundamental rights as that of the Federal Republic, again echoing the "structural congruence" argument found up until the 1964 Kiel meeting. He asked pointedly why authorities should be transferred to a set of institutions without basic rights protection, if they would not be transferred to institutions who would undertake wars of aggression – another constitutional provision of the Basic Law.[177] Wengler's heavy criticism of the Community's institutions came as a result of two of the FCC's major decisions during 1967 in relation to European law.[178] First, the FCC made the long awaited decision on the RTC's referral questioning the constitutionality of the ratification of the Treaties of Rome.[179] The FCC's decision in this case provoked more questions than it answered and many scholars probed the actual legal reasoning of the court.[180] While prointegrationists such as Ipsen and Nicolaysen[181] greeted the referral as a chance for the FCC to rule finally in favor of membership, the FCC did not rule immediately on the case. Instead, the Court used its "delay tactic,"[182] waiting four years before finally dismissing the referral, attempting in this time to achieve two goals: provoking debate and promoting the building of consensus in legal-academic opinion. The former proved considerably easier to achieve than the latter, because the contrasting positions concerning the applicability of European law became ever more entrenched and consolidated.

The result of the case was that the RTC's reference was technically inadmissible, but the point was made that if a single European regulation was unconstitutional, the entire Treaty was not null and void.[183] This judgment only passed by a slender

[175] Schlochauer, "Der Gerichtshof der Europäischen Gemeinschaften als Integrationsfaktor," pp 451–2.

[176] Wilhelm Wengler (1907–95) was a professor of international law at the Free University in Berlin, founding that institution's Department of International and Comparative Law

[177] Wilhelm Wengler, "Aus Wissenschaft und Praxis: Grundrechtsminimum und Equivalenz der Grundrechtsschutzsysteme," *Juristen-Zeitung* 10 (1968), p 327.

[178] Wengler, "Aus Wissenschaft und Praxis: Grundrechtsminimum und Equivalenz der Grundrechtsschutzsysteme," p 327.

[179] Re Tax on Malt Barley (Case III 77/63), BVerfG decision of 5 July 1967, EuR 2 (1967).

[180] Green, *Political Integration by Jurisprudence: The Work of the Court of Justice of the European Communities in European Political Integration*, pp 400–1; Mann, *Function of Judicial Decision in European Economic Integration*, pp 420–4; Alter, *Establishing the Supremacy of European Law*, pp 77–9.

[181] Ipsen and Nicolaysen, "Haager Kongreß fur Europarecht und Bericht uber die Aktuelle Entwicklung des Gemeinschaftsrechts," p 344.

[182] Mann, *Function of Judicial Decision in European Economic Integration*, pp 184, 420–1.

[183] Re Tax on Malt Barley (Case III 77/63), BVerfG decision of 5 July 1967, EuR 2 (1967)

four-three voting majority and demonstrated that the divergent views in the legal-academic community made it impossible for the FCC to form a single, unambiguous position on the question of European law applicability. The result left scholars on both sides of the debate disappointed, and not long after the decision, the FCC was again faced with the problem of judging the applicability of a European norm in the national setting. This time a constitutional complaint was made directly to the FCC against Article 189 Community[184] because it was claimed that it impinged upon many of the fundamental rights of the Basic Law.[185] Again the FCC argued that the case was inadmissible because constitutional complaints can only be heard by the court against "German" public authority. The FCC argued, that despite the use of Article 24 (i) BL to join the Community, it was not exclusively "German" and therefore the court held no special competence to rule on the constitutionality of Community regulations. In this way, the FCC agreed de facto that European law was both directly effective and supreme in its areas of competence within the West German legal framework.

THE SOLANGE ERA, 1970–1974: FINDING A MIDDLE PATH? STRUCTURAL CONGRUENCE, SOLANGE AND BASIC RIGHTS PROTECTION

First, it is important to resituate at this point the legal-academic debate within the evolution of judicial decision making at the time. A number of important cases were heard at the turn of the decade. In November 1969, during the *Stauder v. Ulm* case,[186] the ECJ ruled against its earlier decisions of 1959 and 1960,[187] declaring that fundamental rights protection did actually form a general principle of European law, even if a specific catalog of rights did not yet exist. Following from its *de facto* recognition of the primacy of European law in 1967, the FCC added on to this in the 1971 *Lütticke* decision the positive recognition of the doctrines of primacy and direct effect.[188] In the years 1967 to 1971, the FCC became the first court overall to fully recognize the primacy and direct effectiveness of European law in relation to national law, not however explicitly with regard to constitutional law.[189] The question as to

---

[184] Article 189 Community related to the applicability of European law within national systems.

[185] BVerfG decision of 18 October 1967 [1968] Europarecht 134.

[186] Case 29/69 *Stauder vs. Ulm* [1969] European Court Report 419.

[187] Case 01/58 *Stork vs. High Authority* [1959] European Court Report 17.Case 36–38 and 40/59 *Ruhrkohlenverkaufsgesellschaften vs. High Authority* [1960] European Court Report 423.

[188] 2 BvR 225/69 – *Milk powder decision*, 9 June 1971 – BVerfGE 31, 145.

[189] At this moment then, as Alter points out, the FCC had gone further than any other national court in accepting the radical jurisprudence from the ECJ of the early 1960s – Alter, *Establishing the Supremacy of European Law*, p 79. Mann argues that the reason for the FCC's endorsement of the ECJ at this point was the political "paralysis" of the Community during the mid 1960s, and that a rejection at this

the relationship between national constitutional law and the European legal system remained open and became a particularly controversial topic of discussion among legal-academia. This phase in the debate is then characterized by the disagreement about the comparative virtues of the European and national legal systems. The supranationalists, buoyed by the apparent acceptance of the FCC of European legal independence, came under increasing attack in this period by scholars troubled by the implications of the FCC's *European Regulations* decision. These attacks were highly vitrolic, even polemic and really forced the FCC into rethinking its 1967 decision. The direct result of this counterattack by the traditionalists was the losing of ground by the supranationalists and a change in jurisprudence by the FCC. This is, of course, most apparent in the *Solange* decision at the end of this particular period.

In March 1970, the Administrative Court of Frankfurt (FAC) referred a case concerning a European regulation to the ECJ. The case involved an importing company, which claimed its basic rights had been violated by a deposit scheme created by the Community. The FAC sent the reference fully expecting the ECJ to nullify the regulation. In essence, the FAC's referral asked the ECJ to rule on the question as to whether European law was supreme even over the fundamental rights of the Basic Law: the debate prompted at the end of the 1960s in legal-academia had finally reached a judicial hearing. The ECJ's decision was highly controversial, but at the same time multifaceted. In the *Internationale Handelsgesellschaft*[190] ruling, it declared that in the name of the "uniformity and efficacy of European law," constitutional fundamental rights of Member States may have to be sidelined in the face of conflicting European regulations – in other words, building on the *Costa* case, European law now broke Member States' constitutional law. Yet, the decision was tempered slightly, as the ECJ clearly stated in its wording, that the court's decision making was deeply "inspired by the constitutional traditions common to the Member States." This stressed that despite the primacy of European law over the national constitutions, the spirit of the constitutions, and particularly that of fundamental rights protection, continued to be incorporated in and protected by the ECJ's jurisprudence. An explanation of the reasoning in the case written by several ECJ judges was published, in English, by the Max Planck Research Institute's International Law Journal in 1972.[191]

---

point would have been a body blow for the integration project (Mann, *Function of Judicial Decision in European Economic Integration*, pp 422–3). Weiler maintains a similar argument, seeing closer judicial integration during the 1960s as the corollary to political disintegration within the Council of Ministers (Weiler, *Constitution of Europe – "Do the New Clothes Have an Emperor?"* pp 10–96).

[190] Case 11/70 *Internationale Handelsgesellschaft vs. Einfuhr- und Vorratsstelle für Getriede und Futtermittel* [1970] European Court Report 1125.

[191] Pescatore, "Aspects of the Court of Justice of the European Communities of Interest from the Point of View of International Law."

The ECJ's statement again strongly divided opinion in West German academia. Supporting the ECJ, scholars such as Gert Meier,[192] argued the ECJ was merely restating the autonomy of the European legal order, which was increasingly accepted during the 1960s. Its separateness meant that it could not be bound to the conditions of national legal orders.[193] On the other side, the specialist journal, *Außenwirtschaftsdienst des Betriebs-Beraters*, published a critique of the ECJ's decision by the Hamburg based lawyer Helmut Rittstieg.[194] In this, Rittstieg argued the ECJ's claim to incorporate that spirit of national constitutions was too "vague" and "questionable"[195] to protect an individual's rights. He claimed basic rights remained a "secondary condition" for the ECJ behind that of the general effectiveness of the Community and that this judgment barely represented a successful pursuance of basic rights provisions at the European level.[196] The FAC followed the argument offered by Rittstieg, promptly refusing to apply the ECJ's ruling and again referred the case – this time to the FCC. The FCC's decision on this case was made three years later in the *Solange* decision. In the following three years, 1971 to 1974, the debate around the applicability of European law in West Germany reached its most intense phase.

What stood out most about the FAC's reference however was the heavy influence of a speech given by Hans Heinrich Rupp,[197] a legal professor from Mainz, from whose work the court quoted directly in its referral.[198] In a speech to the German Academy of Judges in January 1970, Rupp launched a polemic attack, rebelling against the so-called Kiel Wave and against the growing acceptance among legal-academic opinion that the transference of sovereignty through Article 24 (i) BL empowered an autonomous supranational legal entity to issue directly effective and supreme regulations within the national constitutional framework. While scholars, for example Wilhelm Wengler,[199] had merely posed the question during the 1960s as to how authorities could be transferred to structurally incongruent institutions, which lacked a comparable sense of democratic legitimacy to their national equivalents. Rupp now openly and strongly criticized this process.[200] He declared the fact that the Basic Law had been sidelined by the ECJ in its 1963–4 jurisprudence as a

---

[192] Gert Meier (1938) is an attorney in Cologne, who was a NATO scholar at Stanford University.
[193] Gert Meier, "Commentary to European Court of Justice Decision 29/69," *Deutsches Verwaltungsblatt* (1970), p 614.
[194] Helmut Rittstieg (1939–2002) was a specialist in international law at the University of Hamburg.
[195] Helmut Rittstieg, "Commentary to European Court of Justice Decision 11/70," *Aussenwirtschaftsdienst des Betriebs-Beraters* 4 (1971), p 184.
[196] Rittstieg, "Commentary to European Court of Justice Decision 11/70," p 184.
[197] Hans Heinrich Rupp (1926) is a professor of public law at the University of Mainz, who also worked at Tübingen (1963–4) and Marburg (1964–8).
[198] Alter, *Establishing the Supremacy of European Law*, pp 88–9.
[199] Wengler, "Aus Wissenschaft und Praxis."
[200] Rupp, "Die Grundrechte und das Europäische Gemeinschaftsrecht," p 353.

"farce"[201] and denied that the Community held any kind of institutional resemblance with the Federal Republic at all.[202] In this, Rupp obviously rejected not only the line taken by supranationalist scholars, such as Ophüls, von der Groeben, Grewe and Ipsen, but also that of the more pragmatic approaches of Jaenicke, Schlochauer, and Riese, who saw a fundamental "structural congruence" between the Community and West Germany as a basis for the conditional acceptance of Community legal primacy. Rupp continued to vent angrily against the Community, describing it famously as "not only a regime without a master, the use of power without a democratic sovereign, but also a regime without fundamental rights.[203]

Rupp's anger was also aimed at the national level; he accused West German scholars of ignoring the Community's lack of basic rights protection – most particularly, he attacked the radical shift in thinking at the Congress of German Public Law Teachers in 1964 – the Kiel Wave – and its leading proponent, Hans Peter Ipsen.[204] Moreover, he identified the rapidly declining political will for integration as being caused by the growing recognition that national democratic sovereignty was being sacrificed to a nondemocratic supranational technocracy – only other Member States had recognized this trend much sooner than West Germany had.[205] Without a radical reform, further integration would prove impossible.[206]

Most importantly for the debate, Rupp rejected the direct effect and primacy of European law, particularly over and above the fundamental rights of the Basic Law. He went against the FCC's 1967 decision, which stated that the FCC had no competence to judge European law, arguing that if the Community norm is adopted into West German law, then the final arbiter of its applicability must be the national judiciary – in this case the FCC. Specifically, Rupp advocated the verification of European regulations by the FCC against national fundamental rights as an important step in the legitimization of the Community. It was not enough, he contended, for scholars such as Ipsen to argue that conflicts with the Basic Law would not arise because of the technical nature of the Community. The Europe that such a policy would create would indeed be unified, but at the cost of being ruled by a bureaucratic technocracy.[207] Only a Europe built and judged by the

---

[201] Rupp, "Die Grundrechte und das Europäische Gemeinschaftsrecht," p 353.

[202] Rupp, "Die Grundrechte und das Europäische Gemeinschaftsrecht," p 354.

[203] "Sie ist nicht nur Herrschaft ohne Herrn, Ausübung von Hoheitsrechten ohne demokratischer Souverän, sondern auch Herrschaft ohne Grundrechte" – Rupp, "Die Grundrechte und das Europäische Gemeinschaftsrecht," p 354.

[204] Rupp, "Die Grundrechte und das Europäische Gemeinschaftsrecht," p 354.

[205] Rupp, "Die Grundrechte und das Europäische Gemeinschaftsrecht," p 354.

[206] "An dieser Stelle wird klar warum die Entwicklung der Europäischen Gemeinschaften ohne eine grundsätzliche Struktur- und Kompetenzveränderung nicht vorwärts kommen kann" – Rupp, "Die Grundrechte und das Europäische Gemeinschaftsrecht," p 354.

[207] Rupp, "Die Grundrechte und das Europäische Gemeinschaftsrecht," p 358.

democratic, legitimate ideals of its constituent parts would be acceptable to future generations.[208]

With Rupp so clearly drawing the battle lines on this issue, it was the turn of his critic, Hans Peter Ipsen, to respond to the charges. Three months later, Ipsen accused Rupp of not fully understanding the nature of the integration process – for Ipsen, it remained a merely technical, economic procedure and therefore basic rights need not mentioned.[209] Rupp was accused of a having a late nineteenth century comprehension of constitutional law,[210] echoing the fundamental schism of the 1964 Bensheim Colloquium, whereas Ipsen prided himself on a more progressive, internationalized understanding.[211]

Ipsen pulled no punches in his attack on Rupp, asking why other more experienced democracies such as Belgium and Holland would be so "suicidal" as to agree to the primacy of European law.[212] He challenged Rupp to name an area of Community competence that would seriously affect the provision of national fundamental rights, and if one were found, he would provide the Community provision that supplied an equal guarantee in this area.[213] In the end, Ipsen highlighted how the *Stauder v. Ulm* decision of 1969 demonstrated the ECJ's commitment to fundamental rights and how these were, at national and Community levels, indistinguishable.[214] In 1972 Ipsen published an extensive survey of European law comprising over fifteen hundred pages, with its implications for the Federal Republic. In this he crystallized his view that fundamental rights are guaranteed in the Community through its inability to affect them in any meaningful way.[215] Calling Rupp a dogmatist, Ipsen conclusively rejected the need for national judicial control over European law.[216]

The question of the relationship between national and European law became the subject of a parliamentary Inquiry Commission in 1972. Under the guidance of Karl Carstens, Helmut Lehmke,[217] the State Premier of Schleswig-Holstein, and legal

---

[208] Rupp, "Die Grundrechte und das Europäische Gemeinschaftsrecht," p 359.

[209] Hans Peter Ipsen, "Verfassungsperspektiven der Europaischen Gemeinschaften – Vortag Gehalten am 17 April 1970," *Berliner Juristischen Gesellschaft* (Berlin: Walter de Gruyter & Co, 1970), pp 10–11.

[210] Ipsen, "Verfassungsperspektiven der Europaischen Gemeinschaften – Vortag Gehalten am 17 April 1970," p 10.

[211] Ipsen, "Verfassungsperspektiven der Europaischen Gemeinschaften, pp 10–11.

[212] Ipsen, "Verfassungsperspektiven der Europaischen Gemeinschaften," vol., pp 14–15.

[213] Ipsen, "Verfassungsperspektiven der Europaischen Gemeinschaften," p 22.

[214] Ipsen, "Verfassungsperspektiven der Europaischen Gemeinschaften, pp 24–5. Manfred Zuleeg also accused Rupp of not being aware of the Stauder vs. Ulm case when delivering his polemic against the ECJ – see Zuleeg, "Fundamental Rights and the Law of the European Communities."

[215] Hans Peter Ipsen, *Europaisches Gemeinschaftsrecht* (Tubingen: JCB Mohr [Paul Siebeck], 1972), pp 716–21.

[216] Ipsen, *Europaisches Gemeinschaftsrecht*, p 716.

[217] Lehmke (1907–90) was a trained lawyer and was involved extensively in the politics of the Federal State of Schleswig Holstein as culture minister, interior minister, and state premier.

expert Professor Karl Joseph Partsch,[218] the Commission was given the task of examining the effect that international and European law had on the domestic constitutional order.[219] For this purpose, the three members of the Commission drew heavily on some of the academic texts published at the beginning of the 1970s, all of which were recorded in the archival material present on this topic. Having been himself involved in the academic and ministerial discussions during the 1960s, Carstens maintained his position of accepting both the primacy and direct effect doctrines. His two copanellists quickly followed suit, despite the fact that the texts chosen as sources for debate reflected the deep divisions in academic opinion at the time.

The first of these texts, from the Cologne based academic, Jörg Manfred Mössner,[220] examined the various arguments for answering the basic rights question, looking first at those scholars who denied that a conflict between European law and the basic rights could possibly arise and called this "unconvincing." Second, he examined the ways in which "supreme" European law could be checked against the national constitutional provision, naming procedural and political measures through which this could occur. Finally, he argued, that if integration were allowed to proceed, then the Community must be accepted as an autonomous legal entity. On this presumption, there was no possible way that independent European law could be measured against the values of another (national) legal order. However, as the Community had taken on authorities beyond that originally given to it by the Member States, it was the right of the Member States to measure European law against national standards of constitutional protection.[221]

The second text, from Walter Seuffert,[222] a Constitutional Judge who later ruled in favor of the *Solange* decision, argued that the question of which measure of basic rights was to be used was merely secondary to the question about who was to decide on their validity.[223] For Seuffert, European law was an independent system, beyond the scrutiny of the FCC in individual cases. The FCC could, in regard to the Community, only measure the constitutionality of the ratification law, which

---

[218] Partsch (1914–96) taught public and international law at the Universities of Kiel, Mainz, and Bonn.

[219] The main topic of debate in the Commission was, above all else, the division of authorities between the federal and *Länder* governments, but also the question as to the protection of the Basic Rights. See BA B106 – 55473 BMI: Unterkommission I: Verhältnis vom Völkerrecht zu nationalem Recht 1972–6.

[220] Jörg Manfred Mössner (1941) worked at the University of Hamburg and is currently teaching at the University of Osnabrück.

[221] Jörg Manfred Mössner, "Einschränkungen von Grundrechten durch Ewg-Recht?" *Aussenwirtschaftsdienst des Betriebs-Beraters* 4 (1971), p 615.

[222] Walter Seuffert (1907–89) was a specialist in tax law, having studied in Munich. He was elected to Parliament (SPD) between 1949 and 1967. From 1967 until 1975, he was a justice on the FCC.

[223] Walter Seuffert, "Grundgesetz und Gemeinschaftsrecht," *Konkretionen Politischer Theorie Un Praxis*, ed. Adolf Arndt, Horst Ehmke, Iring Fetscher and Otwin Massing (Stuttgart: Ernst Klett Verlag, 1972), p 175.

brought the Treaties of Rome into effect domestically. Individual European legislation was not something that could be measured against the national constitution.
He argued that if a case was bought before a national court, then national standards
applied, and vice versa if bought to the ECJ.[224] However, the "wording, content and
function" of the national basic right being impinged upon had to be very closely
scrutinized to prevent unnecessary conflict with European law.[225] For this purpose,
Seuffert claimed, the final expert on the "spirit" of the basic rights and the constitution was the FCC. Combined with his statement about the "monopoly of decision"[226]
on the basic rights held by the FCC, it is hardly surprising that Seuffert was later
instrumental in drawing up the *Solange* decision, the kernel of which is clearly evident
in the text from 1972.

A third text, from the Bavarian legal expert Reinhard Riegel,[227] was highly critical of the FAC's behavior in the preceding years, stating that FAC's rereferral to
the FCC after disagreeing with the ECJ's original advice was procedurally and
materially wrong.[228] He argued, against Seuffert and Mössner that the ECJ had
exclusive right to rule on the validity of European law. The only decision left for
the FCC to make, Riegel disputed, was whether the transference of sovereignty
through Article 24 (i) BL was constitutional and whether the authorities transferred
did not endanger the principle incorporated in Article 79 (iii) BL. This, however,
was the long established position of the supranationalists and was therefore neither
surprising nor original, which Riegel freely admitted.[229] Indeed, Riegel called upon
the Commission to intervene in this argument and work with the ECJ to create a
common system of rights at the European level.[230] Seuffert had already preempted
this suggestion, stating that a political decision on the basic rights question was
highly unlikely, which left it solely the responsibility of the judges at the various
levels.[231] Here, Seuffert argued for a dialogue, rather than a shouting contest to
solve the question.

A final author called upon by the Inquiry Commission was the strongly supranationalist Ernst Werner Fuß.[232] Fuß had been present at the Bensheim Colloquium

[224] Seuffert, "Grundgesetz und Gemeinschaftsrecht," p 181.
[225] Seuffert, "Grundgesetz und Gemeinschaftsrecht," p 183.
[226] "Entscheidungsmonopol"; Seuffert, "Grundgesetz und Gemeinschaftsrecht," p 185.
[227] Reinhard Riegel (1942–2000) was active in the Bavarian and Federal Interior Ministries throughout the 1970s, specializing in police and information law.
[228] Reinhard Riegel, "Zum Verhältnis von Ewg-Recht und Staatlichem Verfassungsrecht," *Bayerische Verwaltungsblätter* 4 (1973), p 99.
[229] Riegel, "Zum Verhältnis von Ewg-Recht und Staatlichem Verfassungsrecht," p 99.
[230] Riegel, "Zum Verhältnis von Ewg-Recht und Staatlichem Verfassungsrecht," p 100.
[231] Seuffert, "Grundgesetz und Gemeinschaftsrecht," p 186.
[232] Ernst Werner Fuss (1924–82) worked on international law with Ipsen at Hamburg, before moving on to positions at the Universities of Mannheim and Würzburg.

in 1964 and was closely associated both with Hallstein and Ipsen. Accordingly, Fuß argued strongly in favor of the European legal order, rejecting completely the position of the FAC, stating that basic rights were sufficiently protected within the Community, even if these were not in the form provided by the Basic Law.[233] He argued that while the Basic Law dictates clear, subjectively applicable rights, the Community held general, objective principles, which were more effective for the Community since agreeing to specific articles at the time of writing the Treaties of Rome would have been difficult. However, like Riegel, Fuß called now for a dialogue between the courts and leaders of the Member States and the Community to fashion a form of basic rights protection at the Community level.[234] Following from this, Fuß argued that the "Masters of the Treaty" remained the Member States, and responsibility for the further development of the European legal order lay as much with them as it did with the ECJ.[235] After all, Fuß claimed, the Member States could still rein in the ECJ if they wanted, as a unanimous treaty revision would not be necessary when a Council decision stating that European law was not directly effective would suffice.[236] This would be particularly undesirable though, as Fuß in another text also used by the Inquiry Commission called for a strengthening of the ECJ and the position of its personnel.[237]

In May 1974, the FCC finally issued its *Solange* decision. Yet, this was not the only important decision on West German basic rights made in this year. Two weeks before *Solange*, the ECJ made a ruling in the *Nold* case,[238] in which it guaranteed to uphold the provision of national fundamental rights in its jurisprudence by judging invalid any regulations incompatible with national constitutions. In a sense, the ECJ sought to preempt the FCC by declaring national constitutional rights safe and protected by European law. However, this did not change the FCC's decision. The criticism against its 1967 decision from Rupp and others, such as Wengler, had greatly alarmed the FCC and it sought to redress the imbalance it had created from its 1967 ruling in its decision of May 1974.[239] It declared that Article 24 (i) BL was limited in its ability to transfer powers of constitutional amendment to international organizations – a question first raised and contrarily answered during the Constitutional Assembly in 1949. Moreover, it moved to deny the autonomy of the European legal

[233] Michael D Goldhaber, *A People's History of the European Court of Human Rights* (New Brunswick, N.J.: Rutgers University Press, 2007), p 50.

[234] Goldhaber, *People's History of the European Court of Human Rights*, p 50.

[235] Goldhaber, *People's History of the European Court of Human Rights*, p 69.

[236] Goldhaber, *People's History of the European Court of Human Rights*, p 69.

[237] Ernst-Werner Fuss, "Rechtsstaatliche Bilanz der Europaeischen Gemeinschaften," *Recht und Staat: Festschrift für Günther Küchenhoff zum 65. Geburtstag am 21.8.1972*, ed. Hans Hablitzel and Michael Wollenschlager (Berlin: Duncker & Humblot, 1972), pp 801–3.

[238] Case 04/73 *Nold vs. Commission* [1974] European Court Report 491.

[239] 2 BvL 52/71 – *Solange I decision*, 29 May 1974 – BVerfGE 37, 271.

order, seeing any European regulation implemented by West German authorities as an exercise of national sovereignty and therefore under the court's judicial remit – in stark contrast to the decision of 1967, which saw Community regulations as entirely "non-German." Finally, the FCC renounced a form of "structural congruence" between the Federal Republic and the Community, which finally provided an answer to the questions posed in this regard by Kraus in the 1950s and Schlochauer in the 1960s stating that it withheld the right to judge the applicability of a Community norm against the basic rights, as long as (*Solange*) the Community lacked a comparable catalog of rights of its own. In one short decision, the FCC had shifted dramatically to favor the side of the legal-academic spectrum that it had angered with its 1967 decision. As a result, it now faced the wrath of those scholars, with whom it had previously sided.

Ipsen was of course quick to react to the decision, describing it as "wrong,"[240] "deceptive, superficial and legally erroneous."[241] He accused the FCC of short-sightedness and that it was crucial to keep in mind that the stage of the Community criticized by the FCC was in fact transitory, and therefore might well lack some basic rights protection. The final stage of the Community would, however, not be helped by the retention of Member State control over its constitutional development.[242] The fact that the FCC retained the power to decide if a regulation was "inapplicable" in West Germany, but not "invalid" was described by Ipsen as "ironic."[243] He questioned the difference between the two terms, seeing this as a deliberate means to confuse what was really being stated by the FCC – that it now sought to control the integration process.[244]

The decision continued to come under attack from other scholars. Reinhard Riegel, who had earlier argued for the exclusive competency of the ECJ to rule on European law, sided strongly with Ipsen on two accounts. First, he argued with Ipsen, that it was for the Community, in dialogue with the Member States, to set its own standards of basic rights protection.[245] Second, he criticized the FCC for demanding a codification of basic rights protection that was neither needed nor

[240] Ipsen, "Bverfg versus Eugh Re "Grundrechte"; Zum Beschuß des Zweiten Senats des Bundesverfassungsgerichts vom 29 Mai 1974 (Bverfge Bd, 37 S, 271)," p 1.
[241] Ipsen, "Bverfg versus Eugh Re "Grundrechte"; Zum Beschuß des Zweiten Senats des Bundesverfassungsgerichts vom 29 Mai 1974 (Bverfge Bd, 37 S, 271)," p 1.
[242] Ipsen, "Bverfg versus Eugh Re "Grundrechte"; Zum Beschuß des Zweiten Senats des Bundesverfassungsgerichts vom 29 Mai 1974 (Bverfge Bd, 37 S, 271)," pp 14–15.
[243] Ipsen, "Bverfg versus Eugh Re "Grundrechte"; Zum Beschuß des Zweiten Senats des Bundesverfassungsgerichts vom 29 Mai 1974 (Bverfge Bd, 37 S, 271)," p 14.
[244] Ipsen, "Bverfg versus Eugh Re "Grundrechte"; Zum Beschuß des Zweiten Senats des Bundesverfassungsgerichts vom 29 Mai 1974 (Bverfge Bd, 37 S, 271)," p 14.
[245] Riegel, "Zum Problem der Allgemeinem Rechtsgrundsätze und Grundrechte im Gemeinschaftsrecht," p 1585.

in the remit of the FCC to demand.[246] He believed the Federal Republic lay open to the charge of not fulfilling its duty to implement Community regulations.[247] Meinhard Hilf[248] and Eckhart Klein[249] argued separately that the FCC had merely opened a "Pandora's Box," with an argumentation that was bound to "infect" other national courts[250] and have "fatal" consequences for the European legal system.[251] He too argued that the Federal Republic now be liable for charges for failing to fulfil its Treaty obligations, although the government itself opposed the FCC's decision.[252] Gert Meier, while recognizing the deficit in basic rights protection in the Community, condemned the *Solange* decision because it went against the principle of autonomy of the European legal system established in the 1960s.[253] Against this wash of criticism, Albert Bleckmann[254] alone saw a positive aspect in the FCC's decision. He argued that in the close wording of the decision, an implicit acceptance of both direct effect and primacy could be found, inasmuch as the FCC was arguing that with a basic rights catalog at the European level, it would no longer have a say in the validity of European law in West Germany.[255]

Indeed, despite suffering extensive and immediate criticism, the FCC's decision does deserve closer attention on two aspects. First, the fact was that a section of the ruling dealing with the applicability of European law and the Basic Rights passed only by the barest of majorities – five votes to three – meaning that a substantial voice in the court opposed the principles espoused in the decision. Like the 1967 ruling, which passed four votes to three, the FCC's support for a clear position was still only lukewarm. Judges Hans G Rupp,[256] Martin Hirsch,[257] and Walter Wand[258] gave in their dissenting opinion several grounds for disagreement. First, they held

---

[246] Reinhard Riegel, "Bundesverfassungsgerichtsbeschluß Anmerkung," *Neue Juristische Wochenschrift* 48 (1974a), p 2176.

[247] Riegel, "Bundesverfassungsgerichtsbeschluß Anmerkung," p 2176.

[248] Meinhard Hilf (1938) is a specialist in European, constitutional, and public law, working at the University of Heidelberg in this period, and later at Hamburg and Bielefeld.

[249] Eckhart Klein (1943) studied at the University of Heidelberg and the Max Planck Institute of the same city during this period, before moving on to the Universities of Mainz and Potsdam.

[250] Hilf, "Sekundäres Gemeinschaftsrecht und Deutsche Grundrechte," p 51.

[251] Klein, "Stellungnahme aus der Sicht des Deutschen Verfassungsrechts," p 77.

[252] Hilf, "Sekundäres Gemeinschaftsrecht und Deutsche Grundrechte," p 64.

[253] Gert Meier, "Bundesverfassungsgerichtsbeschluß Anmerkung," *Neue Juristische Wochenschrift* 48 (1974), p 1704–5.

[254] Albert Bleckmann (1933) studied at and was employed by the University of Heidelberg throughout this period, finally moving to the University of Münster in 1976.

[255] Albert Bleckmann, "Zur Funktion des Art 24 Abs 1 Grundgesetzes," *Zeitschrift für ausländisches offentliches Recht und Volkerrecht* (1975), p 80.

[256] Hans G Rupp (1902–89) was a specialist in Anglo-American and international law, studying in Tübingen and Berlin. He was appointed to the FCC in 1951.

[257] Martin Hirsch (1913–92) was a prominent member of the SPD, a lawyer in Berlin and appointed to the FCC in 1971.

[258] Walter Wand (1928–85) was appointed to the FCC by the Bundesrat in 1970.

the Community to be "autonomous" and "independent" from national law as a result of the transference of authorities under Article 24 (i) BL. Second, they felt that through the *Stauder v. Ulm* and *Nold* decisions, the ECJ had made clear its promise to guarantee basic rights within the Community framework. Third, they did not seek to deny the direct effectiveness and primacy of European law within the Federal Republic. As a result of accepting these doctrines, all three judges felt incapable of having sufficient expertise to rule on the applicability of a Community norm, let alone its overall validity.

The second point to be examined in relation to the decision is that it did not represent a final and unchangeable rejection of Community basic rights protection, as Bleckmann had pointed out. In fact, the wording "as long as" rather implied a challenge to the ECJ to develop a similarly comprehensive catalog of rights as that found in the Basic Law. Whether the FCC had the right to demand this from the ECJ was contested by Riegel,[259] but it was clear from the comments made by the president of the FCC, Ernst Benda,[260] that it was the intention of the FCC to put this pressure on the ECJ.[261] In these two aspects then, the *Solange* decision was not as regressive as it was portrayed by its opponents. Not only was the decision-making process both divided and fraught, reflecting opinion in the wider legal-academic community, but also its demand on the ECJ to develop its own fundamental rights protection has been an important compulsion on subsequent ECJ jurisprudence.

SUMMARY

The reception of the constitutional practice by West German legal-academia can be divided into three chronological periods:

- This period may be known as the "Erlangen" era, named after the Public Law Teachers meeting in 1959, which really encapsulated the spectrum of views across West German legal academia. Between 1949 and 1963, the question as to the openness of the Basic Law to international and supranational law was debated. The question as to whether the newly written Paris and Rome Treaties could actually create truly "supranational" law, autonomous in itself, was the main bone of contention among scholars. Traditionalist opinion rejected the

[259] Riegel, "Bundesverfassungsgerichtsbeschluß Anmerkung," p 2176.
[260] Ernst Benda (1925) completed his studies after the Second World War in America and Berlin; he became politically prominent for the CDU in Berlin and Bonn during the 1950s and 1960s, serving as Kiesinger's interior minister. He was elected as president of the FCC in 1971.
[261] Ernst Benda, "Das Spannungsverhältnis von Grundrechten und Übernationalen Recht," *Deutsches Verwaltungsblatt* 10.11 (1974), pp 395–6. See also subsequent media publications and interviews with Benda in this chapter, especially "Zur Frage der Schaffung eines europäischen Grundrechtskatalog"; interview with Ernst Benda, *Deutsche Welle*, 9 April 1975.

supranationality of European law, viewing it as merely complex international law. A small group of pro-integration scholars, predominately centred around experts close to the government, championed the supranationalist perspective, supporting both the implied effectiveness and primacy of the European legal system.

- In contrast to the "Erlangen Era," we might accurately call this section the "Bensheim era," which would indicate the shift in acceptance in both legal academia and the FCC in this period. In the period 1963 until 1969, the coming to terms with the ECJ's jurisprudence radicalized opinion, with a general shift over the period toward the supranational perspective prompted by the influential conferences at Bensheim and Kiel in 1964. The changes brought about by these meetings were as much driven by the work of the supranationalist scholars as by the successful lobbying of the ECJ, the Commission's Legal Service and the FIDE organization. There was at this point a self-confident and telling penetration of the national arena by European advocates. For many, as a result of the ECJ's jurisprudence, ignoring the supranationality of European law was pointless. Instead, concerns were raised about the democratic credentials and basic rights provision encapsulated in the newly supreme and directly effective European law. Safeguards were sought, predominately in Article 79 (iii) BL, for limiting the impact of European law. These concerns, which were not addressed in the FCC's 1967 de facto acceptance of primacy, prompted an even greater radicalization of debate in the following period.
- The third chronological period is best known as the "*Solange* Era." Between 1970 and 1974, instigated foremost by the writings of Hans-Heinrich Rupp, an intense debate raged about the basic rights provisions at the Community level. Defending fiercely the supranational perspective was Hans Peter Ipsen. The debate reached such intensity that the question of the impact of European law on the national constitution was included in a parliamentary Inquiry Committee on constitutional reform. Watching and waiting for the academic debate to find a settlement, the FCC issued its *Solange* decision in 1974, trying to find a middle path between the viewpoints of Ipsen and Rupp. The decision, which split the Court itself, sought to prompt the ECJ to move on basic rights at the Community level, while not completely rejecting the primacy and direct effect doctrines. As an attempt to appease many views, the *Solange* decision received heavy criticism from both sides of the debate.

Two main conclusions follow from the debates outlined in this chapter. First, the minor allusions to the academic debate in existing literature on the judicial reception of the constitutional practice fail to provide a full account of a contested, nuanced debate, that was formative on subsequent court jurisprudence. Returning to Alter's comment about Rupp's criticism of the FCC,[262] it is now clear to see that Rupp played a key role in shaping the legal academic and judicial reception, but he was merely part of a much longer and much richer reception process. His vitrolic defense of the national realm against the perceived comparative deficiencies of European democracy and rights protection were simply the end point of the structural congruence argument prevalent since the 1950s. Legal academic debates involved actors from the judicial, academic and political spheres, bringing together a variety of opposing opinions. Rather than being a side issue, legal-academic debates were influential on the courts and on government policy, yet in converse ways. In particular, government policy in the period up until the mid-1960s was being shaped by a particularly prointegration political elite, who themselves were extremely persuasive in concomitant academic discussions. Figures such as Ophüls, Hallstein, and Carstens were involved in government and academic debates and proved equally influential in shaping opinion in both.

This realization leads to the second main conclusion, relating to the broader nature of the reception of integration in the FRG. Primarily, mainstream legal-academic opinion rejected the supranationality of European law in the early period. This is reflective of a curious "self-confidence" in the German legal academy about their own traditions and legal system when dealing with or comparing with European counterpart, particularly in view of the recent past at that point and the fact German lawyers and judges were seen as more complicit with the Nazi regime than other German elites and that continuity into the new republic was as great as in any other elite group. This self-confidence might be explained in a number of ways, perhaps primarily through the natural conservatism of the German legal elite, which was unprepared to deal with such a radical reinterpretation of the norms of international law. Additionally, concerns about Europe were above all else in relation to its democratic and rights protection credentials. If German lawyers were critical of Europe on these particular grounds, then this was a good way of demonstrating to their neighbors that there had been a transformation in opinions in that particularly sensitive area. Against this resistant, hesitant background then, the dedication of a small elite group of supranationalist scholars, working with and around the ASEL and FIDE, combined with the practical reality that the ECJ established through its jurisprudence, enabled a minor shift in mainstream opinion toward the conditional acceptance of the primacy and direct effect doctrines. Within a decade, by the mid-1970s, the voices opposing the ECJ and its jurisprudence – scholars such as Rupp or Wengler – were highly vocal, but not necessarily still in the majority. Through the vehicles of regular conferences and the establishment of academic journals, the small grouping of scholars proved the means through which legal-academia

---

[262] See Alter, *Establishing the Supremacy of European Law*, p 88.

ultimately came to accept, with conditions, the constitutional practice. These conferences and meetings were facilitated and prompted by the associations working in and around the pan-European FIDE organization. While not entirely successful in convincing the German legal academy of the constitutionality of European law, they did play an important role in getting at least part of their ideology accepted.

3

National versus Supranational

West German Public Opinion toward the
Constitutionalization of European Law, 1949–1979

INTRODUCTION

As the complexities of debates in legal academia have shown, the development of the European legal system in West Germany had become a highly contentious issue. The book turns now to the question of whether these difficulties were also raised in the public reception of the constitutional practice. Analysis of the public discourse in the media landscape of the FRG in the 1960s and 1970s will highlight just how critical the public voice was toward the ECJ and European law. This was occasioned first by disappointment and disillusionment in the early period caused by the failure to create a truly federal Europe, and second in the later period by the recognition that the Community created did not match up to the high democratic and constitutional standards set by the new national order. This is decidedly coun-terintuitive considering the West Germans' widely documented fondness for the integration project, the perception that criticism of Europe's democratic credentials could hardly sound authentic when originating in the FRG, and the "permissive consensus" idea predominant in studies of European public opinion.

This chapter will demonstrate that this critical public discourse was important in prompting and mandating the FCC's *Solange* decision. The FCC judges were critically aware of and even decided to participate in the media and public debates on European law. They intervened and explained their decisions in the terms set by the media. Even if they would not admit that these debates played a role in their deliberations as judges, there is no doubt that they were conscious of what was being said. The central theme in media debates after the disillusionment of the late 1950s was the necessity for a comparable institutional constellation and system of rights recourse between the national and European levels. This is highly reminis-cent of the "structural congruence" argument found in legal academia. In popular discourse though, this idea is less well articulated and much more emotive in con-tent. There are, for instance, continual references to the "sacrifice" made by the

FRG in its membership in the Community. But this sacrifice had its limits. As the 1960s progressed, the media undertook a number of increasingly direct and explicit comparisons between West German and European public authority. The limits of the sacrifice West Germans were prepared to make were articulated in the post-1968 period as much more public attention focused on "postmaterialist" concerns, not least including qualitative democratic life and the protection of the individual against state authority. The lack of fundamental rights protection against directly effective and supreme European law was simply too much and this chapter will document the open hostility toward Europe from many commentators. It reveals a surprising self-confidence of the West Germans in their own democratic constitutional order, even as early as the 1960s, and shows that *Solange* was a decision well received by the West German public.

PUBLIC OPINION, EUROPE, AND WEST GERMANY

Measuring public opinion on European integration came of age in the mid-1970s with the inception of the Eurobarometer polls in 1974. This development was the result of a growing number of political controversies in the European arena – the Empty Chair Crisis, the question of Enlargement and the membership referenda held in the acceding countries – that stimulated a rising interest in the flows of public opinion toward the Community. In contrast, prior to the mid-1970s, measuring levels of public support for the European project was completed sporadically, in a patchwork manner, or indirectly, only in reference to other questions of national political importance.[1] This was due in particular to the social and administrative dislocation in the immediate postwar period, as well as the lack of concrete developments in the integration process until the mid-1950s. As a result, research on public opinion toward European integration in the period prior to 1974 is dominated by Lindberg and Scheingold's conception of a "permissive consensus,"[2] which highlighted a broad base of popular support for the unspecified idea of a

---

[1]   There are, in contrast, multifarious studies of public opinion for later periods of European integration, particularly in the post-Maastricht period. See, for instance, and nonexhaustively Eva Kolinsky, "The Euro-Germans: National Identity and European Integration in Germany," *Europeans on Europe: Transnational Visions of a New Continent*, ed. Mairi Maclean and Jolyon Howorth (London: Macmillan, 1992); Mark Franklin, Michael Marsh and Lauren McLaren, "Uncorking the Bottle: Popular Opposition to European Unification in the Wake of Maastricht" *Journal of Common Market Studies* 32 (1994); Julia Teschner, "No Longer on Europe's Europhiles? Euroscepticism in Germany in the 1990s," *European Integration* 22 (2000); Frank Brettschneider, Jan van Deth and Edeltraud Roller, "Europaische Integration in der Offentlichen Meinung: Forschungsstand und Forschungsperspektiven," *Europaische Integration in der Offentlichen Meinung*, ed. Frank Brettschneider, Jan van Deth and Edeltraud Roller (Opladen: Leske & Budrich, 2003).

[2]   See Stuart Scheingold and Leon N Lindberg, *Europe's World-Be Polity: Patterns of Change in the European Community* (Englewood Cliffs, N.J.: Prentice-Hall, 1970).

"United Europe," but with little general knowledge of the actual events and institutions governing this process that granted political elites a free hand to pursue integration as they saw fit.[3]

As the FRG has frequently been polled as the most "European" of all the Member States,[4] the assumption of the permissive consensus has been particularly prevalent in surveys looking at West German opinion toward Europe. The permissive consensus was based theoretically on a utilitarian presumption that if there was a perception that the Member State gained from European membership, then the public would acquiesce to developments toward a united Europe. In both economic and political terms, integration provided the FRG with many benefits. The formation of the European communities coincided chronologically with the Wirtschaftswunder, the famous "Economic Miracle" of the late 1950s and 1960s, and the two became closely linked as successes in the mind of the populace.[5] Elisabeth Noelle-Neumann also points out that perceived economic benefit is the "central motive"[6] for public support for integration, especially in the FRG. Eva Kolinsky, on the other hand, tempers this assessment, stating that

> it is worth noting that West Germans have regarded the economic dimension as the key dimension in Europe, their economic performance as the best in the European context, but their gains doubtful overall. Germans tend to see themselves as everybody's paymaster, in Europe and beyond.[7]

It must be added that while this observation is certainly correct, its relevance for the early period of integration under observation in this chapter is more doubtful, as the institutions and structures, particularly the Common Agricultural Policy, which serves as the main bone of financial contention, existed only in a nascent, fledgling form. Politically, integration offered arguably even clearer, further benefits. As Teschner points out, the political choice faced by the early West German elites was perceived, at least by Adenauer, to be between "integration into the

---

[3] See Martin Slater, "Political Elites, Popular Indifference and Community Building," *The European Community: Past, Present and Future*, ed. Loukas Tsoukalis (Oxford: Blackwell Publishing, 1983), for one of the first analyses of elite-public interaction in the formation of the European Communities.

[4] For a range of Eurobarometer results confirming this, see Ronald Inglehart and Karlheinz Reif, *Eurobarometer: The Dynamics of European Public Opinion: Essays in Honour of Jacques-René Rabier* (London: Macmillan, 1991), pp 2–11.

[5] Simon Bulmer and Paterson William, *The Federal Republic of Germany and the European Community* (London: Allen and Unwin, 1987), p 114.

[6] Elisabeth Noelle-Neumann, "Phantom Europe: Thirty Years of Survey Research on German Attitudes toward European Integration," *Contemporary Perspective on European Integration: Attitudes, Non-Governmental Behaviors, and Collective Decision Making*, ed. Leano Hurwitz (London: Aldwych Press, 1980), p 63.

[7] Kolinsky, "Euro-Germans: National Identity and European Integration in Germany," p 174.

West and submission to the USSR."[8] As such, integration into Western Europe was seen generally, after initial partisan disputes between the main political parties, as the means by which to achieve a large number of political goals: the eventual reunification of Germany, protection against Communist agitation, the basis for military alliance, the restoration of full sovereignty, and reconciliation with France – all of which meant, after the shift in SPD policy toward Europe in the mid-1950s,[9] that there was little direct opposition to the broad goal of integration in the FRG.

Taken even further still, Matthew Gabel posits a system of individual self-interest dependent entirely on the perceived national economic benefit derived from the market liberalization resulting from integration.[10] This model is particularly relevant for the FRG as it is the West German export economy that has gained most from the removal of trade barriers within Europe. Eichenberg and Dalton go one stage further and place, in addition to the economic benefits of integration, elements of perceived political gain for the Member State, where the integration is seen to extend the influence and importance of the nation state into the supranational arena.[11] Of crucial importance then for these authors is how political events are portrayed in the media, with negative news coverage having a potentially harmful effect on levels of public support for integration[12] In addition, the habits and tendencies of each Member State's foreign policy choices, in other words its "political culture of foreign policy,"[13] also has a profound effect on public support, with publics in those Member States with a broad tendency to pursue multilateralism and

---

[8] Teschner, "No Longer on Europe's Europhiles?" p 58.

[9] The SPD's Godesberg Programme of 1959 marked a fundamental change in the SPD's manifesto, shifting the party toward becoming a mass-support *Volkspartei*, similar to the model of the CDU. One of the most crucial aspects of these changes was the shift in foreign policy from striving for a unified, neutral Germany to accepting Western-oriented European integration. Changes in the party's policy toward European integration had begun as early as 1955. See William E Paterson, *The Spd and European Integration* (London: Saxon House/Lexington Books, 1974). See also Willy Albrecht, "Europakonzeptionen der Spd in der Gründungszeit der Bundesrepublik," *Personen, Soziale Bewegungen, Parteien. Beitrage zur Neuesten Geschichte: Festschrift für Hartmut Soell*, ed. Oliver Von Mengersen, Matthias Frese, Klaus Kempter, Heide-Marie Lauter and Schober Volker (Heidelburg: Manutius Verlag, 2004); or Jürgen Bellers, *Ewg und die "Gobesberger" Spd* (Siegen: Universität Siegen, 2003).

[10] Matthew Gabel, "European Integration, Voters, and National Politics," *Contentious Europeans: Protest and Politics in an Emerging Polity*, ed. Doug Imig and Sidney Tarrow (Lanham, Md.: Rowman & Littlefield, 2001).

[11] The typical example is the perceived influence of De Gaulle (and France) after the Empty Chair Crisis during the late 1960s. Richard C Eichenberg and Russell J Dalton, "Europeans and the European Community: The Dynamics of Public Support for the European Integration," *International Organisation* 47.4 (1993), p 512–13.

[12] Eichenberg and Dalton, "Europeans and the European Community," p 514.

[13] Eichenberg and Dalton, "Europeans and the European Community," p 514.

sacrifice sovereignty, more appreciative of European integration. West Germany
fits this bill entirely.

Integration also provided a positive stimulus for the West German population,
enabling a surrogate expression for a troubled sense of national identity. Medrano
has argued, for instance, that supporting integration allowed West Germans to come
to terms with the country's violent recent history, pointing out "the Nazi past provided arguments for European integration and facilitated the spread of these arguments to broader groups in the population."[14] Moreover, Western Europe provided
the FRG with a "plausible supranational identity" since "alternative supranational
identities, such as Mitteleuropa.... were thus buried after Germany's defeat."[15] Both
Kolinsky[16] and Teschner agree with this perspective, with Teschner placing particular emphasis on the fact that the West German population has a "far greater affinity"
with integration, rationalized through "strong similarities between the [institutional]
structures" of the FRG and the European polity.[17] This point is particularly interesting for this chapter as perceived institutional affinity – the "structural congruence"
is a key element in the public reception of legal integration, as well as among the
legal-academic community, as demonstrated in the previous chapter. In fact, the
findings provided by this chapter contradict Teschner's statement on institutional
affinity directly, highlighting that it was the perceived lack of affinity between the
Community's and FRG's constitutional orders, especially on the issue of basic rights,
which led to an increasing dissension toward legal integration. Indeed, as Noelle-
Neumann points out, the more the West Germans learned about the "imaginable
and phrased in everyday terms" Community, the more they disassociated themselves
from it.[18] However, Noelle-Neumann's reliance purely on empirical data to demonstrate this point acts as a limit on her study, since she argues dismissively, "these
developments could not have arisen until after 1974, for no symptoms of dissociation
could be ascertained prior to 1974."[19] On the contrary, this chapter will demonstrate
that an increasing lack of affinity with the development of the Community legal
system was quite clear in West German media prior to 1974.

This chapter does not offer a total reassessment of the permissive consensus, but it
does challenge the assumption that West Germans were uninformed, unreflective,

[14] Juan Diez Medrano, *Framing Europe: Attitudes to Europe Integration in Germany, Spain, and the United Kingdom* (Princeton, N.J.: Princeton University Press, 2003), p 179.
[15] Medrano, *Framing Europe*, p 179.
[16] Kolinsky, "Euro-Germans," pp 173–7.
[17] Teschner, "No Longer on Europe's Europhiles?" p 59.
[18] Elisabeth Noelle-Neumann, "Phantom Europe: Thirty Years of Survey Research on German Attitudes toward European Integration," *Contemporary Perspective on European Integration: Attitudes, Non-Governmental Behaviors, and Collective Decision Making*, ed. Leano Hurwitz (London: Aldwych Press, 1980), p 62.
[19] Noelle-Neumann, "Phantom Europe," p 62.

and uncritical about the integration process. What appears most crucial is that the constitutional practice of the European legal system ran side-by-side with the embedding of the new West German constitutional order into the popular consciousness. This chapter presupposes that these two processes were not without tension, and that this tension is reflected both in public opinion data and media reporting. This chapter then seeks to add to and go beyond standard works on the permissive consensus in two ways. First, this chapter seeks to move beyond the permissive consensus in terms of substance, in that it reveals a much greater differentiation in West German public opinion toward European integration, specifically, legal integration, than the permissive consensus concept would acknowledge. Through the examination of press discussion and of public opinion poll data, the chapter charts a large amount of skepticism, even hostility, toward the ECJ's jurisprudence, increasing particularly in the 1970s, when direct and overt comparisons between the national and supranational legal orders were made. As a result, new conclusions will be drawn about West German public opinion toward European integration, at least through the lens of legal integration. Second, in a methodological sense, it breaks new ground in not relying entirely on purely poll data, but seeks to complicate the impression added by the textual analysis of primary sources, in this case newspaper articles, editorials and broadcast media reports. The reason for choosing this approach is that in foreign policy issues, particularly elite projects such as European integration, information is much more difficult for the average citizen to find, so that the ability of the mass media, with its sources and foreign correspondents, to inform and influence public opinion is proportionally that much greater. Newspaper reporting would therefore be the most important source shaping public opinion on the integration process. Moreover, the relationship between the press and the public is strategic, so that as well as having an informative role, the press also has to cater to the perceived interests of its readers in order to increase its distribution and sales. Therefore, press reporting mirrors and articulates the media's interpretation of the public consciousness in a particular period. In this sense, the content of newspaper reporting represents the issues in which the public has an interest.

THE WEST GERMAN MEDIASCAPE

In the West German case, there are a number of distinguishing characteristics that accentuate the public-media relationship even further still. The West German media system, particularly the printed press, is one of the most highly developed in terms of readership, volume, and quality in Europe, despite the disjuncture caused by the Second World War. It has three particularly distinguishing characteristics. First, it is highly decentralized structure with several increasingly important national[20] and specialist papers.[21] By 1955, over half of the Federal states had over thirty different newspapers.[22] Second, the Basic Law guarantees freedom of press expression and outlaws censorship (Article 5 BL).[23] It might be assumed that this would predispose the media to be especially protective of its own position within the West German constitutional order, particularly in relation to unalterable basic rights through which press freedom is secured. Finally, the press has an importance as a reeducative force, or "opinion builder" (*Meinungsbildung*), in society. Its role of disseminating information to the public (*Auskunftspflicht*) has been bolstered through state legislation, which required governmental bodies to have dedicated official press offices through which information could flow freely to media. This quickly extended beyond the public authority to also include individual ministries, parties, MPs, influential nongovernmental groups (trade unions, employer's organizations, churches, and social groups), and above all, the government's Federal Press Office (*Bundespresseamt*).[24] This has helped West German newspapers develop a very high reputation for quality reporting and editorial comment. As a result, newspapers were a particularly important factor in public opinion formation, with high and increasing readership coverage throughout the chosen period of research: Between 1954 and 1976, the number of newspapers sold rose from 13.4 million to 19.5 million.[25] In 1960, the Bild-Zeitung sold 3.2 million copies, die Welt 243,000, the FAZ 227,000, Frankfurter Rundschau 114,000, and the Westdeutsche Allgemeine Zeitung 410,000,[26] making the reach and influence of the media unquestionably powerful.

---

[20] The newspapers traditionally regarded as "national" are the *Frankfurter Allgemeine Zeitung* (*FAZ*), *die Welt, die Zeit*, the *Bild-Zeitung* (tabloid), *Süddeutsche Zeitung*, and the *Frankfurter Rundschau*. Important national "magazines" are *Spiegel* and *Stern*.

[21] The most important specialist economics paper is the *Handelsblatt*, published by the Stuttgart-based publisher Verlagsgruppe Georg von Holtzbrinck.

[22] Number of newspapers in 1955: Baden-Württemberg: 33, Bavaria: 45, Berlin: 10, Bremen: 3, Hamburg: 10, Hessen: 30, Lower Saxony: 27, North-Rhine Westphalia: 41, Rhineland-Palatinate: 13, Schleswig-Holstein: 13. Adapted from Peter Humphreys Media and Media Policy in West Germany: The Press and Broadcasting since 1945. German studies series. (New York: Berg, distributed exclusively in the US and Canada by St. Martin's Press, 1990.), p 67.

[23] Article 5 (1) BL states: "Every person shall have the right freely to express and disseminate his opinions in speech, writing, and pictures and to inform himself without hindrance from generally accessible sources. Freedom of the press and freedom of reporting by means of broadcasts and films shall be guaranteed. There shall be no censorship."

[24] Peter Humphreys, *Media and Media Policy in West Germany: The Press and Broadcasting since 1945* (Leamington Spa: Berg, 1989), p 57.

[25] Humphreys, *Media and Media Policy in West Germany: The Press and Broadcasting since 1945*, p 75.

[26] Adapted from Jeffrey Vanke, "Consensus for Integration: Public Opinion and European Integration in the Federl Republic, 1945–1966," *Die Bundesrepublik Deutschland und die Europäische Einihung 1949–2000: Politische Akteure, Gesellschaftliche Kräfte und Internationale Erfahrungen: Festschrift für Wolf D Gruner zum 60. Geburtstag*, ed. Marieke Konig and Matthias Schulz (Stuttgart: Franz Steiner Verlag, 2004), p 327.

Existing surveys of the West German media reaction to European integration have been restricted exclusively to the political sphere, looking at reactions to high political and foreign policy events. Markus Kiefer's work on the German Question in the West German media is of limited use to this chapter because its time period runs only to 1955. Kiefer does emphasize the importance of "Law" in European policy, but only in relation to negotiations on the Saar and Oder-Neisse issues.[27] Mendrano's review of the Frankfurter Allgemeine Zeitung's (FAZ) and die Zeit's reaction focuses predominately on the "Quest for Sovereignty,"[28] and as such, looks more closely at Franco-German relations in terms of rearmament and the Saar question. His observation, that "the FAZ and die Zeit also welcomed the creation of the [Community] and EURATOM by the Treaties of Rome (1957)" almost appears to be an afterthought.[29] While his choice of papers does accurately represent his description of "quality press," by being so exclusive in his selection, he misses out on a broad, diverse set of arguments about integration, which go beyond the two paper's "unwavering pro-integration attitude."[30] It is the aim of this chapter to overcome the narrow perspectives provided thus far in the literature and instead to provide an overall, aggregate perspective of the media discussion, which cuts across regional and party-political affiliations of the newspapers and media outlets.

Jeffrey Vanke's survey of press opinion to integration up to 1966, although more encompassing in terms of source material than Medrano's work, also focuses primarily on reactions to high political events, especially the Elysee Treaty and the question of West German rearmament. When commenting on the creation of the Communities, Vanke contradicts the findings of Noelle-Neumann in that he cites the perceived popularity of the new organization as a result of its "common institutions for European unity."[31] Noelle-Neumann, as indicated, argued that the creation of concrete institutions was a factor in alienating public opinion from integration, albeit after 1974.[32] Most questionable is Vanke's conclusion that by the mid-1960s, "the Community gave the breadth of West Germans a concrete focus for their hopes for unprecedented European cooperation and unity."[33] In fact, the following discussion of the West German media's reaction to European legal integration will demonstrate that the mid-1960s actually saw a rise in criticism toward the Community's

[27] Marcus Kiefer, *Auf der Suche nach Nationaler Identitaat und Wegen zur Deutschen Einheit: Die Deutsche Frage in der Uberregionalen Tages- und Wochenpresse der Bundesrepublik 1949–1955* (Frankfurt am Main: Peter Lang, [2nd ed.], 1993), p 581.

[28] Medrano, *Framing Europe*, p 118.

[29] Medrano, *Framing Europe*, p 119.

[30] Medrano, *Framing Europe*, p 118.

[31] Vanke, "Consensus for Integration: Public Opinion and European Integration in the Federal Republic, 1945–1966," p 335.

[32] Noelle-Neumann, "Phantom Europe," p 62.

[33] Vanke, "Consensus for Integration," p 339.

legal system, which in itself then broadened out to a much more widespread critique of democracy and legal recourse at the Community level.

CRESTFALLEN, 1949–1963: DASHED HOPES FOR A UNITED EUROPE

A strong idealistic element was prominent throughout the West German media response to the transference of national sovereignty to European institutions in the early 1950s, which matched public opinion poll data on this topic. EMNID polls showed that the desire for a (nonspecified) "United Europe" grew from 36 percent in 1949 to 49 percent by 1951 and to 52 percent by the end of the decade.[34] Moreover, further data revealed that in early 1953, 37 percent of respondents favored a European Parliament having final say on political issues, as opposed to only 14 percent who felt that national parliaments should.[35] The ideas that the pursuit of total and independent national sovereignty were outdated and that only a federalized Europe could answer the existential problems facing the continent at the onset of the cold war were typical of early media coverage. As early as July 1949, the Schwäbisches Tagblatt, a south German daily published an article from a leading Social Democrat parliamentarian, Fritz Erler.[36] In this article, entitled "Europe, a federal state!" Erler outlined the reasons why Europe should be united and what form his proposed "federal state" should take. He saw in the North German Union an archetype for a future European state and economic model, declaring that the illusion of "complete sovereignty and independence" for European states was over and that only a supranational federal system, to which sovereign rights must be transferred, could rescue Europe from the threat of the cold war.[37] This federal state had to hold real powers to legislate and enforce "the general European will" upon its constituent parts, above and against any veto rights at the national level.[38] Such foresight and optimism in the integration project was widespread in the West German media in the early 1950s. Above all, the Schuman declaration and the proposals for the EDC were met with great media enthusiasm, despite apparent indifference and

---

[34] EMNID poll "Nationales oder Europäisches Denken," 1960, in BA B1367–6407 Bundeskanzleramt 1960–2.

[35] Allensbach Archivbericht, "Deutschland und die Europäischen Gemeinschaften," 1950–67.

[36] Fritz Erler (1913–67) was a leading SPD MP and was head of party from 1953 onward. He became leader of the opposition (to Erhard) in 1964, before retiring in 1966 because of illness.

[37] "Es muß aber eine echte Einheit in der Realität sein und nicht nur eine solche des Wortes und Kultur. Dazu gehört, daß der Traum von der vollkommenen Souveränität und Unabhängigkeit jedes einzelnen europäischen Volkes endgültig ausgeträumt ist. Alle europäischen Völker, nicht nur die besiegten des letzten Krieges, müssen einen Teil ihrer Souveränität aufgeben und diesen Teil übertragen auf den gesamteuropäischen Staat" in "Europa ein Bundesstaat!" *Schwäbisches Tagblatt*, 10 July 1949.

[38] "all diese sehr praktischen Fragen sind nur zu lösen, wenn wir dem europäischen Bundesstaat echt bundesstaatliche Organe geben, d.h. ein gesamteuropäisches Parlament und eine gesamteuropäische Regierung" in "Europa ein Bundesstaat!"; *Schwäbisches Tagblatt*, 10 July 1949.

lack of knowledge about the Plan among the public demonstrated in several public opinion polls.[39]

Closely mirroring Adenauer's "policy of strength"[40] views, the Rheinischer Merkur celebrated the Schuman plan as a chance both to strengthen West Germany's political, economic, and social ties to the West and at the same time strengthen its position vis-à-vis the German Democratic Republic (GDR).[41] Later in 1952, the Frankfurter Rundschau welcomed the proposed meeting of a convention in the ECSC Assembly to draw up a European constitution with far reaching powers to issue binding laws, seeing this as an opportunity to add another level of protection to the "democratic institutions and personal fundamental rights" of the ECSC Member States.[42] The opening of the Court of the ECSC on 10 December 1952 was welcomed equally as warmly. The Handelsblatt described the opening ceremony as a "turning point in the history of Justice,"[43] with the Court being the first international court able to issue binding judgments and "step over the boundaries of sovereignty and exercise political functions."[44] The Bulletin der Bundesregierung, published on the same day, was even more generous in its praise of the Court, seeing its creation as the fulfillment of Dante's call for a judge for every dispute, hoping that it would quickly develop into a Supreme European Federal Court.[45] A week later, the Regensburg-

---

[39] An Allensbach poll in April 1951 showed that 30% of those questioned had no opinion on the Schuman Plan and another 17% of respondents had never heard of it. Of the remaining 53%, 18% opposed it. The poll revealed that it was in particular men of middle income, rural workers, and those voting for left-wing parties (SPD, KPD) who particularly opposed the plan. Region, religion, age, and education had no discernible impact on opinion. In a further poll, Allensbach demonstrated that only 9% of regular newspaper readers had no knowledge of the Schuman Plan, whereas 42% of those who never read any newspaper had never heard of it.

[40] Kettenacker, *Germany since 1945*, p 60.

[41] "Deutschland kann nur dann in Freiheit wiedervereinigt werden, wenn sich die Bundesrepublik zuvor politisch, wirtschaftlich und sozial gefestigt hat," in "Wer ist gesamtdeutsch," *Rheinischer Merkur*, 18 January 1952.

[42] "Dem Europäischen Bund sind in dem Brüsseler Entwurf weitgehende Rechte zugedacht, die auch in die innenpolitische Entwicklung der ihm angeschlossenen Länder eingreifen können. Der Bund übernimmt die Verpflichtung, die Regierungen der angeschlossenen Länder bei der Aufrechterhaltung der verfassungsmäßigen Ordnung, der demokratischen Einrichtungen und der persönlichen Grundrechte zu unterstützen" in "So soll der Europäische Bund entstehen," *Frankfurter Rundschau*, 13 November 1952.

[43] "... am 10. Dezember hat sich nun auch die vierte und letzte Institution der Gemeinschaft konstituiert. Ihre Errichtung stellt ... einen Wendepunkt in der Geschichte der Justiz dar" in "Montan-Gerichtshof konstituiert," *Handelsblatt*, 12 December 1952.

[44] "Er überschreite die Grenzen der Souveränität aus und trete damit aus dem rein juristischen Aufgabenkreis heraus" in "Montan-Gerichtshof konstituiert," *Handelsblatt*, 12 December 1952.

[45] "... ergriff Präsident Pilotti das Wort zu einer Ansprache, in der er die Definition des Rechtes durch den universellen Genius Dante Alighieri – daß überall dort, wo die Möglichkeit eines Streitfalls besteht, auch ein Richter vorhanden sein soll, der den Streit schlichtet, als Leitmotiv für das erstmals auf supranationaler Ebene tätig werdende Gericht herausstellte" in "Wendepunkt der internationalen Rechtsgeschichte," *Bulletin der Bundesregierung*, 12 December 1952.

based Deutsche Tagespost published a very similar article to the Bulletin, hailing the Court as the savior to create a true supranational order, which would promote the economic prosperity of the people of Europe.[46] When the ECJ held its first public hearing at the end of 1954, a variety of papers, particularly the business publications, provided good coverage.[47]

However this optimism was soon tempered in the first instance by despair caused by the hesitancy of the French to ratify the EDC and in the second about concerns regarding the transference of authorities to the ECSC. Public opinion data reveals a falling belief in the effectiveness of a European governance system: whereas in 1953, a majority favored final say decision making by a European Parliament,[48] by 1955, this majority turned around with 42 percent now believing in the authority of the Federal Parliament (32 percent in the European Parliament, 26 percent undecided), and 46 percent believing the Federal Parliament's prior agreement to European legislation before it became effective (25 percent disagreeing, 29 percent undecided).[49]

The faltering EDC especially soured the mood in the West German press toward the whole integration project. The FAZ declared the idea of European unity to be in a "difficult crisis," which only the French and their resolute opposition to the rearmament of their eastern neighbor could resolve.[50] Nevertheless, the editorial claimed that despite French rejections, Europe was "already so strong" that it would withstand this setback. Most interestingly, the FAZ saw the proposed constitution of the European Political Community (EPC) as the means forward out of the crisis.[51] Claiming the constitution to be a true reflection of what West Germany desired for Europe, and no doubt for itself too, the FAZ argued that the constitution could play the role of a

[46] "Pilotti sagt weiter, der Gerichtshof … sei durch sein Abkommen von Staaten errichtet worden, die sich keineswegs damit begnügen, ihre Beziehungen untereinander zu regeln, sondern darüber hinaus bestimmte, für das Leben Europas unerlässliche wirtschaftliche Tätigkeiten einer supranationalen Ordnung zu unterstellen mit dem Hauptzweck, das gemeinsame Wohl ihrer Völker zu fördern" in "Montan-Gerichtshof Vorstufe zum Bundesgericht," *Deutsche Tagespost*, 19 December 1952.

[47] "Gerichtshof der Montanunion beginnt seine Arbeit," *die Neue Zeitung*, 18 January 1954; "Montangerichtshof tritt in Funktion," *die Welt*, 23 October 1954; "Wann können Unternehmen klagen?" *Handelsblatt*, 10 November 1954; "Warum klagt der Ruhrbergbau?" *Handelsblatt*, 23 May 1955.

[48] Allensbach Archivbericht, "Deutschland und die Europäischen Gemeinschaften," 1950–67.

[49] Allensbach Archivbericht, "Deutschland und die Europäischen Gemeinschaften," 1950–67.

[50] "Es besteht kein Zweifel, daß sich der Gedanke der europäischen Einigung wieder einmal in einer schweren Krise befindet. Es wäre allerdings unaufrichtig, sich heute darüber überrascht zu zeigen. Die westliche Welt weiß seit dem Tage, da die Idee Europa mit dem Gedanken der deutschen Wiederbewaffnung gekoppelt wurde, daß diesem Europa ein Gegner entstehen musste: Frankreich" in "Was wird aus Europa?" *FAZ*, 16 March 1953.

[51] For a discussion of the European Political Community's constitution and its failure, see Griffiths, *Europe's First Constitution: The European Political Community 1952–1954*.

unifying paragon, which not even the French could deny.[52] The Saarbrücker Zeitung also placed its hopes on the constitution,[53] and reported in May 1953 on Adenauer's strong personal support resulting in the cabinet's approval of the Constitution project.[54] In fact, the protocols of this cabinet meeting[55] point to the lack of expectation among government figures that the French would actually agree to the Constitution, which, of course with hindsight, was much more realistic. The Frankfurter Rundschau shared this outlook, writing after the ratification of the EDC in the Bundestag that the future of European cooperation was now in the hands of the French Parliament.[56]

The disillusionment associated with the faltering EDC also manifested itself in a growing critique of the ECSC. This criticism had two aspects: first, that the ECSC discriminated unfairly against the FRG; second, doubts arose about the wisdom of the transference of sovereignty to institutions qualitatively weaker in democratic terms than their national counterparts. In regard to the first aspect, the first signs of discontent with the High Authority appeared in early 1953. In May, the coalminer's trade union, IG Bergbau, issued a statement complaining about what it claimed to be the unfair bias toward French industry shown by the ECSC's High Authority, resulting in increases to over-all production costs of coal and steel throughout Western Europe. The Constance-based newspaper, Südkurier, carried this story immediately under the broad headline "So Far Only Disadvantages from the ECSC."[57] The attack from heavy industry on the ECSC continued into the early summer,[58]

---

[52] "Wir glauben, daß die europäische Entwicklung, die zuerst aus negativen Momenten einen heftigen Impuls bekam, schon so weit fortgeschritten ist, daß Frankreich den Weg der Negation nicht mehr beschreiten kann. Die europäische Idee hat bereits eine Eigengesetzlichkeit entwickelt ... Dieser Verfassungsentwurf ist ein Spiegelbild des Europas, wie es sich die Deutschen vorstellen" in "Was wird aus Europa?" *FAZ*, 16 March 1953.

[53] A draft EPC treaty was drawn up by the ECSC assembly, including a directly elected assembly, a senate appointed by national parliaments, and a supranational executive accountable to the parliament. See Griffiths, *Europe's First Constitution*.

[54] "Bundesregierung positive für Europa-Verfassung," *Saarbrücker Zeitung*, 9 May 1953.

[55] 291 meeting on 8 May 1953, Kabinettsprotokolle 1953, http://www.bundesarchiv.de/kabinettsprotokolle/web/index.jsp

[56] "Wichtig aber ist und bleibt nach der Debatte: die Bundesrepublik hat sich im Parlament durch Regierungskoalition und Oppositionssprecher eindeutig zum Westen bekannt....Wie alle aber bisher auf Deutschland und die Ratifizierung der Verträge schauten, so schauen wir nunmehr nach Frankreich. Nach Frankreich, von dessen politischen Entscheidungen jetzt die europäische Zusammenarbeit der Zukunft abhängt" in "Bundesrepublik im Bund des Westens," *Frankfurter Rundschau*, 21 March 1953.

[57] "Bisher nur Nachteile durch Montan-Union," *Sudkurier*, 26 May 1953.

[58] Set against the background of the controversial anticartel laws being introduced by Erhard's Economics Ministry at the time, this open and connected critique of the ECSC must have proved awkward for the government. For a discussion of the anticartel legislation, see above all Werner Abelshauser, *Deutsche Wirtschaftsgeschichte seit 1945* (Munich: CH Beck Verlag, 2004), chapter V (3) and pp 30–3; John Gillingham, *European Integration, 1950–2003: Superstate or New Market Economy?* (Cambridge: Cambridge University Press, 2003), pp 41–52.

with Die Welt reporting on protests from major West German industrialists and bankers against High Authority regulations that "penetrated too deeply into the German economy" and created an "Überorganization" to the detriment of the FRG.[59] Further criticism of the ECSC in the FAZ,[60] Süddeutsche Zeitung,[61] and the Frankfurt-based Neue Presse[62] followed throughout 1953, all based on the supposed bias toward French heavy industry.[63] This resulted in the government feeling obliged to publish a counterattack to the widespread condemnation through the Federal Press Office. Citing the need for the "man on the street" to have a fair, balanced view, it countered the cited limitations of the ECSC by reminding its readers that it was merely a step on a much longer path and that the seemingly unfair costs being borne by West German heavy industry were necessary for the long term prosperity of Western Europe.[64] This appeal found little resonance, particularly as, in the following year, the French Parliament officially confirmed its rejection of the EDC.

The media reaction to the failure of the EDC was yet a further disappointment, which reflected on the integration project more generally. The Berlin Tagesspiegel wrote of "the end of an era, which had been filled by European illusionism" and the ushering in of a new phase of "external uncertainty and internal indecision" for the FRG.[65] The liberal Westdeutsche Rundschau declared European unity only for the "romantics,"[66] whereas the Rheinischer Merkur described progress with integration as entering a "frantic nosedive."[67]

---

[59] "Die westdeutsche Montanindustrie und die Banken haben sich bei der Hohen Behörde der Montanunion scharf gegen die Einwürfe einiger Verordnungen gewandt, deren Herausgabe die Hohe Behörde in nächster Zeit plant und die nach deutscher Auffassung einen zu weitgehenden Eingriff in die deutsche Wirtschaft und die Gefahr einer Überorganization zum Nachteil der Bundesrepublik bedeuten" in "Gegen Eingriffe der Hohen Behörde," *die Welt*, 13 June 1953.

[60] "Unzufrieden mit der Montanunion," *FAZ*, 23 June 1953.

[61] "Kranker Mann Montanunion," *Suddeutsche Zeitung*, 31 December 1953.

[62] "Schumanplan – pessimistisch gesehen," *Frankfurter Neue Presse*, 7 December 1953.

[63] When asked in 1953 which countries gained and lost most from ECSC membership, 46% claimed France gained from the ECSC, whereas only 1% saw the FRG as gaining something, and 50% believed the FRG was disadvantaged by membership. Allensbach Archivbericht, "Deutschland und die Europäischen Gemeinschaften," 1950–67.

[64] "Montan-Union im Kreuzfeuer," *Informationsdienst des Bundespresseamts*, 10 July 1953.

[65] "Der Pessimismus, mit dem Staatsmänner auf der Brüssler Konferenz … gingen, bezeichnet das Einde einer Periode, die vom europäischen Illusionismus erfüllt war…. Eine andere Frage ist, in welcher Weise sich die Bundesrepublik auf die beginnende Periode äußerer Unsicherheit und innerer Unentschiedenheit vorbereiten kann" in "Konferenz gegen Europa," *Berlin Tagesspiegel*, 22 August 1954.

[66] "Nur Romantiker der europäischen Einigung konnten jemals annehmen, daß der Weg zu einem politisch vereinten Europa ohne größere Widerstände zu beschreiten wäre" in "Der Weg zu Europa," *Westdeutsche Rundschau*, 26 April 1954.

[67] "Seitdem am 30. August die Europäische Verteidigungsgemeinschaft abgewürzt worden ist, hat ein rasender Absturz stattgefunden" in "Europa am Ende?" *Rheinischer Merkur*, 27 October 1955.

Above all, the bitterness of this defeat could be felt in the reporting of the FAZ, particularly when it complained that its Western neighbors (especially France) misunderstood its desire for integration.[68] It was not the case, it argued, that West Germany was willingly sacrificing sovereignty it did not fully enjoy yet, but more a recognition that full sovereignty was an outdated concept, for which the FRG no longer had any enthusiasm.[69] Answering the criticism of the opposition SPD and FPD[70] to the integration project, who claimed integration precluded unification, the FAZ stated that the more sovereign and less integrated the FRG became, the clearer the division of Germany could be seen.[71] Through integration into a greater, larger whole, the FRG was more likely to solve the question of reunification than it would as a small, but independent state, mirroring the Adenauer's government's stated policy of a "position of strength."[72]

The acrimonious tone caused by the supposed misunderstanding of West German intentions in pursuing integration continued later that month. Calling it "tragic" that the work of great "Europeans," such as Adenauer and von Brentano had been misinterpreted, the FAZ chided the West Germans for being too honest and idealist in dealings with their western neighbors, calling on them to realize that the "epoch of the nation state is not yet finished."[73] Finally, when discussing the replacement of the retiring Jean Monnet, the FAZ expressed its hope that his successor would not be German because the FRG's neighbors would merely continue to misunderstand its enthusiasm in pushing for and leading integration.[74] By the start of 1955, the West German media was in a state of despondency and confusion, with the FAZ questioning "what is Europe worth?"[75]; the Handelsblatt asking how integration might proceed[76]; and the Westdeutsche Allgemeine Zeitung publishing a "Wanted"

---

[68] "Die Europapolitik nach den Verträgen," *FAZ*, 2 November 1954.

[69] "Souveränität und Wiederbewaffnung lösen bei uns keine Begeisterung aus" in "Die Europapolitik nach den Verträgen," *FAZ*, 2 November 1954.

[70] For accounts of the SPD and FPD opposition to integration, see Chapter 4.

[71] "Je mehr dieses westliche Deutschland die Attribute eines selbständigen Staats erhält, desto mehr wird seine Rumpfhaftigkeit in Erscheinung und ins Bewusstsein treten," in "Die Europapolitik nach den Verträgen," *FAZ*, 2 November 1954.

[72] "In die neue Allianz bringen wir sie [die Frage der deutschen Einheit] als das Kernproblem eines der Beteiligten ein" in "Die Europapolitik nach den Verträgen," *FAZ*, 2 November 1954.

[73] "Wir müssen begreifen, daß das Zeitalter der Nationalstaaten noch nicht zu Ende ist" in "Das große Missverständnis," *FAZ*, 26 November 1954.

[74] "Am besten kein Deutscher: Wir Deutschen haben nach dem Zusammenbruch die Fahne Europas mit besonderer Begeisterung ergriffen. Wir haben das ehrlich getan und ohne Hintergedanken.... Die Begeisterung, mit der wir uns an die Mitarbeit gemacht haben, ist draußen nicht überall verstanden, nicht selten sogar missverstanden worden. Daraus müssen wir die Lehre ziehen: Sie heißt: Weiterhin überall mitmachen, wo an die Einigung Europas gearbeitet wird, aber Zurückhaltung üben, wenn es dabei um die Führung geht" in "Nicht vordrängen," *FAZ*, 27 December 1954.

[75] "Was ist Europa wert?" *FAZ*, 24 March 1955.

[76] "Integration ja – aber wie" *Handelsblatt*, 4 May 1955.

headline, seeking the "best way to European unity."[77] The second form of critique against the ECSC was much less predominant than that caused by the perceived bias against the FRG, but was much more lasting in its impact. Namely, it centered on the qualitative nature of the democratic structures at the supranational level and how these did not quite match up to national standards. Here we find – again as early as the 1950s – the articulation of the popular version of the structural congruence argument. The Heidelberg-based Rhein-Neckar-Zeitung had, seemingly inadvertently, added a tone of caution to its reporting. Writing at the very end of 1954, the paper stated that the ECJ was a very "necessary" creation, because it was designed to compensate for the lack of representative democratic controls over the bodies in the ECSC.[78] In particular, the article made a list of democratic weaknesses in the ECSC, which included an overly powerful executive High Authority, the lack of a sovereign territory, a common "Volk," and true democratic representation in the Common Assembly. So, whereas legal academia saw the ECJ as part of the problem, initial media reporting heralded the court as means to protect democracy and the individual in the Member States. These hopes however were to be dashed as time progressed and the ECJ continued to fail to act on the fundamental rights protection issue. These concerns became clearly apparent in media coverage by the mid-1960s.

The FAZ launched further criticism of the level of democratic controls in the ECSC in 1957, questioning the constitutionality of the ECSC Treaty itself.[79] Reporting on a case involving the coal-trading firm *Nold*,[80] the FAZ claimed that if the FCC were to decide that a provision of the ECSC Treaty infringed upon the Basic Rights, then the entire document would have to be declared unconstitutional. Specifically, the report claimed that the ECSC endangered Articles 14[81]

---

[77] "Gesucht wird das beste Weg zur Einheit Europas," *Westdeutsche Allgemeine Zeitung*, 27 May 1955.

[78] "Der Gerichtshof übt weitgehend jene Kontrollfunktion aus, die sonst innerhalb von staatlichen Gemeinschaften der Volksvertretung zukommt. Für die Montanunion erwies sich die Übertragung derartiger Aufgaben an einen Gerichtshof aber als notwendig, weil diese Gemeinschaft zwar übernationale hoheitliche Gewalt für den Bereich von Kohle und Stahl ausübt, bisher aber weder ein Hoheitsgebiet noch ein gemeinschaftliches Volk besitzt" in "Die sieben Wächter des Montanvertrages," *Rhein-Neckar-Zeitung*, 30 December 1954.

[79] "Die Konsequenz einer Verletzung von Grundrechten durch eine Entscheidung der Hohen Behörde, die vom Gerichtshof der Montanunion gebilligt wurde, müsste daher … sein, daß das Bundesverfassungsgericht eine solche Entscheidung für die Bundesrepublik und für deutsche Staatsbürger aufhebe. Damit aber würde sich die folgenschwere Frage ergeben, ob ein Vertrag, der eine Verletzung von Grundrechten ermöglicht, nicht überhaupt für nichtig erklärt werden müsse" in "Ist der Montan-Vertrag verfassungswidrig?" *FAZ*, 16 November 1957.

[80] Case 18/57 *Firma J Nold K.G. v High Authority of the European Coal and Steel Community* [1957] European Court Report 121.

[81] Article 14 BL [Property, inheritance, expropriation] states:
"(1) Property and the right of inheritance shall be guaranteed. Their content and limits shall be defined by the laws.

and 19[82] BL, which necessitated recourse to the law in cases of Basic Rights violation and limited the ability of the state to expropriate private property. If the FCC were to declare the ECSC unconstitutional, the paper writes, the political and economic implications (of a potential withdrawal from the ECSC) would be 'extraordinarily large.' The arguments proposed in the Rhein-Neckar-Zeitung and FAZ are reminiscent of the arguments that occurred in contemporaneous academic debates, in particular to the question of ease of legal recourse to protect Basic Rights provisions and the idea of structural congruence. However, a number of factors suggest that the media and academic debates were not linked at this point in any close way. Primarily, the vehemence of the academic debate is in no way matched by the coverage in the media. Whereas numerous texts were published in the legal-academic framework questioning and probing the legal democratic recourse in the ECSC, merely two articles on this topic made it into the pages of major newspapers. Second, the article in the Rhein-Neckar-Zeitung gives the impression that the critique of the ECSC was more inadvertent than deliberate. The point of the article was to praise the creation of the ECJ as an independent adjudicator, ensuring the control of a potentially dirigiste system of supranational authority. In doing this, the paper concluded by drawing out the democratic failings in the ECSC as a whole. However, the FAZ article is deliberately and quite specifically critical of the lack of Basic Rights provision at the European level. However, it is difficult to ascertain whether the FAZ was aware of the academic debates, since there are no citations of authors or texts predominant in that discussion, nor is there any reference made to the discussions themselves.

After the success of the Messina Conference in 1955,[83] Adenauer traveled to Brussels in late September 1956 for bilateral talks with the Belgian government.

---

(2) Property entails obligations. Its use shall also serve the public good.

(3) Expropriation shall only be permissible for the public good. It may only be ordered by or pursuant to a law that determines the nature and extent of compenzation. Such compenzation shall be determined by establishing an equitable balance between the public interest and the interests of those affected. In case of dispute respecting the amount of compenzation, recourse may be had to the ordinary courts."

[82] Article 19 BL [Restriction of basic rights] states:

"(1) Insofar as, under this Basic Law, a basic right may be restricted by or pursuant to a law, such law must apply generally and not merely to a single case. In addition, the law must specify the basic right affected and the Article in which it appears.

(2) In no case may the essence of a basic right be affected.

(3) The basic rights shall also apply to domestic artificial persons to the extent that the nature of such rights permits.

(4) Should any person's rights be violated by public authority, he may have recourse to the courts. If no other jurisdiction has been established, recourse shall be to the ordinary courts. The second sentence of paragraph (2) of Article 10 shall not be affected by this paragraph."

[83] The Messina Conference relaunched the European integration project after the EDC failure and ultimately resulted in the drafting of the Treaties of Rome in 1957/8.

He took the occasion to reveal his continued belief in a federal Europe,[84] which in turn reignited interest in the West German media about the integration process. The Süddeutsche Zeitung described the speech as "medicine for Europe,"[85] particularly with Western Europe's two leading powers caught up in the tension around the Suez Canal and the Hungarian Uprising, provoked concern of an escalation of the cold war at that time. In a further article, the same newspaper declared Europe was again a topic of converzation[86]; the same point was also made in the Mainz-based Allgemeine Zeitung.[87] However, unlike five years previously, this optimism about the integration project was tempered by more caution. As the Deutsche Tagespost succinctly wrote, "Europeans had burnt their fingers before and could not be expected to be enthusiastic again."[88] Still more typical of this is an article published in the Stuttgarter Nachrichten from the jurist and FDP MP Ewald Bucher, who in the same year also published in the NJW criticizing the provisional Treaties of Rome.[89] In the newspaper article, Bucher asks whether the Europe Adenauer spoke of was really "Europe," citing the need to use the prefix "klein-" (small) with all of the geographically and sectorally limited integration projects existing at that point.[90] Unlike in his article in the NJW, Bucher did not base his argument on a legal-academic argument here, and instead played on the issue of reunification, clearly tailoring his argument to overtly exercise more influence over the average West German reader than the technical legal issue would have. The evidence for this is clear. In multiple opinion polls, the reunification of Germany came out consistently as a more important foreign policy goal than the unification of Europe,[91] and specific technical knowledge about the ECSC and the Treaties of Rome (ToR) was particularly limited, demonstrated in an EMNID poll from 1960 where 41 percent of those questioned were unable to name all six Member States in the Common Market.[92]

---

[84] *Bulletin der Bundesregierung*, 26 September 1956, pp 1725–9.

[85] "Medizin für Europa," *Süddeutsche Zeitung*, 27 September 1956.

[86] "Man spricht wieder von Europa" in "Die guten Vorsätze," *Süddeutsche Zeitung*, 27 November 1956.

[87] "Europa wieder auf der Tagesordnung," *Allgemeine Zeitung*, 27 September 1956.

[88] "Die Europäer sind gebrannte Kinder, von ihnen wird niemand politischen Enthusiasmus erwarten können," in "Hoffnung Europa," *Deutsche Tagespost*, 1 December 1958.

[89] Bucher, "Verfassungsrechtliche Probleme des Gemeinsamen Marktes," pp 850–2.

[90] "Die vielen Europaprojekte, die uns seit Kriegsende beschert wurden, müssen zwangsläufig alle mit dem Präfix 'klein' versehen werden, sei es nun die EVG, die WEU, die OCommunity, oder die EZU. Denn sie umfassen alle nur den Teil Europas, bis zur Elbe reicht, oder wie das letzte, der Gemeinsamer Markt, sogar nur einen Teil von diesem Teil" in "Ist es wirklich Europa?" *Stuttgarter Nachrichten*, 8 March 1957.

[91] For instance, EMNID poll, 1960, "Nationales oder Europäisches Denken," shows that in 1957, 68% of West Germans preferred German reunification to European unity. This figure was down from a high of 76% in 1955 but rose again the following year to 70%. In BA B1367–6407 Bundeskanzleramt 1960–2.

[92] In N1266 1798 Nachlaß: Walter Hallstein: Meinungsumfragen in der BRD.

In March 1957, the FAZ published a full two page spread under the heading "Documents of the Time," highlighting the exact nature of the ToR.[93] Surprisingly, the coming to force of the Treaties of Rome on 1 January 1958 barely made the headlines, reflecting and propagating a general passive indifference to the events among the general population, typical of the "permissive consensus." In January 1958, 44 percent of West Germans had never heard of the Common Market and over one third of West Germans who had, did not know that the Treaties of Rome had been signed and created.[94] Moreover, when asked in January 1958 what event had raised the most interest in the recent past, the creation of the Common Market was selected in 22 percent of the responses, placing it between the rise in bread prices and rise in prices of train tickets.[95] If at all, some areas of the press were openly hostile to the Treaty, with the *Süddeutsche Zeitung* declaring it a "high price" to pay, especially the financial sacrifices being asked of the FRG.[96] The FAZ merely carried a small comment on the bottom of its front page informing readers that the document was now in force,[97] and coverage in the immediate period was not overwhelming in quantity. On 28 January 1958, the FAZ published a small article calling on the ECJ to continue to work "steering the path of European integration,"[98] and a visit by the seven ECJ judges to the Justice Ministry in Bonn in October 1959 received minor coverage in the *Deutsche Zeitung*.[99]

However, the question of transferring sovereignty and the impact of European law on the FRG were no longer considered, with more focus falling on concrete legal cases. Cases involving West German firms received extensive coverage, with continued emphasis on the seeming unfairness of the ECSC High Authority in setting prices of West German goods,[100] or on the heavy fines incurred by Mannesmann in a high profile 1962 case.[101] The *Mannesmann* case provoked an outcry from the *Deutsche Zeitung*, which denounced the lack of legal recourse guaranteed by the ECJ, despite this right being taken for granted in all six Member

---

[93] "So denkt man sich den Gemeinsamen Markt," *FAZ*, 6 March 1957.
[94] Jahrbuch der Öffentlichen Meinung 1958–64, p 543.
[95] "Deutschland und die Europäischen Gemeinschaften," *Allensbacher Archivbericht* 1950–67.
[96] "Ein hoher Preis," *Süddeutsche*, 1 March 1957.
[97] "Jetzt Gemeinsamer Markt," *FAZ*, 1 January 1958.
[98] "Dritte Gewalt in Europa," *FAZ*, 28 January 1958.
[99] "Europa-Richter besuchen Bonn," *Deutsche Zeitung*, 29 October 1959.
[100] For a sample from the year 1958, see cases covered in "Die Klage gegen die Hohe Behörde," *FAZ*, 21 February 1958; "Erhöhte Schrottumlage ist eine Strafe," *FAZ*, 22 February 1958; "Klage gegen Lieferbeschränkungen," *FAZ*, 25 February 1958; "Schrottklagen abgewiesen," *Handelsblatt*, 23 June 1958; "Entscheidendes Gerichtsurteil," *Handelsblatt*, 25 June 1958; "Bonn fühlt sich im Recht," *Industriekurier*, 12 August 1958; "Nold vor dem Europagerichtshof," *FAZ*, 20 November 1958.
[101] Case 19/61, *Mannesmann AG v High Authority of the European Coal and Steel Community* [1962] European Court Report 357.

States.[102] The newspaper predicted the growing importance of European law, stating that so far only large firms had been called before the ECJ, but then asking what would occur when smaller, perhaps even household producers were made to answer to the Court. Mirroring the FAZ article from five years previous,[103] the Deutsche Zeitung called for a much clearer understanding of the rights of the individual and small firms within the Community legal system. Despite these real concerns, important cases within the constitutional practice, particularly in the *Stork v. High Authority*[104] and *Ruhrkohlenverkaufsgesellschaften v. High Authority*[105] went entirely without comment in the media, despite the frantic academic discussion of these cases.[106] Nevertheless, the issues around guaranteed legal recourse and the democratic nature of the Community were raising substantial concerns among the media, even if they were not yet identified as themes of "constitutional" importance.

COMING TO TERMS, 1963–1969:
THE SUCCESS AND FAILINGS OF THE ECJ

The ECJ reached its *Van Gend* decision on 5 February 1963. Immediate newspaper coverage of European events was monopolized not by law, but by politics and diplomacy, namely, the British membership bid and by analysis of the Elysee Treaty signed during the week previous to the ECJ's decision, with the FAZ allocating a full page spread to Adenauer's explanation of the Treaty in the Federal Parliament.[107] Ten days later the first mention of the case was reported in the FAZ, whose article consisted of two brief paragraphs merely outlining relevant details.[108] Most importantly, the report made no mention of the impact of the decision for the constitutional practice, despite clearly identifying that Community law created citizen's rights that could now be called on directly within national courts. Another well-read broadsheet, die Welt, published further information on the decision in the following month, writing that the ToR decisively limited the sovereignty of the Member States

---

[102] "So selbstverständlich diese Rechtsgarantie aber in jedem der sechs Mitgliedsländer von Montanunion und Europäischer Gemeinschaft ist, so unbekannt ist sie noch in der europäischen Rechtssprechung. Es ist erstaunlich, wie … die Rechtssicherheit unbeachtet bleibt, der mit zunehmender Verwirklichung der Gemeinschaft die von ihren Regeln betroffenen Bürger dieser Länder entgegengehen" in "Europagericht ohne Kontrolle," *Deutsche Zeitung*, 4 August 1962.

[103] "Ist der Montan-Vertrag verfassungswidrig?," *FAZ*, 16 November 1957.

[104] Case 1/58 *Stork vs. High Authority* [1959] European Court Report 17.

[105] Case 36–38 and 40/59 *Ruhrkohlenverkaufsgesellschaften vs. High Authority* [1960] European Court Report 423.

[106] See, for instance, the 1959 Erlangen meeting. At this meeting, the two cases invoked concrete fears that Community law might well violate the principles of the national constitution.

[107] "Adenauer: Ohne Freundschaft mit Frankreich kein Europa," *FAZ*, 7 February 1963.

[108] "Zollerhöherungen nicht mehr möglich," *FAZ*, 15 February 1963.

and that the law it created was not simply standard international law, but directly effective law for all Member State citizens.[109] Despite spelling out the implications of this far-reaching decision, no further editorial commentary was provided. An almost identical report appeared in the FAZ soon thereafter.[110]

The Hamburger Echo, a SPD-leaning northern German publication, was one of the first papers to point out the differences between de Gaulle's newly declared nation state-orientated European policy and the ECJ's jurisprudence. Writing in March 1963, the paper heartily backed the ECJ, declaring the "Europe of sovereign nation states belonging legally to the past" and to have this openly stated by the highest of courts only "did good."[111] The article went on to claim that the ECJ had secured the constitutional status of all the European institutions and made their personnel independent from Member State interference. The newspaper asked quite acerbically how "the decision sounds in certain French ears, now that they realise that the Commission had the final say on a whole host of issues."[112] The continual references to de Gaulle and France was characteristic of the coverage from the generalized media given to the *Van Gend* decision. The media's interest in de Gaulle reflected in public opinion data in the period, demonstrated the polarizing effect he had.[113] Rather than being viewed as an event in itself, the *Van Gend* decision was frequently referred to as a blow against Gaullism and the destruction of the idealized version of a federal Europe found so often in the West German media during the 1950s. Clearly, as Weiler predicted, the constitutional practice was seen in the West German media as remedy for the political disintegration occurring within the council of ministers.

Yet, more often than not, the developments in the legal system, despite their importance, simply slipped under the radar of many commentators. They perceived that the interest of the reading public was in high politics, not the law.[114]

---

[109] "Mit dem EWG-Vertrag ist eine supranationale Rechtsordnung geschaffen worden, die die Souveränität der Mitgliedstaaten einschneidend beschränkt" in "EWG-Recht geht nationalem Recht vor," *die Welt*, 11 March 1963.

[110] "EWG-Vertrag wirkt direkt," *FAZ*, 30 March 1963.

[111] "Das Europa der souveränen Vaterländer gehört zumindest rechtlich bereits der Vergangenheit an. Dies zu wissen und von hohen Gerichten bestätigt zu bekommen, tut gut. Gerade jetzt," in "Europa vor den Vaterländern," *Hamburger Echo*, 13 March 1963.

[112] "Wie mag nun in manchen französischen Ohren … klingen, daß die EWG-Kommission in Brüssel die ausschließliche Zuständigkeit für die Entscheidung über … [viele Bereiche] … besitzt?" in "Europa vor den Vaterländern," *Hamburger Echo*, 13 March 1963.

[113] of West Germans 55% opposed de Gaulle's policies in 1963, against 10% who supported them. Also in 1963, 36% of West Germans preferred a closer friendship with Great Britain, as opposed to 24% who favored more cooperation with France. *Jahrbuch der Öffentlichen Meinung, 1958–64*, Institut für Demoskopie Allensbach.

[114] Knowledge of the Community had grown considerably since the first polls in 1957/8 (see Chapter 3). By 1963, 58% of West Germans could name at least four of the six Community Member States, and

For instance, a review of European events from 1963 in die Zeit from Katharina Focke, later Willy Brandt's European secretary in the chancellor's office, concentrated entirely on high political events and did not mention the ECJ at all, despite the importance of the *Van Gend* decision being spelled out clearly, albeit briefly, in all the leading broadsheets.[115]

It was left to specialized economic publications to comment at a more fundamental level on the ECJ's decision. The weekly business magazine, der Volkswirt,[116] again provided evidence to Weiler's argument. It deeply commended the ECJ for swimming against the tide of reactionary economic nationalism, which it claimed was resurgent in the Community.[117] Moreover, the "unexpected" clarity and sharpness of the court's reasoning left it beyond doubt that the decision was equally political as it was judicial in nature. It wrote: "the fundamental importance of this decision can not be underestimated and it would be good for the [Member States] governments to be clear about its consequences."[118] Nevertheless, the commentary warned against too deep a desynchronization between the ECJ and the national governments and judiciaries, who were yet to issue any comment on the case and who might yet undo some of the ECJ's good work. In particular, it highlighted France under de Gaulle as one particular case in which difficulties between the wishes of lawyers and politicians might arise, writing that "despite the independent judiciary's satisfaction about the decisions, one can not escape the concern that the gulf between Europe's legal norms and the much less optimistic political reality has only widened."[119] The Volkswirt continued its coverage of the ECJ's jurisprudence by reporting on a conference held at the University of Cologne, in which it describes a number of "useful" suggestions for improving the Community's legal system, namely greater judicial independence, longer periods of office for justices, and the introduction of published dissenting opinions.

The coverage of this conference by the widely read business daily, Handelsblatt, was far more critical, mainly because of the Court's inactivity, focusing on the

---

only 13% had never heard of the Treaties of Rome. This was considerably better than all the other Member States plus England, except Holland (75%/10%) and Luxembourg (86%/9%)

[115] "De Gaulles politische Union: Europa der Vaterländer oder Europa der Gemeinschaft?" *die Zeit*, 19 July 1963.

[116] *Der Volkswirt* became the current publication *die Wirtschaftswoche* in October 1970.

[117] "Kluft zwischen Justiz und Politik," *der Volkswirt*, 15 May 1963.

[118] "Die grundsätzliche Bedeutung dieses Gerichtsurteils kann gar nicht unterschätzt werden und es wäre gut, wenn die Regierungen sich über die sich daraus ergebenden Folgen klar werden würden," in "Kluft zwischen Justiz und Politik," *der Volkswirt*, 15 May 1963.

[119] "Trotz der Genugtuung über diese Urteile einer unabhängigen Justiz in Frankreich und in Europa kann man sich der Sorge nicht erwehren, daß durch sie die Kluft zwischen den europäischen vertragsjuristischen Normen und den von der Politik gesetzten sehr viel weniger hoffnungsvollen politischen Realitäten noch größer geworden ist" in "Kluft zwischen Justiz und Politik," *der Volkswirt*, 15 May 1963.

argument used during a particular presentation about "in how many (or more exactly: how few) cases, the Court provided sufficient legal argumentation."[120] It emphasized in its coverage the fact that the ECJ had been called a "silent court," akin to the "Corps des Muets," the French parliament under Napoleon, in which the justices, speaking different languages, do not always understand each other.[121] The Handelsblatt remained critical of the ECJ decisions throughout the early 1960s, predominantly for being too reticent in its decision making. Citing the Direct Effect decision as almost "worthless," the article warned that unless the ECJ began to ensure judicially the rights of citizens of the Member States, the Community was in danger of becoming incompatible with the Basic Law.[122] The protection of rights was made weaker because of the difficulty in calling on the ECJ through the Article 267 procedure and the monopolization of the judicial right of action relating to Community law by national governments.

Most interestingly, the Handelsblatt critique of the ECJ stemmed from a direct comparison of the European and West German constitutional systems. It wrote, "according to our constitution, the Basic Law, authority is divided into three: Legislature, Executive and Judiciary. An even supranational law – if it is to be valid in the Federal Republic – is subordinated to the Basic Law. We have to ask if the division of powers in the [Community] is sufficiently observed, and in particular the recourse to the law."[123] The article claimed that the European judiciary remained remarkably "silent" on the issue of legal recourse, despite this being a fundamental principle of both the European Human Rights Convention and of the Basic Law. Very similar criticism was published as a result of the coverage of an FDP Congress by the Frankfurter Rundschau[124] and the Stuttgart-based Südwest-Merkur.[125] This direct comparison of European and West German constitutional systems, with the clear winner being the Basic Law, marked the first point in a quickly evolving and

[120] "So wurde dem Europäischen Gerichtshof vorgerechnet, in wie vielen (oder genauer: wie wenigen) Verfahren er ausreichende Beweiserhebungen vorgenommen habe und daß in der ganzen Praxis diese grundlegende Tätigkeit entschieden zu kurz komme," in "Unzufrieden mit dem Europa-Gericht," *das Handelsblatt*, 21 May 1963.

[121] "Ferner wurde der Befürchtung Ausdruck gegeben, daß die Richter aneinander vorbeireden, wenn sie in einer anderen als ihrer Muttersprache beraten müssen ... schließlich wurde der Gerichtshof als ein schweigendes Gericht gekennzeichnet.... Bis heute biete der Europäische Gerichtshof ein "Corps des Muets, wie das französische Parlament unter Napoleon."

[122] "Mit dem Rechtsschutz hapert es in der EWG," *das Handelsblatt*, 5 May 1964.

[123] "Nach unserer Verfassung, dem Grundgesetz, sind die drei Gewalten Gesetzgebung, Verwaltung und Rechtssprechung geteilt. Auch übernationales Recht – soll es in der Bundesrepublik wirksam werden – ist diesem Grundgesetz unterworfen. Man fragt sich indessen, ob in der EWG die Gewaltentrennung, die zu den Fundamenten aller freiheitlichen Verfassungen zählt, zureichend beachtet wird. Besonders im argen liegt der Rechtsschutz," in "Mit dem Rechtsschutz hapert es in der EWG," *das Handelsblatt*, 5 May 1964.

[124] "Europa-Diktatur," *Frankfurter Rundschau*, 3 April 1964.

[125] "Europäische Politik und Wiedervereinigung," in *Südwest-Merkur*, 13 March 1964.

vigorous public debate in West Germany about the qualitative nature of fundamental rights protection at the European level.

From this point forward, the difficult issue of the Basic Rights and their position in the crystallizing European constitutional order was continually raised, triggered by a number of legal cases, both domestic and European. Most frequently, the comparison of the West German and European constitutions worked out in favor of the national system, despite the reluctance of most West Germans in this period to look favorably on "national" symbols and institutions.

The first of such cases highlighting the differences between the national and European systems was not the *Costa* decision, but instead was the RTC's referral to the FCC in 1963. The RTC claimed that the division of powers in the Community was not sufficiently democratic for its directives to be applicable by West German courts and asked the FCC to make a ruling on this issue. The Handelsblatt was among the first to report on this referral in February 1963. It opened its coverage with the plain question, "are Community directives in accordance with the Basic Law?"[126] Continuing its critique, it cited Chancellor Erhard's speech in the Federal Parliament of the previous month, which had called the democratic credentials of the Community into question.[127] However, the RTC's referral escaped the attention of most broadsheets and it was only after the ECJ reached its *Costa* decision on 15 July 1964 that the issue was taken up again.

The FAZ provided the first factual account of the *Costa* decision two days later,[128] at the same time as the Cologne based paper, the Kölner Stadt-Anzeiger.[129] Yet it was not until the following year, when the court's reasoning was published, that the case gained any kind of prominence. Again it was the FAZ that took up the issue, in February 1965, declaring German judges too "poorly informed" and very "late" in dealing with this enormously important "history making" decision.[130] The FAZ's critique of the ECJ was clear as it welcomed the referral of a case in front of the RTC to the FCC because of the lower court's doubting of the applicability European law with the Basic Law.[131] Die Welt maintained the critical tone, stating that the "German constitution has provided the courts with plenty of opportunities

[126] "Sind die EWG-Verordnungen mit dem Grundgesetz vereinbar?" in "EWG-Verordnungen verfassungswidrig?" *das Handelsblatt*, 13 February 1964.

[127] "Damit stößt das Finanzgericht Rheinland-Pfalz mitten hinein in ein allmählich weit verbreitetes und auch von Bundeskanzler Erhard am 9. Januar geäußertes Unbehagen über die Tatsache, daß immer mehr nationale Souveränitätsrechte nach Brüssel an eine 'im demokratischen Sinne politisch nicht verantwortliche Körperschaft ... ' abgegeben werden," in "EWG-Verordnungen verfassungswidrig?" *das Handelsblatt*, 13 February 1964.

[128] "EWG-Recht hat Vorrang," *FAZ*, 17 July 1964.

[129] "EWG Vertrag hat vor dem nationalen Recht Vorrang," *Kölner Stadt Anzeiger*, 17 July 1964.

[130] "Urteile machen Geschichte," *FAZ*, 22 February 1965.

[131] "Daß die Diskussion, wenn auch ziemlich spät, nun in Gang kommt, ist zu begrüßen," in "Urteile machen Geschichte," *FAZ*, 22 February 1965.

to consider the nature of the Community Treaty."[132] The article continued the trend of comparing national and European systems, distinguishing the inviolable separation of powers in the Basic Law (Article 20 (3) BL) against the less clear-cut institutional balance within the Community, which now had the right to issue the Member States directly effective, supreme legislation.[133] It stated very openly that "the German citizen is in danger of having their Basic Rights removed from without."[134] It called on the FRG government to represent "the German point of view"[135] within the Community, and on the FCC to fully answer the RTC's referral.

However, less critical voices were to be found elsewhere. The Sunday paper, Sonntagsblatt Hamburg, compared the Italian government's attempts to reject the *Costa* decision with de Gaulle's anti-integration policies,[136] which were extremely unpopular in the FRG.[137] It reminded the ECJ that the best way to rein in recalcitrant Member States would be by reinforcing the legal autonomy and authority of the European Communities. Likewise, the Saarbrücker Landeszeitung rejoiced in hearing the voice of a "sovereign Europe for the first time," declaring the European Communities much more than simple economic entities.[138] Nevertheless, the Handelsblatt remained skeptical of the ECJ, reciting the difficulty with which a referral could reach the European level, leaving the Court powerless without somebody willing to take the trouble to call upon it.[139] The FAZ reiterated this problem.[140] Moreover, the primacy doctrine had been too radical, claimed Handelsblatt, and had succeeded in merely alienating further the Gaullist government, and the French acceptance of this doctrine would be more moral than substantive.[141] To contextualize this statement, it must be remembered that at this time the French government's boycott of European institutions had been running for several months

---

[132] "Die deutsche Verfassung hat den Gerichten schon mehrmals Anlass zu Bedenken gegenüber dem EWG-Vertrag gegeben" in no title, *Die Welt*, 6 October 1965.

[133] No title, *Die Welt*, 6 October 1965.

[134] "Der deutsche Bürger läuft also Gefahr, daß von außen her seine Grundrechte ausgeholt werden," *Die Welt*, 6 October 1965.

[135] "Es wird Sache der Bundesregierung sein, den deutschen Standpunkt zu vertreten," in *Die Welt*, 6 October 1965.

[136] "Souverän: EWG und nationales Recht," *Sonntagsblatt Hamburg*, 7 March 1965.

[137] The mass daily *Bild Zeitung* published a cartoon in 1965 of de Gaulle repainting the German initials EWG (Community) as FWG (French Economic Community). *Bild Zeitung*, 9 July 1965.

[138] "Hier sprach zum ersten Mal ein Stück souveränes Europa, wenn auch nur ein ganz kleines Stück," in "Europarecht vor Landesrecht," *Saarbrücker Landeszeitung*, 13 March 1965.

[139] "Der Gerichtshof kann nicht helfen," *Handelsblatt*, 1 October 1965.

[140] "Insbesondere sei der Schutz der Privatperson und Unternehmen zustehe, unzulänglich," in "Mehr Rechtsschutz für den Europäer," *FAZ*, 11 September 1965.

[141] "Denn auf dem Treffen der Präsidenten der obersten Gerichte der sechs Mitgliedsländer … habe ein angesehener französischer Jurist zu den Europäischen Gerichtshofes gesagt, in seinem Lande räume man diesen Vorrang mehr moralische als substantielle Bedeutung ein," in "Der Gerichtshof kann nicht helfen," *Handelsblatt*, 1 October 1965.

and much editorial coverage was given to the issues surrounding the Empty Chair Crisis.[142] The FAZ's European correspondent, Hans-Herbert Götz, even wrote a two-page spread article in October 1965 seeking to explain the nature of the crisis in Brussels.[143] Götz was an economics correspondent for the FAZ until 1963, when he switched to being its European Correspondent until 1975. He was a very close associate of Walter Hallstein, helping him to complete his semiautobiographical "der unvollendete Bundesstaat" in 1969. Götz ensured that the supranationalists in legal academia and the government got a voice in West Germany's leading broadsheet on a regular basis.

After the French return at the beginning of 1966, Götz described the hopes of many who wanted the Community to succeed. Under the title, "A Return to the Everyday in Brussels," Götz declared,

> we can leave the [Community] lame for a while, we can even question its existence, but it appears as though it can no longer be destroyed. This is not because the "European idea" is so alive, not even because of the oft cited "Community Spirit," but because the national political and economic interests of the Member States simply forbid its destruction and they demand its further development.[144]

The West German public clearly agreed, with one of the highest ratings among the Member States when asked if the Common Market was advantageous for the country.[145]

However, just as the EDC had served to destroy the idealism found in the media coverage of European integration during the 1950s, the Empty Chair Crisis also seemed to shake West German belief in the possibility of a legally or constitutionally united Europe. Only 29 percent of those asked in 1965 believed that they would see the creation of a United States of Europe within their lifetime, which was 8 percent

[142] For instance, among many such choices, "EWG-Ministerrat tagt am 25. Oktober," FAZ, 23 September 1965; "De Gaulles Deutschlandpolitik," FAZ, 5 October 1965; "Die neue Verhandlungsbasis in der EWG," FAZ, 12 October 1965; "Mit oder ohne Frankreich," die Welt, 2 December 1965; "Die Zeit arbeitet für Brüssel," FAZ, 22 December 1965.

[143] "Die vaterlandlose Gesellen von Brüssel," in FAZ, 5 October 1965.

[144] "Man kann die Europäische Wirtschaftsgemeinschaft für eine Weile lahm legen, ja ihre Existenz aufs Spiel setzen, aber man kann sie offensichtlich nicht mehr zerstören. Das ist das Ergebnis der Luxemburger Konferenz. Nicht, weil der 'europäische Einigungsgedanke' so lebendig ist, und auch nicht, weil der zu oft beschworene 'Gemeinschaftsgeist' noch wirkt, sondern einfach deshalb, weil die nationalen Interessen der Mitgliedstaaten, die politischen und die wirtschaftlichen, die Zerstörung der Gemeinschaft verbieten und ihre Weiterentwicklung gebieterisch verlangen," in "Zurück zum Alltag in Brüssel," FAZ 31 January 1966.

[145] of West Germans 43% believed that the Common Market was advantageous for the FRG, as opposed to Italy (37%), France (35%), Belgium (37%), England (37%), Holland (51%), and Luxembourg (46%). Allensbach Archivbericht "Deutschland und die Europäischen Gemeinschaften" 1950–67.

lower than even in the immediate post-EDC period.[146] The Industriekurier asked, for instance, whether the "community idea was dying,"[147] whereas the SPD-orientated Kieler Morgen answered partly with the headline, "The ECSC Has Died."[148]

Yet, by the end of 1966, coverage did start returning to normal. For instance, die Welt's analysis of an ECJ pronouncement regarding cartels prompted it to reinvoke the questions asked in the previous year, namely "what happens in a conflict between national and Community law?"[149] It grumbled, the ECJ had avoided the question and as a consequence "Community law was not further developed."[150] The FAZ's Götz also saw the further development of the faltering Community in the hands of legal specialists. Writing at the very end of 1966, Götz claimed that "it was surprising, just how deep the idea of European unity had embedded itself in the legal community,"[151] reflecting perhaps the on-going sea change in legal-academic opinion evident as a consequence of the Bensheim and Kiel Conferences in the previous years.[152] In his article, Götz reviewed the release of the Festschrift tribute to Walter Hallstein's 65th birthday, in which the various authors had surmised that legal integration had long overtaken the development of economic integration, marking a rare and new order of international law.[153] Legal scholars, Götz argued, are in a key position: They educate new students, they advise governments, they publish and they issue law. Götz concluded that with this responsibility comes the influence and power to overcome the stagnation in which the Community found itself at that point.[154] This growing optimism was also reflected in public opinion data. In 1967,

---

[146] In 1955, 37% believed they would live to see the United States of Europe. "Europa-Idee ist mehr als ein Ersatzvaterland," Institut für Demoskopie, 1967.

[147] "Stirbt die Gemeinschaftsidee?" *Industriekurier*, 12 May 1966.

[148] "Die Montanunion ist tot," *Kieler Morgen*, 29 January 1966.

[149] "Geht die Rechnung der Luxemburger Richter auf?" *die Welt*, 18 August 1966.

[150] "Das europäische Recht wurde nicht weiter entwickelt," in "Geht die Rechnung der Luxemburger Richter auf?" *die Welt*, 18 August 1966.

[151] "Es ist überraschend, wie tief die europäische Einigungsidee in die Rechtswissenschaft eingedrungen und dort bereits Wurzeln geschlagen hat, nicht nur in der Bundesrepublik, sondern in ganz Europa," in "Die Juristen und Europa," *FAZ*, 3 December 1966.

[152] Compare with "Hauptvertreter des klassischen Völkerrechts" in Memorandum, 16 July 1964, in BA N1266 1156 Nachlaß Walter Hallstein: Wissenschaftliche Gesellschaft für Europarecht, and "Vermerk an Herrn Präsident Hallstein, betr: Verhältnis von Gemeinschaftsrecht an nationalen Rechten," 11 January 1965, in BA N1226 1796 Nachlaß Walter Hallstein: Verhältnis Gemeinschaftsrecht – Nationales Recht.

[153] "Selten geht die Rechtsetzung den ihr korrespondierenden wirtschaftlichen Phänomenen voraus.... In den Beiträgen … wird demonstriert, wie sich 'die neue Ordnung des Völkerrechts' entfaltet," in "Die Juristen und Europa," *FAZ*, 3 December 1966.

[154] "Juristen, ob als Professoren, ob in der Verwaltung, oder als Richter, wirken in die Tiefe, denn sie bilden Studenten aus, führen Assessoren in die Politik ein, sprechen Recht, publizieren und beraten die Regierungen. Sie tragen Verantwortung … so vermag diese Festschrift ein wenig Zuversicht zu geben, daß die europäische Einigungspolitik ihre derzeitige Schwächeperiode überwinden wird," in "Die Juristen und Europa," *FAZ*, 3 December 1966.

78 percent of West Germans would have voted "Yes" in a vote on the creation of a "United States of Europe," with only 6 percent stating a desire to vote against it.[155] This result was down from the 81 percent, who would have agreed in 1961, but still considerably higher than corresponding figures during the post-EDC period of pessimism of the mid-1950s (68 percent voting for). Once again, Weiler's argument that law was perceived to be an escape from political impasse is given credibility.

One of the prominent jurists cited by Götz was Walter Hallstein himself. The FAZ published his appraisal of ten years of progress of the ToR in die Zeit in March 1967. Hallstein focused predominately on the industrial, agricultural, and commercial aspects of the Community, but he did find time to answer some of the critics of the supposed undemocratic division of powers between the European institutions. He wrote, "the institutions secure a balance in a Community of unequal partners ... Everyone is equal in the eyes of the Law, which itself is created by democratic institutions. The Six agreed in the ToR to transfer these national constitutional principles in the area of the economy to the supranational organs."[156] In the following months, media debates about the ECJ and the nature of Community law died down to an extent, although this decline was probably not a result of Hallstein's explanation. 1967 saw the three Communities combined into a single authority, no longer under Hallstein's leadership, and this process took up most of the space in the columns devoted to European events.

Moreover, the FCC had delayed making decisions on two important cases relating to the position of Community law within the national constitutional system. In July 1967, it made decisions regarding the RTC's referral about the applicability to Community directives.[157] The Industriekurier commented on the case in the following month, stating that the FCC had simply failed to make any decision at all, escaping on a technicality.[158] The Spiegel's single commentary on the development of the European legal system in this period was on the RTC's referral. Heralding Wolfgang Schubert, president of the RTC, as a sort of "heretic" against the perceived wisdom of the Community, the article wrote with an astonished tone that the "self-confident Brussels bureaucrats" fail to recognize a democratic separation of powers and – with reference to the Basic Law – that the Federal Parliament should not be allowed to give up its position as a single legislator of public authority in the

---

[155] Jahrbuch der öffentlichen Meinung, 1965–67, Institut für Demoskopie Allensbach.

[156] "Die Institutionen sichern auch das Gleichgewicht in einer Gemeinschaft ungleicher Partner ... es gilt die Gleichheit vor dem Gesetz, für das demokratische Institutionen verantwortlich sind. Was die sechs Mitgliedstaaten des Vertrages von Rom vereinbart haben, ist, solche nationalen Verfassungsgrundsätze auf die zwischenstaatliche Beziehungen im Bereich der Wirtschaft zu übertragen," in "Was soll aus Europa werden?" die Zeit, 17 March 1967.

[157] 2 BvL 29/63 – Tax on Malt Barley decision, 5 July 1967 – BVerfGE 22, 134.

[158] "Bundesverfassungsgericht traf keine Entscheidung in der EWG-Rechtsfrage," Industriekurier, 15 August 1967.

FRG.[159] The FCC's second decision in which it accepted de facto the primacy of Community law[160] aroused little more interest in the West German media. The FAZ reported on the basic facts about the decision, stating that the FCC would refuse to hear constitutional complaints regarding Community directives because they were issued by non-German authorities.[161] The Süddeutsche Zeitung and die Welt gave much the same information, covering the exact wording of the FCC's reasoning without providing any commentary.[162] The lack of in-depth analysis from even the main broadsheets reflects the fact that the apparent inactivity of the FCC had left as many questions open as it had answered, and not even legal academic specialists could truly foresee the consequences of these decisions. Instead, the focus remained on high politics, reflected in a list of questions on "Europe" sent by the Rheinischer Merkur to Brandt as foreign minister, in which of the ten questions posed, not a single one dealt with legal integration.[163]

Focus instead fell on the ECJ, which celebrated its symbolic tenth anniversary in 1968. The Bremen-based Weser Kurier criticized the ECJ for not being strong enough, both institutionally, in that it held no "policing power," and politically, for not doing enough to further its position vis-à-vis the Member States. It equally criticized the Member States and the Commission for not calling on the ECJ enough to deal with infringements on the ToR, particularly by France.[164] At the beginning of 1969, the weekly parliamentary publication das Parlament provided a story about the ECJ, reviewing its activity over the last decade. Strangely, considering the events that had occurred over the past six years, the article concluded that "simply through the fact of its existence, the ECJ promotes the Community. In order to avoid a possible censuring, authorities and private organizations hold back in cases in doubt … [as] … if there is a policeman at the crossing, then drivers behave better. Because

---

[159] "Tatsächlich kennt die selbstbewusste Brüsseler Eurokratie überhaupt keine Gewaltentrennung in Legislative und Exekutive…. Das in Straßburg tagende Europa-Parlament hat nichts zu sagen….Er [der Bundestag] darf aber auf sein Privileg, einziger Gesetzgeber zu sein, laut Verfassungsartikel 79 Absatz 3 nicht verzichten," in "Gesetz und Gerste," *Spiegel*, 4 March 1964.

[160] Article 189 Community related to the applicability of Community law within national systems. See also 1 BvR 248/63 & 216/6 – *European Regulations decision*, 18 October 1967 – BVerfGE 22, 293.

[161] "Brüssel hat keine Staatsgewalt" in *FAZ*, 27 November 1967.

[162] "Bundesverfassungsgericht hält sich für EWG-Gesetze nicht zuständig," *Süddeutsche Zeitung*, 21 November 1967; "Verfassungsbeschwerde gegen EWG-Akten nicht zulässig," *die Welt*, 22 November 1967.

[163] Of the 10 questions posed, most dealt with closer cooperation in terms of military, economics, foreign policy, and development aid. One question was raised about the British entry to the Community. Memo, betr: Schriftliches Interview des Herrn Bundesministers mit dem "Rheinischen Merkur," in PAA B80–1169 Reden, Interviews, Vorträge, Stellungnahmen, Presse.

[164] "Sowohl die Mitgliedstaaten als auch die Kommission scheuen sich, vor dem Europäischen Gerichtshof Verstöße gegen den EWG-Vertrag anzuklagen, die rein politischer Natur sind. So hat Frankreich bis jetzt mindestens dreimal die Verträge verletzt, ohne daß man eine Lösung beim Gerichtshof suchte," in "Oberste Instanz bleiben die Politiker," *Weser Kurier*, 25 October 1968.

independent judges sit in Luxembourg, there are rarely major infringements against Community law."[165] Clearly, the parliamentary official responsible for the publication of this article had not followed the development of the Community's legal system, nor had any idea of how intense the media debate on the constitutional practice was to become.

During the 1950s, the early idealism toward integration had dissipated because of the setbacks of the EDC failure and the installation of de Gaulle in France, leaving the focus of media attention in regard to the ECJ to fall on the perceived anti-German bias in many of its decisions. Throughout the 1960s, there was an increasing tendency in the West German media to question the desirability of transferring legal sovereignty to a supranational organization in which legal recourse and fundamental rights were not as well protected as they were in the national system.

By the end of the 1960s and into the 1970s, a clear shift is discernible. A new set of priorities in the media was apparent and the tone became much more critical. The end of the 1960s was really the turning point. How do we explain this? In "The Silent Revolution," Ronald Inglehart demonstrated the existence of an "intergenerational value shift"[166] around the end of the 1960s, during which "postmaterial" ideals overtook "materialist" concerns as the overriding focus for political action. This position argues that younger generations, more physically and materially secure than previous generations, would have a different set of political values, namely ones based on "belonging, self-expression, and the quality of life."[167] To this list can also be added issues of "human rights, and the environment."[168] This finds resonance in the writings of Duncan Kennedy, who in his work on the patterns of globalization of law and legal ideas, describes human rights, democracy, and the rule of law as crucial aspects of the post-1945 "legal consciousness."[169] In fact, recent research by Habbo Knoch and others suggests that this shift in focus toward new forms of engagement and civil participation, while strong across Europe in the late 1960s, were particularly so in West Germany.[170] In a similar vein, Martin Slater has emphasized the importance of such "postmaterialist ideas," in particular the demand for more democratic participation in supranational governance since the 1970s, as a reason for growing public dissension. Slater argued that the latent "vast reservoir" of support and a "high level

---

[165] Das Parlament, 10 May 1969.

[166] Inglehart and Reif, *Eurobarometer*, p 2.

[167] Inglehart and Reif, *Eurobarometer*, p 11.

[168] Gabel, "European Integration, Voters, and National Politics," p 10.

[169] Duncan Kennedy, "Two Globalizations of Law & Legal Thought: 1850–1968," *Suffolk University Law Review* 36.3 (2003).

[170] Habbo Knoch, *Bürgersinn Mit Weltgefühl: Politische Moral und Solidarischer Protest in den Sechziger und Siebziger Jahren: Politische Kultur und Solidarischer Protest in den Sechziger und Siebziger Jahren* (Goettingen: Wallstein Verlag, 2007).

of goodwill towards a United Europe"[171] were crucial in allowing elites to pursue integration without "public pressure for popular participation,"[172] which would have raised the potential for conflict and decreased the ability for like-minded elites to reach the necessary level of integrative consensus. Correspondingly, as the salience of issues increased with the Community becoming more influential in citizen's lives, so has the demand for participation in supranational decision-making processes. When this was not forthcoming, public apathy and displeasure toward the Community institutions increased.[173] This postmaterial shift and the resulting discord is clearly apparent in the 1970s West German media landscape.

MAKING THE COMPARISON, 1970–1974: NATIONAL VERSUS SUPRANATIONAL

As a result of the postmaterial shift, the comparisons between the national and supranational systems during the 1970s became ever more explicit and contentious, with the domestic order coming out ever more frequently on the winning side. The turn of the 1970s saw media coverage of events in terms of European integration dominated by several high political discussions, foremost among which were the reorientation of emphasis toward the FRG's Ostpolitik under the new Chancellor Brandt in September 1969, the Hague Conference in December 1969, and the complex negotiations concerning the first enlargement of the Community. As such, and typically also for the first two periods explored, this coverage relegated the multiple important decisions made by the ECJ and the FCC in the period 1969–70 to a topic for sparse coverage. Legal issues once again gained prominence only in 1971, mainly because of the political nature of the case involved.

The FAZ's Hans Herbert Götz writing on the *ERTA*[174] decision of the ECJ in 1971 asked in an article from May that year whether policy goals can be achieved through the use of legal norms.[175] For Götz, it was obvious that they could, as in the Community, a community founded on law,[176] law and politics were inextricably

---

[171] Slater, "Political Elites," p 78.
[172] Slater, "Political Elites," p 80.
[173] Slater, "Political Elites," pp 74–81.
[174] Case 22/70, *Commission of the European Communities vs. Council of the European Communities* [1971] European Court Report 263. For a discussion of the importance of this case in terms of the establishment of the constitutional practice, see Weiler, *Constitution of Europe – "Do the New Clothes Have an Emperor?"* pp 22–3.
[175] "Kann man Politik mit Hilfe von Rechtsnormen durchsetzen?" in "Welche Rechte hat die EWG?" *FAZ*, 27 May 1971.
[176] "Die EWG … ist nicht nur auf gemeinsame Interessen, sondern vor allem auf geschriebenes Recht gegründet," in "Welche Rechte hat die EWG?" *FAZ*, 27 May 1971. This is reminiscent of Hallstein's famous statement from his 1969 memoirs, which opens this book and which Götz himself helped to write.

bound and the more comprehensive the Community's legal system became, the more intensive the political disputes concerning it.[177] In the ERTA decision, the Commission and the Council were in dispute about the division of authorities when drawing up international treaties in areas of Community competency. This raised the perceived interest in the case, as it was the first time two Community institutions had fought against each other judicially, and second, the possible impact of the decision, in which it was ruled that the Community now had the implied competency to agree to external treaties, was a major incision into a traditional area of national sovereignty. In particular, Götz wrote, the French newspaper Le Monde was critical of the decision, citing the ECJ's "overstepping" of its powers and its continual attempts to push the power of the Community legal system.[178] Instead of celebrating the decision as a new locus for discussion about the future of the Community, Götz regarded the French reaction as predictable and disappointing.[179]

Whether Götz's call for a new discussion was heeded in political circles appeared doubtful, as neither Brandt, in an interview in Le Monde shortly thereafter,[180] nor Katharina Focke, in a long article in die Zeit,[181] mentioned the case nor even the ECJ at all. Indeed, the entire effectiveness of the Community legal system was questioned by the Frankfurter Rundschau, which reported on the growing number of legal offenses committed by Member States against European law.[182] It claimed the Community was worried by the increasing tendency of Member States, particularly France and Italy to ignore Community legislation and demonstrated that the FRG was also involved in twenty cases of presumed or proven offense. However, the article claimed that this could also be explained by the increasing complexity and broadness of the Community legal system.[183]

---

[177] "Der Gerichtshof … hat zur Entwicklung des gemeinschaftlichen Rechts und Rechtsbewußtseins Entscheidendes beigetragen. Es ist unvermeidlich, daß er angesichts des mit zunehmender Intensität geführten politischen Ringens um den Charakter der EWG in diesen Konflikt hineingezogen wird. Er kann und darf diesem Konflikt nicht ausweichen. Die Auseinandersetzungen um das Urteil vom 31. März 1971 … macht deutlich, um welche politische Dimensionen es inzwischen geht"in "Welche Rechte hat die EWG?" *FAZ*, 27 May 1971.

[178] "Dieser fachkundiger französischer Jurist wirft dem Gerichtshof vor, er habe seine Zuständigkeit überschritten; anders als der Supreme Court in den Vereinigten Staaten stehe dem Luxemburger Gericht nicht zu, das Gemeinschaftsrecht dynamisch weiterzuentwickeln," in "Welche Rechte hat die EWG?" *FAZ*, 27 May 1971.

[179] "Wer die französischen Vorstellungen von diesem Europa kennt, wundert sich über die Urteilsschelte aus französischem Munde allerdings nicht," in "Welche Rechte hat die EWG?" *FAZ*, 27 May 1971.

[180] Bulletin der Bundesregierung, 104, 7 July 1971.

[181] "Europa ohne Zauberformel," *die Zeit*, 23 July 1971.

[182] "Verstöße gegen EWG-Vertragsbestimmungen," *Frankfurter Rundschau*, 4 January 1972.

[183] "Inwieweit diese Entwicklung jedoch schlicht durch den Umstand begründet ist, daß das Gemeinschaftsrecht von Jahr zu Jahr breiteren Umfang einnimmt, würde nach Ansicht von Experten einer detaillerten Untersuchung bedürfen," in "Verstöße gegen EWG-Vertragsbestimmungen," *Frankfurter Rundschau*, 4 January 1972.

However, while media reports also refused to engage in Götz's proposed discussion, they did continue the growing trend apparent through the 1960s of contrasting national and European legal systems. Whereas these comparisons had taken place on specific issues in the 1960s, the 1970s saw a growth in impact-making, generalized headlines about a perceived intrusion on the national legal system. For instance, the *Handelsblatt* ran the headline "Conflict: German and Community Law" in August 1971 for a story covering an ongoing and complicated case before the FCC involving the importation of milk powder.[184] Shortly thereafter, *die Welt* newspaper declared "Foreign Law Is Supreme" in its headline on a story involving a Berlin based furniture importer.[185] On the same story, the *Hamburger Abendblatt* published under the headline "Legal Differences."[186] This continued tendency from the 1960s to compare and contrast national and European systems, coupled with the FCC's de facto acceptance of the ECJ's jurisprudence at the end of the 1960s, prompted the media, as had happened in academia, to examine the relationship between the Basic Law and Community legislation. The examination of this question began in earnest at the start of 1972.

In April 1972, the Ludwigshafen-based newspaper, the *Rheinpfalz*, published a commentary on a television broadcast, "Recht im Gespräch," from the Mainz-based public service station ZDF involving an interview with the president of the FCC, Ernst Benda. In the program, Benda had advocated the creation of a catalog of fundamental rights for the Community, similar to the basic rights in the FRG's constitution.[187] He claimed this to be the solution to the complex dilemma posed by the penetration of European law into the FRG's constitutional life, namely the recognition of supreme, effective Community legislation juxtaposed against the urgency in not simply abandoning "legitimate German interests" and the carefully created West German constitutional order.[188] Benda saw his role, holding such an influential position, as a mediator to ensure an avoidance of conflict between the

---

[184] "Konflikt: Deutsches und EWG-Recht," *Handelsblatt*, 20 August 1971.

[185] "Ausländisches Recht hat Vorrang," *die Welt*, 3 November 1971.

[186] "Rechtsunterschiede," *Hamburger Abendblatt*, 19 July 1972.

[187] "Für die Schaffung europäischer Grundrechte für den Bereich der EWG hat sich der Präsident des Bundesverfassungsgericht, Benda, ausgesprochen. Benda wies dabei auf den ausgeprägten Grundrechtskatalog der Bundesrepublik hin," in "Für europäische Grundrechte," *die Rheinpfalz*, 18 April 1972.

[188] "Man müsse ... das Dilemma sehen, in dem sich das deutsche Verfassungslebens angesichts des Vordringens europäischen Recht befinde. Einerseitz müsse das EWG-Recht Vorrang auch vor einzelnen deutschen Grundrechten haben, andererseits bestehe auch das legitime deutsche Interesse, das vom Grundgesetz verordnete, vom Bundesverfassungsgericht und allen anderen staatlichen Instanzen oft mühsam aufgebaute und verteidigte freiheitlich-demokratische Verfassungsrecht nicht einfach preiszugeben" in "Für europäische Grundrechte," *die Rheinpfalz*, 18 April 1972.

two legal systems.[189] This was to be achieved through a transposition of the FRG's basic rights to a general community wide fundamental rights provision.[190] Here too is clear evidence that the FCC had been paying attention to public and media discourse and its president was even willing to appear on television to ensure that his message got across. This strongly suggests that the media discourse, if clearly not decisive in the FCC's later *Solange* decision, at least provided a public mandate for such an outcome. Benda's clear and strong belief in the value of the West German constitutional order was countered only partly in the program by the ECJ's German judge, Hans Kutscher,[191] who claimed that the growth of European law had actually increased the provision of fundamental rights to European citizens.[192]

Shortly thereafter, Benda's wish to influence the creation of European basic rights began to come into fruition, as the Frankfurt Administrative Court (FAC) made its reference to the FCC that would result in the latter's *Solange* decision. Coverage of this reference was unsurprisingly limited geographically to the Frankfurt papers. The Frankfurter Rundschau reported factually on the reference in May 1972, citing the astonishment of European lawyers that the FAC would question the constitutionality of European law again, after the FCC had already ruled on this issue in 1967.[193] Such action raised potentially difficult consequences for the Community. In a further editorial in the same issue, the paper wrote that every West German citizen should have full judicial protection against potentially unconstitutional European law, and therefore it could not criticize the FAC's reference to the FCC.[194] It conceded that the Communities were extremely complex legal institutions, in which

---

[189] "Er selbst würde such dafür einsetzen, sagte Benda, daß aus der Konkurrenz zwischen dem übergeordneten EWG-Recht und dem nationalen Verfassungsrecht keine Konflikt entstünden," in "Für europäische Grundrechte," *die Rheinpfalz*, 18 April 1972.

[190] "In der ZDF-Sendung sagte er wörtlich: "Kein Mensch könnte vernünftigerweise Einwendungen dagegen erheben, wenn die Rechtsgarantien, die etwa das Grundgesetz den Bürgern der Bundesrepublik gibt, europäischen Allgemeingut bei den Mitgliedern der Gemeinschaft würden," in "Für europäische Grundrechte," *die Rheinpfalz*, 18 April 1972.

[191] Hans Kutscher (1911–93) was a justice on the First Senate of the FCC between 1955 and 1956, and then on the Second Senate from 1956 to 1970. In 1970, he became the German representative to the ECJ's panel of judges.

[192] "Dabei dürfte jedoch nicht übersehen warden, daß die Bürger der Europäischen Wirtschaftsgemeinschaft zahlreiche zusätzliche Rechte innerhalb des ganzen EWG-Bereichs erhielten," in "Für europäische Grundrechte," *die Rheinpfalz*, 18 April 1972.

[193] "EWG-Juristen sind erstaunt, daß das Frankfurter Verwaltungsgericht den Fall nun auch dem Bundesverfassungsgericht in Karlsruhe vorgelegt hat, zumal die Karlsruhe Verfassungsrichter in einer anderen Sache schon früher entschieden hatten, das Recht der [EG] stelle eine eigene Rechtsordnung dar. Sollte Karlsruhe diesmal anders urteilen, befürchtet man in Brüssel eine Rechtsunsicherheit, die für den wirtschaftlichen Integrationsprozeß der EWG schwerwiegende Folge hätte," in "EWG-Verordnung in Karlsruhe unter der Lupe," *Frankfurter Rundschau*, 12 May 1972.

[194] "Jeder deutsche Bürger … hat das Recht auf vollen Schutz vor gerichtlichen Entscheidungen, die gegen das Grundgesetz verstoßen würden," in "Rechtssicherheit hat Vorrang," *Frankfurter Rundschau*, 12 May 1972.

national interest had to play a cursory role, but it also asserted that the rights of the citizen must always take precedence.[195]

The FAC's reference and the general question of the constitutionality of Community legislation had in this way become an important news story. It must also be remembered that in this period of the mid-1970s, the FCC had gained both political and public prominence because of a series of high profile political cases held before it, not the least its decision on the constitutionality of Brandt's Ostpolitik in 1973.[196] As a result, the question of how to protect the Basic Rights was never far from the headlines over the following two years. In October 1973, the Augsburger Allgemeine Zeitung examined the question not from the national viewpoint, but at what the ECJ had been doing to accommodate national concerns, in particular with reference to two cases involving the ECJ from the local region. In one case, the Court conferred the same guaranteed rights of German workers to an Italian migrant worker in Augsburg, which the paper welcomed as a confirmation that rights can be protected through the European legal mechanisms without costs for the individual. The second case was the *Stauder v. Ulm*[197] decision, in which the ECJ declared fundamental rights protection was an integral part of Community legislation. The paper referred to the case, if not specifically by name or with an assessment of its true importance, as a "triumph of the individual,"[198] declaring in conclusion that such successes were a reason to forget the smaller problems of domestic politics.[199]

Another regional paper, the Mannheimer Morgenpost, reported on the meeting of the judges from the various levels of federal and state constitutional courts[200] found in the FRG's legal system. It stated that the main talking point was the relationship between the Basic Law and Community legislation and that the most difficult task facing the West German legal community was the transposition of a comparable fundamental rights catalog, with the Basic Law as a model, to the Community. The problem, the article claimed, stemmed from the inability of the Member States to agree on a suitable level of rights protection in the original treaties. This proved, according to the judges in discussion, particularly disadvantageous to the FRG,

---

[195] "Nationale Interessen sollten dabei keine Rolle spielen – aber das Recht des Bürgers muß an erster Stelle stehen," in "Rechtssicherheit hat Vorrang," *Frankfurter Rundschau*, 12 May 1972.

[196] See Horst Säcker, *Das Bundesverfassungsgericht* (Bonn: Bundeszentrale für politische Bildung, 2003), pp 20–31.

[197] Case 29/69 *Stauder vs. Ulm* [1969] European Court Report 419.

[198] "Ein Triumph des Individuums auch in Ulm," in "In Europa jedem sein Recht," *Augsburger Allgemeine Zeitung*, 19 October 1973.

[199] "Ein Grund für Politiker und Bürger, etwas großzügiger auch gegenüber den kleinen politischen Problemen des heimatlichen Bereichs zu sein …," in "In Europa jedem sein Recht," *Augsburger Allgemeine Zeitung*, 19 October 1973.

[200] As well as the ECJ judge, Hans Kutscher.

whose "system of Basic Rights is more developed than anywhere else."[201] This political failure would make it almost impossible to introduce a catalog through the political arena and instead the judges agreed that it was best left to the judiciary, i.e. the ECJ to develop its own fundamental rights provisions.[202] This provides a further insight that, alongside Ernst Benda's revelation from the previous year,[203] the highest levels of the West German judiciary were openly seeking to prompt the ECJ through judicial, public and academic dialogue into developing a basic rights catalog comparable to that of the FRG. Clearly, they believed that the ECJ would give credence to such debates at the national level.

The Handelsblatt however remained critical that such an approach could work. It wrote that there was no guarantee that if the ECJ were to undertake such a task, it would choose to mimic the West German model. Instead it was far more likely to use the lowest common denominator between the Member States, resulting in a dimunation of the Basic Law, the "most progressive national constitution" and its basic rights.[204] With the media awaiting the FCC's decision on the FAC's reference, and leading judicial personalities raising the possibility of an intercourt dialogue to solve the basic rights dilemma, the tension entering 1974 was palpable as newspapers tried to keep the issue in the public's attention. Under the headline "Here Is Where the National Cow Is Slaughtered," the Rheinische Post published a long and detailed survey of the composition and activities of the ECJ since its inception in 1952.[205] Claiming that despite its importance, ruling over nine states and 250 million citizens, the existence of the Court was unknown to many.[206] After outlining the nature of the Court, the paper decided that the ECJ held an overtly political role, deciding independently from and between national interests.[207]

---

[201] "Das würde insbesondere für die Bundesrepublik nachteilig werden, weil hierzulande das System der Grundrechte weiter ausgebaut ist als anderswo," in "Grundrechte auf dem europäischen Markt," *Mannheimer Morgenpost*, 26 October 1973.

[202] "Das wäre voraussichtlich auch die praktisch einfachste Lösung auf dem Weg des geringsten Widerstands im Vergleich zu der politisch kaum durchführbaren Wirklichkeit, einen zufriedenstellenden Grundrechtskatalog für Europa nach deutschem Vorbild in Kraft zu setzen," in "In Europa jedem sein Recht," *Augsburger Allgemeine Zeitung*, 19 October 1973.

[203] "Für europäische Grundrechte," *die Rheinpfalz*, 18 April 1972.

[204] "Jedoch besteht kein Garantie, daß die Europa-Richter die aus neun Ländern mit ganz unterschiedlicher Rechtsentwicklung und Rechtsauffasung kommen, stets ihren Spielraum nutzen und sich der in Fragen einzelner Grundrechte jeweils am weitesten fortgeschrittenen nationalen Verfassun anschließen werden. Eher würden sich in bestimmten Punkten sogar retardierende Einflüsse unter den neun Europarichtern erwarten lassen," in "Europarecht bricht das nationale Verfassungsrecht," *Handelsblatt*, 30 October 1973.

[205] "Hier wird die nationale Kuh geschlachtet," *Rheinische Post*, 31 May 1974.

[206] "Viele wissen nichts von der Existenz des Europäischen Gerichtshofes und vielleicht ebensoviele verwechseln ihn mit dem Internationalen Gerichtshof in Den Haag," in "Hier wird die nationale Kuh geschlachtet," *Rheinische Post*, 31 May 1974.

[207] "So ist der Europäische Gerichtshof nicht die Summe von weisungsgebundenen Staatsvertretern, er ist keine Schiedsinstanz, sondern ein Gericht, das zur Rechtsprechung berufen ist abseits der nationalen

Shortly after the Rheinische Post published its critique of the ECJ, the FCC made its *Solange* decision. Coverage of the decision occurred throughout the media spectrum, with some newspapers going beyond the mere factual reports and dedicating editorial opinion to the situation. The reaction to the decision was divided, mirroring the opinion in the FCC itself. The Hannoverische Allgemeine Zeitung was critical of the FCC in the extreme. It wrote that the already shaken Community had received a further "knock" from the FCC, which could unleash dangerous long-term consequences for the Community.[208] The damage was two-fold, with the decision raising the danger that the European legal system could splinter, and denying the ECJ an "earned" vote of confidence from the national level.[209] The result was the threat that the Community legal order could simply "fall apart," before it really had been fully completed.[210] Admittedly, the article conceded, the FCC had limited its power of review until that time that the Community held its own comparable set of basic rights, but the paper argued this condition would be impossible to fulfill in the "foreseeable future," because only Italy, out of the other eight Member States, had a comparable constitution to the Basic Law.[211] Moreover, the chance of reaching the political agreement needed to bolster the European Parliament according to the terms of the FCC was unthinkable.[212] The article went on to cast doubt on the validity of the decision by highlighting the fact that the FCC's opinion was so divided, and that the argument posited by the majority opinion felt "suspiciously self-righteous."[213] It concluded that the FCC had dealt Europe yet another defeat.[214]

Interessen. Und darin liegt seine politische Rolle" in "Hier wird die nationale Kuh geschlachtet," *Rheinische Post*, 31 May 1974.

[208] "Die durch Angriffe auf die Agrarmarktordnung und die Zollunion ohnehin erschütterte Europäische Gemeinschaft hat aus Karlsruhe einen Stoß erhalten, der gefährliche Langzeitwirkungen entfalten könnte," in "Stoß aus Karlsruhe," *Hannoverische Allgemeine Zeitung*, 14 August 1974.

[209] "Mit ihrer Entscheidung . . . haben die Karlsruhe Richter nicht nur die Gefahr der Rechtszersplitterung heraufbeschworen, sondern auch einer noch jungen, aber bereits angesehenen europäischen Institution den verdienten Vertrauensvorschuß verweigert," in "Stoß aus Karlsruhe," *Hannoverische Allgemeine Zeitung*, 14 August 1974.

[210] "Die ohnehin erst in dürftigen Ansätzen vorhandene europäische Rechtsordnung droht auseinanderzufallen, bevor sie richtig entstehen kann," in "Stoß aus Karlsruhe," *Hannoverische Allgemeine Zeitung*, 14 August 1974.

[211] "Aber wenn man bedenkt, daß von den Mitgliedsländern der Europäischen Gemeinschaft nur Italien einem dem deutschen vergleichbaren Grundrechtskatalog besitzt, mag man berechtigte Zweifel haben, ob es in absehbarer Zeit gelingen wird, den EWG-Vertrag durch einen solchen Katalog zu ergänzen," in "Stoß aus Karlsruhe," *Hannoverische Allgemeine Zeitung*, 14 August 1974.

[212] "Von den politischen Chancen eines direct gewählten Europaparlaments ganz zu schweigen," in "Stoß aus Karlsruhe," *Hannoverische Allgemeine Zeitung*, 14 August 1974.

[213] "Das Argument des besseren Bürgerschutzes vermag den Verdacht der Selbstgerechtigkeit nicht zu verdrängen," in "Stoß aus Karlsruhe," *Hannoverische Allgemeine Zeitung*, 14 August 1974.

[214] "In Karlsruhe hat das von Dauerkrisen geschültelte Europa eine weitere Niederlage erlitten," in "Stoß aus Karlsruhe," *Hannoverische Allgemeine Zeitung*, 14 August 1974.

In a second article on the decision, the paper stressed the further "disagreeable" result of the decision: a patchwork of Community legislation, valid in some Member States and not in others.[215] The opinion provided by the Süddeutsche Zeitung was similar, although not so extreme. It also referred to the *Solange* decision as a "knock" for the integration process, but emphasized over several paragraphs that the decision was limited both in scope – the FCC had turned out the initial complaint and still refused to hear cases directly against European law – and time – the decision was valid only as long as the Community did not have a comparable fundamental rights provision.[216] The Stuttgarter Zeitung was also critical of the decision, believing it to have created a "special status" for the FRG and exposed that danger, under which the Community legal order stood.[217] The Stuttgarter Nachrichten also carried a commentary laced with irony on the decision, asking whether it was right or not that European law be measured against "our good constitution."[218]

However, several voices in the media supported the FCC's decision. The most active support was issued by the Kieler Nachrichten. Writing under the headline "European malaise," the article praised the "courage" of the FCC in voicing the opinion of the "great majority of Europeans" toward the European integration process and calling into question the democratic failings of the Community.[219] It claimed the FCC had, through its decision, underlined the lack of democratic legitimacy in a Community run by a "bureaucratic apparatus" (Commission), a Council, which was not answerable to any parliament, and a European Parliament, whose existence was merely "theoretical."[220] Moreover, the ECJ had based its jurisprudence on the

---

[215] "Die Entscheidung des Bundesverfassungsgerichts führe außerdem zu unannehmbaren Ergebnissen. Es könne der Fall eintreten, daß einzelne Vorschriften der Europäischen Gemeinschafte in einigen Mitgliedstaaten anwendbar seien, in anderen nicht," in "Bundesverfassungsgericht will EG-Recht überprüfen," *Hannoverische Allgemeine Zeitung*, 14 August 1974.

[216] "Mit dieser Entscheidung hat der 2. Senat des Bundeverfassungsgerichts der europäischen Integration einen Stoß versetzt...," in "Grundgesetz geht vor EG-Recht," *Süddeutsche Zeitung*, 14 August 1974.

[217] "... mit dieser Entscheidung ... hat das Bundesverfassungsgericht seine Kompetenzen erweitert und damit ... einen Sonderstatus für die Bundesrepublik Deutschland geschaffen und sie dem berechtigen Vorwurf ... der Gefährdung der Gemeinschaftsrechtsordnung ausgesetzt," in "Grundgesetz geht vor EG-Recht," *Süddeutsche Zeitung*, 14 August 1974.

[218] "War es nicht eine Brüskierung der Europäischen Gemeinschaft, von ihr erlassene Verordnungen an unserem guten Grundgesetz zu messen?" in "Kautionsklauseln," *Stuttgarter Nachrichten*, August 15, 1974.

[219] "Das Bundesverfassungsgericht hat den Mut gehabt, durcheine grundsätzliche Entscheidung das europäische Übel, nämlich das Fehlen demokratischer Institutionen in der Gemeinschaft, beim Namen zu nennen.... Wir meinen, daß dieser Standpunkt mit seiner politischen Untermauerung genau der Denkweise der großen Mehrheit der Europäer entspricht," in "Europäisches Übel," *Kieler Nachrichten*, 15 August 1974.

[220] "In der Tat ist die Europäische Kommission in Brüssel eine reine Beamtenapparatur.... Dieser Ministerrat ist keinem Parlament verantwortlich.... Das 'Europäische Parlament' führt in Straßburg ein theoretisches Dasein, irgendwelche ins Gewicht fallenden Kontrollfunktionen hat es nicht," in "Europäisches Übel," *Kieler Nachrichten*, 15 August 1974.

presumption of primacy of European law over national law without actually considering the importance that this law should stem from a "democratic" system.[221] Other sources, while not openly critical of the decision, remained only lukewarm in their support for the FCC. For instance, die Welt newspaper published merely a cursory mention of the case, despite it making the headlines in the other broadsheets.[222] The Mannheimer Morgenpost also printed just a factual reconstruction of the case, without any commentary pro or contra the decision.[223] The Frankfurter Rundschau, which had earlier welcomed the reference made by the FAC to the FCC, placed a lot of emphasis on the reasoning made by the FAC, rather than the FCC, with almost a third of the article dedicated to the Frankfurt Court, but it also made no commentary on the nature of the FCC's decision.

The other Frankfurt newspaper, the FAZ, provided the most subtle, even covert, support for the FCC's decision. In its wording of its report, the FAZ frequently referred to the Basic Law as "our" constitution[224] or to "our" basic rights catalog,[225] implying an implicit association with the FCC's choice to defend the national constitution against the externalized European order. The wording of the FAZ's article stands out, as in all of the coverage of the *Solange* decision; it is the only time that this possessive pronoun is used (except for the singular ironic use in the Stuttgarter Nachrichten[226]) and is particularly unusual for the FAZ's otherwise measured style. In a further commentary in its economics section, the FAZ denied some of the critique levelled at the decision. In particular, it claimed that the fears that the Community legal system would disintegrate were unfounded and that the wording of the FCC's decision had made the *Solange*-clause a last minute "emergency brake" to prevent an infringement on the basic rights.[227] Moreover, it claimed that instead of complaining, the ECJ should understand the *Solange* decision as a call for strengthening and

[221] "Für ihn (ECJ) war die politische Frage, ob es ein demokratisches Europa gibt oder nicht, unerheblich," in "Europäisches Übel," *Kieler Nachrichten*, 15 August 1974.

[222] "Verfassungsgericht schränkt EG-Recht ein," *die Welt*, 15 August 1974.

[223] "Deutsches Recht geht vor Europarecht," *Mannheimer Morgenpost*, 14 August 1974.

[224] "Steht das Gemeinschaftsrecht mit den Grundrechtsgarantien unserer Verfassung in Widerspruch, so hat ausnahmsweise das nationale Recht den Vorrang," in "Vorrang der Grundrechte vor dem europäischen Gemeinschaftsrecht," *FAZ*, 15 August 1974.

[225] "Eine Überprüfung von europäischem Recht durch das Bundesverfassungsgericht ist, nach der neuen Entscheidung so lange zulässig, bis der Integrationsprozeß der Gemeinschaft so weit fortgeschritten ist, daß auch das Gemeinschaftsrecht einen von einem Parlament beschlossenen Grundrechtskatalog enthält, der mit unserem Grundrechtskatalog vergleichbar ist," in "Vorrang der Grundrechte vor dem europäischen Gemeinschaftsrechtz," *FAZ*, 15 August 1974.

[226] See "Grundgesetz geht vor EG-Recht," *Süddeutsche Zeitung*, 14 August 1974.

[227] "Solche Befürchtung scheinen aber zumindest verfrüht. Man kann die Entscheidung aus Karlsruhe nämlich auch so verstehen, daß nur eine letzte Notbremse eingebaut werden sollte, wenn der Europäische Gerichtshof eine Norm passieren läßt, die unsere Grundrechte gröblich verletzt," in "Kein Tiefschlag für Europa," *FAZ*, 16 September 1974.

improving the Community legal system.[228] Following the logic of the decision, the ECJ should introduce a catalog of fundamental rights, which, if not identical to the West German model, should use this as a paragon for their development.[229] This was not, so claimed the FAZ, an "axe to the roots" of the Community.[230]

However, the immediate reaction from the European institutions, in particular the Commission, was to criticize the *Solange* decision, a fact that received plenty of attention in the West German press. The FAZ reported on the "dramatic tone"[231] of the letter of complaint written by the Commission and given to the Federal Government. It argued that the letter was paradoxical, since it was addressed to a government that actually shared the Commission's view on the case, but was nominally responsible externally for all the acts of the federal institutions – in this case the FCC. Die Welt, after only reporting cursorily on the *Solange* decision itself, published two articles on the Commission's angry reaction to the FCC. Covering extensively the arguments given by the Commission's chosen spokesman, Guido Brunner, one of the FRG's Commissioners, the report stated that the vast majority of legal academic opinion had accepted the autonomy of the Community legal system and this precluded any right of the FCC to judge the validity of Community legislation.[232] In a second article on the subject, the paper was much more critical of the Commission's position. Stating that it had taken the Commission more than six months to respond to the *Solange* decision in this manner, the die Welt article called into question the working effectiveness of the Commission as an institution.[233] Its

---

[228] "Aber man kann aus der Karlsruhe Entscheidung auch gerade einen Aufruf für eine Verbesserung der Rechtseinheit herauslesen. Denn die Richter nehmen eine Verfassungskontrolle nur so lang für sich in Anspruch, bis der Integrationsprozeß der Gemeinschaft so weit fortgeschritten ist, daß das Gemeinschaftsrecht selbst einen unseren Grundrechten vergleichbaren Katalog enthält," in "Kein Tiefschlag für Europa," *FAZ*, 16 September 1974.

[229] "An den deutschen Grundrechten soll Europa nicht genesen – aber sie könnten immerhin als Leitschur dienen," in "Kein Tiefschlag für Europa," *FAZ*, 16 September 1974.

[230] "Die Karlsruher Entscheidung hat, *Solange* sie nur als ein ferner Wink mit dem Grundgesetz verstanden werden kann, nicht die Axt an die Wurzel der Europäischen Gemeinschaft gelegt," in "Kein Tiefschlag für Europa," *FAZ*, 16 September 1974.

[231] "Die seit dem … Urteil des Bundesverfassungsgericht über die Beziehung zwischen Grundrechten und EWG-Recht in Gang gesetzte politische Diskussion hat durch ein Schreiben der Europäischen Kommission an die Bundesregierung eine neue, nahezu dramatische Note bekommen," in "Die Kommission kritisiert das Bundeverfassungsgericht," *FAZ*, 21 December 1974.

[232] "Brunner wies jetzt darauf hin, daß ebenso wie von den drei Richtern des Bundesverfassungsgerichtes auch im weit überwiegenden Teil der gegenwärtigen juristischen Literatur die Auffassung vertreten werde, daß europäisches Recht autonomes Recht sei," in "Brüssel pocht auf Vorrang für EG-Recht," *die Welt*, 23 December 1974.

[233] "Man wundert sich allerdings, daß die Brüsseler Kommission mehr als ein halbes Jahr für eine Antwort auf den Beschluß des Bundesverfassungsgericht gebraucht hat….Es wirft nicht gerade ein vorteilhaftes Licht auf die Effektivität dieses Gemeinschaftsorgans, wenn es in einer für die EG vitalen Frage zunächst einmal nahezu sieben Monate die Hände in den Schoß legt und so tut, als ob nichts geschehen sei," in "Späte Reaktion aus Brüssel," *die Welt*, 30 December 1974.

reaction was fuel for the widespread critique of the Brussels "technocracy."[234] Noting too the difficulty in which the Commission was placing the Federal Government, the article believed this was an attempt to close the lid on a "Pandora's box" of legal consequences emanating from the decision.[235] The report continued to state that, if other supreme courts followed the FCC's suit, then, similar to the FAZ's reasoning,[236] the *Solange* decision would indeed represent an axe blow to the core of the Community.[237] The die Welt article also demonstrated, however, that this could prove to be an overreaction to the situation, as it claimed, the *Solange* doctrine was intellectually limited, binding neither the First Senate of the FCC, which had denied the ability to rule on European law in 1967, nor truly taking into account the nature of the transference of sovereignty made initially in the 1950s through Article 24 (i) BL.[238]

Similarly recalling earlier debates on the issue of Article 24 (i) BL, the continually prointegration FAZ published a full page spread in November 1974 to remind its readers that national sovereignty was a thing of the past, and that European unity was in the interests of all Member States, especially the FRG.[239] An analogous article had appeared in die Welt a few months previously.[240] Despite the FAZ's concerns that this message might be lost in the arguments around the *Solange* decision, public opinion data from the period demonstrated that the West German public never lost its belief that Europe might be united, or that the Common Market benefited West Germany in particular. The first Eurobarometer polls demonstrate that the demise of the Common Market would have been regretted by citizens of the FRG most

[234] "Die Kritik an der Schwerfälligkeit des bürokratischen Beamtenapparates der Brüsseler 'Technokraten' erhält dadurch zwangsläufig neue Nährung," in "Späte Reaktion aus Brüssel," *die Welt*, 30 December 1974.
[235] "Wenn jetzt die EG-Kommission die Bundesregierung offiziell auffordert, gegenüber der Gemeinschaft eine politische Stellungnahme abzugeben, dann vor allem, um…sicherzustellen, daß diese Büchse der Pandora fest verschlossen bleibt," in "Späte Reaktion aus Brüssel," *die Welt*, 30 December 1974.
[236] See "Kein Tiefschlag für Europa," *FAZ*, 16 September 1974.
[237] "Die Kommission hat spat zwar, hoffentlich aber nicht zu spat erkannt, daß mit dem Urteil des Bundesverfassungsgerichts die Axt an die Fundamente der Gemeinschaft gelegt wird. Wenn diese Urteil des Zweiten Senats Schule macht und von den Gerichten anderer Mitgliedstaaten ähnliche Urteile gefällt werden, dann droht früher oder später das ganze System der als 'autonomes Recht' anerkannten Gemeinschaftsregelungen zusammenzubrechen," in "Späte Reaktion aus Brüssel," *die Welt*, 30 December 1974.
[238] "Das Urteil des Bundesverfassungsgerichts scheint überdies auf schwachen Füßen zu stehen. Abgesehen davon, daß Artikel 24 … nicht nur die Übertragung von Hoheitsrechten an zwischenstaatlichen Institutionen vorsieht, sind nach einem Urteil des Bundesverfassungsgericht Hoheitsakte der zwischenstaatlichen Einrichtungen von der Bundesrepublik auch anzuerkennen. Im übrigen hat der Erste Senat sich bei der Behandlung von Fragen der gleichen Substanz auch an deise Prinzipien gehalten," in "Späte Reaktion aus Brüssel," *die Welt*, 30 December 1974.
[239] "Aüch ein 'Starker Mann' kann Europa nicht retten," *FAZ*, 6 November 1974.
[240] "Die deutsche Wirtschaft braucht die Märkte der EG," *die Welt*, 7 March 1974.

(57 percent), compared with only 20 percent in the UK or 42 percent in France.[241] When asked if they would favor a politically "united Europe," 69 percent of West Germans responded favorably in 1970, 73 percent in 1972 and 72 percent in March 1974.[242] Moreover, in 1974 over half of the respondents (55 percent) agreed to a European supranational government having final say on issues of foreign policy, defense and economy, over and above the Federal Government (1970 = 56 percent, 1971 = 58 percent).[243] Furthermore, in 1971, FRG citizens were far more willing to accept leaders from other Member States to run this form of supranational government, with 68 percent willing to vote for a non-German leader, whereas at the time, only 43 percent of British voters (lowest) and 59 percent of Dutch (second highest after the FRG) would vote for a foreign candidate.[244] Even by 1975, after the *Solange* debates, Eurobarometer polls showed that West Germany (43 percent) came second only to Luxembourg (48 percent) in "very much" favoring a United Europe.[245] Clearly throughout this period in the 1970s, and throughout the entire period since the inception of the Federal Republic, West Germans regarded the idea of European unity in progressive, positive terms.

With only the Federal Government having the responsibility to respond officially to the Commission, and with widespread criticism in legal-academia and public debates, the FCC used the media to respond to the criticism. In April 1975, the president of the FCC, Ernst Benda, took part in a radio interview on the Deutsche Welle broadcasting station. He responded directly to the Commission's letter demanding clarity from the Federal Government, stating that the FCC was forced to react to the lack of basic rights protection in the Community legal system. He believed the *Solange* decision was meant progressively and should be viewed as an invitation to improve this discrepancy at the European level.[246] Benda stated that the press criticism of the FCC was unfair, as the Court had ruled on the legal issue at hand and was not attempting to be either pro- or contra-Europe.[247] In fact, he denied that the

[241] Eurobarometer Poll, 1, April–May 1974.
[242] "Europa ist die grosse Heimat," Allensbacher Berichte, 29, 1974.
[243] Only 22% of British voters (lowest) and 52% of Italian voters (second highest after the FRG) would view this favorably. "Europa ist die grosse Heimat," Allensbacher Berichte, 29, 1974.
[244] *Jahrbuch der Öffentlichen Meinung* 1968–73, Allensbach.
[245] Eurobarometer Poll, 3, June–July 1975.
[246] "Wenn ich die Entscheidung richtig verstehe, zugleich die Aufforderung an die politischen Kräfte zu sehen, den gegenwärtig vom Gericht als nicht voll berfriedigend erachteten Zsutand in einem Sinne zu verändern und zu verbessern, daß die vom Gericht geäußerten Bedenken für die Zukunft entfallen könnten," from "Zur Frage der Schaffung eines europäischen Grundrechtskatalog," interview with Ernst Benda, *Deutsche Welle*, 9 April 1975.
[247] "Das Gericht hat die verfassungsrechtlichen Fragen zu beurteilen gehabt und die Beurteilung der Verfassungsrechtsfragen kann in sich weder europafreundlich noch euro-feindlich sein.... Insofern glaube ich, daß man politische Bewertungen einer gerichtlichen Entscheidung doch nicht ohne Schwerigkeiten vornehmen kann," from "Zur Frage der Schaffung eines europäischen Grundrechtskatalog," interview with Ernst Benda, *Deutsche Welle*, 9 April 1975.

FCC had made a political decision in any sense, as the media accused. When asked by the interviewer how the FCC was able to reconcile what on the surface appeared to be an "anti-European" decision with Article 24 (i) BL and the preamble of the constitution, Benda argued that the question about the relationship of national constitutional and European law was still very much open in legal-academic circles, which indeed it was, and that it was the responsibility of the FCC to make a clear judgment on this difficult question.[248]

Benda finished the interview with several revealing statements. First, he once again reiterated his belief that the *Solange* decision was an attempt by the FCC to enter into discussion with the Community institutions about the creation of European basic rights.[249] It was not a judgment on the desirability per se of European legal integration for the FRG. Second, Benda made a subtle nod to the acceptance of the direct effect and primacy doctrines of the ECJ by stating that European unity could be achieved if the Community legal system was allowed to apply in all Member States to its fullest possible extent.[250] This basis, he argued, should form the core of future political discussions within the Community. This remarkable example of judicial-public discourse really provides a key insight into the final period of the reception in the public and media opinion. As the saliency of issues such as democratic participation and the protection of fundamental rights increased with the shift in political priorities around 1968, so too does the importance of constitutional practice in the media discussion. It became increasingly apparent that the legal system established in the Community had a number of deficiencies when compared to its national equivalent. As a result of these ever more overt comparisons, the national constitution gradually gained an elevated position within media commentary. It was held out as a model toward which the ECJ could strive. As such, Benda's remarks

---

[248] "Nach den Bestimmungen des Grundgesetzes, Artikel 24, ist die Übertragung von Hoheitsrechten zugunsten einer supranationalen Regelung … möglich. Wo die Grenzen einer solchen Möglichkeit liegen, ist in der Rechtsprechung und Wissenschaft in der Bundesrepublik Deutschland und auch in anderen Mitgliedsländern der Europäischen Gemeinschaft gegenwärtig noch lebhaft umstritten. Daß den freiheitlich-demokratische System des Grundgesetzes nicht völlig aufgegeben werden könnte … darüber sollte Klarheit bestehen," from "Zur Frage der Schaffung eines europäischen Grundrechtskatalog," interview with Ernst Benda, *Deutsche Welle*, 9 April 1975.

[249] "Ich glaube, daß die Entscheidung des Bundesverfassungsgerichts, die vielfach kritisiert worden ist, jedenfalls das Verdienst hat, auf ein gegenwärtig noch bestehendes Dilemma hingewiesen zu haben.… Dieses Dilemma kann nur beseitigt werden … durch die Schaffung möglichst einheitlicher übernationler Verfassungsnormen, die einer Grundrechtskatalog enthalten," from "Zur Frage der Schaffung eines europäischen Grundrechtskatalog," interview with Ernst Benda, *Deutsche Welle*, 9 April 1975.

[250] "Es ist richtig, daß auf der einen Seite eine wirkliche europäische Einigung nicht zustandkommen kann, wenn jades der Mitgliedsländer für sich in Anspruch nimmt, eine eigene Rechtsordnung zu haben, und das europäische Recht nur insoweit gelten zu lassen, als es mit seiner eigenen Rechtsordnung übereinstimmt," from "Zur Frage der Schaffung eines europäischen Grundrechtskatalog," interview with Ernst Benda, *Deutsche Welle*, 9 April 1975.

about the FCC acting as an instigator in a discussion to create European basic rights then also reflects the wider public view that the Community could learn from the West German constitutional experience.

SUMMARY

The nature of the West German public's response to the constitutionalization of the European legal order can be characterized into three distinct periods:

In the period 1949 to 1963, public opinion toward European integration was at first idealistic, and then disillusioned following several political disappointments and a perceived unfairness of European institutions toward West German interests. The predominant question posed in this period was that of the nature of legal sovereignty itself. Most, if not all commentators, rejected the idea of a legally sovereign West German state in favor of a European constitutional order. Many commentators at first welcomed the idea of a European legal order as adding an extra level of protection to the new democratic and constitutional order in the FRG, as well as being a turning point in intra-European relations, after which disputes were now legal cases, not potential sparks of violent conflict. More often than not, support was based on political grounds, with a strong legal order not only visualized as tying West Germany closer to its Western allies, but joining it as an equal with all the other states in the eyes of the law. However, as the disillusionment with French dithering over the EDC, the failure of the EPC and the perception of unfair treatment of West German companies within the ECSC increased, so did the lack of interest in European integration. This is typified by the muted response to the Treaties of Rome in all the major dailies, as well as sparing coverage of the key ECJ decisions in 1963 and 1964.

The phase 1963–9 was characterized by a coming to terms with the implications of the ECJ's jurisprudence. At first, the public uninterest meant that coverage of the decisions was scarce, particularly as political events (British accession attempts and the Elysees Treaty) monopolized the coverage of European events. As a result, it was left to many specialized economic publications to begin the discussion on the new legal order emerging from Luxembourg. Predominant among these was the coverage of the Handelsblatt, whose initial lauding of the ECJ was soon overtaken by its concerns that the ECJ had made two important mistakes: It had gone so far as to polarize the French against integration, but not actually done enough to consolidate the European legal system. It is in this second observation that the most far reaching West German critique of the ECJ lay. By the mid-1960s, many commentators were drawing on the West German constitution to highlight weaknesses in the European order, particularly on questions of the division of powers and the protection of the basic rights. The juxtaposition of the two constitutional systems was provided with more substance by the coverage on the important RTC's referral to the FCC of the question of the constitutionality of Community Law. While many newspapers were critical of the ECJ's failure to take into account the special nature of the Basic Law, this criticism was abated by the perceived threat to the integration process as a whole posed by De Gaulle during this period. As a result of this and the perceived issue-dodging in the FCC's 1967 decision, interest in the issue again dissipated.

The final period between 1970 and 1974 can be characterized by a much fiercer polarization of opinion on the question of the applicability of European law. There are two main reasons for this. First, as Inglehart points out, a generational shift in value occurs at the beginning of the 1970s, which sees issues of basic rights and qualitative democracy come to the forefront. Kennedy reaffirms this shift in values, specifically in notions of the law.[251] Whereas in the mid-1960s, the perceived threat to the whole European project posed by De Gaulle was enough to mute the critique about the European legal system, by the 1970s the issue of fundamental rights protection would not go away. Moreover, these generalized concerns where given real substantive quality through the coverage of the *Internationale Handelsgesellschaft* case, which ultimately, through rereferral, resulted in the FCC's *Solange* decision. The case provoked many newspapers to set up open and direct comparisons between the national and supranational systems, with invariably the effectiveness of the national constitution in securing and guaranteeing individual freedoms coming out on top. Not only does this challenge Noelle-Neumann's idea that dissatisfaction with the Community did not exist prior to 1974,[252] but also goes a long way in undermining the perception of a "permissive consensus," with its disinterested and uninformed public opinion toward the processes of European integration.

However, there remains the issue of public opinion polls, which do indeed add support to the permissive consensus theory. Despite this criticism in the media, West German poll support for European integration remained consistently high throughout this entire period, and even after the *Solange* decision, West German public opinion was second only to Luxembourg's in favoring a more United Europe.[253] Even when the utilitarian cost-benefit analysis of membership seemed to decline during the 1950s, with the perceived unfairness of the ECSC toward West German industry, generalized support for the Community remained high. Similarly, when the perceived deficiency in democratic and fundamental rights protection at the end the 1960s became more perceptible, there is again no discernible decrease in polled support for the Community, and in fact there is an increase in the face of de

[251] Duncan Kennedy, "Two Globalizations of Law & Legal Thought: 1850–1968," *Suffolk University Law Review* 36.3 (2003).
[252] See Noelle-Neumann, "Phantom Europe: Thirty Years of Survey Research on German Attitudes toward European Integration," p 62.
[253] See *Jahrbuch der Öffentlichen Meinung* 1968–73, Allensbach.

Gaulle's policies. We can only surmise two things from this. Opinion poll analysis is a blunt instrument that cannot do justice to the nuance and complexity of political and legal debates. Second, and specifically to the West German case, the broad and general desire for integration continually outweighed the perceived frailties of the system itself. When de Gaulle threatened integration as a whole, support increased, despite greater awareness that the system itself was far from perfect. It is only after the generational shift at the start of the 1970s, which Inglehart and Slater both predict increases the importance of "postmaterialist" concerns that the weaknesses of the European legal system truly make front-page news. In substantive terms, this is reflected in the increasing relevance of the issue of basic rights in the media discussion and the close coverage of the FCC's deliberations on the *Solange* case, as well as the president of the FCC's perceived need to explain the decision in radio and newspaper interviews. Perhaps by the start of the 1970s, Europe seemed sufficiently consolidated to be openly criticized. More likely was the growing impatience with its failings and a growing self-confidence in the qualities of the national order.

The growth of the basic rights issue does not merely point to the separate models of Inglehart, Kennedy or Knoch of a postmaterialist shift occurring in the late 1960s holding true, but it also highlights the fact that the permissive consensus of the 1950s was well and truly dead. No longer was public opinion toward European integration uninformed, uninterested and inert. On concrete issues, such as the protection of basic legal provisions, the media and public were over time ever more vociferousness in their criticism of insufficient European standards. Increasingly, the inadequacy of the supranational level was compared with the seeming superiority of the national constitutional order. The confrontation with the external system of European law promoted a discussion, and endorsement, of the domestic system, increasing support for the national institutions and a sense of pride in the own constitution.

This is an important supposition because the West German constitutional order was almost as new as that of the European Communities themselves and support for the idea that such a level of self-identification with the national institutions existed at such an early stage is difficult to find. Nevertheless, the evidence is clear: The West German media were increasingly overt in their comparison between national and supranational levels and not ashamed to admit that the national level was superior to the European. As such, many newspapers saw the FCC's *Solange* decision not as nationalist retrenchment or legal parochialism, but as a welcome wake-up call for the ECJ to respond to the issue of basic rights in its later jurisprudence. The various perspectives offered by the newspapers indicate the need for future research as to whether the regional and party-political affiliations of the newspapers played a role in shaping their opinions toward the constitutional practice: Are border region newspapers more open to the idea of a supranational legal system? Do newspapers found in towns and cities that depend on intra-European trade favor the ECJ and its rulings? How do changes in government and party European policy affect the opinions of closely affiliated newspapers?

Finally, an important last consideration to be made concerns the perceived nature and role of European law among the West German public. According to Weiler's theory, the constitutionalization of the Community legal order was accepted by national governments as a substitute for the stagnated political situation resulting from De Gaulle's European policy. Whereas Weiler makes no comment on the nature of the public acceptance of the constitutional practice, it is clear from this discussion that the ECJ was seen by the West German media as a champion of European integration in opposition to De Gaulle. Much of this advocacy was put in indirect terms – for instance the Volkswirt's commendation of the ECJ's *Van Gend* decision on economic grounds[254] – but the contextualization of Law and Politics, of the ECJ and De Gaulle was also made explicit – for instance, the Bild-Zeitung's satirical cartoon[255] or the Hamburg Echo's acerbic crowing at the ECJ's actions against French wishes. This is powerful evidence in favor of Weiler's model, at least in the realm of public opinion. In fact, the West German critique of the ECJ stemmed predominately from the ECJ constitutionalizing a legal system in which political guarantees of the separation of powers and the qualitative nature of democracy were not yet in place. As such, demands were being made by the public of the government and national administration to bring about reforms that matched the level of integration already achieved in the legal arena. Clearly now, the debates outlined in this and the previous chapter raise the question about how the constitutional practice was being received in political and bureaucratic circles.

---

[254] See "Kluft zwischen Justiz und Politik," *der Volkswirt*, 15 May 1963.
[255] See *Bild Zeitung*, 9 July 1965.

4

Competition and Authorities

The West German Government's Response to the Constitutionalization of European Law, 1949–1979

So far, this book has demonstrated that the reception of the constitutional practice in academic opinion and in the public sphere was highly polarized and contentious. Yet, the question remains of why the West German government, as opposed to the judicial branch, did so little to articulate this in terms of attempting to rein in or influence the ECJ. The disconnect between expert and public opinion and government policy is one of the most intriguing aspects of the constitutional practice, and will be dealt with in this chapter. It will first deal with current explanations of why the government stayed so inactive in this period, discussing both the possible options as well as limitations for official resistance. It will then describe the peculiarities of the West German ministerial constellation, which, as will be shown, is essential for understanding why so little was done against the ECJ despite concerns in broader society. Predominantly the cause for this is the fact that the supranationalist elite, so vocal and yet ultimately ineffective in the academic and public debates, "locked" the FRG into a default prointegration position from a very early point. This was possibly caused by the long tenure of Konrad Adenauer at the start of the FRG's history, the competitive nature of guarding authorities among West German ministries, the sidelining of those officials who had the most concerns about the ECJ actions, and a parliament that was both generally prointegration and was ignorant of the legal consequences of the ECJ and FCC's decisions.[1]

Even from a more abstract level, European integration in general and most particularly the developments in the legal arena should have caused some consternation among West German officials. The classical theorist of (German) bureaucracy, Max Weber, depicted a model of bureaucratic behavior in the modern state, in which a

---

[1] For an excellent account of the Bundestag's broad and rather docile prointegration stance in this period, see Deniz Alkan, "Der Duldsame Souverän: Zur Haltung des Deutschen Bundestags Gegenüber der Rechtlichen Integration Europas durch die Rechtsprechungdes Europäischen Gerichtshofs 1963–1978," Heinrich-Heine-Universität 2011.

system of rational-legal, monopolized power is concentrated in the hands of administrative figures, who are both unwilling to relinquish their authorities and who are in fact continually seeking to expand them.[2] As such, European integration in the postwar period, in which governments chose to voluntarily surrender competency and control of the national economy, seemed to challenge the Weberian model of behavior. Yet, national governments and their administrations played a decisive role in negotiating how and which authorities were to be supranationally ordered, providing for a large element of control and influence still being exercised by national bureaucracies. However, the establishment of a constitutional practice of European law led by the ECJ fundamentally undermined this model, making far-reaching inroads into national legal sovereignty that were not included in the founding treaties nor then agreed upon by national administrations. Yet despite all these factors, there seems to be remarkably little strong, direct action taken against the ECJ by national bureaucracies. The aim of this chapter is to discuss why, in particular, the West Germany government was either unwilling or unable, even in the face of hostile public and academic opinion, to respond to the ECJ in this period.

The debate as to why national administrations chose not to respond to the establishment of a constitutional practice of European law has raged for over four decades. These deliberations have resulted in four main schools of thought under the rubric of ITL that have been outlined already in the introduction and will be recounted here only in brief. These are the legalist, realist, neofunctionalist, and contextualist approaches. We will illustrate especially where each of these schools of thought has a particular relevance for explaining the behavior of national bureaucracies.

The first of these, the legalist perspective, focuses on the special, independent nature of legal discourse and of legal institutions,[3] implying that bureaucracies failed to act because they did not fully understand either the consequences or the terminology of the ECJ's decisions. Moreover, if they had done so, they were not in a position to act overtly against the judiciary because of the traditional separation of powers. This is even more relevant in the West German case because of the nominal adherence to the separation of powers principle in the postwar constitutional order. This chapter will demonstrate that the importance placed on not being seen to interfere

---

[2] Max Weber, *Schriften zur Sozialgeschichte und Politik* (Stuttgart: Reclam, 1997), pp 271–339.

[3] Positions in this field range from the perspective offered by Pescatore, "Aspects of the Court of Justice of the European Communities of Interest from the Point of View of International Law," which focuses on the powerful codified institutional position of the ECJ; that of Stein, "Toward Supremacy of Treaty – Constitution by Judicial Fiat: On the Margin of the Costa Case," which focuses on the role played by litigants; or that of Joxerramon Bengoetxea, Neil MacCormick and Leonor Moral Soriano, "Integration and Integrity in the Legal Reasoning of the European Court of Justice," in Gráinne de Búrca and J. H. H. Weiler (eds.), *European Court of Justice* (Oxford and New York: Oxford University Press, 2001), which explains the ECJ's decisions as an attempt to maintain the coherence of the European legal system.

with the boundaries of separated power did indeed play an important role in the government's reluctance to act, yet in the fallout of the *Solange* decision, discussed in Chapter 5, West German ministry officials were less reluctant in trying to intervene with FCC judges to have them to change their decision. The legalist perspective is equally undermined in the West German case by the widespread diffusion of legally trained personnel that is typical of the West German administrative systems. This implied a better than average understanding, if not of the ECJ's decisions, then at least of legal terminology in general among West German bureaucrats.[4] Indeed, as has been discussed previously, many members of the government were also heavily involved in contemporaneous legal academic debates on the constitutional practice of European law. In many cases, such as those of Karl Carstens or Carl-Friedrich Ophüls, they published key articles in that debate at the same time as being leading government officials. The interrelation of bureaucratic and judicial personnel in West Germany was extremely high, a tradition in Germany dating back to the early nineteenth century. For instance, judges on the FCC during the 1950s and 1960s were, above all, drawn from the ranks of government, rather than academia or the legal profession. Between 1951 and 1962, ten FCC Judges had been high ranking officials (*Ministerialräte, Sonstige Beamte*) immediately before appointment, compared to six drawn from academia, six from Land and Federal Parliaments, and five from other Federal Courts. Only one practicing lawyer was called to the Court in this period.

Second, the realist perspective, based on the perceived national interest of the Member States in pursuing integration, would argue that the West German government's reluctance to act against the court reflects an understanding that in allowing the ECJ room to fill contractual lacuna in the Treaties, the national bureaucracies were also acting in their own interest.[5] By not having to scramble and negotiate every single detail with all the other Member States, requiring extensive use of resources – financial and personnel – national bureaucrats could leave the supranational institutions to fill in the blanks in generally beneficial packages deals. There are, however, a number of questions regarding this approach, predominantly about through whom and how the perceived interest of the national administration was formed. Weber predicted that bureaucracies are inherently opposed to losing their powers.[6] Further

---

4   See Johannes Feest, "Die Bundesrichter: Herkunft, Karriere und Auswahl der Juristischen Elite," *Beitrage zur Analyse der Deutschen Oberschicht*, ed. Manfred Zapf, 2nd ed. (Munich: R Piper & Co Verlag, 1965), p 101.

5   See, for instance, Andrew Moravcsik, *The Choice for Europe: Social Purpose and the State Power from Messina to Maastricht* (London: UCL Press, 1998), pp 67–72, or Geoffrey Garrett, Daniel R Keleman and Heiner Schulz, "The European Court of Justice, National Governments and Legal Integration in the European Union," *International Organisation* 52.1 (1998).

6   Weber, *Schriften zur Sozialgeschichte und Politik*, p 273.

questions lie in the role played by national bureaucrats working in the European environment, or whether the contentious high political context of the 1960s made for a willing submission of authorities, particularly in the legal field. Moreover, the suggestion of a single definable national perspective that was to be fulfilled by the supranational authorities is highly questionable. The following narrative will show that not only was opinion on the ECJ divided between the ministries – in this case between the prointegration Foreign and Economics ministries and the much more reluctant Justice Ministry, but even within the former too. In essence, the "West German" position on the ECJ was merely the opinion of a thin level of supranationalist elites with direct access to the means of policy making. This gives credence to Garrett's "political power" approach,[7] which indicates that governments must have supported ECJ activism, but it also represents a massive oversimplification of the debates occurring within the government, the judiciary and broader society.

Third, the neofunctionalist approach focuses specifically on the circumvention of nation state authority by nonstate actors at the sub- and supranational levels, namely in the case of legal integration, the ECJ, judges, lawyers, and litigants using the preliminary ruling mechanism enshrined in Article 267.[8] Neofunctionalists argue that the autonomy of legal reasoning and the circumvention of national administration would leave the West German government unaware of or unable to respond to maneuverings of the nonstate groups. Yet, it is again undeniable that many in the West German administration were legally trained and therefore potentially capable of following the judicial developments of the 1960s and 1970s. This book has already demonstrated, both in the media and academic discussion, that there was a large amount of resistance and hostility to the ECJ and this was massively fueled by references by lower national courts reluctant to sacrifice the integrity of the Basic Law to the European ideal. Of course, as demonstrated in Chapter 2, many of the commentators in the academic discourse were also themselves members of the administration, notably Justice Minister Ewald Bucher and Foreign Ministry State Secretary Karl Carstens. It is simply impossible to believe that the national government was unaware of the main judicial events, even if the question as to why they were unable or unwilling to act remains open.

---

[7] Garrett, Keleman and Schulz, "European Court of Justice, National Governments and Legal Integration in the European Union."

[8] For the role of lawyers, see Eric Stein, "Lawyers, Judges and the Making of a Transnational Constitution," *American Journal of International Law* 75.1 (1981). The archetype neofunctionalist account can be found in Walter Mattli and Anne-Marie Slaughter, "Law and Politics in the European Union: A Reply to Garrett," *International Organisation* 49.1 (1995); Walter Mattli and Anne-Marie Slaughter, "The Role of National Courts in the Process of European Integration: Accounting for Judicial Preferences and Constraints," *The European Courts and the National Courts – Doctrine and Jurisprudence: Legal Change in Its Social Context*, ed. Anne-Marie Slaughter, Alex Stone-Sweet and JHH Weiler (Oxford: Hart Publishing, 1998).

Finally, the contextualist school examines the sociopolitical environment in which the establishment of a constitutional practice of European law occurred. Notably, Joseph Weiler's work argues that national governments allowed an unchecked ECJ to expand its remit as fundamentally as it did as a response to the concomitant Gaullism emanating from France.[9] As a result, the West German government should be seen as weighing the options of opposing the ECJ against the threat this posed to the integration project as a whole and using this calculation to decide not to intervene against the court. There is clear evidence for this, as the narrative will show, but at the same time, this is equally just a minor consideration, usually given as an after-thought on policy documents and certainly not a coherent and definitive policy of the ministries. Karen Alter alternatively understands the constitutional practice as a "negotiated compromise" between national and supranational court systems.[10] As such, she argues that the ECJ was careful in its decision making not to cause a reactionary response from national bureaucracies to the expansion of its powers. There are a number of factors that helped build the immunity of the ECJ from such a national reaction, namely the differing "time horizons" of political actors, their response to short term stimuli ("fire alarms"), the greater expertise in (European) legal reasoning within the ECJ, and the "credibility gap" created by bureaucrats seen to be meddling in judicial affairs.[11] As a result of these factors, national administrations were unable to work against the ECJ in any substantial way, except for the occasional submission of dissenting opinions in ECJ hearings, particularly when the case in hand involved Member State nationals or companies. The only option realistically available to national governments was the so-called nuclear option of Treaty revision to rein in the court. However, as Scharpf's classic work on the intricacies of the Joint Decision trap has demonstrated, this option was considered to be an extreme and unlikely course of action.[12]

In summary, the theories that focus on factors "external" to the West German government itself cite a number of recurring themes to explain why the national administration, against expectations, failed to act against the ECJ. These are (a) the autonomy and specialization of legal terminology and reasoning, (b) the inability to act caused by (i) the role played by nonstate actors, (ii) the lack of viable courses of action, (iii) differing time priorities of politicians and justices,

[9] JHH Weiler, *The Constitution of Europe – "Do the New Clothes Have an Emperor?" and Other Essays on European Integration* (Cambridge: Cambridge University Press, 1999).

[10] Karen Alter, *Establishing the Supremacy of European Law: The Making of an International Rule of Law in Europe*, Oxford Studies in European Law (Oxford; New York: Oxford University Press, 2001).

[11] See Alter, *Establishing the Supremacy of European Law*.

[12] Fritz W Scharpf, "The Joint Decision Trap: Lessons from German Federalism and European Integration," *Public Administration* 66.3 (1988).

(c) the perceived desirability of independence between judicial and bureaucratic politics, and (d) the favorable political context for allowing rapid legal integration to continue.

What all of the ITL theories share is a focus on factors "external" to the West German government. They concentrate on themes that do not deal with the idiosyncrasies unique to the FRG's policy-making system to explain why the national administration, against expectations, failed to act against the ECJ. These are:

1. The autonomy and specialization of legal terminology and reasoning,
2. The inability to act cause by:
   a. the role played by nonstate actors
   b. the lack of viable courses of resistant action
   c. differing time priorities of politicians and justices
3. The perceived desirability of independence between judicial and bureaucratic politics
4. The favorable political context for allowing rapid legal integration to continue.

However, we already have indications that none of these factors truly explain why the FRG government remained so passive. It stretches credibility to believe that first, national bureaucrats were unaware of the implications of the ECJ's actions or second, that the role played by nonstate actors was sufficient to entirely circumvent the national administration. Both the preponderance of jurists in the government and the fact that so many of the supranationalists were also the highest members of the administration are evidence enough to undermine these views. Clearly there is something missing in these analyses. We have already seen that a critical national reception of the ECJ and the constitutional practice occurred at all levels of the national judiciary and also in the intellectual and public spheres. Why did the government choose not to articulate this? The answer to this conundrum must lie in the factors specific and internal to the West German administration that conditioned its response to the ECJ.

Two of the most far-reaching and important analyses of the West German ministerial constellation are those offered by Peter Katzenstein[13] and those by Simon Bulmer and William Patterson.[14] Katzenstein describes the Federal Republic as a "tamed power" because of its particular historical and societal context, where power is decentralized among many bodies and institutions and change in policy

[13] Peter J Katzenstein, *Policy and Politics in West Germany: The Growth of a Semi-Sovereign State* (Philadelphia: Temple University Press, 1987).
[14] Simon Bulmer and Paterson William, *The Federal Republic of Germany and the European Community* (London: Allen and Unwin, 1987).

formation is achieved only slowly, incrementally and in a cooperative manner. The "semi sovereign" state has four structural characteristics.

- First, power is dispersed geographically, with the constitutionally defined authorities of the Länder and Bundesrat acting as counterbalances to the power of the center.
- Second, the FCC has an extremely powerful legal and moral position within the government framework, acting both as a legal guardian for the constitution and also as a final arbiter on many contentious political issues, such as abortion, banning of political parties and membership of the European Economic and Monetary Union.
- Third, the formal power of the chancellor is very limited, appointing ministers and having competence to guide general policy (*Richtlinienkompetenz*). The appointed ministers are in turn very powerful within their own remit, particularly in those specialist areas where the Chancellor has little or no expertise.
- Finally, and most importantly, Katzenstein describes a system of very strong ministerial independence, with highly formalized structures within administrations, and a clear separation of powers and authorities between individual ministries (*Ressortsprinzip*). He argues that the *Ressortsprinzip* limits the influence of the highest political authorities, particularly the Chancellor, because information, expertise and administrative functions are guarded fiercely by each of the ministries. As a result, for policy formation to occur there needs to be a good deal of cooperation and accord between governmental and societal groups, or nodes, as Katzenstein calls them. The result of this is slow, incremental action and a political system that is extremely stable, inclusive and consensus based, but plagued by inertia when faced with making quick responses to short term issues.

Katzenstein also argues that West Germany's membership in the Community was an external facet of its semisovereignty, limiting both its scope for an independent or aggressive diplomatic and economic foreign policy. Applying Katzenstein's model to the constitutional practice, the lack of an administrative response in the West German case can be explained by the following factors: (i) a bureaucratic segregation of information, (ii) too much inertia in policy formation to respond to the Court in such a short time,[15] and (iii) a willingness to accept the rulings of the ECJ born out of a tradition of high regard for the court system, a particularly strong stance on

---

[15] The president of the ECJ decides how long the period should be for submitting observations on the Court's decisions, which is when the national government might submit a dissenting opinion – this cannot be shorter than 15 days, but is rarely longer than 60 days.

the separation of powers born out of the German historical experience, and a belief in consensual decision making.

A second model for bureaucratic behavior is proposed by Simon Bulmer and William Paterson. While this model is similar to that of Katzenstein's, there are a number of factors that result in a particularly contrasting set of conclusions about the formation of European policy in the administrative system. Bulmer and Paterson describe a system characterized by three factors: "sectorization," "incrementalism," and "consensualism." Sectorization refers to the Ressortsprinzip and the strict ministerial independence, which results in a specialized sectoralized concentration of information and expertise within the individual administrative departments. Incrementalism refers to the tendency among the ministries to offer particularly technical, inward oriented suggestions for policy change, which often results in slow but stable government action. Consensualism refers not to the form of decision making in relation to the separate bodies within the government, but more to the cross party agreement and perceived permissive consensus among the public that European integration was a very positive goal for the Federal Republic to follow.

The major difference from Katzenstein's model lies in the role played by the Chancellor. For Katzenstein, the Chancellor is a more or less mute figure, "a political hostage" caught between a multitude of powerful bodies and sharing formalized power with a whole host of other institutions. Bulmer and Paterson alternatively describe a "troubleshooting" chancellor, whose powers are in fact increased by the decentralization and sectorization of the policy mechanism. Not only does the Chancellor have the political clout to shape general policy toward Europe, but the Chancellor's Office can act as central collection point for the information coming from the ministries, and with its nontechnical staff, can see beyond incremental changes and can keep in sight medium and longer-term agendas for European policy. As a result, the Chancellor becomes the key figure in European policy, particularly, Bulmer and Patterson argue, when they have a strong personal commitment to the European project, as was the case, for instance, with the first Chancellor, Adenauer. Applying Bulmer and Paterson's model to the constitutional practice, we see a slow changing, stable, and positive administrative response determined predominantly by the attitude toward Europe of the Chancellor at the time.

From the survey of literature examining why Member State bureaucracies generally, and also the West German administration specifically, were so inactive toward the ECJ's jurisprudence, it is possible to illustrate three common explanatory factors, which provide a thematic framework of reference for understanding the period:

1. The role of political leadership, specifically that of the Chancellor and of party preferences toward integration

2. The question of "ministerial competency," predominantly which department was to hold the responsibility for European policy in general and more specifically, who was to follow and respond to developments in the Community legal system.

3. The coherence of "legal reasoning" as a specialist, technical terminology, and the separation of powers doctrine prompting bureaucracies to be extremely wary of meddling in judicial affairs.

This chapter is ordered chronologically, structured around changes in government that also coincide with some of the major developments in the national court-ECJ dialogue.

The first section (1949–63) discusses Adenauer's government attitude toward European law, with equal focus on the opposition of the SPD and FDP to European integration and to what extent both sides' support of or resistance to integration was determined by legal concerns. It will also look at the reception of the early European legal system in the West German government, notably raising the issue of which ministry was to hold the competency for European legal matters and how these disputes affected the government's response to the *Van Gend* decision.

The second section (1963–9) discusses how the Erhard government was combined with that of the Grand Coalition. This period represents a major phase in the ECJ-national court dialogue, from the *Costa* decision through to the FCC's de facto acceptance of the ECJ decisions. It also combines two competing foreign policy preferences of the Atlanticist leaning Erhard government with that of the Grand Coalition, whose dominant figure was the Foreign Minister Brandt, who favored a closer engagement with Eastern Europe. It also incorporates the far-reaching social changes in West German society during the 1960s that forced issues of qualitative democracy and basic rights protection to the forefront of political and civil debate.

The third section (1969–74), examines the implications of the first SPD-FPD government, under Brandt, in regard to the European legal system; it closely analyzes the national administration's reactions to the series of important European and national legal cases taking place in the early 1970s, resulting in the FCC's *Solange* decision. The predominance of the basic rights question and the continued disputes between ministries about the competency to assess European law will prove crucial to understanding this period.

FOUNDATIONS, 1949–1963: LOCKING IN EUROPEAN INTEGRATION

West German politics in general during the first decade of the new Republic were unquestionably dominated by the personality of Konrad Adenauer. His stubborn, semiauthoritarian leadership style coupled with his high moral standing for his resistance to the Nazi regime have been analyzed in countless studies,[16] and these factors, combined with his role of chancellor and foreign minister,[17] meant that Adenauer could make an indelible mark on the Federal Republic's European policy.

In his autobiography, Adenauer asserted that he aimed to tie West Germany to its western neighbors in a staged process of "small steps," thus to "reawaken confidence in the Germans,"[18] protect Europe's "Christian and humanistic ideology" from the threat of Communism,[19] bolster the social cohesion within West Germany itself,[20] and to overcome the "centuries of … war, destruction and bloodlettings" created by European conflicts.[21] In particular, he saw a close relationship with France as key to these ambitions and it is in Adenauer's concept of Franco-German relations within a unifying Europe that his attitudes toward the development of a European legal order can be found. Adenauer saw in the unification of Germany during the late nineteenth century a historical precedent for the path of European integration. He analogized the hundreds of small German states of that period with the nation states of Europe and described how, through common institutions – "a customs union and customs parliament"[22] – these states were molded into a single political entity. This would take time and, of course, the continual "small steps" as well. However, the ultimate ideal of a united, peaceful, and prosperous Europe, free, naturally from Adenauer's Christian Democrat perspective,[23] of the threat of Communism was worth waiting through a transitory period of executive driven, technocratic European governance. Structural congruence between the institutions of the national democracy and the Community could wait until Europe's future was secure. Certainly it was helpful too, looked at more cynically, that Adenauer and his CDU cohort led

---

[16] See, among many others, Kurt Sontheimer, *Die Adenauer-Ära* (Munich: Deutscher Taschenbuch Verlag, 2003); Wilfried Loth, "Konrad Adenauer und die Europäische Einigung," *Die Bundesrepublik Deutschland und die Europäische Einigung 1949–2000: Politische Akteure, Gesellschaftliche Kräfte un Internationale Erfahrungen: Festschrift für Wolf D Gruner zum 60. Geburtstag*, ed. Marieke Konig and Matthias Schulz (Stuttgart: Franz Steiner Verlag, 2004); and the numerous biographies of Hans Peter Schwarz. Also Adenauer's own memoirs of the period in Konrad Adenauer, *Memoirs 1945–1963* (London: Weidenfeld and Nicolson, 1966).

[17] Adenauer served this double role from 1951 until 1955, when he was succeeded by Heinrich von Brentano

[18] Adenauer, *Memoirs 1945–1963*, p 79.

[19] Adenauer, *Memoirs 1945–1963*, p 79.

[20] Adenauer, *Memoirs 1945–1963*, p 184.

[21] Adenauer, *Memoirs 1945–1963*, p 190.

[22] Adenauer, *Memoirs 1945–1963*, pp 246–7.

[23] For the most important account of the visions and role of Christian Democracy in postwar European integration, see the seminal work by Wolfram Kaiser, *Christian Democracy and the Origins of European Union*, New Studies in European History (Cambridge; New York: Cambridge University Press, 2007). or Kaiser, "Institutionelle Ordnung und Strategische Interessen: Die Christdemokraten und 'Europa' nach 1945."

the executive at this time and even worked to sideline the oversight of the legislative branch in this formative period.[24] These goals were reflected, in fact, in his policies and pronouncements as Chancellor. Adenauer had no doubt that this was also the way for Europe to be reshaped and also that the economic integration proposed in the Treaties of Paris and Rome were nothing less than the first stages in a politically united Europe.[25] A united Europe, political or economic, was however foremost a legal entity, formed on a "basis of law and liberty" and guaranteeing "equal rights for all."[26] However, despite being a trained lawyer, Adenauer's opinions on the nascent European legal system never went beyond a generalized support based on the principle of equal treatment for all Member States, a key goal for West Germany. Nevertheless, those working with and around Adenauer in the administration could be in no doubt of the Chancellor's equally pragmatic and idealist support for any form of integration that brought West Germany equal footing with its neighbors. A strong and influential legal order based on judicial equality was perceived to bring this about. In terms of the thematic approach outlined above, "Political Leadership" in this period can be defined as favorably, if unspecifically, toward greater legal integration and the constitutional practice.

Despite Adenauer's strong leadership enabling him to bring about his chosen orientation for the Federal Republic's European policy, his goals were not without vocal critics both across the political spectrum and within his own party. The Social Democratic Party (SPD) was stridently opposed to Adenauer's *Westintegration* policy in the early 1950s, seeing it as precluding the more desirable unification with the eastern half of Germany.[27] However, SPD opposition was not entirely based on

[24] See again the work by Alkan, "Der Duldsame Souverän," on the "deparliamentization" of German European policy in this period.

[25] "Die EWG ist in der Hauptsache ein politischer Vertrag, der bezweckt, auf dem Wege über die Gemeinschaft der Wirtschaft zu einer politischen Integration Europas zu kommen," speech from Adenauer, Bonn, 9 September 1959, in *Die Protokolle des CDU-Bundesvorstands 1957–61*, p 440.

[26] Adenauer, *Memoirs 1945–1963*, pp 190–1.

[27] For SPD opposition to European integration during the 1950s see Willy Albrecht, "Europakonzeptionen der Spd in der Gründungszeit der Bundesrepublik," *Personen, Soziale Bewegungen, Parteie: Beiträge zur Neuesten Geschichte: Festschrift für Hartmut Soell*, ed. Oliver Von Mengersen, Matthias Frese, Klaus Kempter, Heide-Marie Lauter and Schober Volker (Heidelburg: Manutius Verlag, 2004); Jürgen Bellers, *Ewg und die "Gobesberger" Spd* (Siegen: Universität Siegen, 2003); Detlef Rogosch, "Sozialdemokratie Zwischen Nationaler Orientierung und Westintegration 1945–1957," *Die Bundesrepublik Deutschland und die Europäische Einigung 1949–2000: Politische Akteure, Gesellschaftliche Kräfte und Internationale Erfahrungen: Festschrift Für Wolf D Gruner zum 60. Geburtstag*, ed. Marieke Konig and Matthias Schulz (Stuttgart: Franz Steiner Verlag, 2004); Wolfgang Müller, *Die Europapolitischen Vorstellungen Von Kurt Schumacher 1945–1952: Eine Alternative für Deutschland und Europa?* (Stuttgart: Ibidem Verlag, 2003); Frederic Hartweg, "Kurt Schumacher, die Spd und die Protestantisch Orientierte Opposition gegen Adenauers Deutschland- und Europapolitik," *Kurt Schumacher als Deutscher und Europaischer Sozialist*, ed. Friedrich-Ebert-Stiftung (Bonn: Friedrich-Ebert-Stiftung, 1988); Friedrich Heine, *Dr. Kurt Schumacher: Ein Demokratischer Sozialist Europaischer Pragung* (Gottingen: Musterschmidt Verlag, 1969).

these political considerations; and, indeed, some leading SPD figures at the time also raised an opposition to the form of legal integration that the Community was pursuing.

As early as 1951, the West German SPD provided material for its Swiss counterpart's journal, "die Rote Revue," to explain its criticism of the proposed European Coal and Steel Community, in which the proposed court system was deemed too weak to be effective in the face of conflicting national interest.[28] In the same year, the head of the SPD, Kurt Schumacher, made a similar claim at an SPD conference in Gelsenkirchen, stating that the party's opposition to integration was as much about the weak democratic and judicial control of the High Authority as it was about reunification.[29] This view was again reiterated in a pamphlet published by the SPD entitled "What Do You Know about the Schuman Plan?" in which the court system was criticized for not having sufficient influence over the executive; and its credentials as a neutral, supranational institution were called into question because of the appointment procedure was organized by national governments.[30] The main trade union, the Deutsche Gewerkschafts Bund (DGB), closely linked to the SPD, also commented on the purely technical-judicial role played by the court, both in the ECSC and the Community, despite the need for more control of the Commission/High Authority and of the Member States in both organizations.[31]

The SPD's opposition to European integration made the task of ratifying the Treaties of Rome in the parliamentary arena potentially difficult for the Adenauer government and therefore required a great deal of hard work explaining the impact the Treaties would have. One such example occurred in June 1951 at the Bundesrat where Walter Hallstein[32] and Carl-Friedrich Ophüls[33] sought to convince the House that legal integration resulting from the ECSC would only benefit the Federal Republic.[34] However, the question concerning the nature of the transference of national authorities to supranational organs through Article 24 BL, as in the concomitant academic debate, was quickly raised. Ophüls argued that transference of national sovereignty was increasingly commonplace and that this posed very little

[28] Article: "Die deutsche Sozialdemokratie und der Schumanplan," in AdsD, Bestand Kurt Schumacher 255 Schuman Plan: Materialen.

[29] AdsD, Bestand Erich Ollenhauer, 443 Europapolitik: Europafragen, Gemeinsamer Markt und Euratom 1951–60.

[30] Pamphlet: "Was weißt du vom Schumanplan?" in KAS, 1–237–018/2.

[31] "Die Konsequenzen, die sich für die Gewerkschaften aus dem Abschluss der neuen Verträge über die Europäische Wirtschaftsgemeinschaft und Euratom ergeben," in AdsD, DGB-Archiv, DGB-Bundesvorstand Abteilung Vorsitzender 5/DGAI001941.

[32] Hallstein was at this time state secretary in the Foreign Ministry

[33] Ophüls was at this time part of the German delegation to the negotiations and employed by the Justice Ministry

[34] Session report, Sondersitzung des Deutschen Bundesrates in Bonn am 15. Juni 1951, in KAS 1–237–018/2.

threat to the Basic Law, as the supranational authority had the right to guide policy but not tell the Federal Republic how exactly to fulfill its obligations – this remained the prerogative of the national government and the government was bound by the national constitution. Moreover, the role of the Court was to ensure a nondiscriminatory community, in which every state and even every company was treated equally, and one where executive power was kept in check through the courts. As such, Ophüls stated openly, the ECJ was not designed just as an administrative court, but also as a constitutional court too.

However, it is important to note that the possible litigants in front of the ECJ listed by Ophüls at this point were companies and national governments – not individual citizens as became increasingly the case after the introduction of direct effect. That Ophüls had not seen this possibility is made even clearer by the protocols of a "Judicial Committee" based in the Foreign Ministry examining the ECSC Treaty. Ophüls, along with several important figures of the academic world – Mosler, Schlochauer, Roemer, Jaenicke – and government officials, including Walter Hallstein, reached the same conclusions about who was allowed access to the court over several meetings through the summer of 1950, complaining the court was not as powerful as the West German delegation had hoped for.[35]

Despite the lack of clarity about the exact workings of the new legal system, the Adenauer government managed after a long, heated parliamentary debate to pass the ratification of the ECSC against the opposition of the SPD and liberal Free Democratic Party (FDP). While the SPD's opposition to European integration had altered radically by the time of the Treaties of Rome, thanks mainly to a change in leadership, but also to the influence of Jean Monnet through the Action Committee for the United States of Europe,[36] there were still heated discussions between factions in the Parliamentary Committee examining the Treaties of Rome, both in the Bundestag and Bundesrat principally concerning the European legal order. The Committee in the Bundesrat was above all else focused on the transference by the federal level of authorities that actually belonged to the Länder, and this dominated the bulk of the discussion. This would become a topic of particular contention in later periods, resulting even in a constitutional amendment to safeguard Länder authorities.[37] However, concerns were also raised about the possibility of

---

[35] BA, B146–277, Juristischer Sachverständigenausschuss für den Schumanplan. Schriftstück 10: "Bemerkungen zu dem deutschem Memorandum," 14 August 1950.

[36] The leading SPD figures at the time, Willy Brandt, Herbert Wehner, and Fritz Erler, all regularly attended Action Committee meetings: See, for instance, AdsD, DGB-Archiv, DGB-Bundesvorstand Abteilung Vorsitzender 5/DGAI002366. Bark and Gress agree with this perspective in Dennis L Bark and David R Gress, *West Germany: From Shadow to Substance 1945–1963* (London: Blackwell Publishing, 1989), p 385.

[37] See the amendments to Article 23 Basic Law.

infringements of the basic rights at the supranational level, although predominantly through the Euratom Treaty, which were after subsequent investigation deemed unnoteworthy.[38]

Matters were more contentious in the Bundestag. In May 1957, the FDP parliamentarian, Ewald Bucher, published an article concerning the constitutional problems around the transference of national authorities to a supranational organization without sufficient constitutional provisions guaranteeing basic rights and the separation of powers. The article had already prompted a heated discussion in academic circles, and was now raised in the Bundestag's committee by both the SPD and FDP to attack the ToR. Defending the government's position, Carl Friedrich Ophüls and Karl Carstens argued that all foreign treaties were subject to the conditions of the national constitution and that the Federal Constitutional Court (FCC) had previously made this statement itself in its case law. When asked what would happen were the supranational authority to issue a decision contrary to the Basic Law, Carstens argued strongly that the Basic Law was the final and supreme source of authority for all German government agencies and that conflicting norms would simply be unenforceable.[39] Despite this, the issue did not disappear and was raised again later in the month. The SPD parliamentarian, Ludwig Metzger, challenged Carstens to explain why the government had accepted transferring authorities to an organization with such a weak understanding of the separation of powers at the supranational level. When Carstens argued that the ECSC had a comparably stronger executive power than that proposed in the Treaties of Rome, Metzger retorted that the government was lucky that the ECSC ratification was not given to the FCC for proofing against the Basic Law.[40] Carstens simply responded that making the European level identical to the national would be impossible in the face of six different national systems, and the idea was simply to create something workable at the beginning, whether this corresponded with national standards or not.

It is particularly important to note at this juncture that the Bundestag became increasingly sidelined by the government when dealing with Europe. Recent research has shown that this was a deliberate policy on behalf of the government and resulted in a clear and strong "de-parliamentalization" of West Germany's European policy making.[41] Indeed, little if any substantial debate took place in plenary sessions

---

[38] Meeting on 24 April 1957 in BA, B102–10876 Bundeswirtschaftsministerium: Ratizierung des EWG-Vertrags: Sonderausschuss Gemeinsamer Markt/Euratom des Bundesrats.

[39] Third Meeting on 21 May 1957 of Sonderausschuss "Gemeinsamer Markt-Euratom" des Bundestages, in PAA B020–200–14.

[40] "Dort sind die verfassungsrechtlichen Bedenken auch erhoben worden. Sie hatten Glück, daß es nicht an das Bundesverfassungsgericht gekommen ist," Eleventh Meeting on 29 May 1957 of Sonderausschuss "Gemeinsamer Markt-Euratom" des Bundestages, in PAA B020–200–14.

[41] Alkan, "Der Duldsame Souverän."

of either parliamentary house about the constitutional practice and it was not until the Brandt government of the early 1970s that regular reporting on European affairs to the Bundestag became the norm. It is however doubtful that the FCC's insistence in *Solange* on parliamentary involvement in drawing up a fundamental rights charter referred specifically to the *national* parliament. Rather, it seems the FCC was more interested in strengthening the European Parliament, at least if we consider the outcomes accepted by the FCC during the fallout to the *Solange* decision. These will be described in Chapter 5.

However, the argument regarding the necessary amount of "structural congruence"[42] between the national and European constitutional orders was far from settled at this point. The principle of congruence emerged from the writings of the academic Hans-Jürgen Schlochauer the previous year[43] and provoked discussion not just among legal specialists, but also within the administration too. As early as 1953, discussions between the Federal Justice Ministry and the Foreign Ministry, again represented by Ophüls, raised the issue of too many authorities being transferred to the supranational level than had been foreseen by the writers of the Basic Law.[44] In fact, the Justice Ministry official, Roemer, stated his fear that too zealous a use of Article 24 BL would simply create an *Überstaat* (superstate) that would subsume the Member States, a prospect guaranteed to wake opposition to the project, not least within the Bundestag.[45] The terminology here is remarkably similar to that used by British eurosceptics two or three decades later. On behalf of the Justice Ministry, Roemer was again involved in similar discussions concerning the negotiations on the Treaties of Rome and acted as an advisor on an interministerial committee advising the West German delegation of judicial matters. Here again, concerns were raised by the Justice Ministry about the nature of competency transfer through Article 24 BL, which resulted in advice being given to the delegation that the democratic controls of the supranational executive be

---

[42] Hans Jürgen Schlochauer, "Rechtsformen der Europäischen Ordnung," *Archiv des Völkerrechts* 5 (1955); Hans Jürgen Schlochauer, "Zur Frage der Rechtsnatur der Europäischen Gemeinschaft für Kohle und Stahle," *Rechtsfragen der Internationalem Organisation, Festschrift für Hans Wehberg zum Seinem 70. Geburtstag*, ed. Walter Schätzel and Hans-Jürgen Schlochauer (Frankfurt am Main: Vittorio Klostermann, 1956), p 367.

[43] Schlochauer, "Zur Frage der Rechtsnatur," p 367.

[44] Memo, btr. Besprechung mit Herrn Min Dir Roemer vom Bundesjustizministerium über Fragen der Verfassungsmäßigkeit des Entwurfs der Satzung einer Europäischen Gemeinschaft, PAA B10–893.

[45] "Einem Überstaat würde die Tendenz innewohnen, schrittweise zur totalen Überlagerung der Staaten führen. Es sei zu erwarten, nicht zuletzt wegen der mit der Opposition bereits geführten Diskussion über die Auslegung von Artikel 24 GG, daß die Europäische Gemeinschaft im Bundestag auf Widerspruch stoßen würde," in Memo, btr. Besprechung mit Herrn Min Dir Roemer vom Bundesjustizministerium über Fragen der Verfassungsmäßigkeit des Entwurfs der Satzung einer Europäischen Gemeinschaft, PAA B10–89.

strengthened, particularly if the executive were given the right to issue directly effective legislation.[46]

The question about the applicability of directly effective supranational legislation was difficult for the Justice Ministry to answer and it frequently wrote to the Foreign Ministry for clarification on treaty points during the year preceding its establishment in law.[47] Indeed, the Justice Ministry continued to be concerned by the transfer question throughout the period and sought to reassure itself about the integrity of the national constitution by asserting that the Basic Law could be protected in the face of conflicting supranational or international law in successive meetings with other ministries, either through legal reform of calling on Article 79 (iii) BL.[48] For instance, in discussions with the Foreign Ministry in April 1957, a Justice Ministry delegation reached agreement with the Foreign Ministry representative that the Basic Law guaranteed the Republic's legislator the right to issue national law over-riding conflicting international law, albeit through the alternative Article 25 BL. However, despite the Justice Ministry's attempts to keep a grip on the development of the European legal system, its influence was waning because of a series of arguments between the federal ministries concerning which department actually held the responsibility for monitoring and guiding West German European policy. As a result of these disputes, the Justice Ministry was increasingly sidelined in matters relating to the Community and its legal order.

The causes of these disputes lay within the governing elite itself. As stated earlier, Adenauer faced battles with the opposition parties in implementing his policy of western integration. But even within his own party, in fact among his closest advisers, there were major differences about the form that European integration should take. These disputes proved to have a major, if indirect, impact on the nature of the administrative reaction to the ECJ throughout the entire period. The fundamental division within the CDU itself lay between the conceptions of Adenauer and his economics minister, Ludwig Erhard. Erhard and a grouping within the Federal Economics Ministry advocated a much looser alignment of the Western European states in favor of a larger Atlantic-based free trade network, which opposed Adenauer's attempts to reassure France by tying West Germany institutionally to a tighter knit European community.[49]

---

[46] Entwurf eines Vetrages über den Gemeinsamen Marktes: hier: Institutionelle Fragen, 3. Dez. 1956 in PAA B80 255 EWG 1955–58.

[47] See B141–11050 Bundesjustizministerium: Verhandlungen über die Europäische Integration: Gemeinsamer Markt November 1956–January 1957 and B141–11051 Bundesjustizministerium: Verhandlungen über die Europäische Integration: Gemeinsamer Markt January 1957–May 1957.

[48] See, for instance, memos regarding the Brussels Conference from October to November 1956 in BA B141–11049.

[49] See Hans-Peter Schwarz, *Adenauer: Der Staatsman: 1952–1967* (Stuttgart: Deutsche Verlags-Anstalt, 1991); and Bernhard Löffler, *Soziale Markwirtschaft und Administrative Praxis, das*

Using his influence both as chancellor and foreign minister, Adenauer was able to put forward his own conception of European policy, but it was undeniable even to him that the economic nature of integration provided the Economics Ministry with a great deal of influence over how policy was formed. As a result, Erhard began to push ever harder for the Economics Ministry to take over responsibility for integration from the Foreign Ministry. This prompted a flurry of secret memos from Carstens on behalf of the Foreign Ministry and Erhard for the Economics Ministry with the result that in October 1957, Adenauer formally gave control for matters of economic integration to the Economics Ministry.[50] By late 1958 however, through a round of negotiations, the Economics Ministry and Foreign Ministry had reached agreement that the Foreign Ministry would also be involved in the coordination of policy, at least on issues concerning foreign policy and political coordination. Due to the competition between the two biggest, most influential ministries, there was increasingly little room for compromises to be made for the smaller ministries, particularly those of Justice and Interior – the so-called *Verfassungsressorts* – who were responsible for monitoring judicial and legal affairs.

This was particularly evident when deciding on the personnel for the Permanent Representation in Brussels. In a meeting at the Foreign Ministry in July 1958, the Justice Ministry and the Federal Interior Ministry both insisted on sending one representative each to Brussels, arguing that the huge legal importance of the Community required a number of constitutional and legal specialists to be on hand. The Interior Ministry had argued strongly, like the Justice Ministry, throughout the negotiations on the Treaties of Rome that a much closer structural congruence, particularly in terms of the separation of powers, was needed between the European and national levels, particularly in terms of strengthening the European Parliament.[51] The Chairman of the meeting, Herbert Müller-Roschach, standing in for Carstens at the time, immediately questioned the relevance of sending personnel from the Interior Ministry and Justice Ministry, despite the written interventions of the justice minister himself and the state secretary of the interior ministry, stating that the current head of the Representation had more than a sufficient understanding of the European legal system – this was, of course, Carl Friedrich Ophüls.[52]

Bundeswirtschaftsministerium unter Ludwig Erhard (Stuttgart: Franz Steiner Verlag, 2002), esp. pp 43off.

[50] See BA N1266 1462 Nachlaß Walter Hallstein: Institutionelle Fragen: Ressorts Zuständigkeiten and BA B146–598 Ministerbüro Schumanplan.

[51] See Memo, Referat I A 4 (von Meibom) 29 October 1956, betr. Euratom, hier: Gemeinsame Unternehmen, bezugL Franz. Entwurf vom 24 October 1956 in BA B141–11046 Bundes-justizministeriumL Verhandlungen über die Europäische Integration: Gemeinsamer Markt October 1956–November 1956.

[52] Protokoll der Ressortsbesprechung im Auswärtigen Amt am 28. Juli 1958 betr. Die Errichtung einer ständigen Vertretung der Bundesrepublik bei den Europäischen Gemeinschaften, in PAA B020–200–123 Vertretung der BRD der der EWG.

However, when asked about the situation in Brussels, Ophüls admitted in a letter in August 1958 that he was simply unable to cope with the legal work being given to him and recommended strongly that both *Verfassungsressorts* be allowed to send trained personnel as soon as possible.[53] Despite this, Adenauer intervened personally in the debate, denying both the Interior Ministry and Justice Ministry the chance to send personnel to the Representation, sighting "overstaffing" as the reason.[54] The result of the discussions was that the Foreign Ministry promised the two *Verfassungsressorts* that its chosen representative would be a fully trained jurist and that he would keep the two ministries informed of all legal developments. When questioned by the Interior Ministry two months later as to the chosen personnel, the Foreign Ministry failed to provide any kind of response. By the time a Working Group for Affairs of the European Community was established in a cabinet meeting of 1962, both the Justice Ministry and Interior Ministry had been completely sidelined from the European policy formation mechanism, with only the State Secretaries of the Foreign Ministry, Economics Ministry, Agricultural, Transport and Social Ministries being invited to participate.[55]

The importance of the ECJ as an institution had not been underestimated by the Federal Republic in the Brussels negotiations, demonstrated by the heated dispute with Italy about securing the second Advocate General's position for a German lawyer during 1958,[56] and the initial assessments of the Court's case law were positive – deemed to be restricted, exact and independent.[57] ECJ-administration relations were improved still further by a visit of the ECJ to West Germany in late 1959.[58] However, with the fight for ministerial competency going on in the background, the ECJ was being faced with an increasing number of court cases, many involving West German companies.[59] In the media discussion, the perceived unfairness of the ECJ toward these companies raised an increasing public hostility toward the court, and this trend is mirrored by opinion in the West German government. Members of the legal section of the Foreign Ministry felt compelled to write to the state secretary to warn him that by continually losing its cases, the Federal Republic was considered to be acting imprudently among judicial circles

---

[53] Fernschreiben von Ophüls, 6 August 1959, in PAA B020–200–123 Vertretung der BRD der EWG.
[54] Letter from Chancellor's Office to Foreign Ministry, 6 August 1958, in PAA B020–200–123 Vertretung der BRD der EWG.
[55] See BA B141 61069 Bundesjustizministerium: Institutionelle Entwicklung der Europäischen Gemeinschaft July 1959–June 1965.
[56] See PAA B020–200–IA2–1 Die Europäische politische Integration.
[57] File note betr. Urteile des Gerichtshofs der EGKS vom 21. Dezember 1954, in PAA B80–129.
[58] Besuch des Gerichthofs der Europäischen Gemeinschaften in der Bundesrepublik vom 26–29 Oktober 1959, in PAA B20–200–420.
[59] The high-profile cases involving Mannesmann in the early 1960s are discussed in Chapter 3. See, as an example, Case 19/61 *Mannesmann AG v High Authority of the European Coal and Steel Community* [1962] European Court Report 357.

and suggested that the government take more care about what cases it fights and who it chooses to represent it.[60]

Strikingly, then, from this point on, the relevant legal personnel in the Economics Ministry and Foreign Ministry responsible for recording cases at the ECJ were more interested in whether a case was won or lost than looking at the implications that the case had for the national constitutional order. Clearly the perception of national prestige was taking attention away from the much more fundamental process of constitutionalization. Evidence for this is provided by the recording of the *Ruhrkohlengesellschaften* and *Storck* cases.[61] Whereas high profile cases involving substantive financial losses for West German firms gathered large folders of documentation in the ministry archives, these two cases, both of which had crucial importance for the constitutional practice,[62] were filed without commentary in long lists of other, less important court cases.[63]

However, the *Van Gend* decision did start a number of alarm bells ringing throughout the ministries. The case however was first commented on by a specialist in the European law section of the Economics Ministry, Ulrich Everling,[64] who raised concerns at the ECJ's proposed direction in its advice to the Dutch court system and asked his equivalent in the Foreign Ministry, Justice Ministry, Finance and Agricultural Ministries whether the Federal Government should make an official statement on the case. Everling suggested making clear to the ECJ that the West German government rejected the principle of direct effect and regarded only itself as a state, and not its citizens, as able to bring cases before the ECJ European legal norms.[65] The response from the other ministries did not reflect the urgency of Everling's concern. The Legal Section of the Foreign Ministry's laconic response stated that it agreed with Everling's rejection of direct effect but did not know if making a statement would be worthwhile.[66] The Ministries of Finance and Agriculture

---

[60] Letter from Von Haeften to State Secretary, 18 July 1961 in PAA B20–200–500 Gerichtshof: Streitfälle.

[61] See Chapters 2 and 3 for academic and public reaction: Case 1/58 *Stork vs. High Authority* [1959] European Court Report 17, Case 36–38 and 40/59 *Ruhrkohlenverkaufsgesellschaften vs. High Authority* [1960] European Court Report 423.

[62] Case 1/58 *Stork vs. High Authority* [1959] European Court Report 17 and Case 36–38 and 40/59 *Ruhrkohlenverkaufsgesellschaften vs. High Authority* [1960] European Court Report 18.

[63] See PAA B20–200–181 Rechtsachen 9/57 11/57 12/57 27–29/57 31–34/57 1/58 and PAA B20–200–422 Gerichtshof (Urteile von 30/59 bis 42/59).

[64] Ulrich Everling was a recurring and central figure in the bureaucratic response to the ECJ, holding key roles in the legal departments of the Economics Ministry from 1953 until 1980, when he became a judge at the ECJ itself.

[65] Express notice from Everling, 21 September 1962, in PAA B20–200–712 Gerichtshof der Europäischen Gemeinschaften: Rechtssache 26/62.

[66] Letter from Referat 500, 23 September 1962, in PAA B20–200–712 Gerichtshof der Europäischen Gemeinschaften: Rechtssache 26/62.

also agreed with the Foreign Ministry, with the former stating that it could not see any difficulties arising from the decision and therefore a statement would not be necessary.[67] Two weeks after Everling's initial memo, the Justice Ministry finally responded, agreeing with the rejection of direct effect, but stated that for clarity's sake, it would be a good idea to issue the ECJ a government statement so that the court would feel obliged to explain its reasoning more fully.[68] The Foreign Ministry finally agreed the next day with the Justice Ministry's suggestion and Everling began work constructing the government position.

Everling circulated the draft of his response to the other ministries on 17 October 1962, in which he rejected the special nature of European law, regarding its effect as not different from that of standard international law, mirroring concomitant debates in academic circles. He argued that citizens retained the rights of their own national constitutions, guaranteed through the actions of their elected public authority, and while the Rome Treaty bound these public authorities, it was not qualitatively different from other international agreements and therefore did not have direct effect for Member State's citizens. Moreover, Everling argued, it was not the responsibility or within the competence of the ECJ to decide on the applicability of norms for citizens, and citizens did not have the right to use supranational norms to challenge national laws. Only the Member States themselves and the Commission had the right to access the court.[69] Everling's suggestion met widespread approval among the other ministries, with the Foreign Ministry adding to the draft the question as to what happens in cases of collisions of conflicting supranational and national rights.[70] With this amendment, a final statement was completed and submitted officially to the ECJ on 7 November 1962.

Over the following months, the ECJ continued its deliberations and announced its decision in February 1963, ignoring and ruling against the West German position. Two months after this, the legal section of the Foreign Ministry wrote a summary to the state secretary, the ardently prointegration Karl Carstens, explaining the rejection of direct effect adopted in the government statement and the fact that the ECJ had entirely ignored this opinion.[71] Carstens' response to this was furious. He described the submission as riddled with errors, and the overall opinion given

---

[67] Express notice, 27 September 1962, in PAA B20–200–712 Gerichtshof der Europäischen Gemeinschaften: Rechtssache 26/62.

[68] Express notice, 5 October 1962, in PAA B20–200–712 Gerichtshof der Europäischen Gemeinschaften: Rechtssache 26/62.

[69] Express notice und Anlage, 17 October 1962, in PAA B20–200–712 Gerichtshof der Europäischen Gemeinschaften: Rechtssache 26/62.

[70] Express notice, 22 October 1962, in PAA B20–200–712 Gerichtshof der Europäischen Gemeinschaften: Rechtssache 26/62.

[71] File note, 5 April 1963, in PAA B20–200–712 Gerichtshof der Europäischen Gemeinschaften: Rechtssache 26/62.

as far from watertight, since the implications of direct effect was still "highly controversial" among academic circles, which was indeed the case at this time. Indeed, Carstens pointed out that he himself agreed with the principle of direct effect and regarded the actions of the legal section, and all those involved in the submission, as "politically extremely unseemly."[72] He demanded that this opinion be made clear in writing to the Economics Ministry and that from that point forward, that he be involved in any submissions to the ECJ. This scolding clearly made an impression. When Everling suggested another submission to the ECJ in further legal cases that year, the Foreign Ministry's Legal Section clearly stated that any submission was to go through Carstens, and no longer exclusively through the Economics Ministry.[73]

The debate around the submission of an opinion to the ECJ in the *Van Gend* case is astonishing. In effect, the West German government submitted an opinion based on the thoughts of relatively minor administrative figures who held a completely different position on the case at hand than both their bureaucratic and political seniors. That this could occur is due to the segregation and tight guarding of responsibility for monitoring European events between ministries without the specialist expertise in legal-constitutional affairs (Foreign Ministry and Economics Ministry), and the complete sidelining from European policy of the ministries with that specialist knowledge – the Justice Ministry and Interior Ministry. However, the Justice Ministry was involved in the submission of opinion to the Court, yet its involvement seem strangely remote, with limited involvement in the drafting and replies to questions and suggestions taking several weeks to arrive. Clearly Everling and the Legal Section in the Foreign Ministry took the initiative to respond, excluding both other ministries and also the personnel around and above them.

The response of the specific ministries to the behavior from their legal specialists is also noteworthy. In the case of the Economics Ministry, no action was taken against Everling and he continued to actively follow and pursue the development of the European legal order unabated, perhaps reflecting the lack of interest among his seniors in the Economics Ministry to matters of European law. On the other hand, the Legal Section at the Foreign Ministry was severely chided by their state secretary, a figure with legal training and a keen interest in European law. This reflected the established differences between the Economics Ministry and the Foreign Ministry regarding their ambitions for European integration, with the former's focus falling entirely on economic issues and the latter being more interested in moving toward a politically (and legally) united Europe.

---

[72] "Ich halte es auch politisch für höchst untunlich, derartige Erklärungen gegenüber den europäischen Gemeinschaftsorganen abzugeben," Memo, 10 April 1963, in PAA B20–200–712 Gerichtshof der Europäischen Gemeinschaften: Rechtssache 26/62.
[73] Letter, 18 September 1963, in PAA B20–200–871 Rechtssache.

The period from 1949 to 1963 can be characterized in many ways. In terms of political leadership, Adenauer's tenure brought a clearly prointegration government, even when faced with opposition to his favored tight-knit, closed community approach from within the parliamentary chamber and the closest circles of his own party. With his close control of the Foreign Ministry, Adenauer was able to install similar minded thinkers in key positions, particularly Hallstein and Carstens, both of whom had a close interest in the development of the European legal system. The fact that such a response could be produced was caused by the particularly unclear demarcation of ministerial competency, which as both internal theories predict, would lead to indecisive and unstable decision making in the West German system, where the Ressortsprinzip is so important. Without a clear determination of the responsibility to respond to the developments in European law, the response was piecemeal and contradictory, with members of the same ministry arguing over the nature and quality of the government response provided.

The response to *Van Gend* also points to three other important conclusions. First, opinion toward the European legal system among the administration was divided, just as it was in the academic and public arenas. It was difficult to reach agreement not just between ministries, but indeed even within certain ministries. Second, the reaction of Carstens in the Foreign Ministry contrasted greatly with the nonreaction of his equivalents in the Economics Ministry – clearly Everling had much more room for maneuver in determining the Economics Ministry's reaction to the ECJ, demonstrating either an underestimation of the growing importance of European law or a distinct lack of interest in legal-constitutional affairs, or a broad, if unspecific agreement with the developments. Third, by the end of the period, it was clear that the two departments, which had a huge interest in such matters – the *Verfassungsressorts* – the Justice and Interior Ministries – were completely sidelined from European policy making. With these factors in the background, the West German government was faced in the next period with several major court decisions regarding European law from both the ECJ and national courts, which are arguably even more fundamental to the constitutional practice than *Van Gend*, namely the primacy Doctrine and the Rhineland Tax Court's (RTC) reference to the FCC on the constitutionality of the Rome Treaty.

GENERATIONAL SHIFTS, 1963–1969: DISINTEREST AND SOCIAL CHANGE

This period is best characterized by rapid and far reaching change in the political, legal and social spheres. In politics, the Federal Republic experienced its first change in leadership as Ludwig Erhard moved from the Economics Ministry to replace Adenauer as Chancellor. As seen already, Erhard's views toward European integration differed greatly from Adenauer's, with Erhard taking a much stronger pro-Atlantic line than his predecessor. At the end of 1966, there followed a change in government to include the SPD for the first time in a Grand Coalition with the CDU under the CDU Chancellor Kurt Georg Kiesinger. Kiesinger's deputy and foreign minister, Willy Brandt, held a particularly high profile among younger voters, whose unrest at the conservative nature of West German democracy up until this point was finding ever greater expression throughout the decade.

Accompanying the changes in the party constellation was a much more far-reaching change in civil society. As discussed in Chapter 3, a generational shift occurred around the mid- to late 1960s, which resonated deeply in the political sphere, most visible in West Germany in the turbulence and protests of 1968. This change raised the salience of issues of qualitative democracy to the forefront, raising public awareness of issues such as the separation of powers, democratic participation and of course fundamental rights, all of which had been concerns in academia and the government in regard to European law for many years. The shift in ideas was accompanied by a governing coalition with a potentially sufficient majority to bring about constitutional change. In particular, the Emergency Acts legislation of 1968, which limited some of the basic constitutional rights under certain conditions, provided a further context in which the questioning of the applicability of European legal norms in the national sphere could blossom.[74] This was reflected in the fact that the question of the protection of the basic rights became a key preoccupation for the administration by the end of the period. This was also, however, prompted by a number of developments in the legal sphere, namely the *Costa* and RTC cases, which dominated the affairs of the legal sections in the Economics Ministry and Foreign Ministry throughout the mid-1960s.

The most important development in European law in this period was undoubtedly the dialogue between the Italian Constitutional Court and the ECJ in the *Costa* case. The Italian Constitutional Court reached its decision on the case in February 1964, the text of which arrived at Ulrich Everling's desk in the Economics Ministry on 20 March 1964 and the Legal Section of the Foreign Ministry three days later.[75] The text from the *Costa* decisions was inexplicably routed through the ministerial office (*Ministerbüro*) of the Foreign Ministry before arriving at the Legal Section. Why this should happen was queried, without reply, by the *Ministerbüro*. Why this particular case was circulated at the highest political office against normal

[74] For a survey on the debates around the Emergency Acts (Notstandsgesetze), see Michael Schneider, *Demokratie in Gefahr? Der Konflikt um die Notstandsgesetze Sozialdemokratie, Gewerkschaften und Intellektueller Protest 1958–1968* (Bonn: Neue Gesellschaft, 1986); and Nick Thomas, *Protest Movements in 1960s West Germany: A Social History of Dissent and Democracy* (Oxford; New York: Berg, 2003).

[75] See PAA B20–200–874 Rechtssache.

practice remains a mystery to the author. While this prompted no immediate reaction from either department, by the early summer, the question of primacy began to increase in importance as first the Italian court's decision to deny primacy was questioned by a Dutch MEP in May 1964,[76] and second by a high profile speech supporting primacy by Hallstein at the European Parliament in June.[77] On 8 July 1964, a week before the ECJ published its *Costa* decision, the Foreign Ministry Legal Section crafted its position on the primacy question. In the position it recommended that West Germany keep a "reserved" position in any discussions of the questions, because it believed it unlikely that either the FCC would accept such a legal doctrine or that the Bundestag would accept such a limitation of its power through the use of Article 24 BL. It concluded that the transference of authorities should be limited to those explicitly named in the Treaties of Rome and any judicial expansion of these was problematic.[78]

In the following week, the Legal Section sent its opinion secretly, under request, to the Interior Ministry, which promptly disagreed with the Foreign Ministry. The Interior Ministry argued that it was irrelevant if the Bundestag should attempt to legislate against existing European law because in a legal dispute, the fact that the Bundestag was attempting to legislate in an area of competence already transferred to the Community would undermine the legality of its attempt. As such, any national or European justice would rule against the subsequent national law.[79] Moreover, it argued, it was impossible to imagine that two competing laws could stand together, as this would imply that the supranational system had a legal will entirely "independent" and "original" from the Member States, and since this was based on a transference of competency from the Member States, it could hardly be original or independent.[80] In effect, the Interior Ministry accepted that primacy was an inevitable consequence of the transference under Article 24 BL.

As a result of this fundamental disagreement, a meeting was arranged between the members of the Foreign Ministry and the Interior Ministry to discuss this issue. The meeting, which took place on the 12th August, was extremely revealing about the attitude of the Foreign Ministry to developments in the European legal system. First, the Interior Ministry's representative, von Meibom, had to make it clear that

---

[76] See Written Question by Van der Goes van Naters, in BA B106–39770 Bundesinnenministerium: EWG Rechtsystematik: Urteil des Italienischen Verfassungsgericht von 24 February 1964 (Schriftliche Anfrage des Herrn van der Goes van Naters).

[77] See KAS-IX-001–033/1 Korrespondenz: Ausgänge (CD Fraktion im EP) 1965.

[78] Memo 8 July 1964, in PAA B80–620.

[79] Memo, 10 August 1964, in BA B106–39770 Bundesinnenministerium: EWG Rechtsystematik: Urteil des Italienischen Verfassungsgericht von 24 February 1964 (Schriftliche Anfrage des Herrn van der Goes van Naters).

[80] Memo, 8 August 1964, in Bundesinnenministerium: EWG Rechtsystematik: Urteil des Italienischen Verfassungsgericht von 24 February 1964 (Schriftliche Anfrage des Herrn van der Goes van Naters).

the rejection of primacy would fundamentally undermine the functioning of the Community, which in turn would seriously damage the West German economy. The Legal Section of the Foreign Ministry was forced to admit that it had never seen the question from this viewpoint before, being more interested in the political considerations involved in the possible accession of the UK, which primacy made more problematic. Second, von Meibom complained that the Foreign Ministry had clearly misunderstood the Interior Ministry's position on Article 24 BL, stating that the transference of authorities was not irreversible and that the Bundestag still held the competency to legislate in all areas where the Community had not been clearly delegated. This left von Meibom with the impression that while the meeting had been open and in good humor, the "Legal Section of the Foreign Ministry had only very barely dealt with the [legal] problems in the Community."[81]

Evidently from the meeting between the Interior Ministry and Foreign Ministry, it was the political events of European integration, particularly De Gaulle and the British accession that held the attention of the key decision makers at the Foreign Ministry. Moreover, from the files of the level of ministerial office and state secretary – the leading coordinators of Foreign Ministry policy – it is clear that European law was not a topic of discussion, being left entirely to the Legal Section to deal with.[82] There was simply no record of matters of European law being discussed on a regular basis. Indeed, even after Carsten's decision that opinions to the ECJ should pass through state secretary level prior to submission, his correspondence on matters of European law with the Legal Section for the rest of his tenure was limited to asking the Legal Section to proofread an essay he had written in 1963 on European law.[83] Perhaps this was seen to be the most adroit way to convince the Legal Section of their political master's views. This is strong evidence to suggest that Weiler's approach to the constitutional practice – that legal integration was allowed to happen unabated as a response to the continued political problems dealing with De Gaulle – can not hold true in the West German case. The link between politics and law in the sense proposed by Weiler is simply not evident, even if certain personnel, such as Carstens were equally aware of the concomitant legal and political developments.

More evident is that the complex legal terminology involved in the ECJ-national court dialogue was simply too difficult for many figures in the administration to follow. The misunderstandings between the Foreign Ministry and the Interior Ministry – excluded from European policy formation by the competition for

---

[81]   Memo, 12 August 1964 in Bundesinnenministerium: EWG Rechtsystematik: Urteil des Italienischen Verfassungsgericht von 24 February 1964 (Schriftliche Anfrage des Herrn van der Goes van Naters).

[82]   See files under PAA B21.

[83]   PAA B20–200–1168 Reden, Interviews, Vorträge, Stellungnahmen, Presse.

competency – demonstrate that those figures in the *Verfassungsressorts* were more ideally suited to follow the developments. Indeed, there is further evidence from actions of the Economics Ministry, where Everling, commenting in 1965 that he would focus his attention only on those cases with "vital importance," fails to provide a submission to the ECJ regarding *Costa*, but does so for subsequent cases of more material or economic importance involving West German firms.[84] Clearly, as with the Foreign Ministry, the main focus when monitoring the European legal system falls on the ministerial specialism – political or economic – and not the constitutional element, which the marginalized *Verfassungsressorts* undoubtedly could have brought. That law was seen as a means of achieving progress during the Empty Chair Crisis was beyond question: The Justice Ministry undertook a study to find which legal mechanisms could be used against the French for nonparticipation, resulting in the choice of Article 175 Community, which referred to negligence of duties by Member States.[85] However, this option was never taken.

The sidelining of the *Verfassungsressorts* continued into the late 1960s as the competition between the ministries for European competence was far from over. It was in fact the concerns raised in the Justice Ministry and Interior Ministry by the ECJ that prompted another round of ministerial disputes. On 12 July 1967, the state secretary in the Justice Ministry, Horst Ehmke, wrote to his counterparts in the Foreign Ministry and Economics Ministry asking whether it was time for a reassessment of the division of authorities between the ministries, particularly as the legal aspects of the integration project were becoming ever more important and common.[86] Accompanying this was a Justice Ministry memorandum on the authorities held by the ministries concerning European policy, in which the ministry voiced its concern at how close European law was to breaking certain basic rights (Art. 2, 12, 13, 14) and that questions of democratic legitimacy and basic rights protection were becoming increasingly prevalent.[87] Despite this, the state secretary in the economics ministry, Fritz Neef, rejected the proposal out of hand, stating that after discussions with colleagues, there was no evidence that European law was becoming more important or more voluminous. Moreover, the legal sections in the Economics Ministry and Foreign Ministry, he argued, had developed a system of "close and trusting" cooperation regarding European law and that further discussion of competency division should be discussed through the more formal means

---

[84] See, for instance, Case 58/64 *Grundig-Verkaufs GmbH vs. Commission* [1966] European Court Report 299.

[85] B141–23616 Bundesjustizministerium: EWG Krise.

[86] Letter, 12 July 1967, in BA B141–61070 Bundesjustizministerium: Institutionelle Entwicklung der EG 1965–8.

[87] Memo, 25 July 1967, in BA B141–61070 Bundesjustizministerium: Institutionelle Entwicklung der EG 1965–8.

of the state secretary committee.[88] The state secretary in the foreign ministry, Klaus Schütz, instigated an investigation into the division of authorities concerning European law within his own ministry. This study demonstrated that there was no formal division for European legal matters. Practically the relevant ministries handled those of a specific, technical nature and those requiring transposition into national law, while the Legal Section of the Foreign Ministry handled legal issues of political importance.[89]

Given this logic, it is not surprising that the Justice Ministry and Interior Ministry were excluded from issues of European law. Legal issues of a "political" nature – meaning issues concerning primacy and direct effect – fell under the remit of the Foreign Ministry, despite being the natural constituency of the *Verfassungsressorts*. Because the Community was still understood as an external, international organization (the Foreign Ministry report stated that most European law issues were dealt with in the "International Law Section"),[90] and the *Verfassungsressorts* dealt with domestic constitutional issues, they were marginalized, despite their concerns that European law was increasingly affecting the national constitutional order. As a result of the report, Schütz was equally dismissive of Ehmke's suggestion as Neef had been.[91] This attitude infuriated Ehmke. In his reply to his counterparts, he claimed issues such as the demarcation of limits of national and supranational law and the use of the preliminary ruling mechanism by West German courts were increasingly urgent. Most importantly, action needed to be taken against the continued undermining of national parliamentary power through strengthening of its European equivalent, preferably through treaty amendment.[92] Nevertheless, Neef quickly brushed aside Ehmke's concerns, stating that the essence of integration was that Member States were not fully in control of its development and that the growth of a European legal system was caused by the impossibility of predicting the path integration might follow.

Indeed, the expansion of European law and the continued weakness of the European Parliament were in the interest of West Germany as it helped achieved certain political goals: namely the sidelining of French obstructionism within the Community by making the necessity of continued and more legitimate integration

[88] Letter, 4 August 1967 in BA B141–61070 Bundesjustizministerium: Institutionelle Entwicklung der EG 1965–8.

[89] Memo, 6 September 1967 in PAA-B20–200–1662 Allgemeine Rechtsfragen nicht Institutionelle Art (4 November 1966–30 June 1970).

[90] Page 5, Memo, 6 September 1967 in PAA-B20–200–1662 Allgemeine Rechtsfragen nicht Institutionelle Art (4 November 1966–30 June 1970).

[91] Letter, 12 September 1967, in BA B141–61070 Bundesjustizministerium: Institutionelle Entwicklung der EG 1965–8.

[92] Letter, 29 September 1967, in PAA-B20–200–1662 Allgemeine Rechtsfragen nicht Institutionelle Art (4 November 1966–30 June 1970).

inevitable.[93] Without a doubt, Neef's instrumentalization of legal integration to achieve political goals, against French wishes, matches Weiler's contextual model perfectly, but there is little evidence that this policy was followed in a systematic way. If this were a conscious policy on behalf of the West German administration, then the decision making level at the Foreign Ministry – responsible for the political strategy of European policy – would mention the European legal system, or even at some point discuss it. As already seen, this simply does not occur. The end result of Ehmke's attempt to bring the Justice Ministry closer to the European policy formation mechanism ended in failure, and the Justice Ministry was given merely the opportunity to prepare a report on the medium and long-term development of the European legal system for the state secretary committee meeting in January 1968. The report's weak conclusion was that the *Verfassungsressorts* should be more involved in the monitoring of European law than the current situation allowed for, without making any concrete suggestions.[94]

However, there was also tension between the Justice Ministry and Interior Ministry. The Interior Ministry had proven to be a supporter of the constitutional practice, if somewhat unimpressed by the Foreign Ministry's analysis of the developments. The Justice Ministry on the other hand was continually questioning the democratic credentials of the Community and whether the expansion of European legal order was in fact a positive phenomenon. In 1964, this difference of opinion really came to a head as the two ministries discussed the merits of the RTC's reference to the FCC to question the constitutionality of the Treaties of Rome. The Interior Ministry's von Meibom was quick to point out that Justice Minister Ewald Bucher was a member of the FDP, which had opposed the ratification of the Treaties of Rome, and he himself had published an academic article in 1957 questioning the constitutionality of the Treaty. Von Meibom, in discussion with members of the Justice Ministry, even found that some were embarrassed by their minister's attitude toward European integration[95] on a number of issues, including its reserved reception of the direct

---

[93] "Eine Diskussion in der EWG über die Stärkung des Europäischen Parlaments ist leider angesichts der französischen Haltung gegenwärtig völlig ausgeschlossen. Daraus sollte jedoch nicht die Folgerung gezogen werden, den Ausbau des EWG-Rechts zu verzögern oder einzuschränken. Vielmehr müssen wir darauf vertrauen, dass die Situation mit fortschreitender Entwicklung schliesslich so unhaltbar wird, dass sich keine Regierung mehr der notwendigkeit, das Europäische Parlament zu stärken, entziehen kann," Letter, 28 November 1967, in PAA-B20–200–1662 Allgemeine Rechtsfragen nicht Institutionelle Art (4 November 1966–30 June 1970).

[94] The *Verfassungsressorts* were excluded from State Secretary Committee meetings on European policy; see Letter, 13 May 1964, in BA B106–39573 Bundesinnenministerium: Einstellung des BMJ zu EWG-Fragen 1964. For the Justice Ministry report, see Memo, 12 January 1968 in PAA B20–200–991 Rechtsfragen der Europäischen Gemeinschaft.

[95] "ORR Dr Bülow (EWG-Referat der BMJ) wurde scherzhaft darauf angesprochen, daß bei der FDP-Zugehörigkeit seines Herrn Ministers ja wohl einer leicht zur negativen Beurteilung des EWG-Vertrages hin tendierenden, abweichenden Stellungnahme des BMJ zu dem Vorlagebeschluß des

effect and primacy doctrines. The main bone of contention between the two ministries was, however, that the Justice Ministry seemed reluctant to criticize the RTC for its reference to the FCC, despite the Interior Ministry's suggestion to do so. The RTC case remained a major issue for the West German government throughout the entire period.

The RTC case began in mid-1963 when the Ministry of Finance was contacted by the Finance Office in Koblenz regarding the proposed referral of a case before the Rhineland Tax Court to the FCC questioning the constitutionality of the ratification of the ToR.[96] Circulated immediately, the proposal was quickly picked up by the Justice Ministry and Economics Ministry, with the latter issuing an especially strong critique of the RTC's reasoning.[97] When the RTC submitted its referral to the FCC in November of the same year, the ministries moved to provide commentaries on the case – exclusively opposed to the RTC's position, either regarding a technicality of the particularly complex financial aspects of the case, or more importantly on the question of constitutionality. While the RTC argued that the transference of competency through Article 24 BL endangered the constitutionally enshrined separation of powers caused by a lack of structural congruence between supranational and national systems, all of the ministries agreed that the competency transference through parliamentary ratification was indeed constitutional. Even the Foreign Ministry, not directly involved in machinations of a domestic court case, issued a strong criticism of the lower court,[98] and State Secretary Carstens asked to be informed on the creation of any government opinion on the case.[99]

At the same time, President Hallstein at the Commission was informed of the case and the Legal Service of the Commission took up contacts with West German representatives at the Bensheim Colloquium in July 1964, which had proven so important in shifting West German academic opinion toward the ECJ. As a result of these contacts, both Hallstein and Hans von der Groeben were secretly forwarded the proposed statements from the ministries and Bundestag by the Economics Ministry State Secretary Fritz Neef and asked whether the

Finanzgerichts Rheinland-Pfalz zu rechnen sei. ORR Dr Bülow blieb in offensichtlicher Verlegenheit die Antwort darauf schuldig," in Memo, 9 June 1964, in BA B106–39573 Bundesinnenministerium: Einstellung des BMJ zu EWG-Fragen 1964.

96 File note, 18 July 1963 in PAA B80–416 EWG Rechtsakten: Vorlagebeschluß des Finanzgerichts Rheinland-Pfalz.
97 Letter, 19 August 1963 in PAA B80–416 EWG Rechtsakten: Vorlagebeschluß des Finanzgerichts Rheinland-Pfalz.
98 Memo, 8 June 1964 in PAA B80–416 EWG Rechtsakten: Vorlagebeschluß des Finanzgerichts Rheinland-Pfalz.
99 Letter, 8 May 1964 in PAA B80–416 EWG Rechtsakten: Vorlagebeschluß des Finanzgerichts Rheinland-Pfalz.

Commission would like to comment on the case.[100] When the Judicial Service said that this was not legally possible, both the BMJ and Interior Ministry instituted unofficial contacts with the Judicial Service to ensure its concerns were taken into account in the official government position being coordinated by the Economics Ministry.[101]

In June 1964, the Bundestag discussed the referral, with Ophüls reviving his role from the late 1950s to represent the Foreign Ministry in the discussion committee.[102] This, however, was already fertile ground, as parliamentarians unanimously rejected the RTC position, dismissing it as "judicial games" and deciding to submit an opinion to the FCC in favor of the constitutionality of the Treaties of Rome.[103] Over the next few months, both the Bundestag and the administration crafted official opinions on the case, with that of the Bundestag placing much more emphasis on the need for greater democracy and a guaranteed separation of powers than that of the ministries, which was highly detailed in relation to the financial aspects of the case.[104] The opinion provided by the administration, however, picked up an issue raised by the RTC in its referral, which was the constitutional protection of the basic rights through Article 79 (iii) BL. As the drafts progressed through to final version of January 1965, the issue of fundamental rights became increasingly important.[105] In particular, Carstens was adamant that Article 79 (iii) BL be clearly stated as the limit for the transference of sovereignty and he sought to influence, in particular, the Justice Ministry through a number of phone calls in January 1965 so that this was included in the final submission.[106] Despite Carstens' effort, the Justice Ministry rejected the need for such a clear statement, citing that it was impractical for the Treaties of Rome to be limited by national constitutional rights.[107] This was a surprising result, considering the Justice Ministry's continued attempts prior to this to maintain the integrity of the national constitutional order in the face of the

---

[100] See BA N1266 1200 Nachlaß Walter Hallstein: Verfassungsmäßigkeit des deutschen Zustimmungsgesetz zum EWG Vertrag and KAS-I-659–042/3 Nachlaß: Hans von der Groeben.

[101] See Memo, 24 July 1964 in BA N1266 1200 Nachlaß Walter Hallstein: Verfassungsmäßigkeit des deutschen Zustimmungsgesetz zum EWG Vertrag.

[102] Memo, 16 June 1964 in PAA B80–416 EWG Rechtsakten: Vorlagebeschluß des Finanzgerichts Rheinland-Pfalz.

[103] Memo, 16 June 1964 in PAA B80–416 EWG Rechtsakten: Vorlagebeschluß des Finanzgerichts Rheinland-Pfalz.

[104] See BA N1266 1200 Nachlaß Walter Hallstein: Verfassungsmäßigkeit des deutschen Zustimmungsgesetz zum EWG Vertrag for both official opinions.

[105] See modifications suggested by the Foreign Ministry in PAA B80–997 and the Justice Ministry in BA N1266 1200 Nachlaß Walter Hallstein: Verfassungsmäßigkeit des deutschen Zustimmungsgesetz zum EWG Vertrag.

[106] See Memo, 14 January 1965 in PAA B80–997.

[107] This statement is a direct contradiction of the FCC's eventual *Solange* decision of 1974. For this statement, see Memo, 14 January 1965 in PAA B80–997.

constitutional practice. With the drafting completed, the Bundestag submitted its opinion on the case to the FCC in December 1964, the Economics Ministry that of the government on 21 January 1965. The FCC then spent the next two years deliberating on the case.

When the FCC's decision arrived in July 1967, it proved to be a disappointment to most sides of the argument, as it appeared that by dismissing the case on a technicality, that the FCC had simply avoided the question. In the time taken to deliberate, the issue of basic rights protection raised in the case became a mainstream topic of discussion both in academia and the media, and also among the ministries. Over the summer of 1968, a series of meetings between Economics Ministry, Interior Ministry, Justice Ministry and Foreign Ministry officials, including von Meibom (Interior Ministry), Bülow (Justice Ministry) and Ophüls (Foreign Ministry), took place to discuss the impact of the Treaties of Rome of the basic rights in the Basic Law.[108] At this initial meeting, a number of important conclusions relating the basic rights were agreed upon:

1. It was agreed by all that the Community itself was not bound by the basic rights, but had to adhere to a "European standard of rights." Any law by the Community needing transposition into the national system did have to meet the standards of the Basic Law.
2. The Community held certain principles similar to basic rights provisions, but these were not comparable in scope or depth to the Basic Law and therefore a conflict could potentially occur to the detriment of the national constitution, however unlikely.
3. The transference of competency through Article 24 BL could occur through a simple parliamentary majority, although this could result in constitutional change through supranational intervention that would normally require a qualified majority. However, Article 24 BL did not allow constitutional change beyond the principle established in Article 79 (iii) BL.
4. West German public authority remained strictly bound to the basic rights in all modes of legislation and execution.
5. That constitutional amendment to include the principle of primacy for European law is undertaken, as well as establishing the principle that the basic rights might be infringed upon in certain cases in order to implement Community obligations.
6. West German officials should avoid possible conflicts between the European law and the basic rights at all stages, particularly at the Council stage.

[108] Memo, 28 July 1968, and Memo, 23 August 1968, in PAA B20–200–1894 EWG-Vertrag und Grundrechte 1 July 1967–10 September 1968.

By the end of the period then, the West German government had agreed upon and established its opinion on the relationship between European law and the basic rights, just as in the public and academic arenas, this same question was also being discussed. However, at the turn of the decade, these principles were questioned and reexamined several times, prompted by the number of court cases both before the FCC and the ECJ, which resulted in the FCC's *Solange* ruling in 1974.

To summarize the period 1963–9, there was a more complex political environment in which the leadership figures had much less interest in the growth of a tightly integrated legal system, yet saw some benefits in the expansion of European law to overcome diplomatic problems, particularly with the French. However, there is little evidence to suggest that there was a systematic attempt to pursue or allow legal integration because political integration was so stagnant. In the political decision making areas of the Foreign Ministry, the developments in the European legal system were rarely discussed, even though State Secretary Carstens held a keen interest in European law. The evidence instead points to the unprompted attempt to tie the French to the integration project through legal integration and strengthening of the European Parliament.

Furthermore, a systematic approach to the constitutional practice was again hindered by the battle raging between departments for competency on European affairs. As before, the result of these disputes was that the *Verfassungsressorts* were marginalized and the monitoring of politically sensitive legal cases remained the responsibility of the Foreign Ministry, whose legal team had not been handling the task very well, as Interior Ministry officials admitted. As the period progressed and the implications of the ECJ jurisprudence became clearer, the welcoming of the constitutional practice became tempered with the realization that the acceptance of primacy and direct effect should not occur at the expense of the national constitution, in particular its basic rights provision. Prompted by the RTC case, the West German government entered the 1970s making far-reaching analyses of the relationship between European law and the basic rights.

DISTRACTION AND DIVISION, 1969–1974: BRANDT, SCHMIDT, AND SOLANGE

The Brandt government completed the trend begun under the Grand Coalition of following a policy of engagement with the Federal Republic's eastern neighbors. Due to Brandt's well known foreign policy predilection, the new government sought to reassure its western allies that its interest in integration was not waning. As such, Brandt instigated a number of institutional reforms to show that the Community was still a key concern, even though his own personal attention would turn eastwards.[109] First, he appointed Katharina Focke as the parliamentary state secretary within the Chancellor's Office; her special assignment was to coordinate the Federal Republic's integration policy. Focke was a specialist in supranational organization, having written her doctoral dissertation on the topic, in which she described the ECJ as a constitutional court for the Community and accepted the primacy and direct effect of European law.[110]

Her first task as Brandt's integration policy coordinator was to bring those officials with roles in the European policy formation below state secretary level together at a series of "working breakfasts" at the Chancellor's Office to enable an exchange of information and opinion and to bring about a much more coherent policy toward the Community. However, the results of these meetings, as well as those of the "European Co-ordination Group" established in the Chancellor's Office itself, tended to focus on short-term, highly visible modes of cooperation, such as improving public information work, creation of European universities, and increased border tourism.[111] This was probably caused by Brandt's and Focke's attempts to show that the Hague Conference had successfully enlivened integration from the rigors of the mid-1960s and to provide reassurance about the focus on Ostpolitik. When the Justice Ministry attempted to raise the issue of preparing a constitution for the Community, the suggestion fell mostly on deaf ears with the final version watered down to a suggestion for "legal harmonization."[112] Clearly, the political leadership in this period, distracted by its concentration on Ostpolitik, was more interested in quick and evident gains in integration, rather than facing the politically sensitive, longer term issues at stake caused by the constitutional practice.

Of these, the main areas of contention remained, first, the division of authorities for European policy between the ministries, with the continued exclusion of the *Verfassungsressorts* causing them great consternation, and second the question of basic rights protection in the face of supreme and directly effective European legislation. The first of these two issues was raised again in May 1971 when the Foreign Ministry suggested the creation of a state secretary position for the Permanent Representative in Brussels for him to act as a "European minister" for the Federal Republic.[113] This new state secretary would, of course, come under the remit of

---

[109] Brandt's files show a total preoccupation with high political events, especially in regard to Ostpolitik, in which events relating to the Community, the Hague Conference, and the British accession are featured heavily. There are no references to the European legal system. See FES Depositum Willy Brandt Bundeskanzler/Bundesregierung.

[110] Doctoral thesis entitled "Das Wesen der Übernational" in FES Nachlaß Katharine Focke 118 Publizistische Äußerungen.

[111] See BA B106 39563 Bundesinnenministerium: Fragen der Weiterführung der Integration in den Europäischen Gemeinschaften Band 2.

[112] See Letter, 1 September 1970, in BA B106 39563 Bundesinnenministerium: Fragen der Weiterführung der Integration in den Europäischen Gemeinschaften Band 2.

[113] Protocol, 5 May 1971, in BA B136 6418 Bundeskanzleramt.

the Foreign Ministry itself. The other departments reacted strongly against the suggestion, with the two *Verfassungsressorts* quickly finding constitutionally grounded reasoning why an extra state secretary could not be named in the Foreign Ministry. The Economics Ministry was more open, stating simply the rigors of "ministerial competition" for its resistance.[114] The argument continued into 1972, with Everling in particular, forcefully arguing to his minister and state secretary the necessity that the economics ministry not give up its coordination of European policy.[115]

While nothing came of the debate on the naming of a Europe minister, the Foreign Ministry continued to gain influence over European policy by calling a series of specialist roundtable discussions, under the leadership of Foreign Minister Walter Scheel and his State Secretary Sigismund Freiherr von Braun. These discussions, which began in 1972, brought together such figures as Hallstein, Carstens, Furler and Klaus Meyer,[116] and raised issues deemed to be the most important to the Federal Republic regarding European integration during the 1970s. Among the list were the strengthening of the European Parliament, the institutionalization of the European Councils, the resurrection of the Fouchet Plan, the creation of a European minister and a general strengthening of the European institutions vis-à-vis the Member States.[117] When the Justice Ministry sent a report to the meeting suggesting on this last point that the principle of legal protection and recourse be improved, possibly by strengthening the ECJ, in order to protect the national basic rights, it was again marginalized, and focus instead fell on the campaign to strengthen the European Parliament.[118] The strengthening of the EP campaign had gathered momentum throughout the early 1970s independent of the later calls by the FCC in the *Solange* decision and procedures to instigate its first direct elections were finalized at the Paris Council summit in 1974.[119]

The entire West German administration remained engrossed with the question of how best to protect the basic rights throughout the early 1970s, particularly as the Frankfurt Administrative Court's (FAC) references on the question of European legal primacy vis-à-vis the basic rights bounced between the ECJ and the FCC, the result of which was the FCC's *Solange* decision. Initially, the FAC's original Article 267 reference to the ECJ passed without much notice, with both the Foreign Ministry

---

[114] Protocol, 5 May 1971, in BA B136 6418 Bundeskanzleramt.
[115] Memo, 21 December 1972, in BA B102 229775 Bundeswirtschaftsministerium: Entwicklung der EG (allgemein).
[116] Klaus Meyer was Hallstein's chef de cabinet from 1959 to 1967, then director of the Chancellor's Office until 1969.
[117] See Protocols in PAA B1 497.
[118] See Letter, 12 June 1972, in BA B141 76400 Bundesjustizministerium: Institutionelle Entwicklung der Europäischen Gemeinschaft June 1972–June 1973.
[119] See http://www.europarl.europa.eu/sides/getDoc.do?type=IM-PRESS&reference=20080226BKG22350& language=EN#title2 (last accessed 31 May 2011).

and Economics Ministry's legal sections recording the ECJ's judgment in 1970 without making comment.[120] Instead, focus fell on the ECJ's judgment of the same year in which directives and decisions were given potential direct effect.[121] During an interministerial meeting to discuss the latter case, the Justice Ministry found its opposition to the ECJ's judgment in the minority, with the Economics Ministry in particular critical of its position. The wariness of the administration toward the ECJ had nevertheless clearly grown. In fact, the report in particular stated

> the ministerial representatives all agreed that it would not be sensible to "play down" the decision. It can not be expected that the ECJ would not further expand the effects of it in later decisions in the face of the development of its previous jurisprudence.[122]

The conclusion of the conference was that informal contact needed to be made with the Judicial Service of the Commission to try and understand the full implications of the case. When it was discovered that the Judicial Service supported the ECJ's decision, and that both Dutch and Italian Permanent Representatives had no intention of discussing the case, the issue petered out.

This issue, however, was not without one major implication. By focusing attention on this case in particular, it distracted personnel from the far more fundamental decision issued by the ECJ two cases later– *Internationale Handelsgesellschaft*.[123] This, of course, when rereferred to the FCC by the FAC, became *Solange*. It was actually the Ministry of Agriculture,[124] which was first informed of the FAC's intention to rerefer the judgment of the ECJ to the FCC on 15 September 1971. It is important to note here that it was only after the case became "national" and not "European" (the FAC originally used the preliminary ruling mechanism to refer to the ECJ) that the administration became truly interested in the case. When the other departments were informed, a flurry of meetings to decide on a government position took place. More than anything they highlighted the disjointed, argumentative tone that had dominated any discussion of European law between the ministries since the early 1960s. The first meeting took place on 27 September 1971,

---

[120] For the Foreign Ministry see: PAA B20–200–1958 Rechtsurteile. For the Economics Ministry see: Letter, 12 October 1970 in PAA B80 1114.

[121] In Case 9/70 *Grad v Finanzamt Traunstein* [1970] European Court Report 825. See Interministerial Discussion Report, 21 October 1970, in PAA B20–200–1958 Rechtsurteile.

[122] "Die Ressortvertreter neigten überwiegend dazu, daß es nicht sinnvoll sei, das Urteil 'herunterzuspielen.' Angesichts der bisherigen Entwicklung der Rechtssprechung des EuGH könne nicht erwartet werden, daß der Gerichtshof in späteren Entscheidungen die Auswirkungen dieses Urteils eingrenzen werde," in Interministerial Discussion Report, 21 October 1970, in PAA B20–200–1958 Rechtsurteile.

[123] Case 11/70 Internationale Handelsgesellschaft vs. Einfuhr- und Vorratsstelle für Getriede und Futtermittel [1970], European Court Reports 1125.

[124] Ministry of Nutrition, Agriculture and Forestry.

during which it was immediately clear that reaching a unified position would be extremely difficult. Procedurally, all involved agreed that the case in point would be lost by the FAC, possibly dismissed as inadmissible by the FCC. However, on the point of principle, three opinions quickly emerged. The representative of the Economics Ministry and Foreign Ministry argued that the Community and national legal systems were entirely separate and independent and therefore the FCC had no jurisdiction to rule on the applicability of European law, whether it infringed on the basic rights or not. The Agricultural Ministry, which was involved in the case because of its subject matter, believed it was more important to defend European law both specifically in the case and more generally. The two *Verfassungsressorts*, on the other hand, spoke strongly in defense of the basic rights and suggested that the FCC indeed become the point of reference for assessing the constitutionality of European law, even in the face of the potentially divisive political consequences this might provoke.[125] With the battle lines so quickly and decisively drawn, the situation was eased somewhat by a technical mistake in the submission by the FAC that forced it to resubmit, moving the deadline for submission of opinions to May 1972. Moreover, the Agriculture Ministry stepped out of the fray and committed itself to merely providing a commentary on the concrete, technical nature of the case, which it prepared by December of that year.[126]

By April 1972, it had still not been possible to reach a common position for submission, predominantly because of feet-dragging by the Justice Ministry, whose lack of activity in preparing its opinion to the case had caused a number of meetings to be postponed. The continued delays by the Justice Ministry clearly revealed problems within the ministry itself at forming an opinion on European law. The other ministries slowly began to pick up on this. Yet as such, the Agriculture Ministry, which had already completed its part of the submission, suggested that if the Justice Ministry was unable to produce a report, then no government opinion should be submitted. The other ministries were not happy with this, in particular the long standing differences in opinion within the *Verfassungsressorts* themselves since the mid-1960s became ever more evident.

By mid-April, the Interior Ministry stated that if the Justice Ministry remained silent, then the Interior Ministry would simply agree to the position proposed by the Economics Ministry in order that at least an opinion be given.[127] However, the

---

[125] Positions established through initial meetings (September 1971–November 1971). See PAA B80–1195 Rechtsnatur des Gemeinschaftsrechts (Verhältnis zum nationalen Recht) 1965–72 and BA B106 39568 Bundesinnenministerium: Vereinbarkeit von EWG-Recht mit dem Grundgesetz. Band 1: September 1971–September 1972.

[126] Opinion, 9 December 1971, in BA B106 39568 Bundesinnenministerium: Vereinbarkeit von EWG-Recht mit dem Grundgesetz. Band 1: September 1971–September 1972.

[127] Letter, 10th April 1972 in BA B106 39568 Bundesinnenministerium: Vereinbarkeit von EWG-Recht mit dem Grundgesetz. Band 1: September 1971–September 1972.

Foreign Ministry and Agriculture Ministry were able to negotiate with Judge Wandt on the FCC for an extension to the submission deadline. It was granted only after Judge Wandt spoke to the Justice Ministry representative Kai Bahlmann directly.[128] To the other departments, it seemed unlikely that the promises made by Bahlmann, Head of the Public Law Section of the Justice Ministry, could be kept. In a letter to the Interior Ministry, the Agriculture Ministry stated that the reason for the delay made public by the Justice Ministry – that it was overburdened by the cases involving the constitutionality of Brandt's Ostpolitik – was in fact a charade, and that the real reason was the deep differences of opinion on the case within the Justice Ministry itself, which would make any submission impossible.[129] It is also interesting to note the symmetry of division in the academic discussion and division of opinion within the Justice Ministry at this time.

This was indeed the case, as by June 1972, the Justice Ministry had still not submitted its opinion on the case, forcing the Agriculture Ministry to apply for a second extension for submission. When questioned in late July as to the reason for the delay, the Justice Ministry representative stated that it had heard from the FCC that the ECJ planned to submit its own opinion on the case and that the Justice Ministry was considering this before completing its review. The reaction of the Interior Ministry to this was highly revealing, with the memo sent by the Agriculture Ministry hand annotated with disparaging comments such as "what is all this?" and questioning the initiative taken by the Justice Ministry in taking up contact with the FCC and ECJ for itself.[130] Finally, on 29 August 1972, the Justice Ministry submitted its opinion to the other ministries, in which it also denied knowing the intentions of the ECJ to submit its own opinion. The opinion of the Justice Ministry, although several months late, did help reach an agreement, as its stance was much more integration-friendly, so that in early September 1972, the Foreign Ministry could foresee a quick end to the drama.[131] This was, however, again wishful thinking. At subsequent editing committees toward the end of the year, it was clear that divisions still remained between the ministries, particularly between the Foreign Ministry and Economics Ministry on the one side and the *Verfassungsressorts* on the other. The former favored a critical response to the FAC on political grounds, whereas the latter really thought it time that the question of

[128] Memo, 25th May 1972 in BA B106 39568 Bundesinnenministerium: Vereinbarkeit von EWG-Recht mit dem Grundgesetz. Band 1: September 1971–September 1972.

[129] Letter, 21 April 1972 in BA B106 39568 Bundesinnenministerium: Vereinbarkeit von EWG-Recht mit dem Grundgesetz. Band 1: September 1971–September 1972.

[130] "Was soll das alles?" in (Handwritten comments by Schwinne, Interior Ministry), Letter, 24 July 1972 in BA B106 39568 Bundesinnenministerium: Vereinbarkeit von EWG-Recht mit dem Grundgesetz. Band 1: September 1971–September 1972.

[131] Letter, 8 September 1972, in BA B106 39568 Bundesinnenministerium: Vereinbarkeit von EWG-Recht mit dem Grundgesetz. Band 1: September 1971–September 1972.

basic rights protection in the Community be brought to a head, regardless of the political consequences.[132] By mid-December, the FCC was forced to extend the submission deadline yet again, this time until February 1973.[133] By January 1973, the Interior Ministry was forced to admit that the confusing situation regarding the basic rights and European law in academic writings and in previous FCC decision making was making an agreement between the departments almost impossible.[134] As such, it was clear by January 1973 that the only way forward would be to attack the FAC on procedural grounds, not on the political issue. When finally submitted on 15 February 1973, the government's opinion represented a highly technical, specialized rejection of the FAC's referral based on Article 100 BL, which determined the right to call upon the FCC to rule on the normative constitutionality of a particular rule or law.

One final twist remained in this prolonged drama that reinforces the recurring theme of high political events conspiring to distract attention away from the key moments in legal integration. On 6 May 1974, just three weeks before the *Solange* decision, the West German government became embroiled in a cold war spy scandal that reached to the highest echelons. On that particular day, Brandt resigned because one of his closest advisers, Günter Guillaume, was outed as an East German spy. His replacement, Helmut Schmidt, only took up the Chancellorship on 16th May. Before that the Federal President Walter Scheel had been running the government on an emergency basis. To say that these were tumultuous times would be understatement in the extreme and we must consider the difficulties faced by those working in the FRG government in trying to deal with the fallout to the *Solange* decision. This will be the subject of the next chapter.

The period 1969 to 1974 was remarkable for the distractions and divisions among the West German government's ministries. The Brandt government was focused primarily on the success of its Ostpolitik and despite the appointment of Focke to coordinate integration policy, this represented little more than a delegation of responsibility from the top. Indeed, the appointment of a coordinating figure did little to ease the tensions between the ministries when it came to issues in European law. If anything, the increased importance of the issues at stake – particularly the protection of the basic rights as the central theme of the period – increased the bitterness of the dispute and revealed a new division in the administration. Whereas previously the main dispute had been between the Foreign Ministry and the

[132] Protocol, 5 October 1972, in PAA B80–1195 Rechtsnatur des Gemeinschaftsrechts (Verhältnis zum nationalen Recht) 1965–72.
[133] Protocol, 13 December 1972, in BA B106 39568 Bundesinnenministerium: Vereinbarkeit von EWG-Recht mit dem Grundgesetz. Band 2: October 1972–December 1972.
[134] Letter, 4 January 1973 in BA B106 39568 Bundesinnenministerium: Vereinbarkeit von EWG-Recht mit dem Grundgesetz. Band 3: January 1973.

Economics Ministry, the constitutional practice had transformed European law into an issue fundamentally affecting the national legal system, introducing the *Verfassungsressorts*, who sought to wield some influence, unsuccessfully, on the two ministries who had already fought hard to win their stake in policy formation. The difficulties in finding a common position in the *Solange* case forcefully highlighted the detrimental effect that the unclear division of competency had on the ability of the West German government to react to developments in the ECJ-national court dialogue.

SUMMARY

This chapter has shown that the broader theoretical approaches attempting to explain the unresponsiveness of Member State bureaucracies to the ECJ and the constitutional practice can only provide a partly complete picture. While there is certainly a need to look at the autonomy of legal terminology and the court system (legalist), perceived national interest (realist), the role of nonstate actors (neofunctionalist), and the broader political environment (contextualist), a full understanding of why bureaucracies were so inert can only be achieved by additionally including the domestic-institutional factors peculiar to each Member State. In the case of West Germany, three factors have proven to be most important:

First, the indecisiveness created by a tradition of ministerial independence coupled with an unclear demarcation of ministerial responsibility in dealing with developments in the European legal system. The initial confusion concerned whether the Foreign Ministry or Economics Ministry was to be responsible for leading European policy formation. The fact that this competency was shared, despite the Community being a primarily economic entity, reflected Adenauer's personal interest in the integration policy and his disagreement with Erhard about the path integration should follow. Surprisingly, party politics seemed to have played only a minor role in the bureaucratic constellation, with ministerial ethos overriding partisan concerns. Only once, in the case of the controversial Justice Minister Bucher were party alignments raised as a concern. The division of responsibility resulted in the exclusion of other ministries, particularly the *Verfassungsressorts*, as both the Foreign Ministry and the Economics Ministry were reluctant to share power because they feared a further loss of position. As a result, the Legal Sections of both ministries failed to recognize the full domestic legal implications of the ECJ jurisprudence.

It is telling that the International Law section within the Foreign Ministry continued monitor the ECJ, when clearly the constitutional practice had transformed European law to much more than that. Even in domestic court cases – in particular the referrals of the RTC and the FAC – which clearly fall into the remit of the *Verfassungsressorts*, the intervention of both the Economics Ministry and the Foreign Ministry ensured that government opinion on the cases was divided and submissions watered down in content. The fact that the submission during the *Solange* case had to revert back to a minimalist, technical argument, which failed to influence the FCC at all, damaged the Federal Republic's relations with the ECJ and the Commission, and almost prompted legal action against the West German government. It was only at this point that the ministries came to fully understand the potential domestic importance of European law – all of a sudden, the constitutional practice had transformed the issue into one with real domestic political implications.

Second, an unusual temporal coincidence of political crises and change of government with developments in the ECJ-national court dialogue created a vacuum of decisive political leadership at key points. The most obvious of these was the resignation of Brandt one week before the FCC's crucial *Solange* decision in May 1974, but changes also occurred in the early 1960s, with the direct effect and primacy doctrines divided between the Adenauer and Erhard governments. What this meant was that changes in senior personnel at crucial times inhibited political "trouble-shooting" and centralized information coordination, which as the "internal theories" outlined previously highlighted, could have helped produce a more coherent, powerful response to these developments. As such, it was often the lower officials, particularly those in the Legal Sections in the Foreign Ministry and Economics Ministry, who, as discussed, were not in some cases the best qualified to respond, were responsible for drawing up government responses to the constitutional practice. That the Federal Republic's response to a case as crucial as *Van Gend* to the European legal system, to European integration as a whole, was drafted by lower administrators, who had not passed their drafts to any higher bureaucratic or political figure, is simply astonishing.

Moreover, the changes in political leadership tell only half the story. The regular ministerial disputes for competency on European law outlined above also coincided chronologically with the key developments in the constitutional practice: 1958, 1964, 1967, and 1974 – each year crucial in the ECJ-West German court dialogue and in each year, the disputes between the ministries reach a high point. As demonstrated above in relation to the *Solange* case, these divisions at crucial points fundamentally weakened the ability of the West German government to formulate a coherent response to the ECJ's jurisprudence. As Katzenstein and Bulmer and Patterson describe, the weakness of the strong ministerial principle becomes particularly evident at the point at which new policy fields challenge the traditional understanding of ministerial competency. In this case, a strong and clear coordinating body was required – in Bulmer and Patterson's model, this would be the

Chancellor. However, due to the continual political distractions at key moments and a generalized will in favor of integration, this strong political leadership was always lacking.

The third and final factor was the autonomy of legal terminology and the court system, coupled with reluctance on the part of the government to be seen as meddling in judicial affairs. It is clear on a number of occasions that the "newness" of the European legal system and the ECJ itself posed problems for bureaucrats unaccustomed in many cases, to dealing with the national legal system. This was indeed also true for many academic commentators, as Chapter 2 demonstrates. Yet this problem was exacerbated further within the administration. The lack of understanding of the workings of the ECJ and the full implications of its jurisprudence meant that the *Verfassungsressorts*, who potentially could have followed the constitutional practice more closely, were marginalized in favor of the Foreign Ministry and the Economics Ministry. The latter two ministries saw the political goal of further integration as much more important to the Federal Republic than, ultimately, the coherence of the national constitution and its basic rights provision.

The interplay of law and politics in the West German reception of the constitutional practice is extremely striking. While the coordinating ministries placed primacy on the political goals of integration, the conscious pursuance of legal integration was never used systematically. In the political decision making levels of the Foreign Ministry and the Economics Ministry, European law rarely, if at all, was a topic of discussion. If many of the decision makers in these ministries were aware of the ECJ's jurisprudence, as undoubtedly the highly influential Carstens was, then there was no deliberate attempt to exploit the constitutional practice to achieve political ends. Perhaps by revealing European law as a tool of diplomatic leverage, the government feared making the ECJ a target for the French and undermining the apparent success of the Court's jurisprudence. Only at one time did this suggestion get raised, and in this case, it was used to dismiss the concerns of the Justice Ministry and preempt its attempt to become involved in monitoring European legal developments. As such, it was a tool of domestic politics, not one of diplomatic maneuver. This represents a fundamental undermining of the exit-voice model proposed by Weiler, at least in the West German case.

This chapter has demonstrated the necessity of looking at the special cases within each Member State when looking at the ECJ-Member State relationships. Such analytical particularism does not undermine the worth of the broader theories however, as each has shown a real relevance in explaining government inertia during the 1960s and 1970s. Nevertheless, each Member State had, of course, its own unique set of circumstances and as this analysis of the West German administration has shown, these idiosyncrasies are crucial to understanding how and why each Member State government reacted in the manner it did toward the constitutional practice. It is perhaps most remarkable, that because of its internal constellation, West Germany, one of the most important Member States in shaping the future path of integration and the European legal system, appeared too slow, ineffective and incapable of restraining the ECJ and the constitutional practice.

5

Dealing with the Fallout

German and European Responses to the Solange *Decision*

In this chapter we consider the consequences of the FCC's *Solange* decision. We have seen in the previous three chapters how the terms of the decision reflected long-lasting concerns in broader elements of West German society about the nature of legal integration that were not, nor could not, be articulated by the FRG government. The FCC, under its remit as guardian of the Basic Law, could, after observing an intellectual and popular mandate for the decision emerge, challenge the integration process and the nature of European governance from the "safe harbor" of legal reasoning. It would, in a sense, be immune to accusations of nationalism that would have been particularly sensitive for West Germans in the postwar period. The Normalization Thesis of William Patterson and Simon Bulmer suggests strongly that it had become increasingly acceptable for postunification Germany to relate its European policy in terms of "national interest" as more and more time passed from the end of the Second World War.[1] The willingness to continually "sacrifice" (see the constant mentions of this term in academic and media discussions during the 1950s and 1960s) for Europe remains, but has certainly dulled. Essentially, "two decades after unification, Germany is prepared to conduct diplomacy like any other member state."[2] This is perhaps best reflected in contemporary developments in the Eurozone, where there is neither public nor consensual political support for the bailout of struggling peripheral economies,[3] which marks a huge change in comparison to the generosity in the early 1980s in funding the accession bids of these very same Member States.[4] West Germany

---

[1] Simon Bulmer and William E Paterson, "Germany and the European Union: From 'Tamed Power' to Normalized Power?" *International Affairs* 86.5 (2010).

[2] Bulmer and Paterson, "Germany and the European Union," p 1071.

[3] http://www.bloomberg.com/news/2011-06-17/greek-bailout-leaves-french-unruffled-while-germany-seethes.html (last accessed 20 June 2011).

[4] For instance, West Germany provided the main body of funding for aiding Greek transition to membership. Complaints about the huge sums of money being supplied were evident in the West German

was, however, not a "normalized power" in the period of our study. West Germany, politically if not judicially, remained instead a "tamed power," desperately trying to avoid insinuations that it was working against integration in any way.[5] As such, the government was acutely embarrassed by the FCC's *Solange* decision and found itself frantically trying to calm the fears raised in Europe by the decision's apparent implications.

We showed in Chapter 2 how the compromise found in legal academia between the supranationalist and traditionalist positions resulted in the requirement for sufficient structural congruence for a just and legitimate transfer of sovereignty between the FRG and the European Community. Over the 1960s, particularly toward the end of that decade, continued academic analysis revealed that the Community was neither satisfactorily democratic nor afforded enough protection of fundamental rights to be institutionally similar enough for the surrender of sovereignty to be unproblematic. This position was expressed most vehemently by Hans-Heinrich Rupp, who himself came under attack from the supranationalist camp led by Hans-Peter Ipsen. These arguments built the intellectual skeleton and defined the terminology for the FCC's *Solange* decision, in which the court maintained final say on the validity of European law in the FRG. Chapter 3 detailed how the awareness of comparative fundamental rights and democratic deficiencies came later and from different sources in media and public debates. Ironically, this emerged from a sense that the ECJ had begun to create an effective legal system for the Community, but had not yet gone far enough in completing it. Of particular concern in the public was the lack of direct legal recourse when European law threatened basic rights. Contributions from the academic arena to the West German media fueled this emphasis. These powerful currents of recalcitrant public opinion were sufficient to transform the academic debate into one in which the FCC felt enough popular mandate to act. Chapter 4 showed that although the government was aware of the dissent in the public and academic spheres, the institutional sidelining of the *Verfassungressorts*, the competitive guarding of authorities by the prointegration Foreign Ministry and Economics Ministry, and the FRG's historically conditioned self-effacement prevented its articulation in actual policy. Moreover, the default prointegration position of the highest elite throughout the period meant that those with access to power limited and suppressed the one minor political attempt to reign in the ECJ, the dissenting submission at the *Van Gend* hearing. As such, the FCC became the single West German institution capable of articulating popular and intellectual concerns about legal integration.

press, although this did not inhibit the government action. See, for instance, "Man hat uns in den Sack gesteckt," *Der Spiegel*, 29 December 1980.
[5] Peter J Katzenstein, *Tamed Power: Germany in Europe* (Ithaca, N.Y.: Cornell University Press, 1997).

This chapter will now take the story beyond *Solange* to document the extensive fallout for the West German government, the FCC, and the European institutions resulting from the decision. In addition, it will demonstrate that *Solange* has had a lasting and formative impact on European governance far beyond the well known, purely judicial narrative of the *Solange* series of decisions made by the FCC described in Chapter 1. In fact, our understanding of the development of basic rights provisions in European governance needs to be reconfigured because of the information presented in this chapter. Existing analyses of the consequences of *Solange* have come, above all else, from the legal sphere.[6] This is, of course, entirely natural, with the issue being an obvious jurisprudential matter. These analyses recall the narrative of *Solange* decisions that have continually redefined the FCC's position on European law as well as set new limits and goals for the integration process. This narrative includes, in its most essential form, the *Solange II*,[7] *Maastricht*[8] and *Lisbon*[9] decisions, and will include the recent *Bailout*[10] decision. Political science accounts of *Solange* make frequent assertions such as "the institutionalization of human rights in the EU started when the ECJ began to make references to fundamental rights in its jurisprudence in the late 1960s."[11] If we take the evidence presented in this book seriously, namely that the resistance – found in academic notions of structural congruence combined with an increasing popular mandate to act – could only be articulated by the FCC in *Solange*, then, to be more precise, we must say that human rights in the EU have their origins in the *resistance in the national realm* shown to the weaknesses in rights provisions in the European system that were not dealt with before the ECJ attempted to constitutionalize Community law. This was less an issue of "competition" between judicial bodies,[12] and much more about

---

6 See Armin Von Bogdany, "A Bird's Eye View on the Science of European Law: Structures, Debates and Development Prospects of Basic Research on the Law of the European Union in a German Perspective," *European Law Journal* 6.3 (2000); Dieter H Scheuring, "The Approach to European Law in German Jurisprudence," *German Law Journal* 5.6 (2004); Christian Tomuschat, "Alle Guten Dinge Sind Iii? Zur Diskussion um die Solange-Rechtsprechung des Bverfg," *Europarecht* 25.4 (1990); Gunnar Folke Schuppert, "Public Law: Towards a Post-National Model," *Germany, Europe and the Politics of Constraint*, ed. K Dyson and KH Goetz (Oxford: Published for the British Academy by Oxford University Press, 2003); Arthur Dyevre, "The German Federal Constitutional Court and European Judicial Politics," *West European Politics* 34.2 (2011).
7 2 BvR 197/83 – *Solange II*, 22 October 1986 – BVerfGE 73, 339.
8 2 BvR 2134, 2159/92 – *Maastricht*, 12 October 1993 – BVerfGE 89, 155.
9 2 BvE 2/08, 2 BvE 5/08, 2 BvR 1010/08, 2 BvR 1022/08, 2 BvR 1259/08, 2 BvR 182/09 – *Lisbon*, 30 June 2009 – BVerfGE 123, 267.
10 2 BvR 987/10, 2 BvR 1485/10, 2 BvR 1099/10 – *Euro Bailout*, 7 September 2011.
11 Frank Schimmelfennig, "Competition and Community: Constitutional Courts, Rhetorical Action, and the Institutionalization of Human Rights in the European Union," *Journal of European Public Policy* 13.8 (2006).
12 Schimmelfennig, "Competition and Community."

the unresponsive governance of West Germany in relation to concerns about European legal integration.

Moreover and separately from this issue, closer evaluation of the events in the fallout from the original *Solange* decision actually reveals that important developments not just in the judicial, but also in the *political* governance of Europe emerged in the late 1970s and early 1980s. In actual fact, this chapter will show unmistakably that the ECJ and the Commission took national resistance to the constitutional practice extremely seriously, as, of course, Alter's theory of backlash would suggest.[13] Here now, we can document for the first time the direct and immediate political consequences of the FCC's conditional acceptance of European legal primacy. It resulted in fundamental rights protection becoming a top item on the European agenda throughout the late 1970s and early 1980s. In real terms, the FCC's resistance resulted directly in a number of European initiatives, namely:

1. The 1977 Joint Declaration of the European Parliament, Commission and Council on the European Convention for Human Rights[14];
2. The 1978 Copenhagen Declaration of Democracy;
3. The reinforcing of fundamental rights protection in ECJ jurisprudence in the 1979 *Hauer* decision;
4. The Commission proposal for Community accession to the ECHR in 1979.[15]

More significantly, the debates about possible Community accession to the ECHR are still contemporary and relevant: Only the inclusion of Article 17 of Protocol 14 of the 2010 Convention for the Protection of Human Rights and Fundamental Freedoms[16] has resolved the dilemmas identified in the late 1970s concerning Community accession. *Solange* prompted questions in European governance that are only being resolved thirty years later and clearly adds material to be incorporated into the blossoming body of analyses of the growth of international (humanitarian) legal systems since the Second World War.[17] None of these are

---

[13] Alter, *Establishing the Supremacy of European Law.*

[14] "Joint Declaration by the European Parliament, the Council and the Commission," in *Official Journal of the European Communities (OJEC)*. 27 April 1977, No C 103, p 1.

[15] Case 44/79 *Hauer vs. Land Rheinland Pfalz* [1979] European Court Report 321.

[16] http://conventions.coe.int/Treaty/EN/Treaties/html/194.htm (last accessed: 31 May 2011).

[17] The amount of work being completed on the development of international humanitarian law since the Second World War is much too long to be meaningfully listed here. Of the recent books that look much more at the relationship between European courts and human rights, we might include Alter, *Establishing the Supremacy of European Law: The Making of an International Rule of Law in Europe*; Alter, *The European Court's Political Power: Selected Essays*; Goldhaber, *A People's History of the European Court of Human Rights*; Keller and Stone-Sweet, *A Europe of Rights: The Impact of the Echr on National Legal Systems*; Stefan-Ludwig Hoffmann, *Human Rights in the Twentieth Century* (Cambridge; New York: Cambridge University Press, 2010); Bates, *The Evolution of the European Convention on Human Rights: From Its Inception to the Creation*

fully aware of the central significance of the *Solange* decision in prompting serious consideration and, in fact, actual moves toward the European Union becoming a signatory to the European Convention on Human Rights. Beyond this, the decision has also served as a model of judicial behavior for Member States acceding to the Union much later on.[18] We might add to this list too, that the *Solange* decision gave extra impetus to the on-going negotiations for direct elections to the European Parliament, finally initiated in 1979, although these had been a long-standing goal for the West German government since long before the FCC issued its decision and official policy of the Community from the Paris Council meeting in 1974 on.

To recapitulate from Chapter 1 briefly the FCC's *Solange* decision: On May 29, 1974, the court gave a long awaited and highly controversial judgment in a case that had bounced between the national and European court systems for a number of years. A main protagonist in this protracted courtroom drama was the Administrative Court of Frankfurt am Main (FAC), which, when asked to rule on the applicability of a European regulation by a West German export firm, had first requested a preliminary ruling from the ECJ[19] but then rereferred the case to the FCC a short while later.[20] While the FCC's Second Senate did not find a problem with the technical details in the case at hand, it did take the opportunity to articulate its opinion on the relationship between European law and the national constitutional order. It explained that it would accept submissions by its own national courts on the constitutionality of European legislation, as long as ("*Solange*" in German) the European Community lacked a fundamental rights provision, drawn up through a parliamentary mechanism, equivalent to that given in the West German Basic Law. This was a direct U-turn from the court's earlier First Senate decision in 1967, in which it ruled European legislation was separate from the national order and therefore inadmissible for adjudication by German public authorities.[21] Instead, it reflected increasingly strident calls from among the West German legal academy and media for checks on the ECJ's growing power, predominantly through ensuring "greater structural

---

of a Permanent Court of Human Rights; Christoffersen, *The European Court of Human Rights between Law and Politics.*

[18] For a fascinating discussion of the influence of *Solange* on the Central and Eastern European states see Wojciech Sadurski, "'Solange, Chapter 3': Constitutional Courts in Central Europe – Democracy – European Union," *EUI Working Paper* 2006/40 (2006).

[19] Case 11/70 *Internationale Handelsgesellschaft vs. Einfuhr- und Vorratsstelle für Getriede und Futtermittel* [1970] European Court Report 1125.

[20] 2 BvL 52/71 – *Solange I*, 29 May 1974 – BVerfGE 37, 27.

[21] 1 BvR 248/63 & 216/6 – *European Regulations*, 18 October 1967 – BVerfGE 22, 293. It is worth highlighting at this point that this decision was made by the First Senate of the FCC. The later *Solange* decision was made by the Second Senate. The implications of this will become apparent as the government attempts to deal with the political fallout to the case.

congruence"[22] between the European institutions and the Federal Republic. In essence, as the president of the FCC confirmed in subsequent writings and media interviews,[23] the court deliberately aimed to place pressure on the ECJ and the supranational institutions to improve rights protection and parliamentary representation to a standard equivalent to that at the national level. Increasing congruence was the court's goal, not an attempt to grab power back from the ECJ.

REVISITING THE ACADEMIC AND MEDIA RESPONSE, 1974–1976

The nature and formative power of the debates in academia, the public sphere, and in the relevant government ministries leading up to and immediately following the *Solange* decision have been the predominant focus of this book thus far. As we have seen from Chapters 2 and 3, the academic and media response to *Solange* was mixed. The FCC, when asked to rule on European legal primacy, found itself drawn into a maelstrom of competing perceptions of the postwar FRG. The two options the court faced – deny primacy and protect national rights provisions, or accept primacy and potentially undermine national constitutional integrity – were in their own way equally unpalatable and destined to raise debate and controversy. The path that the FCC finally chose – to defend the national order – ultimately provoked the European institutions to act. Academics on the whole came out against the FCC, with the most vocal of the supranationalists, Hans-Peter Ipsen calling the decision "wrong,"[24] "deceptive, superficial and legally erroneous."[25] Others still ventured that the FCC had opened a "Pandora's Box," and the court's recalcitrance would "infect" other national courts,[26] having "fatal" consequences for the European legal system.[27] A minority of academic opinion welcomed the decision for calling out the European institutions on the deficiencies in their fundamental rights provisions.[28]

---

[22] Hans Jürgen Schlochauer, "Der Übernationale Charakter der Europäischen Gemeinschaft für Kohle und Stahl," *Juristen-Zeitung* 10 (1951); Hans Jürgen Schlochauer, "Rechtsformen der Europäischen Ordnung," *Archiv des Völkerrechts* 5 (1955); Hans Jürgen Schlochauer, "Das Verhältnis des Rechts der Europäischen Wirtschaftsgemeinschaft zu den Nationalen Rechtsordnung der Mitgliedstaaten," *Archiv des Völkerrechts* 11.1 (1963).

[23] Benda, "Das Spannungsverhältnis Von Grundrechten Und Übernationalen Recht." See also subsequent media interviews: "Zur Frage der Schaffung eines europäischen Grundrechtskatalog," interview with Ernst Benda, *Deutsche Welle*, 9 April 1975.

[24] Ipsen, "Bverfg Versus Eugh Re 'Grundrechte,' Zum Beschuß des Zweiten Senats des Bundesverfassungsgerichts vom 29 Mai 1974 (Bverfge Bd, 37 S, 271)," p 1.

[25] Ipsen, "Bverfg Versus Eugh Re 'Grundrechte,'" p 1.

[26] Meinhard Hilf, "Sekundares Gemeinschaftsrecht und Deutsche Grundrechte: Zum Beschluss des Bundesverfassungsgericht vom 29. Mai 1974," *Zeitschrift für ausländisches offentliches Recht und Volkerrecht* (1975), p 51.

[27] Eckart Klein, "Stellungnahme aus der Sicht des Deutschen Verfassungsrechts," *Zeitschrift fur auslandisches offentliches Recht un Volkerrecht* (1975), p 77.

[28] Bleckmann, "Zur Funktion des Art 24 Abs 1 Grundgesetzes."

Of course, members of the FCC defended their decision in the academic presses and journals. FCC President Ernst Benda made contributions to both the academic and public arenas, reinforcing his view and the view of the five judges who voted in favor of *Solange* that this was a wake up call to the European institutions, rather than a power grab by the FCC to take back some of the authorities perceived to be stolen by the expansionist ECJ. Benda's foray into the media world reflected the massive interest in the decision in West German newspapers and, in some cases, television and radio. The Kieler Nachrichten maintained the "contagion" analogy evident in academic writings, congratulating the FCC on finally naming the "European malaise."[29] Whereas legal integration had until that point taken somewhat of a back seat to affairs of high politics and economics, by 1974 on, it was a front-page issue. In this sense, a new phase of critically aware public perception of legal integration really begins with *Solange*, different from the relatively abstract concerns about evidently "foreign" cases like *Van Gend* and *Costa*. From this point forward, European law became a West German concern, and as will be shown in the rest of this chapter, West German concerns became European law in the sense that *Solange* brought about substantive and lasting changes in European judicial and political governance.

THE SOLANGE STANDOFF PART ONE: GOVERNMENT AGAINST THE COMMISSION

Ultimately, the fallout from the *Solange* decision hit the FRG government hardest. It followed the reaction to the FCC's decision in May 1974 with interest, with newspaper clippings and academic reviews collected by the Interior Ministry.[30] In August 1974, Justice Minister Hans-Jochen Vogel verbally informed the new cabinet under Chancellor Schmidt of the implications of the *Solange* decision, warning of a potential conflict between the ECJ and the FCC.[31] No one had the desire to see the largest Member State's constitutional guardian go face-to-face with the Community's highest court. It must be remembered too that the context of the early to mid-1970s was not particularly conducive for the European project. The proposed currency union detailed in the Werner Plan had failed, destroyed by the oil price crisis that was

---

[29] "Das Bundesverfassungsgericht hat den Mut gehabt, durch eine grundsätzliche Entscheidung das europäische Übel, nämlich das Fehlen demokratischer Institutionen in der Gemeinschaft, beim Namen zu nennen.... Wir meinen, daß dieser Standpunkt mit seiner politischen Untermauerung genau der Denkweise der großen Mehrheit der Europäer entspricht," in "Europäisches Übel," *Kieler Nachrichten*, 15 August 1974.

[30] BA B106 39568 Bundesinnenministerium: Vereinbarkeit von EWG-Recht mit dem Grundgesetz. Band 4: February 1973–December 1974.

[31] See Letter, 5 September 1974 in BA B106 39568 Bundesinnenministerium: Vereinbarkeit von EWG-Recht mit dem Grundgesetz. Band 4: February 1973–December 1974.

ravaging many of the European economies by the middle of the decade. Member States retreated to protectionist national remedies to shield themselves from the heaviest damage and the paralysis this prompted in European governance meant that the 1970s are often described as suffering from "Eurosclerosis." Of most immediate concern at the start of 1974 was the electoral gains made by the Labour Party in the United Kingdom, which had garnered much support from voters by promising a referendum on continued membership of the Community. It seemed far from certain that the Community of Nine would stay that for much longer. And on top of all this, there was the FCC threatening the autonomy and integrity of the European legal system.

In order to minimize the potential for this, the Justice Ministry was instructed to take up unofficial contacts with the Commission's Legal Service to assess the mood in Brussels toward the FCC and West Germany as a whole. The first of these meetings took place in October 1974 and revealed that the Commission felt an obligation to make a strong response to the FCC, even to the point of taking West Germany to the ECJ under the infringement proceeding of Article 169 TEC.[32] A French MEP had even written to the Commission to instigate this and the Legal Committee of the European Parliament had initiated an inquiry into the decision.[33] As part of that inquiry, the long-serving West German representative to the Commission's Legal Service, Walter Much,[34] delivered an exposé on the Service's position on *Solange*.[35] This opinion, as recent research has increasingly demonstrated, was of crucial importance because the Legal Service played a central role in framing and even driving the constitutionalization agenda.[36]

In his exposé, Much described the dismay in the Commission, first that the Frankfurt court, the lower national court that had rereferred the *Solange* case to the FCC, had refused to accept the ECJ's preliminary ruling on the first referral. This alluded to the fact that not all lower national courts were as prointegration has had been believed. If anything, Much continued, the FCC had been one of the most prointegration courts in West Germany – until now. Much was also careful to

---

[32] Memo, 9 October 1974 in BA B106 39568 Bundesinnenministerium: Vereinbarkeit von EWG-Recht mit dem Grundgesetz. Band 4: February 1973–December 1974.

[33] See Memo, 9 October 1974 in BA B106 39568 Bundesinnenministerium: Vereinbarkeit von EWG-Recht mit dem Grundgesetz. Band 4: February 1973–December 1974. The French Gaullist MEP Coustet raised this proposal in a written question (414/74) on 8 October 1974.

[34] Much had been involved with the supranationalist group in the 1950s, helping negotiate the Treaties of Paris and Rome alongside Carl-Friedrich Ophüls, and was one of the original West German nominations to the Legal Service. See especially Morten Rasmussen, "Exploring the Secret History of the Legal Service of the European Executives, 1952–1967," *Contemporary European History*, forthcoming.

[35] Exposé by Walter Much, 7 February 1975, in PAA Zwischenarchiv 121875 424.

[36] Rasmussen, "Exploring the Secret History of the Legal Service of the European Executives, 1952–1967."

distinguish between the position of the FCC and the position of the government, which had rejected the *Solange* reasoning and actually stood in full agreement with the Commission. Moreover, he stressed, the decision itself had deeply divided the Second Senate, much like academic opinion in West Germany as a whole. Clearly, the supranational authorities had been paying attention to these debates. The most dangerous aspect of the decision for Much was the potential for the reasoning in the case to spread to other Member States. Much also cited the regular meetings of constitutional court judges across Europe as a point where the contagion might spread. That was to be avoided at all costs. This was particularly prescient of Much, as both British and Italian judges were increasingly recalcitrant in their dealings with European law at this point and would point to *Solange* for their own purposes as the 1970s progressed.[37] In particular Much pointed to the *Frontini* decision of the Italian Constitutional Court from December 1973, in which the Italian court had dealt with a similar basic rights problem, but through a much more "impeccable and elegant" construction.[38] This detailed the right of the Italian court to rule on fundamental rights only in the most extreme cases of rights infringements by European institutions.[39]

What was most disappointing from the Legal Service's point of view, however, was that the FCC had chosen to ignore the ECJ's *Nold*[40] ruling just prior to the *Solange* decision. As hinted at in the Introduction, this seemed to be an attempt by the ECJ to preempt the FCC by emphasizing the importance of fundamental rights in European law. Much's exposé confirms this, stating that *Nold* was indeed the ECJ's attempt to mollify the FCC and showed the ECJ's focus on a "maximum standard" of rights protection.[41] As such, *Solange* represented a "significant attack" on the integrity of the European legal system and that the FCC was attempting to relegate the ECJ to second order court in Europe.[42] Had the FCC found that the European legislation did indeed infringe on a West German basic right, infringement proceedings would have already begun. However, the FCC had not ruled in that way – and here came the olive branch – if it continued to find interpretations of the basic rights that were compatiable with Community law, the Commission might hold off initiating embarrassing infringement proceedings against the government, which essentially agreed with the Commission's own permission.

---

[37] Of particular importance here are the Italian Constitutional Court rulings in *Frontini* and *Chimiche*. Their connection to *Solange* and its fallout will be explained as the chapter progresses. See 27 December 1973, n. 183, *Frontini e a.*, in *Giur. Cost.*, 2401 & 30 October 1975, n. 232, *Società industrie chimiche Italia centrale (I.C.I.C.)*, in *Giur. Cost.* 2211.

[38] Exposé by Walter Much, 7 February 1975, in PAA Zwischenarchiv 121875 424.

[39] 27 December 1973, n. 183, *Frontini e a.*, in *Giur. Cost.*, 2401.

[40] Case 04/73 *Nold vs. Commission* [1974] European Court Report 491.

[41] Case 04/73 *Nold vs. Commission* [1974] European Court Report 491.

[42] Exposé by Walter Much, 7 February 1975, in PAA Zwischenarchiv 121875 424.

The FRG government was desperate to avoid an infringement proceeding hearing.[43] Not only would this be highly embarrassing, but it would also ignore the fact that the FCC had ignored the opinion of the government, which was basically identical to that of the Commission. If the Commission were to attack the government, this would add fuel to growing antiintegration feeling in the national realm. One possible solution suggested by the Justice Ministry was to hope that the First Senate would disagree at the earliest possible opportunity with the Second Senate, so that a full Plenary of the FCC could be called and the *Solange* decision might ultimately be overturned.[44] Justice Minister Hans Jochen Vogel reported back to Schmidt in a cabinet meeting at the end of October 1974 about ministerial deliberations on the decision. He, like Much, stressed the danger that other Member States might see inspiration in the FCC's reasoning, which would be all the more "regrettable" considering the government's impeccable prointegration credentials until that point.[45] Top priority was, according to the results of one such meeting, giving the press and other commentators no reasons to play up the importance of the story.[46] The government indicated it had no desire to play the role of poster-boy for elements within the Community keen to undermine the power and integrity of its legal system.[47] This was not entirely successful as, in July 1975, the British Embassy in Bonn forwarded a letter to the Foreign Ministry asking to host a Parliamentary Scrutiny Committee coming from London, which wanted to learn more from the West Germans about promoting national oversight over the Community institutions![48] In response, the Chancellor stated the urgent need for West German representatives at the Community to ensure all legislation would meet the basic rights standards of the Basic Law. At this point then, the West Germans were, at best, desperately treading water, attempting to minimize the fallout from *Solange*.

However, these attempts appeared to be failing as the battlelines became increasingly clear. The Commission could not back down from its role as the "guardian of the treaties" and urged on by MEPs positively braying for an infringement proceeding, the Commission was forced to square up to the FRG. In December 1974, president of the Commission, Francois-Xavier Ortoli, wrote to Foreign Minister Hans-Dietrich Genscher to criticize the *Solange* decision and called upon the government to consider ways in which the damage to the integration process by the

---

[43] See Memo, 8 October 1974, in PAA Zwischenarchiv 121874 424.50SB1.
[44] See Outline, 5 September 1974, in PAA Zwischenarchiv 121874 424.50SB1.
[45] See Report, 17 October 1974, in PAA Zwischenarchiv 121874 424.50SB1.
[46] Ressortsbesprechung, 6 January 1975 in PAA Zwischenarchiv 121874 424.50.
[47] A point that was emphasized in a letter to a cabinet meeting at the Chancellor's Office by the justice minister in October, 1974 – Letter from Vogel to Bundeskanzleramt, 17 October 1974 in PAA Zwischenarchiv 121874 424.50.
[48] Letter from British Embassy, 9 July 1975 in PAA Zwischenarchiv 121874 424.50.

FCC could be reduced.[49] If it did not, the government would face infringement proceedings for failing to fulfil its treaty obligations. At the same time, the press received a copy of the letter, which the media roundly attacked.[50] Europe's largest Member State, its biggest economy, and most generous paymaster was being accused of attacking the integrity of the Community's legal system. Events were coming to a head.

THE SOLANGE STANDOFF PART TWO: GOVERNMENT AGAINST THE FCC

The battle with the Commission was only half of the struggle facing the FRG government at this point. There was also the issue of dealing with the concerns raised by the FCC in a reasonable and appropriate way. Being stuck between its own constitutional court and the European Commission was never going to be easy for the government, but the measures it took in trying to sideline the FCC really tested the limits of the separation of powers doctrine. Conversely, the FCC equally did not seem reluctant to meddle in political affairs, with some justices using their political and social capital to ensure the FCC participated in the drafting of a response letter to the Commission, even though this was exclusively the remit of the Foreign Ministry. The ministries had already discussed several possible ways of working around the court's decision. One suggestion involved using the historically prointegration First Senate of the court (which had ruled in the *European Regulations* case in 1967) against the Second (which had ruled in *Solange*).[51] Other more drastic options floated – originating notably from the Legal Service's Much (who, as a massively experienced scholar in German constitutional law, must have known how radical his suggestions were) – included changing the laws that established the FCC, as well as constitutional amendment to make integration easier.[52] While none of these options was deemed viable or even desirable, German representatives in the Community were asked through a direct intervention of the Chancellor to doubly ensure that Community legislation did not conflict with any national fundamental rights provisions.[53]

In addition, the government took explicit steps to isolate and exclude the Second Senate of the FCC, particularly its vice-president, Walter Seuffert, from its dealings

[49] See Letter, 19 December 1974, in BA B106 39568 Bundesinnenministerium: Vereinbarkeit von EWG-Recht mit dem Grundgesetz. Band 4: February 1973–December 1974.

[50] See, for example, "Die Kommission kritisiert das Bundeverfassungsgericht," *FAZ*, 21 December 1974.

[51] Outline from Justice Ministry on 5 September 1974, in PAA Zwischenarchiv 121874 424.50.

[52] Memo from Foreign Ministry on 8 October 1974, in PAA Zwischenarchiv 121874 424.50.

[53] Protocols of the 87 Meeting of the Cabinet of the Federal Government on 6 November 1974.

with the Commission and the Legal Service.[54] Seuffert wrote to the Foreign Ministry to inquire more about the Commission's letter to Germany in December 1974, and on receipt of the reply went straight to Genscher to express his dismay with the Commission's actions, asking the government to show solidarity with the court and to allow the FCC aid in drafting the government's response. This, however, was something that the ministries were not willing to do. Instead, Seuffert, despite repeated requests through January and February 1975, was denied access to the drafts of the government's response to the Commission's letters. Indeed, the Justice Ministry sent later ECJ judge, Kai Bahlmann (who then led its Public Law section), to speak with Seuffert and pass on news of his exclusion on the grounds that this was now a political, not a legal issue.[55] Seuffert did not take the news well[56] and appealed directly to Chancellor Schmidt, who in the presence of both foreign and justice ministers ensured that Seuffert would see the government's response before it was sent. As a result, the Chancellor's Office requested, in late March 1975, a copy of the ministries' draft letter to the Commission, which then, the ministries had deemed unnecessary to send to the cabinet level. Reluctantly, and wary of provoking a domestic constitutional battle with the FCC, the Foreign and Justice Ministries sent the letter to the Chancellor's Office in April 1975.[57]

At a premeeting briefing for the cabinet discussion, the Foreign Ministry's legal section informed the Justice and Foreign Ministry State Secretaries that at all costs, Seuffert should be excluded from adding to the draft; notably this point was capitalized and underlined in the document.[58] The Foreign Ministry claimed that this was now a political matter and the government could neither have its "hands tied" by the court nor have Seuffert "cause problems." It is somewhat ironic then that the result of the cabinet meeting was the decision to have the two State Secretaries meet Seuffert to discuss the contents of the letter.[59] It was even more so that, when the meeting took place at the end of May 1975, Seuffert had a paragraph prepared that he demanded be included in the letter and declared that he would call the Foreign Ministry with additional amendments in June.[60] The paragraph, which denied the claim that the FCC was trying to undermine the coherence of the Community legal system, was ultimately included in the German response. After Seuffert kept

---

[54] PAA Zwischenarchiv 121874 424.50.
[55] Report from the State Secretary Committee on European Affairs on 21 February 1975, in PAA Zwischenarchiv 121874 424.50.
[56] Letter from Bahlmann to Foreign Ministry on 18 March 1975, in PAA Zwischenarchiv 121874 424.50.
[57] Letter from state secretary of justice to state foreign secretary containing letter to Chancellor's Office with combined Foreign-Justice Ministry position from 24 April 1975 in PAA Zwischenarchiv 121874 424.50.
[58] Letter from Legal Section on 29 April 1975 in PAA Zwischenarchiv 121874 424.50.
[59] Cabinet Protocol from 20 April 1975.
[60] Meeting report from 23 May 1975 in PAA Zwischenarchiv 121874 424.50.

his promise of calling again in June, this time with no additional amendments, the letter was signed, sealed, and delivered to the Commission on 16 June 1975. It was concillatory in nature, emphasizing the common positions of all sides on the need for basic rights provisions and the necessity for an integral and effective Community legal system. The letter welcomed the ECJ's *Nold* decision, but also suggested that the FRG would work to ensure that the ECJ had a real catalog of rights in the Treaties on which to call.[61]

THE REISCHL COMPROMISE:
THE 1977 JOINT DECLARATION AND BEYOND

It was during these negotiations with the Commission, Legal Service, and the FCC that a solution to the dilemma facing all sides emerged. In the face of a concillatory government letter and the fact that a prolonged battle on this issue would only increase the publicity of the fact that fundamental rights provisions in European law were perceived as deficient, the Commission was willing to delay the threatened infringement proceedings.[62] This suited the West German approach perfectly. Instead, behind the scenes, negotiations began about a compromise first suggested by the German Advocate General (AG) at the ECJ, Gerhard Reischl, in late 1974, which would see the Community tied officially to the standards of rights protection found in the European Convention of Human Rights.[63] In 1973 Reischl had become the FRG's second appointment to the AG's position after his predecessor, Karl Roemer, had become embroiled as a witness in a difficult case in front of the Berlin State Court, involving the purchasing of Jewish property during the Third Reich.[64] Roemer had served as the FRG's AG since the inception of the European Communities, but his claim of diplomatic immunity to prevent having to appear before the Berlin court had caused some embarrassment and concern in the ministries. His term was due to expire in October 1973 and rather than considering reappointing him, the Justice and Foreign Ministries decided to go with Reischl instead. Reischl's resume was impeccable. Born in Munich at the end of the First

---

[61] See Letter from Genscher, 16 June 1975 in PAA Zwischenarchiv 121874 424.50SB1.

[62] Letter from Seidel (Economics) to Teske (Justice) and Foreign Ministry, 12 January 1976 in PAA Zwischenarchiv 121874 424.50.

[63] Letter to Chancellor Schmidt from Reischl from 14 November 1974, in PAA Zwischenarchiv 121825.

[64] Roemer and an associate had been responsible for the purchase of a Jewish-owned company, Firma Wartenberg, in Berlin in 1938. Roemer, on orders from the Third Reich's Economics Ministry, had been replaced at the last minute in the deal by another party. Roemer was called by the Berlin State Court to serve as a witness on the terms of purchase after the original owner of the firm had died in England and his will was to be enforced. See case *Ruckerstattungssache Krüger u.a/Deutsches Reich –* 151/155/157/142 WGK 69/57 und 161/57 (Landgericht Berlin) and the ministerial discussions of the case and Roemer's attempt to use diplomatic immunity in PAA Zwischenarchiv 121825.

World War, he had graduated third in a class of 275 law school students, spoke fluent French, English and Italian, and had served for eleven years as a member of the Bundestag and for two years as an MEP.

Just two weeks into the job, Reischl received an invitation for a thirty-minute conversation with Chancellor Brandt to the Chancellor's Office to discuss his role at the ECJ.[65] The first topic of discussion was to be the lack of fundamental rights provisions in European law and Brandt, under prompting from the Foreign and Justice Ministries, suggested in no uncertain terms that Reischl consider ways in which the ECJ might make improvements in this area. While his fellow AG, Alberto Trabucchi, eventually served on the *Nold* case, decided just a few months later, we must wonder to what extent, if any, Reischl's priming by the FRG government had played a role in the ECJ's emphasis on drawing from both national and international human rights standards in the case. It would seem that there must have been some connection involved, as the *Nold* case went further than the ECJ's previous attempt to mollify national concerns on basic rights in the *Stauder v. Ulm* case. It did this by explicitly naming the European Convention on Human Rights as a potential source of "inspiration" in its decision-making. In this lay the kernel of an idea, which, when the time came, served as a basis for Reischl's suggestion for ending the *Solange* stand-off between the government, Commission and FCC.

After another thirty-minute conversation in the Chancellor's Office, this time with the new incumbent Schmidt on 8 November 1974, Reischl wrote a letter back to the Chancellor just six days later making the point that, given the current political atmosphere in the Community (1970s Eurosclerosis), getting any kind of agreement on a fundamental rights catalog, as demanded by the FCC, would simply be impossible. The European Parliament, too, would be too slow and ungainly in drafting a document, even if parliamentary involvement were a necessary condition in the *Solange* decision. Another solution had to be found and Reischl suggested that perhaps a political declaration by the European institutions, initiated by the European Parliament, would be sufficient in getting the FCC to change its mind. While the Chancellor himself found the suggestion "sufficient and practical,"[66] there were some significant reservations in the Justice Ministry about whether this would go far enough to satisfy the FCC.[67] In fact the ministry undertook a fifty-page comparative study of the provisions of the ECHR and the Basic Law, finding many similarities between the two, but also areas where the ECHR was insufficient. Despite these, the Justice Ministry seemed willing to accept this on an on-going basis as a compromise, especially in light of two subsequent events in 1975. First, the British membership

---

[65]   PAA Zwischenarchiv 121825.

[66]   Letter to Reischl from Chancellor Schmidt from 9 December 1974, in PAA Zwischenarchiv 121825.

[67]   Outline from Justice to Foreign Ministry from 16 April 1975, in PAA Zwischenarchiv 121874 424.50.

referendum was just around the corner[68] and then second, it had received notification from the Embassy in Rome later that year that the Italian Constitutional Court ruled in its *Chimiche* case[69] in a manner mirroring the FCC's *Solange* reasoning. It seemed that the overarching goal of a functioning, effective Community legal system was more important to the West Germans at this point and compromise seemed the lesser of two evils. The contagion was spreading and the threat of growing fragmentation of the Community's legal system at the hands of the constitutional courts in Germany and Italy was too great to bear.[70]

The dilemma now arose about how to get the European Parliament to initiate a declaration binding the European institutions to the ECHR without it appearing that the Commission was bowing to pressure from the FCC or that the West German government was trying to do an unseemly runaround of its own constitutional court. This proved tricky to solve. Eventually, though, a solution became apparent in that the Paris Summit meeting in December 1974 had created a Working Group on European Social Rights. At a ministerial roundtable in April 1975, it was decided to use this Working Group to push the issue of improving basic rights provisions.[71] This was not entirely in the plan of work for the Group, but the government seemed happy to simply hijack the meetings for the purpose of getting the issue on the agenda of the European Parliament. Then, in addition, two pieces of fortunate timing helped relieve the pressure on the situation. First, a year-long inquiry by the European Parliament on the consequences of the *Solange* decision was published in October 1975. The inquiry report was massively critical of the FCC – so much so that even the FRG government felt compelled to defend the FCC against the "one-sided negative portrayal of the decision."[72] Yet it did allow the government to get its views across strongly to the West German MEPs, who were ordered to defend the FCC's position at every opportunity. To do this, the Justice Ministry even drew up "educational documents" for use by the MEPs in plenary discussions. As a result, the European Parliament held a sitting specifically on the *Solange* decision in October 1976, which became part of the basis for the Joint Declaration by the European institutions in 1977. The rest of the basis for the Joint Declaration related to the second piece of good timing, which was the release of a three-year long report into basic rights protection by the Commission in February 1976.[73] The Commission

---

[68]   It was held on 5 June 1975.
[69]   30 October 1975, n. 232, Società industrie chimiche Italia centrale (I.C.I.C.), in Giur. Cost. 2211.
[70]   See "Joint Declaration by the European Parliament, the Council and the Commission," in *Official Journal of the European Communities (OJEC)*. 27 April 27, 1977, No C 103, p 1.
[71]   See PAA Zwischenarchiv 121875 424.50SB3.
[72]   See Meeting Report, 10 November 1975 in PAA Zwischenarchiv 121875 424.50SB3.
[73]   See Report of the Commission submittted to the European Parliament and the Council. COM (76) 37 final, 4 February 1976. *Bulletin of the European Community*, Supplement 5/76.

had been requested to undertake the study by the European Parliament in 1973, but because of the difficulties created by *Solange* and by the fact that the Commission had been patiently waiting for some kind of "balance" to be reached in legal academic opinion, the report had been delayed. In particular, the report waited on the outcome of the seventh FIDE conference held in Brussels in 1975, at which the Luxembourgian ECJ justice Pierre Pescatore delivered a particularly important assessment of European fundamental rights. In it, the Commission stated that it believed that the ECJ had done enough in its *Nold* jurisprudence, but as this had not satisfied the FCC, a Joint Declaration by the political institutions of the Community (Commission, Parliament and Council) on the importance of fundamental rights would suffice until such a time that a rights catalog could be completed.

The West German response to the idea of a Joint Declaration was only lukewarm. The Foreign Ministry wanted to push for a legally binding initiative, not merely a declaratory statement.[74] Both the Foreign and Justice Ministries wanted to continue with their euphemistically named "special initiative" (read: colonization) in the European Social Rights Working Group. After all, it was claimed, the Commission had gotten the idea of a Joint Declaration from West German suggestions in that forum.[75] As such, neither ministry was particularly opposed to the Joint Declaration as a starting point in a longer conversation on fundamental rights. By now, the European Parliament sitting on the *Solange* decision had taken place and had reached the conclusion that a Joint Declaration would be a practical and sufficient step forward, even though the ECJ had continued its expansion of fundamental rights jurisprudence in the *Rutili* decision in October 1975.[76] The momentum for a Joint Declaration was gathering.

The question now was to which set of human rights the Community institutions would bind themselves? It was apparent to everyone that creating a unique document for the Community itself would be politically impossible,[77] and so we return to the Reischl Compromise, which identified the ECHR as a suitable paradigm. This would not be without problems though, as the Justice Ministry had already found the ECHR deficient in comparison to the Basic Law in many respects. West German legal academia agreed. In October 1976, a colloquium on European basic rights was held at Heidelberg University. The participant list at the meeting was a genuine

---

[74] See Telegram, 18 February 1976 in PAA Zwischenarchiv 121875 424.50SB3.
[75] See Letter, 16 September 1976 in PAA Zwischenarchiv 121875 424.50SB3.
[76] Case 36/75 *Roland Rutili vs. Minister of the Interior* [1975] European Court Report 1219.
[77] This is prescient of the difficulties in ratifying the Charter of Fundamental Rights of the European Union in the decade between its creation in 2000 and the coming to force of the Treaty of Lisbon in 2009. Germany had been one of the strongest advocates for the charter, as is readily understood in the context of these discussions in the 1970s. See Dario Castiglione, Justus Schönlau and Chris Longman, *Constitutional Politics in the European Union: The Convention Moment and Its Aftermath* (New York: Palgrave Macmillan, 2008).

who's who of West German jurisprudence at the time, not least among whom were luminaries such as FCC President Ernst Benda, ECJ President Hans Kutscher, and General Advcoate Reischl himself. The Economics, Justice, and Foreign Ministries all sent their European specialists too, including people like Ulrich Everling and Erich Bülow, who were so central to the story told in Chapter 4. The three-day event discussed specifically the Joint Declaration proposal, the limitations of the ECHR and the best way forward after *Solange*. What was striking about this meeting, especially considering the attendance by Benda, was the much more concillatory tone toward the European institutions. Overall, the participants did not overestimate the importance of the basic rights problem for the overall fate and destiny of European integration. The project itself was too important to let one problem bring it down. It was clear to many that a single attempt to create a basic rights catalog would be insufficient and that this issue was only going to be solved through a gradual evolution toward sufficient rights protection. Most even went so far as to say that the rights protection afforded at that time by the European institutions would be sufficient for the time being.

So, by the end of 1976, it was quite clear that the Joint Declaration, though far from perfect, would be the best way forward. It was drafted over the course of the next few months and published on 5 April 1977. To reinforce the point, the European Council made an official "Declaration on Democracy" at the Copenhagen Council meeting a year later in April 1978, which reiterate the Community's belief in human rights and parliamentary democracy.[78] What stands out most about the 1977 Joint Declaration though was, in fact, the opening speeches made by the respective presidents of the institutions. Then British foreign secretary and president of the council, David Owen, stated clearly that "this proposal came from the European Parliament" and European Parliament President Emilio Colombo thanked "the courageous and determined Members of Parliament who originated this Declaration."[79] We now know quite clearly that the Joint Declaration had definitively not begun in the European Parliament – it was instead the product of a thirty minute conversation between the Advocate General and the West German Chancellor in the latter's office on what we can imagine to be a cold November day in Bonn. Nonetheless, these speeches assigning ownership of the Declaration to the European Parliament rather adroitly dealt with the FCC's demand that a parliamentary body settle the fundamental rights issue,[80] while saving face for the Commission and the FRG government. As resolutions to tricky disputes go, this was a particularly nimble-fingered example.

[78] Conclusions to Session of the European Council, Copenhagen, 7–8 April 1978.
[79] See Speeches, 5 April 1977 in PAA Zwischenarchiv 121875 424.
[80] 2 BvL 52/71 – *Solange I decision*, 29 May 1974 – BVerfGE 37, 271.

It would however be wishful thinking to expect everyone to be pleased with this outcome. Some voices in the West German legal academy spoke out against the compromise. The academic, Meinhard Hilf, who between 1973 and 1976, had worked for both the FCC and the Commission's Legal Service, was critical of the nonlegal nature of the enterprise,[81] being confused by the purely rhetorical nature of the Declaration – the institutions were still not, in effect, legally bound by any fundamental rights provisions. Moreover, Hilf argued, the ECJ had not been party to the document – it "bound" only the three political institutions of the Community, and yet it had been the court's expansive interpretation of its duties that had caused the problems in the first place. Even the West German media remained critical, with the leading broadsheet, FAZ, writing in June 1979 that the Community "still does not have basic rights."[82] By this time, the ECJ was extremely sensitive to criticism emerging from the West German arena. In October 1975, the ECJ had expanded on its rather equivocal reference to the ECHR in the *Nold* decision to actually use Protocol 4 of the Convention to rule in the *Rutili* case.[83] This marked a substantive step forward in incorporating the ECHR into the body of ECJ case law. The ECJ also extended the checks against the ECHR for not just European legislation, but to Member States actions too.[84] However, with both the Commission and the ECJ now monitoring the responses in the national realm, particularly in the FRG,[85] we can imagine that the ECJ felt that the criticism that it had not taken part in the Joint Declaration was sufficient to further strengthen its fundamental rights jurisprudence. It did so in the *Hauer* judgment of December 1979. In this case, ironically, we return to the wine-growing region of the Rhineland, where the very first reference to the FCC about the validity of European legislation in the FRG originated.[86] When asked to rule on a case involving the planting of a vineyard, the ECJ boldly reiterated the developments in its basic rights case law throughout the 1970s, ultimately and rather self-confidently addressing the conditional approach adopted by the FCC in *Solange*, stating:

> The question of a possible infringement of fundamental rights by a measure of the Community institutions can only be judged in the light of Community law itself. The introduction of special criteria for assessment stemming from the legislation

[81] Hilf had provided commentary on the *Solange* decision, which is detailed in Chapter 2. Meinhard Hilf, "Die Gemeinsame Grundrechtserklärung des Europaischen Parlaments, des Rates und der Kommission vom 5. April 1977," *Europäische Grundrechte Zeitschrift* 4 (1977).

[82] "Die Neuner-Gemeinschaft kennt noch keine Grundrechte," *FAZ* 23 June 1979.

[83] Case 36/75 *Roland Rutili vs. Minister of the Interior* [1975] European Court Report 1219.

[84] Andrew Drzemczewski, "Protection of Fundamental Human Rights in the European Community," *Notre Dame International Law Journal* 1.57 (1983).

[85] C.E. Archives Historiques de la Commission H00-h01-h02-h03-h08 BAC 201–1989 1976–8.

[86] 2 BvL 29/63 – *Tax on Malt Barley decision*, 5 July 1967 – BVerfGE 22, 134.

or constitutional law of a particular Member State would, by damaging the substantive unity and efficacy of Community law, lead inevitably to the destruction of the unity of the Common Market and the jeopardizing of the cohesion of the Community.

Convinced that it and its fellow European institutions had done enough to appease the FCC, the ECJ listed its reasoning the developments since 1974 in European basic rights provision and to reinforce the point, ruled against the planting of the vineyard using Protocol 1 of the ECHR combined with its own interpretation of the Member States constitutional traditions.

The ECJ appeared to be correct in its assumption. Although the FCC had left open the relationship between European legislation and the Basic Law right though to 1979,[87] by 1986, in its *Solange II* decision,[88] the FCC rescinded the earlier *Solange* conditions. It stated:

> In the judgment of this Chamber a measure of protection of fundamental rights has been established in the meantime within the sovereign jurisdiction of the European Communities which in its conception, substance and manner of implementation is essentially comparable with the standards of fundamental rights provided for in the Basic Law. All the main institutions of the Community have since acknowledged in a legally significant manner that in the exercise of their powers and the pursuit of the objectives of the Community they will be guided as a legal duty by respect for fundamental rights, in particular as established by the constitutions of member states and by the European Convention on Human Rights. There are no decisive factors to lead one to conclude that the standard of fundamental rights which has been achieved under Community law is not adequately consolidated and is only of a transitory nature.

The FCC went on to list the grounds for its change in view, foremost of which were the Joint Declaration and the *Nold* and *Hauer* decisions. It had taken twelve years, but finally the confrontation between the FCC and the ECJ was over – at least on the issue of fundamental rights. The often forgotten secondary clause to *Solange* – the need for greater parliamentary input – in essence, the need for greater "structural congruence" between the federal parliamentary democracy in the FRG and the institutions of European governance – did not. In this, we find the genesis of the FCC's subsequent and highly controversial Maastricht,[89] Lisbon[90] and Euro Bailout[91] decisions.

[87] 2 BvL 6/77 – *Perhaps decision*, 25 July 1979 – BVerfGE 52, 187.
[88] 2 BvR 197/83 – *Solange II decision*, 22 October 1986 – BVerfGE 73, 339.
[89] 2 BvR 2134, 2159/92 – *Maastricht Decision*, 12 October 1993 – BVerfGE 89, 155.
[90] 2 BvE 2/08, 2 BvE 5/08, 2 BvR 1010/08, 2 BvR 1022/08, 2 BvR 1259/08, 2 BvR 182/09 – *Lisbon Decision*, 30 June 2009 – BVerfGE 123, 267.
[91] 2 BvR 987/10, 2 BvR 1485/10, 2 BvR 1099/10 – *Euro Bailout*, 7 September 2011.

EPILOGUE: TO ACCEDE OR NOT TO ACCEDE?

The final part to this story concerns Community deliberations as to whether full accession to the ECHR for the European institutions was possible or even desirable. This would take the Reischl Compromise far beyond its original remit of just a simple political declaration of the importance of the ECHR. Actual membership posed a number of difficult questions about legal recourse, final competence and legal representation that was as complex, if not more so, than the original process involved in legally integrating the Member States of the Community.

The initial impulse for this move came from a cross-party grouping of Socialists and Liberals within the European Parliament toward the end of 1978. Having referred the issue to the Parliament's Legal Committee on 14 December 1978 and getting a statement of intent from the Political Committee in April 1979, the Commission's Legal Service quickly drew up Green Paper SJ/229/79-EN, which addressed some of the difficulties involved in accession to the ECHR.[92] The Legal Service stated that because of the concerns raised in the *Solange*, and to a lesser extent the *Frontini* case of the Italian Constitutional Court, there was a real and pressing need to create some kind of rights catalog for the Community. However, political circumstances, specifically the difficulties in the relationship between the United Kingdom and Ireland in the late 1970s, meant that this was going to be a nigh on impossible task. Joining the ECHR, according to the Legal Service, would still be difficult, but as all the Member States were already signatories, it would be the easier of the than trying to create a new rights document. The Green Paper outlined some of the advantages and disadvantages of accession. Foremost in favor was the lessening of the threat that Member States would fragment the European legal system by holding Community legislation accountable to national constitutional provisions. However, it was noted on the reverse side, that the ECHR was not as complete as most national provisions, lacked clear procedures for individual recourse, and most importantly, as a nonsovereign state entity, it was not entirely clear if the Community could accede or not.[93]

The Commission, now under the Presidency of Roy Jenkins, seemed determined to push ahead with the suggestion and published a memorandum with its intent to consider accession to the ECHR. Jenkins sent the Legal Service out to the Member States at the end of 1979 to sound out the possible reactions toward accession. The then General Director of the Legal Service, Claus-Dieter Ehlermann, made contacts in the FRG and the United Kingdom. The FRG, understandably, was open

[92] C.E. Archives Historiques de la Commission H19-H20 BAC 201–1989 1979–80.
[93] See Green Paper SJ/229/79-EN in C.E. Archives Historiques de la Commission H00-h01-h02-h03-h08 BAC 201–1989 1976–8.

to the suggestion. The Justice Ministry's Erich Bülow passed Ehlermann several internal documents intended for West German MEPs and the Legal Committee of the Bundestag, which revealed the intention to draft a favorable reply to the Commission's memorandum.[94] Ehlermann's visit to the House of Lords in London however did not go so well with the British giving the suggestion a frosty response.[95] His visit right at the start of 1980 was during the height of the Irish Troubles, with Lord Mountbatten having been assassinated just a few months earlier and the death toll of the conflict rising on both sides. Britain had long faced criticism for its tactics in dealing with Northern Ireland, not least from the European Parliament itself.[96] Additionally, across the Channel, the battle continued in France to abolish the death penalty and allow the right to individual petition for French citizens to the ECHR. This came about finally in 1981 after a successfully contested campaign spearheaded by the Minister of Justice, Robert Badinter.[97] The French could not have given the green light to accession while this issue remained unresolved. The final nail in the coffin of the accession suggestion came from the ECJ itself. Its German president, Hans Kutscher, was reluctant to agree to the suggestion because of questions about who would represent the Community in actions at the ECHR and the fact that the ECHR was not always compatible, in Kutscher's view, with European law. Moreover, Kutscher was particularly worried about relegating the ECJ to being a subsidiary court to the ECHR.[98] It seemed that the hierarchies among courts mattered beyond just the Member States.

In June 2010, Article 17 of Protocol 14 to the Convention for the Protection of Human Rights and Fundamental Freedoms was amended to allow the European Union to accede to the treaty.[99] Given that, since the introduction of the Treaty of Lisbon the European Union now has a single legal personality, no legal difficulties would stand in the way of EU accession. At that point, another important part of the *Solange* legacy would have been finally fulfilled.

---

[94] C.E. Archives Historiques de la Commission 536–538 BAC 39–1989.

[95] C.E. Archives Historiques de la Commission H85A+B BAC 103–1992.

[96] See, for instance, the European Parliament session on the British treatment of prisoners in Northern Ireland on 14 March 1980.

[97] For the history of this campaign, see Robert Badinter, *Abolition: One Man's Battle Against the Death Penalty* (Boston: Northeastern University Press; Hanover: University Press of New England, 2008).

[98] C.E. Archives Historiques de la Commission 536–538 BAC 39–1989.

[99] http://conventions.coe.int/Treaty/EN/Treaties/Html/194.htm (last accessed: 31 May 2011).

Conclusion

Legal Integration in Europe, the United States, and Beyond

I send you enclos'd the propos'd new Federal Constitution for these States. I was engag'd 4 Months of the last Summer in the Convention that form'd it. It is now sent by Congress to the several States for their Confirmation. If it succeeds, I do not see why you might not in Europe carry the Project of good Henry the 4th into Execution, by forming a Federal Union and One Grand Republick of all its different States & Kingdoms; by means of a like Convention; for we had many interests to reconcile.[1]

SUMMARY OF FINDINGS

This book has documented the resistance against the ECJ's issuing of the doctrines of primacy and direct effect in the Federal Republic of Germany. It has demonstrated that far from being a permissive, eager participant the constitutional practice, a broad swath of West German intellectual and public discourse was dedicated to analyzing critically, comparing, and ultimately rejecting the path chosen by the ECJ for the European legal system. The intellectual framework and terminology of this critique were born in the legal academy, where concerns about sufficient levels of structural congruence between national and supranational institutions, particularly in terms of democratic accountability, and, above all else, basic rights provisions, moved to the fore. This was supplemented by a tendency in public and media discourse to compare national and European systems. Ultimately, in those comparisons, against expectations, the young institutions of the FRG seemed to trump those of Europe again, especially in the same areas of accountability and rights provisions. Because of the political constraints of the FRG's postwar position, institutional blockages in the domestic system, and the close handling of policy by a dedicated supranational elite, these concerns could or would not be uttered by the

---

[1] James Brown Scott, *James Madison's Notes of Debates in the Federal Convention of 1787 and Their Relation to a More Perfect Society of Nations* (New York: Oxford University Press, 1918).

government in the European political arena. Instead, it fell upon the FCC to articulate the critiques. The Court had waited for a consensus to emerge in the academic
and media spheres and its *Solange* decision represented these views closely: There
simply was not enough similarity, or congruence, between the Basic Law and the
European "constitutional" system for the unconditional acceptance of European
legal primacy and direct effect. The message of the Court was clear: With certain
improvements, the situation would be different. Faced with this act of resistance by
the largest Member State's most legitimate public body, the Commission and Court
backed down, implementing important and lasting changes to the European system of judicial and political governance. Through West German resistance, human
rights were institutionalized at the Community level.

What, then, is the importance of this narrative? How has it changed our understanding of the formative period of the European legal system? Does it confirm or
question the ITL theories? And what remains to be done on the historical analysis of
European law? And how does what we have discovered fit into broader, more comparative trends in European and legal historical analysis?

"WE USE THE MEMORY OF OUR OWN HISTORY AS A GUIDELINE FOR OUR FUTURE BEHAVIOR"

The ongoing judicial dialogue between the ECJ and FCC, particularly from its
Maastricht decision on, has its intellectual and terminological origins in the debates
of the 1950s.[2] The arguments about structural congruence still matter. It is still the
comparative qualities of the national and European system today that provide inspiration for the FCC to condition its acceptance of European legislation and modes of
governance. The failure to have comparative parliamentary controls over the executive at the European level provided much of the ground for the FCC's recent *Lisbon*
and *Euro Bailout* decisions. Europe has yet to meet the demands of *Solange* fully,
and we might expect the FCC to keep banging on the door until this is achieved.
In this way, knowing the history of the resistance proffered by Germany allows us to
understand in large part why the FCC has made – and will continue to make – the
decisions on European affairs that it has.

WHY RESISTANCE MATTERS AND WHY IT WORKS

Now we have a narrative that records that at least one of the Member States
has resisted the ECJ, not just in the courtroom, but far beyond. It would not be

---

[2]   The quote is from a speech by Richard von Weizsacker, president of the Federal Republic of Germany,
      in the Bundestag during the Ceremony Commemorating the 40th Anniversary of the End of the War
      in Europe and of National Socialist Tyranny, 8 May 1985.

unreasonable to suspect resistance has occurred in other Member States, certainly comparing the otherwise pro-European tendencies in Germany with the profound Euro skepticism of the Danes, Brits, and even some of the Central European states. But what have we learned, and why is this important? The documentation of West German resistance to developments in the European legal arena matters because the changes that this prompted force us to recast our understanding of the formative period of the European legal system. We know now that the court decision that led to the institutionalization of human rights in European jurisprudence and governance has its initial impulse in discourse in West Germany in the early 1950s. The structural congruence argument, raised originally in relation to the European Defense Community, remained alive and relevant in West German legal academia until it was taken up as a template for the *Solange* decision in 1974. Even the public sphere, assumed by most to be disinterested and inertly permissive of European affairs in this period, took note of the ECJ's actions and in the same methodology of comparison increasingly found better qualities in the domestic system. Even if legal integration was not headline news at the start of the period, it was by the mid-1970s. The FCC, already the proactive guardian of the Basic Law, watched this consensus emerge before issuing the 1974 judgment.

Why was West German resistance so effective? We know that other Member State judiciaries – Italian, British, and French – have all had problematic relationships with the ECJ yet on the face of things have not had such a profound influence on the nature of European governance as the FCC. There are at least three reasons why *Solange* proved so effective. First, the Community institutions were willing to compromise. In fact, they had little other choice. Already facing political and financial crises of its own in the mid-1970s, the Commission was keen to hold back infringement proceedings against the FRG government while backroom negotiations for a compromise took place. It helped too that the Commission and FRG government essentially shared the same position against the FCC. Equally, though, it is understandable, with the crises of the 1970s as context, why the Commission and ECJ had no desire for a showdown with the largest and richest Member State, the Member State that held all of the purse strings. As such, the timing of West German resistance – occurring in a period of crisis for Europe – was conducive to its being effective. In a nutshell, Germany matters. In one way, the institutional export of human rights protection from Germany to Europe is another example of the already well-identified potential of the Germans to "shape the European milieu."[3] We saw it already in the structures of governance of the European Central Bank, and it is

---

[3]   Simon Bulmer, Charlie Jeffery and William E Paterson, *Germany's European Diplomacy: Shaping the Regional Milieu*, Issues in German Politics (Manchester, UK; New York: Manchester University Press, 2000).

likely – in the view of this author – that the eventual fallout from the contemporary financial crisis will allow Germany again to shape the dynamics of European integration in a way that matches its own interests. Second, there is the substance of the argument. It was simply too difficult for the European institutions to argue that the citizens of the Member States (West Germany) required *less* fundamental rights protection, while proclaiming the successes of European legal integration and the effectiveness of the European legal system. Given the context of the generational shift in values at the end of the 1960s and the increased salience of notions of qualitative democracy and rights protection, the Community institutions could not, politically at least, find substance against the FCC argument.

Finally, the nature of the FCC's argumentation was, to an extent, conciliatory. Without a doubt, the *Solange* decision represented a warning shot across the bows of the ECJ, but there was always a possibility of changing the jurisprudence once the suggested improvements in rights provisions had been made. The FCC remained true to its word in 1986, when it did indeed modify its decision in *Solange II*. In essence, the first decision was less a threatening ultimatum, and much more a conversation starter with the European legal system and the ECJ, which continues to this day. There was room for the ECJ and the Community institutions to maneuver, albeit in a direction dictated by the FCC. Even with that in mind, the eventual compromise – a modification in political and judicial governance to incorporate aspects of the ECHR –still left some West German commentators desiring more. In effect, the FCC did not totally have its own way. It had to meet Europe somewhere in the middle. As such, the *Solange II* decision of 1986, when the FCC rescinded its earlier decision, is perfectly representative of the "negotiated compromise" that Alter describes in her contextualist model. This does, however, beg the question as to whether the conditions for the impact of *Solange* represented somewhat the "perfect storm." Was the exact combination of the timing, substance, and nature of the argument so conducive to changes in European governance, or can national resistance to the ECJ make a difference at any time and on any issue? After all, the ECJ is still, to a large extent, reliant on national court compliance for the enforcement of European law. To spread its influence and consolidate and explain its case law in the Member States, especially in the formative period, the ECJ and the Legal Service relied on a dedicated group of scholars and practitioners to spread the supranational gospel. These transnational groups played an important, if ultimately unsuccessful, role in the West German reception.

THE (UN)IMPORTANCE OF TRANSNATIONAL ELITES

Recent scholarship has frequently made mention of the central importance of transnational knowledge and ideological communities in the formation of the European legal system.[4] Above all, these were sponsored by the Community institutions to go out to the Member States, explain case law, organize conferences and meetings, drive through references to the ECJ, and generally expound the benefits of European legal integration. These elites drove the process of legal integration from positions within the ECJ, the Legal Service, and international legal associations, such as FIDE, or from within the domestic system itself. This was a battle of ideas – of mastery of the postwar legal consciousness. In West Germany, the battle lines were drawn by a small group of supranationalists fighting in the early period against the traditionalist view that European law was simply the same as standard international law. As the reality of *Van Gend* and *Costa* set in, the supranationalists had some successes in promulgating their view, especially in the mid-1960s. However, ultimately and surprisingly, the supranationalists *lost* the battle of ideas in West Germany. The *Solange* decision represented a victory for the more traditionalist view, which opposed a transfer of sovereignty to institutions not suitably similar enough to the West German system. As such, in this case, the work of the transnational, prointegration elites was not entirely successful. Historians need to bear this in mind when analyzing the power and influence of these groupings.

WHY THE INTERCONNECTIVITIES MATTER: THE DEMOCRATIC DEFICIT?

However, it is equally important to remember that, at least in West Germany, these very same convinced supranationalists controlled the levers of power and were able to steer European policy and lock in a preference for integration for subsequent administrations. This "locking in" of the integration preference meant that the government was unwilling or unable to articulate resistance to the ECJ, leaving it instead to the FCC. The severed connection between public and academic discourse and government policy is a central explanatory theme in the West German reception. It is important to stress, though, how interconnected these grouping actually were, and despite these interlinkages, it is exactly in the lack of responsiveness in the political elites that the origins of *Solange* can be found.[5] The interlinkages among the groupings really drive home just how thoroughly permeated legal considerations were with contemporaneous public and political debates. In the West German case, with the high level of legal training among German bureaucrats and

---

4   Karen J Alter, "Jurist Advocacy Movements in Europe and the Andes: How Lawyers Help Promote International Legal Integration," *SSRN eLibrary* (2008); Morten Rasmussen, "Exploring the Secret History of the Legal Service of the European Executives, 1952–1967," *Contemporary European History*, forthcoming.
5   The role played by figures who were active in all three debates –such as Hallstein, Carstens, Bucher, Focke, and Ophüls – highlights the interlinkages of the three "groups."

politicians,[6] this was even more striking. Simply, for the FRG, the political and economic impulses for integration were more important than the legal consequences of the constitutional practice. *Solange* and its potential spreading to courts in Italy and the United Kingdom threatened the disintegration of the European legal system. As a result, the FRG government was very willing to seek compromise, even at the expense of alienating – jurisprudentially, and in the case of Justice Seuffert, literally – its own constitutional court. Yet, it was legal integration that brought about the most radical changes in European governance – primacy and direct effect were a real revolution in the political organization of the European continent. This begs the question of the extent to which governments of other Member States, or even subsequently the FRG, have deliberately ignored public and intellectual critiques of European integration in the name of "ever closer union." Could it be that the perceived disconnect between citizens and European institutions is, in fact, more related to the unresponsiveness of national institutions to the concerns of national electorates? Rather than a problem of too much delegation too far from the locus of popular sovereignty, as Lindseth posits,[7] perhaps the democratic deficit might be located in the choice of national governments to dedemocratize and deparliamentarize European policy making in the domestic arena? There is evidence here, at least, that this is the case, and further studies of cases of resistance other Member States may or may not confirm this intuition.

RECEPTION STUDIES MATTER AND MORE ARE NEEDED

Clearly then, of the new research being undertaken by historians on the EU's legal system, reception studies of European law within the Member States are some of the most important. Such analyses face the complexity of coming to grips with the national idiosyncrasies of the Member States. In the case reviewed here, we must first locate the dynamics of reception within the unique political culture of the FRG. Its willingness to "sacrifice" national interests and financial aid in the name of an ever closer union is a product of an exceptional set of circumstances that the FRG found itself in at its founding in 1949. The bureaucratic and institutional constellations and traditions – with ministries at competitive loggerheads over authorities and a supremely powerful and legitimate constitutional court – are equally products of the national historical context. Without these factors in place in our narrative, it is impossible to explain accurately why the *Solange* case came about and why

---

[6]   See Chapter 1 and Ralf Dahrendorf, *Gesellschaft and Freiheit*, 2nd ed. (Munich: R Piper Verlag & Co, 1963), pp 267–75.

[7]   Peter L Lindseth, *Power and Legitimacy: Reconciling Europe and the Nation-State* (Oxford; New York: Oxford University Press, 2010).

it was the FCC and not the FRG government that resisted the ECJ. Focus on the national, on the particular, is crucial in explaining the formation of European law, even if our first instincts point us toward the ECJ, the Legal Service, and the other supra- or transnational elements of the system. As is evident from this study, the national reaction has been of particular importance in the molding of the European legal system.

By establishing this argument for the case of West Germany, this book establishes the need for much closer historical scrutiny of these same debates in two other areas. First, in later periods of West German history, particularly around the Maastricht Treaty,[8] it is true to say that each Member State is different from the next, but it is also accurate to say that each Member State also changes within time. Political and legal cultures are not constants, but in a continual process of renewal, reassessment, and change. No one would doubt that the Germany of 1951 is an entirely different subject of analysis from the Germany of 2011. Reception studies across time are of great importance. Second, focusing on the national reception in other Member States might yet yield further gold mines of information on how the European legal system has developed. We know that the judicial reception of European legal integration has been, for instance, in Italy or in the United Kingdom, as problematic as it was in West Germany, albeit for different reasons, depending on the specific national context. Just as the West German case has a claim for being a particularly "special case," considering the position of the West German state in the postwar period, each and every other Member State also has its own specific cultural, structural, and legal idiosyncrasies. For instance, does the existence of a Constitutional Court in the Italian system make it more likely to resemble the West German reception? How does the British tradition of common law determine interaction with the European legal system? Do the smaller Member States have the same concerns with primacy, direct effect, and the ECJ, considering that legal integration makes all states regardless of size or stature equal in the eyes of the law? To what extent do debates within Member States cross geographical, cultural, and linguistic barriers? What is the role played by interest groups, such as the Academic Society for European Law or FIDE, in disseminating such debates? The possible implications of such research for understanding and

---

[8] Julianne Kokott has looked at the national reception of FCC's decisions regarding the Maastricht Treaty but focuses on the court dialog, not the academic, public, and bureaucratic elements. See Julianne Kokott, "German Constitutional Jurisprudence and European Legal Integration: Part I," *European Public Law* 2.2 (1996a); Julianne Kokott, "German Constitutional Jurisprudence and European Legal Integration: Part Ii," *European Public Law* 2.3 (1996b); Julianne Kokott, "Report on Germany," *The European Courts and National Courts – Doctrine and Jurisprudence: Legal Change in Its Social Context*, ed. Anne-Marie Slaughter, Alex Stone-Sweet and JHH Weiler (Oxford: Hart Publishing, 1998).

informing contemporary debates on European constitutionalism are likely to be important, allowing for the creation of more reliable and accurate ITL models, as well as providing new insights into national historiography.

This book also prompts questions concerning the reception debates in the academic, public, and bureaucratic spheres themselves. For instance, did such debates also occur outside the "constitutional" cases, namely, in those areas where European law also deeply penetrated the national order in agriculture, trade, and economics? Also, while there is little evidence that party political affiliation played a major role in the nature of the reception of European law, this factor has potentially major scope for future research. While it was not the aim or intention to incorporate political affiliation into the discussion of the reception in this book, even a cursory reading into the material presented here reveals that this indeed played some role. For instance, during the bureaucratic discussions, the justice minister Bucher was deemed unreliable as an authority on European law because he was a member of the FDP, a party that had opposed European integration in its early phases. It would be revealing to look at political preference as a determining factor in the nature of the personal, institutional, and organizational (in terms of the media) reception process. Linked closely to this is the question of geography, particularly in the case of the highly decentralized media. Did newspapers based in towns near border regions accept the expansion of European law faster or more thoroughly than those farther away? What was the dynamic between national and regional newspapers within the reception process? Were national newspapers more focused on "high politics" and therefore less aware of legal developments potentially originating in small, local court cases? Were regional papers able to provide a sufficient overview to fully grasp fully the implications of the constitutional practice? All these questions, which could not be answered within the remit of this book, would provide still further insight into the nature of the reception process and are as valid in the West German case as they would be in examinations of other Member States.

Equally so, examining the national reception of European law might provide insight into how international or transnational law affects the domestic arena. Recently, Ban Ki-Moon declared that the existence of the International Criminal Court had "altered" the behavior of many of its signatory states.[9] This is an interesting and contentious claim, indicating that the actions of nonnational courts may hold some sway in the national arena. In addition, international law is becoming more effective and influential, even in domestic systems most resistant to its norms. Such an effect is also slowly being recognized among the more liberal of U.S. Supreme Court justices, who claim that international legal standards on the

---

[9]   http://news.bbc.co.uk/2/hi/africa/10196907.stm (last accessed: 31 May 2011).

death penalty and homosexuality should influence American legislation.[10] Clearly the idea that international courts make decisions and nation states passively receive and alter their behavior is increasingly too one-dimensional and, in reality, factually incorrect. National courts react, public opinion reacts, and governments react. Ultimately, there should be a complex negotiation among all of these elements if an international norm is to take hold in a national arena. In all national cases, there are different cultural, legal, and institutional factors in play that radically alter this reception process. Ban Ki-Moon's comments show that this is not just important to Europeans and scholars of European integration, but has wider application. The globe is becoming increasingly juridified under the sway of international courts seeking to prosecute genocide, promote human rights, and change the politics of murderous national governments across the world. If these issues matter, then we need a good understanding of how national systems react to international legal norms and how best to tailor these to ensure the most effective uptake of their standards in national systems.

In the case of the EU judiciary, we have an outstanding case to test the validity of the secretary general's claim. Without doubt, the ECJ has gone further than any other international court in claiming powers for itself to impact the life and effectiveness of national legislation. It has done this to such an extent that it now seems strange to think of the ECJ as an international court comparable to judicial bodies in The Hague or Strasbourg. Like the EU, it is itself sui generis, a truly supranational court. In a few short years in the early 1960s, the ECJ attempted to sweep away the Westphalian principle and undo the centuries-old doctrine of national legal sovereignty – and for the most part, it was successful. Yet how much do we truly know about the reception process of European law in the Member States that could serve as a model with broader application? Are enough studies being undertaken? Can they be molded together to form a coherent narrative? And what would that narrative look like in comparison to the existing ITL theories that seek to explain the ECJ's success?

ITL THEORIES ONLY PARTLY STAND UP TO THE HISTORIAN'S SCRUTINY

If we return now to one of the original stated goals for the exploration of these particular historical sources – the testing of the Integration through Law models – we predominantly find support, if only partially, for the contextualist perspective of Karen Alter and, to a much lesser extent, Joseph Weiler. Evidently, there are as many strengths in all the ITL models examined as there are weaknesses. Where

---

[10] http://www.nytimes.com/2009/04/12/us/12ginsburg.html (last accessed: 31 May 2011).

and how does the historical evidence in this book confirm the suggestions of the body of ITL literature?

The legalist's focus on the autonomy of legal reasoning does indeed hold true, but in the West German example, it has been apparent that the legal terminology used in the judicial dialogue could be understood, interpreted, and debated among a wide range of groups in society. The media, if somewhat more emotive and less technically aware than legal academia, still carried frequent stories on legal developments, and these stories evolved from the specialist sections to the front pages as the period progressed. Legal integration did not occur in a specialist vacuum, and the ECJ, particularly in the early formative years, could not rely on its decisions being unnoticed and misunderstood by uneducated and disinterested populations. The legal autonomy suggested by the legalist perspective is only partially in evidence. The law cannot be completely independent of broader social forces. The legal consciousness described by Kennedy is dependent on the social structure in which it emerges.[11] In this case, there were sufficient concerns in intellectual and public discourse for the FCC to act against the constitutional practice. The ECJ was not received as the stalwart institution merely interpreting the Treaties, or the hero saving the integration project from its enemies, as it would sometimes have us believe. It was perceived as overstepping its mark or of not raising the European legal system to national standards. It was resisted. The FCC, while also attacked for its *Solange* decision, maintained massive levels of legitimacy and support among the populace. Able to cite this backing, the FCC was always likely to win this particular battle. The ECJ was, and remains, susceptible to pressure from outside the courtroom.

From the realist perspective, the main problem lies in how to define the "national interest," both in terms of prescribing or predicting government policy and in defining the parameters in which the ECJ could work without provoking a response from the governments. It is beyond question possible in the case of the FRG to focus on the generalized support and perceived national interest in pursuing integration. However, as shown, this national interest was really determined by a small and very powerful elite with close control over the mechanism of policy formation. To talk of this as the "West German position" is to make a massively superficial oversimplification. The FCC clearly articulated a different "interest" to the FRG government. Even among and within the different ministries in the government, there were huge differences in attitudes toward the ECJ and legal integration – it is impossible to talk of one common interest or attitude in terms of the government. This is even more valid for the opinions voiced in the public and in academic debates. Clearly, it is

---

[11] Duncan Kennedy, *The Rise and Fall of Classical Legal Thought* (Washington, D.C.: Beard Books, 1975); Duncan Kennedy, "Two Globalizations of Law & Legal Thought: 1850–1968," *Suffolk University Law Review* 36.3 (2003).

impossible to talk of a single interest for and within each Member State. By delving into the archives and analyzing the debates held at the time, this book only further complicates and differentiates this already diffuse picture. Even with the clarity of historical hindsight, the picture of West German interest is muddy and scattered. If we were to play the role of the ECJ in the realist model, we then need to multiply this picture by six, nine, or even twenty-seven. How then should we realistically expect the ECJ to be able to tailor its decision making to stay always on the side of the Member States?

The neofunctionalist model is extremely accurate in describing how a small elite of advocates could shape opinion on a national level toward integration. In terms of legal-academia, just such a small grouping was highly influential in disseminating ideas and arguments in favor of the ECJ's jurisprudence, even if they eventually lost this particular argument. Yet, in each case and analysis, the voices of opposition and resistance to legal integration were just as vocal as those in favor. Resistance arose from lower national courts – the Rheinland Tax Court and the Frankfurt Administrative Court – as well as from the highest judicial levels. An anti-integration grouping was at least as successful as the prointegration constituency in having its cases heard and referred to the ECJ and FCC. This book argues that the FCC's attempts to condition the constitutional practice – particularly in the *Solange* decision – represented an articulation of the critique of the legal integration process and concerns about the loss of basic rights protections and judicial protection. At least from the media perspective, these concerns were born out of the early "successes" of the ECJ in *Van Gend* and *Costa* and then the subsequent failure to complete a comparatively accessible legal framework. As such, the *Solange* decision represents the opposite of the "spill-over" effect proposed by the neofunctionalists, where in fact the continued successes of the ECJ in integration prompted a reprimand from the national realm. This is the backlash that the contextualist model proposed by Alter describes.

Alter's model of a "negotiated compromise," with the ECJ working carefully to circumvent political concerns and avoid a "backlash" from the political level, appears therefore to be much more predictive in actually describing the judicial maneuvering at the national and supranational levels. However, Alter's model cannot possibly provide a full narrative of all the forces at work in the reception process – this is a work of political science, not history, so the focus and methodology of the model are oriented in a different way. In fact, it is remarkable that the model is so accurate despite lacking the historical sources on which to build. Yet, the details of the historical narrative are important and cannot be ignored. As demonstrated, the FCC was deeply influenced by debates occurring within academia and the wider public. Through the inclusion of these debates and discourse, we can begin to draw a complete picture of the origins, terms, and evolution of the "negotiated compromise" that the European legal system clearly represents.

Finally, this book provides some, at best coincidental, historical substance to the framework of Weiler's "exit" and "voice" model, which has inspired so much thought and research on European law. At the same time, it shows that the rational choice suggested by the model was simply not made, and even barely recognized by actors in the narrative described. Central to the explanation of the ECJ's successful expansionism was the willingness of other Member States to circumvent French Gaullist obstructionism in the mid-1960s. This gains very little credence in the narrative told here. The idea of allowing legal integration to occur because the French attitude to integration was halting the process was, indeed, briefly mentioned in the discussion between state secretaries in the mid-1960s, as Chapter 4 describes,[12] yet this was the single mention of such a deliberate choice of diplomacy throughout the period. As such, it is hard to provide any evidence that the West German administration systematically instrumentalized the constitutional practice to get around De Gaulle. It never arose as an issue among legal academics. In fact, quite remarkably, the most vocal and persistent advocacy of such a policy can be found in the West German media, where the unpopularity of De Gaulle was matched only by the early enthusiasm for the ECJ as a means of overcoming the Gaullist vision of Europe.[13] As described, one commentator even asked, when writing on the *Van Gend* decision, how that decision sounded in certain French ears![14] Yet, is this enough to support Weiler's model? The answer to this question must be a cautious "no." With further research into the reception of the constitutional practice in other Member States, it is entirely possible that further evidence of the utilization of the ECJ and its jurisprudence to overcome political stagnation will be found. However, in the West German case, the evidence for this is simply too unsystematic and too cursory for credence to be given to the exit-voice dichotomy.

Clearly then, even the most sophisticated models of ITL theories, such as those of Alter and Weiler, are not entirely suitable for revealing why the ECJ was able to constitutionalize the European legal system during the 1960s with so little political reaction. Alter's description of "negotiated compromises" between national and supranational courts, similar in essence to Stone-Sweet's "judicial dialogue," focuses too much on the judicial discourse, without incorporating the broader law-in-context perspective. What was said around the courtroom was as influential in this case as what happened inside it. Weiler's perspective, while seeking explicitly to overcome the division between politics and law, fails to look beyond a narrow

---

[12] Letter, 29 September 1967, in PAA-B20–200–1662 Allgemeine Rechtsfragen nicht Institutionelle Art (4 November 1966–30 June 1970).

[13] See "Europa vor den Vaterländern," *Hamburger Echo*, 13 March 13, 1963.

[14] "Wie mag nun in manchen französischen Ohren … klingen, daß die EWG-Kommission in Brüssel die ausschließliche Zuständigkeit für die Entscheidung über … [viele Bereiche] … besitzt?" in "Europa vor den Vaterländern," *Hamburger Echo*, 13 March 1963.

definition of "politics" as high politics and diplomacy. This book had demonstrated that in the West German case, there were rich, complex, and contentious debates concerning the reception of the European law beyond the judicial and high political realms, which were central in determining the conflicts between the legal systems. Politicians and judges, identified superficially as the main players in determining the national reception in existing literature, have in fact been massively influenced by academic, public, and bureaucratic debates, which have not, until now, been examined in any detail.

How ITL theories will adapt and incorporate the findings from the new studies being undertaken by historians on the formative period of European legal integration is really a fascinating prospect. Can ITL theories be adapted to match historical reality more closely? Or will the apparent complexities inherent within the dynamics of reception, action, and inaction by each Member State make the task of creating a generally applicable model simply impossible? Can we perhaps learn about the creation of a federallike constitutional legal system from comparison to other systems? What might the EU learn from the United States?

LOOKING IN THE MIRROR? THE U.S. COMPARISON

The original ITL study of Weiler, Capelletti, and Seccombe was, of course, undertaken in part as a comparative exercise, examining European legal integration with the lens of the American experience. This has been a recurring theme for studying European law, as the United States is the only remotely comparable political entity in terms of size, political system, and federal framework to the European Union in the contemporary world. Rarely, however, are such comparisons undertaken from a historical perspective.[15] In the United States, history can be, and often is, retold through a series of court cases and legal moments. Many Americans can recognize the importance of *Marbury v. Madison*,[16] *Dred Scott*,[17] and *Brown v. Board of Education*,[18] even if they might not be able to retell the exact details of each case. American politics is closely entwined with the law and the judiciary, and any attempt to disconnect the legal history from the political and economic history of the United States would be doomed to failure. The U.S. Constitution, its development, and its interpretation really matter in the United States, and knowledge of it and its amendments is widespread and accessible to popular culture. The judicial branch of government is ever more influential. This is increasingly true as the

---

[15] For an exception, see the conference "The EU and US in Comparison: The Constitutional Genesis and Evolution of Federalized Democracy" held at American University, 6 December 2010.
[16] *Marbury v. Madison*, 5 U.S. (Cranch 1) 137 (1803).
[17] *Dred Scott v. Sandford*, 60 U.S. 393 (1857).
[18] *Brown v. Board of Education of Topeka*, 347 U.S. 483 (1954).

Supreme Court assumes more and more salience in the vociferous political atmosphere of twenty-first-century America. One of the major political debates of the last few years in the United States was the Supreme Court's *Citizens United* decision. Appointments to the Supreme Court are one of the most important and contentious moments faced by any president and Senate.

Yet, can we say the same for Europe? How many Europeans can name one of the twenty-seven ECJ justices? How many Europeans can recall *Van Gend, Costa,* or *Solange?* How many can differentiate between the ECHR and the Charter of Fundamental Rights? How many could even locate the ECJ within Europe? Why this disparity? This is probably, in no small part, caused by the fact that the histories available to chronicle the development of Europe's legal system are few and far between. The development of the U.S. Constitution is a mainstream historical narrative in America. Rich and minutely detailed accounts of the Founding Fathers, the Supreme Court, nullification crises, the New Deal disputes, and the civil rights movement, all aimed at and written for a mass audience, proliferate in the bookstores. This is an area sorely in need of redress in Europe, both as a European narrative in itself, and as a comparative one with the United States. Did, for instance, the *Solange* decision represent Europe's nullification crisis? To what extent can we regard Hans-Heinrich Rupp and the FCC West Germany's equivalent to equivalent to Jefferson or Madison writing the Kentucky and Virigina Resolutions? While some accounts[19] exist examining the comparative legal history of the EU and United States, there is much room for more work to be done.

EUROPEAN LEGAL INTEGRATION IN ITS BROADER HISTORICAL AND JUDICIAL CONTEXT

Incorporating European legal integration into comparative narratives with the United States is just one avenue that further research in this area can take. Perhaps much more apparent is the need to integrate the development of the European Union's constitutional order into accounts of the development of broader frameworks of international courts, human rights regimes, transnational judiciaries, and postwar European constitutionalism. Scholars such Karen Alter, Martin Shapiro, Alec Stone-Sweet, and Mikael Risk Madsen have already taken huge and important

[19] See, for instance, the work of Leslie Friedman Goldstein, *Constituting Federal Sovereignty: The European Union in Comparative Context,* Johns Hopkins Series in Constitutional Thought (Baltimore: Johns Hopkins University Press, 2001); or Andrew Glencross, *What Makes the EU Viable?: European Integration in the Light of the Antebellum Us Experience* (Basingstoke, England; New York: Palgrave Macmillan, 2009); Andrew Glencross and Alexandre H Trechsel, *EU Federalism and Constitutionalism: The Legacy of Altiero Spinelli* (Lanham, Md.: Lexington Books, 2010).

strides in this area.[20] How the multiple systems of international law originated, function, and evolved is a massively complex question, even more so in Europe, where the overlapping functionality of the system leaves it famously looking on paper like a "spaghetti bowl."[21] Indeed, some research has highlighted the fact that a small group of scholars worked on all of the foundational documents and in the various international legal institutions found in Europe.[22] What this connectivity means in terms of the compatibility, goals, and outcomes of these legal systems remains unclear. It certainly, however, begs the question as to the influence of these lawyer elites and the prolific and successful consolidation of international judiciaries in Europe since the Second World War.

In addition, we must also consider how the legal integration narrative told in this book fits in with accounts focusing more on the domestic legal arena. The constitution has undoubtedly become the source of political legitimacy across Europe, and the rule of law is the fundament of each modern state on the continent. It appears, at least in this sense, that the national legal order is more robust than ever before in Europe. This is a remarkable change in the two short generations since the horrors of the 1940s. How does European legal integration fit into this narrative? In this context, can we really think of the European Union as a constitutional order "supreme" above the Member States? Or is European legal integration best understood as a political compromise, affecting just a tiny minority of Europeans?[23] Or merely a complex means of international organization that relies a lot more on mutuality than the norm?[24] Of

[20] Karen Alter, *Establishing the Supremacy of European Law: The Making of an International Rule of Law in Europe*, Oxford Studies in European Law (Oxford; New York: Oxford University Press, 2001); Karen Alter, *The European Court's Political Power: Selected Essays* (Oxford; New York: Oxford University Press, 2009); Karen J Alter and Sophie Meunier-Aitsahalia, "The Politics of International Regime Complexity Symposium," *Perspectives on Politics* 7.1 (2009): 13–24 (2009); Helen Keller and Alec Stone-Sweet, *A Europe of Rights: The Impact of the Echr on National Legal Systems* (Oxford; New York: Oxford University Press, 2008); Alec Stone-Sweet, *Governing with Judges: Constitutional Politics in Europe* (Oxford: Oxford University Press, 2000); Martin M Shapiro and Alec Stone-Sweet, *On Law, Politics, and Judicialization* (Oxford; New York: Oxford University Press, 2002); Jonas Christoffersen, *The European Court of Human Rights between Law and Politics*, New Book ed. (New York: Oxford University Press, 2011); Stefan-Ludwig Hoffmann, *Human Rights in the Twentieth Century* (Cambridge; New York: Cambridge University Press, 2010).

[21] Karen J Alter and Sophie Meunier-Aitsahalia, "The Politics of International Regime Complexity Symposium," *Perspectives on Politics* 7.1 (2009): 13–24.

[22] Antonin Cohen, "Constitutionalism without Constitution: Transnational Elites between Political Mobilization and Legal Expertise (1940–1960)," *Law and Social Inquiry* 1 (2007); Michael Risk Madsen, "From Cold War Instrument to Supreme European Court: The European Court at the Crossroads of International and National Law and Politics," *Law and Social Inquiry* 1 (2007).

[23] Hjalte Rasmussen, *On Law and Policy in the European Court of Justice: A Comparative Study in Judicial Policymaking* (Dordrecht; Boston; Lancaster: Martinus Nijhoff Publishers, 1986).

[24] Will Phelan, "Why Do EU Member States Offer a 'Constitutional' Obedience to EU Obligations? Encompassing Domestic Institutions and Costly International Obligations," *TCD Institute for International Integration Studies* 256 (June 2008).

particular importance here is the exploration of delegation, legitimacy, and power by Peter Lindseth, who seeks to tie European integration to longer-term trends of delegation to administrative bodies beyond the successful oversight of democratic institutions. Is, for instance, the structural congruence argument in 1950s West Germany a nascent expression of this sense of distance between electorate and authority?

LEGAL HISTORY IS MORE THAN JUST THE LAW

Herodotus invariably seems to be an excellent starting place for any historian, but here we will finish with him. At the very beginning of European civilization, the term *historia* referred to a sort of inquiry, a search to explain why the world was the way it was. To write his own work, Herodotus scoured the sources of the eastern Mediterranean, weaving together the narrative that is now so familiar to us. His purpose in writing his *Histories* was to ensure that "the deeds of man" were not "forgotten in the lapse of time," and "especially the causes be remembered" for why Greeks and Persians were at war for most of Herodotus's life.[25] In other words, his research, his inquiry, was to find the reason why contemporary events and structures had come about. This, ultimately, became the customary template of action for the academic field that Herodotus founded. We enter the archives, collate our findings, and recreate the chronology of events so that we can best understand why matters are the way that they are. This too has to be the ultimate purpose of European integration historiography of all different types, but most particularly for accounting for how "the majesty of the law" has achieved in Europe "what centuries of blood and iron could not."[26]

In one sense – the historian's sense – documenting these events is important and interesting simply because this narrative does not exist anywhere else. However, this narrative also matters beyond filling in the gaps in our historical knowledge. It is crucial to those interested in comprehending the full mechanics of European legal integration and the development of the EU's political and judicial system, particularly in light of the changes in European governance prompted by the *Solange* decision. Moreover, this narrative delivers additional fare for those hoping to understand the dynamics of the spheres of law, society, politics, and public opinion. This is a complex relationship at the best of times. In this case, however, the complexity is multiplied by the fact that the law under question is not strictly one's own. This book demonstrates the importance of law as a medium of historical research, both for West Germany and for the European Union. Through the historicization of the establishment of the constitutional practice, and in particular the reception of

---

[25] http://www.gutenberg.org/files/2707/2707-h/main1.htm (Last accessed: 31 May 2011).
[26] Walter Hallstein, *Europe in the Making* (London: Allen and Unwin, 1972).

this at the Member State level, this book draws innovative conclusions that reveal new insights into the development of legal integration at the supranational level, as well as into the development of a new postwar self-understanding of the German nation.

In the case of the FRG, this book shows that by the late 1960s, West Germans were increasingly comfortable with their own national constitution and were happy to use it as a standard to which the Community should aspire. Unfortunately, in the ever more explicit comparisons between national and supranational constitutional orders, both in academic and in public spheres, the success of the national merely highlighted the democratic and judicial failings of the European. The increased pride in the national constitutional order was at the expense of greater disillusionment with the integration project. This conclusion has two important implications. First, for national historiography, it adds credence to terminology used in the Left-liberal perspective during the "constitutional patriotism" debate of the Historikerstreit of the 1980s. This is even more surprising as the evidence for a nascent form of constitutional patriotism emerges as early as the mid-1960s. The fact that European integration, at least through the medium of law, was openly debated within a public discourse at such an early stage is revealing for the theories of the "permissive consensus" that dominate our understanding of early public opinion formation toward the Community.

Second, for integration historiography, it demonstrates the importance of understanding the legal nature of European integration as both an independent process in itself and inextricably linked to the economic and political forces that the legal framework determines and governs. Above all else, such a historicization serves as a reminder that the integration process has been and is predominantly a process of law. Law – in all the various forms found at the European level – has defined and shaped integration from its origins in the Coal and Steel Community, through the continued widening and deepening of the Community, to the contemporary discussion of a European constitution. Despite this, the law has been forgotten by integration historians. As discussed in the Introduction, the major works of integration historiography – Lipgens, Haas, Milward, Moravcsik, and Gillingham – have all focused at various times on the political, economic, and ideological elements of the development of an integrated Europe. This imbalance has led to the neglect of a rich and fruitful area of historical research. By historicizing the reception of European law at the Member State level, beyond the traditional judicial accounts focusing on court and case-law dialogue, this book has enabled a revision of several long-established presumptions in integration historiography.

Initially, this book has made clear that the debates concerning the constitutional practice penetrated deeply into West German society, way beyond the boundaries set by the long established idea of a "permissive consensus" and its disinterested masses.[27] There is irrefutable evidence that legal integration prompted a far-reaching and complex public discourse during the 1950s and 1960s, which undermines the perception that the ordinary citizen was both unaware of and apathetic toward integration.[28] Law, as a medium for historical research, has provided insight not only into debates of interested intellectuals and the bureaucrats trying to keep up with the rapid changes in the legal sphere – where, of course, it should be expected – but also into how it shaped the everyday debates in public and media discussion. The insights into the public debates revealed how the West Germans – and by logical extension, possibly Europeans in general – have come to understand themselves in the postwar period – as communities defined and bounded by legal standards, by constitutional provisions, and by the adherence to and protection of basic fundamental rights.

Next, the model proposed initially by Haas[29] of an elite-driven project does indeed hold true, as elites in the West German case were crucial in determining the bifurcated nature of the reception of the constitutional practice. If we take the legal-academic reception alone, the role played by the Academic Society for European Law in propagating information and ideas through the *Europarecht* journal and the holding of conferences and meetings, most notably the Bensheim Colloquium in 1964, was crucial in promoting the wider acceptance of the supranationality of European law in mainstream academic opinion during the 1960s. However, this book has also revealed that public awareness and public debate of the integration process, here at least in relation to legal integration, did take place, and at a much earlier period than described by scholars thus far. It is therefore only accurate to describe a double dynamic of public debate and elite-driven action. The defining moment in the inaction of the West German government toward the ECJ was not the ignorance of public and intellectual concerns about the national constitution, but rather the institutional inertia of the bureaucratic apparatus toward the Community. As such, this raises issues concerning the perceived democratic deficit,[30] in that, it

[27] See Stuart Scheingold and Leon N Lindberg, *Europe's World-Be Polity: Patterns of Change in the European Community* (Englewood Cliffs, N.J.: Prentice-Hall, 1970).

[28] See, for instance, Noelle-Neumann's statement describing a lack of evidence of public dissension toward European institutions before 1974. See Elisabeth Noelle-Neumann, "Phantom Europe: Thirty Years of Survey Research on German Attitudes toward European Integration," *Contemporary Perspective on European Integration: Attitudes, Non-Governmental Behaviors, and Collective Decision Making*, ed. Leano Hurwitz (London: Aldwych Press, 1980), p 62.

[29] See Ernst Haas, *The Uniting of Europe: Political, Social and Economic Forces 1950–1957* (Stanford, Calif.: Stanford University Press, 1968).

[30] On the existence of a "democratic deficit" in the EU debate, see Yves Mény, "De La Democracie en Europe: Old Concepts and New Challenges," *Journal of Common Market Studies* 41 (2003); or Andrew Moravcsik, "In Defence of The 'Democratic Deficit': Reassessing Legitimacy in the European Union," *Journal of Common Market Studies* 40 (2002).

appears, at least in this case, that the deficiency in responding to developments in the European sphere lay less with the supranational institutions themselves than with the inability at the national level to react quickly and forcibly enough to the demands of the public sphere. Perhaps the fault in accountability lies not with the European institutions, but in the inability or unwillingness of national governments to allow popular opinion to sway their European policies?

In fact, quite surprisingly, the issues raised in the public and academic debates – most specifically, the concerns about the protection of the fundamental rights provisions of the Basic Law – were in reality expressed by the jurisprudence of the FCC in the *Solange* decision. Far from being an "extreme position,"[31] the *Solange* case in fact reflected, to a large extent, opinion in both academia and the public. At the time, the FCC was heavily criticized for the decision. Many scholars and commentators saw the FCC's actions as merely means to secure its power vis-à-vis the ECJ, something that prointegrationists found entirely undesirable.[32] Yet, when the words of two FCC justices[33] are taken into account, it is clear that the intention of the FCC was to provoke the ECJ into action regarding the creation and protection of fundamental rights at the supranational level. It could, of course, be countered that Benda and Seuffert were hiding the true intentions of the FCC behind the façade of promoting basic rights, while in reality securing the position of the FCC against the ECJ. Subsequent FCC jurisprudence, most notably the *Solange II* decision,[34] in which the FCC renounced its desire to test European law against the fundamental rights, also demonstrates that the FCC was happy to accept primacy and direct effect after the ECJ had worked to develop fundamental rights protection at the European level in *Stauder v. Ulm* and *Nold*. While Alter[35] and Stone-Sweet[36] argue that *Solange* was indeed the cue for the ECJ to move on basic rights, other scholars, particularly Tomuschat, have accused the FCC of pursuing

[31] Scheuring, "The Approach to European Law in German Jurisprudence," p 16.
[32] See, above all else, the legal academic reception of the *Solange* case in Chapter 2. Scholars such as Ipsen, Riegel, Hilf, and Meier were outspoken in their critique of the decision.
[33] See Walter Seuffert, "Grundgesetz und Gemeinschaftsrecht," *Konkretionen Politischer Theorie un Praxis*, ed. Adolf Arndt, Horst Ehmke, Iring Fetscher and Otwin Massing (Stuttgart: Ernst Klett Verlag, 1972); Ernst Benda, "Das Spannungsverhältnis von Grundrechten und Übernationalen Recht," *Deutsches Verwaltungsblatt* 10.11 (1974), pp 395–6. See also subsequent media publications and interviews with Benda, especially "Zur Frage der Schaffung eines europäischen Grundrechtskatalog," interview with Ernst Benda, *Deutsche Welle*, 9 April 1975, and "Für europäische Grundrechte," *die Rheinpfalz*, 18 April 1972.
[34] 2 BvR 197/83 – *Solange II decision*, 22 October 1986 – BVerfGE 73, 339. The FCC has, since *Solange II*, reiterated its desire to test European law against the Basic Law following the Maastricht Treaty.
[35] Alter, *Establishing the Supremacy of European Law: The Making of an International Rule of Law in Europe*, p 98.
[36] Stone-Sweet, *Governing with Judges: Constitutional Politics in Europe*, p 172.

a policy of "basic rights imperialism,"[37] forcing the West German model onto the
European stage. By contrast, this book reveals quite evidently that the securing of
fundamental rights both in the national constitution and at the European level
was a central concern for both the public and legal academia for almost a decade
before the *Solange* decision.

That, in either case, the national constitution could be seen by West Germans as
a model for the whole of (integrated) Europe provides new insights into the double
process through which West Germans reshaped their own self-understanding and
the image portrayed to the outside world. In regard to the latter, there was evident concern among public and ministerial opinion that the *Solange* case be interpreted by the other Member States as the start of a period of national recalcitrance.
Clearly, a positive reception of European legal integration was also a means for the
West Germans to prove to their neighbors that the new state really did wish to subsume its own interests for the good of an integrated Europe.[38] Many scholars did
indeed call the acceptance of lesser basic rights provision at the supranational level
a "sacrifice" that the Federal Republic had to make in the name of integration.[39]
Yet despite this, the FCC did indeed see fit to act, even if this provoked the highly
embarrassing threat of infringement proceedings from the Commission.[40] This is
clear evidence that the West German political and judicial system was increasingly
comfortable within itself and self-confident enough to propose its own principles
as a model for Europe. In this sense, the economic and social patterns that defined
West Germany in the mid- to late 1970s as *Modell Deutschland*, the paradigm toward
which the rest of Western Europe strove, also hold true in a judicial sense. As the
ECJ sought to build a basic rights jurisprudence for the Community, it surely must
have had in mind a kind of legal *Modell Deutschland* as the standard to which it
should aim. As such, this book has demonstrated that the interaction between the
Community and the Member States is indeed a two-way, dynamic process. While,
on the one hand, primacy and direct effect and the use of the preliminary ruling

[37] Christian Tomuschat, "Alle Guten Dinge Sind Iii? Zur Diskussion um die Solange-Rechtsprechung des Bverfg," *Europarecht* 25.4 (1990), p 351.

[38] To circumvent the threat of potential conflict, negotiations took place between the Commission and the West German government to ensure that the implementation of European law within the FRG could never potentially threaten the Basic Law, thereby calling on the FCC to act. See Alter, *Establishing the Supremacy of European Law: The Making of an International Rule of Law in Europe*, p 93.

[39] Georg Erler and Werner Theime, "Das Grundgesetz und die Offentliches Gewalt Internationaler Staatengemeinschaften," *Veroffentlichungen der Vereinigung der Deutschen Staatsrechtslehrer* 18 (1959), pp 48, 110.

[40] See Memo, 9 October 1974 in BA B106 39568 Bundesinnenministerium: Vereinbarkeit von EWG-Recht mit dem Grundgesetz. Band 4: February 1973–December 1974. The French Gaullist MEP Coustet raised the idea of infringement proceedings against Germany in a written question (414/74) on 8 October 1974.

mechanism served to Europeanize national legal orders in a "top-down" sense, the uploading effect of the FCC's *Solange* jurisprudence served to Europeanize a national tradition in a "bottom-up" manner.[41]

Just as important is the other part of this double process, namely, the impact of the constitutional practice on the introspective recasting of West German identity. Recent German historiography has begun a trend of recognizing the role that justice and law have played in molding the new German state, with particular focus on the democratic "learning process" brought about by legal modernization and liberalization.[42] This book adds concrete evidence to such debates, demonstrating how contact with the external European legal system prompted a much greater awareness and appreciation of the national constitutional order. The strengths of the West German constitution – the democratic and judicial controls over the executive, clear channels of legal recourse, and, above all, the inviolable basic rights – became provisions to respect and protect against the failings of the European system. In some cases, particularly in the public debates, there was clearly a sense of pride in the national order.[43] Indeed, it is absolutely remarkable how quickly and how thoroughly the attachment to the new constitutional order had developed, particularly when it is considered how ambiguous the German experience with constitutionalism had historically been in all the previous incarnations of the German state.[44] Within a generation of the Federal Republic, a new myth had been created – a myth of the West German *Rechtsstaat* – a state defined by the binding of government authority to constitutional principles and guaranteed legal recourse of all citizens and in which the law and the constitution defined identity, both domestically and to the outside world. The strength and depth of this myth were such that the perceived endangering of the Basic Law through the Community polarized public and academic opinion and called upon the FCC to act against the ECJ, thereby potentially undermining another pillar of the West German identity – European integration. Evidently, the centrality of law and the constitution in post-1945 West Germany can in no way be underestimated.

---

[41] For literature on Europeanization and the "top-down" and "bottom-up" dynamics, see as a starting point Kevin Featherstone and Claudio Radaelli, *The Politics of Europeanisation* (Oxford: Oxford University Press, 2003).

[42] See Ulrich Herbert, "Liberalisierung als Lemprozeß: Die Bundesrepublik in der Deutschen Geschichte – Eine Skizze," *Wandlungsprozesse in Westdeutschland: Belastung, Integration, Liberalisierung, 1945 bis 1980*, ed. Ulrich Herbert (Gottingen: Wallstein, 2002), p 49.

[43] See, for instance, "Vorrang der Grundrechte vor dem europäischen Gemeinschaftsrecht," *FAZ*, 15 August 1974.

[44] See Christoph Gusy, *Die Weimarer Reichsverfassung* (Tübingen: Mohr Siebeck, 1997); John, Michael, *Politics and the Law in the Late Nineteenth-Century Germany: The Origins of the Civil Code* (Oxford: Oxford Historical Monographs, 1999); Hesselberger, Dieter, *Das Grundgesetz. Kommentar Fur Die Politische Bildung* (Bonn: Bundeszentrale fur Politische Bildung, 2001), pp 17–20.

From this perspective then, much credence is given to the terminology employed by the Left-liberal thinkers of the Historikerstreit,[45] who talked of a sense of "constitutional patriotism." Based on the writings of Jürgen Habermas, these thinkers argued that a sense of identity could be rationalized through the discussion and codification of common values and principles within a constitutional document. The constitution would then serve as a rallying point for a common identity, usurping less rational media of national identity. While this position was heavily criticized during the debates by those who argued that rationalized identity could never be as powerful or as binding as identities forged on common history, symbols, and myths, this book clearly demonstrates that the attachment to constitutional principles did indeed form the basis of a common West German identity. Yet more interesting is the fact that many West Germans, both in the public and academic arenas, called upon the West German state to act to secure the fundamental rights provisions vis-à-vis the Community. This is much more evocative of Dolf Sternberger's original conception of "constitutional patriotism," which was much more state-centered, with the institutions acting to guarantee the rights and freedoms of the constitution.[46] In fact, both forms of "constitutional patriotism" – one proposed by Sternberger, one by Habermas – are evident in the chosen period of study, with the former being predominant in the earlier years and the Habermasian model at the forefront after the "generational shift" around 1968. At this point, the debate changed to become a fight for fundamental rights as principles and ideals, and not merely freedom and right to be secured by and from the state.

Finally, the book demonstrates the need for a much more thorough inclusion of the European integration process into the writings of national history. Europe's twentieth century has been extraordinarily well documented by historians for many, very obvious reasons, but we all already know that the European Union has enjoyed only a very diminished role in these. The focus for historians has overwhelmingly been on the national dimension and at best expands to a comparative perspective. With an increasing recognition of the impact of Europeanization on the nation-states, this is clearly changing, but slowly. European integration is of fundamental importance to the European nation state. Yet, national histories tend to sideline or relegate the European project as a "foreign policy" initiative, a means to gain economic prosperity or secure peace in Europe. Integration has been much more than this, and as this book has sought to prove, the force of Europeanization has left an indelible mark on areas of West German history that have long been understood as purely national debates. For instance, the discussion about the use of "constitutional

---

[45] The best recollection of the Historikerstreit can be found in Jürgen Peter, *Der Historikerstriet und die Suche nach Einer Nationalen Identität der Achtziger Jahre* (Frankfurt am Main; Berlin; Bern; New York; Paris; Vienna: Peter Lang, 1995).

[46] See Sternberger, "Verfassungspatriotismus, Aus: *Frankfurter Allgemeine Zeitung Vom 23.5.1979*," pp 2–4.

patriotism" emerged from one of the most introspective national debates in modern West German historiography and has since been debated quite apart from the Historikerstreit, broadening out to a European level discussion.[47] At the same time, an understanding of how the FRG received the constitutional practice – comparing the failures of the European legal sphere with the success of the national constitutional order – adds an extra dimension to the questions about how a West German self-understanding was remolded in the postwar period. Clearly, contact with the European legal system promoted a greater sense of self-identification with its national equivalent. European integration thus played a central role not only in redefining the West German state to its neighbors, but also in recasting German identity itself.

[47] See, for instance, the discussions about the value of a European Constitution in terms of identity formation between Jürgen Habermas, "Remarks on Dieter Grimm's 'Does Europe Need a Constitution?'" *European Law Journal* 1 (1995), and Dieter Grimm, "Does Europe Need a Constitution?" *European Law Journal* 1 (1995).

Bibliography

Abelshauser, Werner. *Deutsche Wirtschaftsgeschichte Seit 1945*. Munich: CH Beck Verlag, 2004.

Adenauer, Konrad. *Memoirs 1945–1963*. London: Weidenfeld and Nicolson, 1966.

Albrecht, Willy. "Europakonzeptionen Der Spd in Der Gründungszeit Der Bundesrepublik." *Personen, Soziale Bewegungen, Parteien. Beitrage Zur Neuesten Geschichte. Festschrift Für Hartmut Soell*. Eds. Von Mengersen, Oliver, et al. Heidelburg: Manutius Verlag, 2004. 365–75.

Alkan, Deniz. "Der Duldsame Souverän. Zur Haltung Des Deutschen Bundestags Gegenüber Der Rechtlichen Integration Europas Durch Die Rechtsprechungdes Europäischen Gerichtshofs 1963–1978." Dissertation, Heinrich-Heine-Universität, 2011.

Alter, Karen. *Establishing the Supremacy of European Law: The Making of an International Rule of Law in Europe*. Oxford Studies in European Law. Oxford; New York: Oxford University Press, 2001.

 The European Court's Political Power: Selected Essays. Oxford; New York: Oxford University Press, 2009.

 "Who Are the 'Masters of the Treaty'? European Governments and the European Court of Justice." *International Organisation* 52 1 (1998): 121–47.

Alter, Karen J. "Jurist Advocacy Movements in Europe and the Andes: How Lawyers Help Promote International Legal Integration." *SSRN eLibrary* (2008).

Alter, Karen J, and Sophie Meunier-Aitsahalia. "The Politics of International Regime Complexity Symposium." *Perspectives on Politics* 7 1 (2009): 13–24.

Avenarius, Hermann. *Die Rechtsordnung Der Bundesrepublik Deutschland*. Bonn: Bundeszentrale für Bildung, 2002.

Bahlmann, Kai. "Der Grundrechtsshutz in Der Europäischen Gemeinschaft – Wege Der Verwirklichung." *Europarecht* 17 1 (1982): 1–20.

Bark, Dennis L, and David R Gress. *West Germany: From Shadow to Substance 1945–1963*. London: Blackwell Publishing, 1989.

Bates, Ed. *The Evolution of the European Convention on Human Rights: From Its Inception to the Creation of a Permanent Court of Human Rights*. Oxford; New York: Oxford University Press, 2010.

Bellers, Jürgen. *Ewg Und Die "Gobesberger" Spd*. Siegen: Universität Siegen, 2003.

Benda, Ernst. "Das Spannungsverhåltnis Von Grundrechten Und Übernationalen Recht." *Deutsches Verwaltungsblatt* 10 11 (1974): 389–96.

Bengoetxea, Joxerramon, Neil MacCormick, and Leonor Moral Soriano. "Integration and Integrity in the Legal Reasoning of the European Court of Justice," in De Burca, Grainne & Jhh Weiler (Eds.). *The European Court of Justice*. 2nd ed. Oxford: Oxford University Press, 2005. 43–85.

Bernier, Alexandre. "Constructing and Legitimating. Transnational Jurist Networks and the Making of a Constitutional Practice of European Law, 1950–1970." *Contemporary European History*. 21 3 (2012).

Betts, Paul. "Germany, International Justice and the Twentieth Century" *History and Memory* 17 1/2 (2005): 45–86.

Bignami, Francesca. "Comparative Law and the Rise of the European Court of Justice." *European Union Studies Association*. Delivered on 4 March 2011 at the EUSA meeting in Boston.

Blankenburg, Ethard. "Changes in Political Regimes and Continuity of the Rule of Law in Germany." *Courts, Law and Politics in Comparative Perspective*. Eds. Jacob, H, et al. New Haven, Conn: Yale University Press, 1996. 249–316.

Bleckmann, Albert. "Zur Funktion Des Art 24 Abs 1 Grundgesetzes." *Zeitschrift für ausländisches offentliches Recht und Volkerrecht* (1975): 79–84.

Bockenforde, Ernst-Wolfgang. *Recht, Staat, Freiheit. Studien Zur Rechtsphilosophie, Staatstheorie Und Verfassungsgeschichte*. Frankfurt am Main: Suhrkamp, 1991.

Boerger, Anne. "La Cour De Justice Dans Les Négociations Du Traité De Paris Instituant La Ceca." *Journal of European Integration History* 14 2 (2008): 27.

Brettschneider, Frank, Jan van Deth, and Edeltraud Roller. "Europaische Integration in Der Offentlichen Meinung: Forschungsstand Und Forschungsperspektiven." *Europaische Integration in Der Offentlichen Meinung*. Eds. Brettschneider, Frank, Jan van Deth and Edeltraud Roller. Opladen: Leske & Budrich, 2003. 9–28.

Bryde, Brun-Otto. "Fundamental Rights as Guidelines and Inspiration." *Wisconsin International Law Journal* 25 2 (2006): 189–208.

Bucher, Ewald. "Verfassungsrechtliche Probleme Des Gemeinsamen Marktes." *Neue Juristische Wochenschrift* 10 (1957): 850–2.

Bulmer, Simon, Charlie Jeffery, and Stephen Padgett. *Rethinking Germany and Europe: Democracy and Diplomacy in a Semi-Sovereign State*. Houndmills, UK; New York: Palgrave Macmillan, 2010.

Bulmer, Simon, Charlie Jeffery, and William E Paterson. *Germany's European Diplomacy: Shaping the Regional Milieu*. Issues in German Politics. Manchester, UK; New York: Manchester University Press; distributed exclusively in the United States by St. Martin's Press, 2000.

Bulmer, Simon, and William Paterson. *The Federal Republic of Germany and the European Community*. London: Allen and Unwin, 1987.

Bulmer, Simon, and William E Paterson. "Germany and the European Union: From 'Tamed Power' to Normalized Power?" *International Affairs* 86 5 (2010): 1051–73.

Bülow, Erich. "Das Verhaltnis Des Rechts Der Europaischen Gemeinschaften Zum Nationalen Recht." Aktuelle Fragen des europaischen Gemeinschaftsrechts, Gemeinschaftsrecht und nationales Rechts Niederlassungsfreiheit und Rechtsangleichung – Europarechtliches Kolloqium. Ed. Hans Peter Ipsen. Stuttgart: Enke, 1965.

Burley, Anne Marie, and Walter Mattli. "Europe before the Court: A Political Theory of Legal Integration." *International Organisation* 47 (1993): 41–76.

Cappelletti, Mauro, Monica Seccombe, and Joseph Weiler. *Integration through Law: Europe and the American Federal Experience*. Series a, Law/European University Institute = Series a, Droit/Institut Universitaire Européen. Berlin; New York: W de Gruyter, 1985.

Castiglione, Dario, Justus Schönlau, and Chris Longman. *Constitutional Politics in the European Union: The Convention Moment and Its Aftermath*. New York: Palgrave Macmillan, 2008.

Christoffersen, Jonas. *The European Court of Human Rights between Law and Politics*. New book ed. New York: Oxford University Press, 2011.

Cohen, Antonin. "Constitutionalism without Constitution; Transnational Elites between Political Mobilization and Legal Expertise (1940–1960)." *Law and Social Inquiry* 1 (2007): 109–35.

Scarlet Robes, Dark Suits: The Social Recruitment of the European Court of Justice. Florence: European University Institute (EUI), Robert Schuman Centre of Advanced Studies (RSCAS), 2008. Conant, Lisa J *Justice Contained: Law and Politics in the European Union*. Ithaca, N.Y.: Cornell University Press, 2002.

Conradt, David P. *The German Polity*. Comparative Studies of Political Life. New York: Longman, 1978.

Council of Europe. Directorate of Human Rights. "Information Sheet." 23 vols. Strasbourg: The Directorate, 1984.

Craig, PP, and G De Búrca. *The Evolution of Eu Law*. 2nd ed. Oxford; New York: Oxford University Press, 2011.

Craig, Paul, and Grainne De Burca. *Eu Law. Text, Cases and Materials*. 4th ed. Oxford: Oxford University Press, 2007.

Dahrendorf, Ralf. Gesellschaft and Freiheit. 2nd ed. Munich: R Piper Verlag & Co, 1963. *Society and Democracy in Germany*. London: Weidenfeld & Nicolson, 1967.

Davies, Bill. "Constitutionalising the European Community: West Germany between Legal Sovereignty and European Integration, 1949–1975." King's College London, 2007. "Meek Acceptance? The West German Ministeries' Reaction to the Van Gend En Loos and Costa Decisions." *Journal of European Integration History* 14 2 (2008): 20.

Dehousse, Renaud. *The European Court of Justice*. London: MacMillan Palgrave, 1998.

Dinan, Desmond. *Europe Recast: A History of European Union*. Basingstoke & New York: Palgrave MacMillan, 2004. *Ever Closer Union: An Introduction to European Integration*. 4th ed. Boulder, Colo.: Lynne Rienner Publishers, 2010. *Origins and Evolution of the European Union*. The New European Union Series. Oxford; New York: Oxford University Press, 2006.

Drzemczewski, Andrew "Protection of Fundamental Human Rights in the European Community." *Notre Dame International Law Journal* 1 57 (1983).

Dyevre, Arthur. "The German Federal Constitutional Court and European Judicial Politics." *West European Politics* 34 2 (2011): 346–61.

Egan, Michelle P, Neill Nugent, and William E Paterson. *Research Agendas in Eu Studies: Stalking the Elephant*. Palgrave Studies in European Union Politics. Basingstoke; New York: Palgrave Macmillan, 2010.

Ehle, Deitriche. "Commentary to European Court of the Justice Decision 26/62." *Neue Juristische Wochenschrift* 21 (1963): 974–6.

Ehle, Dietrich. "Verhaltnis Des Europaischen Gemeinschaftsrechts Zum Nationalen Recht." *Neue Juristische Wochenschrift* 50 (1964): 2331–3.

Eichenberg, Richard C, and Russell J Dalton. "Europeans and the European Community: The Dynamics of Public Support for the European Integration." *International Organisation* 47 4 (1993): 507–34.

Erler, Georg, and Werner Theime. "Das Grundgesetz Und Die Offentliches Gewalt Internationaler Staatengemeinschaften." *Veroffentlichungen der Vereinigung der Deutschen Staatsrechtslehrer* 18 (1959).

Espagne, Michel, and Michael Werner. *Les Relations Interculturelles Dans L'espace Franco-Allemand (Xviiie Et Xixe Siècle)*. Transferts. Paris: Editions Recherche sur les civilisations, 1988.

Featherstone, Kevin, and Claudio Radaelli. *The Politics of Europeanisation*. Oxford: Oxford University Press, 2003.

Feest, Johannes. "Die Bundesrichter: Herkunft, Karriere Und Auswahl Der Juristischen Elite." *Beitrage Zur Analyse Der Deutschen Oberschicht*. Ed. Zapf, Manfred. 2nd ed. Munich: R Piper & Co Verlag, 1965. 95–113.

Fischer, Fritz. *Bündnis Der Eliten: Zur Kontinuität D. Machtstrukturen in Deutschland 1871–1945*. Düsseldorf: Droste, 1979.

  Griff Nach Der Weltmacht; Die Kriegszielpolitik Des Kaiserlichen Deutschland 1914/18. Düsseldorf: Droste, 1961.

Franklin, Mark, Michael Marsh, and Lauren McLaren. "Uncorking the Bottle: Popular Opposition to European Unification in the Wake of Maastricht." *Journal of Common Market Studies* 32 1994 (1994): 455–72.

Frevert, Ute. "Europeanizing Germany's Twentieth Century" *History and Memory* 17 1/2 (2005): 87/116.

Fuss, Ernst-Werner. "Rechtsstaatliche Bilanz Der Europaeischen Gemeinschaften." *Recht Und Staat: Festschrift Für Günther Küchenhoff Zum 65. Geburtstag Am 21.8.1972*. Eds. Hablitzel, Hans and Michael Wollenschlager. Berlin: Duncker & Humblot, 1972. 781–803.

Gabel, Matthew. "European Integration, Voters, and National Politics." *Contentious European: Protest and Politics in an Emerging Polity*. Eds. Imig, Doug and Sidney Tarrow. Lanham, Md.: Rowman and Littlefield, 2001.

Garrett, Geoffrey. "The Politics of Legal Integration in the European Union." *International Organisation* 49 (1995): 171–81.

Garrett, Geoffrey, Daniel R Keleman, and Heiner Schulz. "The European Court of Justice, National Governments and Legal Integration in the European Union." *International Organisation* 52 1 (1998): 149–76.

Geyer, Michael. "Historical Fictions of Autonomy and the Europeanization of National History." *Central European History* 22 3 (1989): 316–42.

Gillingham, John. *European Integration, 1950–2003: Superstate or New Market Economy?* Cambridge: Cambridge University Press, 2003.

Glencross, Andrew. *What Makes the Eu Viable? European Integration in the Light of the Antebellum Us Experience*. Basingstoke, England; New York: Palgrave Macmillan, 2009.

Glencross, Andrew, and Alexandre H Trechsel. *Eu Federalism and Constitutionalism: The Legacy of Altiero Spinelli*. Lanham, Md.: Lexington Books, 2010.

Goldhaber, Michael D. *A People's History of the European Court of Human Rights*. New Brunswick, N.J.: Rutgers University Press, 2007.

Goldstein, Leslie Friedman. *Constituting Federal Sovereignty: The European Union in Comparative Context.* The Johns Hopkins Series in Constitutional Thought. Baltimore: Johns Hopkins University Press, 2001.

Golub, Jonathan. "The Politics of Judicial Discretion: Rethinking the Interaction between National Courts and the European Court of Justice." *West European Politics* 19 (April 1996): 360–85.

Gordon, Robert W. "Critical Legal Studies." *Legal Studies Forum* 10 3 (1986): 335–40.

——— "Recent Trends in Legal Historiography." *Law Library Journal* 69 (1976): 462–8.

Gortemaker, Manfred. *Kleine Geschichte Der Bundesrepublik Deutschland.* Munich: CH Beck Verlag, 2005.

Green, Andrew Wilson. *Political Integration by Jurisprudence: The Work of the Court of Justice of the European Communities in European Political Integration.* Amsterdam: AW Sijthoff-Leyden, 1969.

Grewe, Wilhelm. "Die Auswärtige Gewalt Der Bundesrepublik." *Veroffentlichungen der Vereinigung der Deutschen Staatsrechtslehrer* 12 (1954): 129–78.

Griffiths, Richard T. *Europe's First Constitution. The European Political Community 1952–1954.* London: Federal Trust, 2000.

Grimm, Dieter. "Does Europe Need a Constitution?" *European Law Journal* 1 (1995): 282–301.

Gusy, Christoph. *Die Weimarer Reichsverfassung.* Tübingen: Mohr Siebeck, 1997.

Haas, Ernst. *The Uniting of Europe: Political, Social and Economic Forces 1950–1957.* Stanford, Calif.: Stanford Press, 1968.

Haas, Peter M. "Introduction: Epistemic Communities and International Policy Coordination." *International Organization* 46 1 (1992): 1–35.

Habermas, Jurgen. "Remarks on Dieter Grimm's "Does Europe Need a Constitution?"" *European Law Journal* 1 (1995): 303–7.

——— "Staatsburgerschaft Und Nationale Identitat." *Faktizitat Und Geltung.* Ed. Habermas, Jurgen. Frankfurt: Suhrkamp, 1992.

Hallstein, Walter. *Europe in the Making.* London: Allen and Unwin, 1972.

Haltern, Ulrich. "Integration Durch Recht." *Theorien Der Europaischen Integration.* Eds. Bieling, Hans Jurgen and Marika Lerch. Wiesbaden: VS Verlag fur Sozialwissenschaften, 2005. 399–426.

Hanrieder, Wolfram F. *Germany, America, Europe: Forty Years of German Foreign Policy.* New Haven, Conn; London: Yale University Press, 1989.

Hartweg, Frederic. "Kurt Schumacher, Die Spd Und Die Protestantisch Orientierte Opposition Gegen Adenauers Deutschland – Und Europapolitik." *Kurt Schumacher Als Deutscher Und Europaischer Sozialist.* Ed. Friedrich-Ebert-Stiftung. Bonn: Friedrich-Ebert-Stiftung, 1988. 188–207.

Heine, Friedrich. *Dr. Kurt Schumacher: Ein Demokratischer Sozialist Europaischer Pragung.* Gottingen: Musterschmidt Verlag, 1969.

Herbert, Ulrich. "Liberalisierung Als Lemprozeß. Die Bundesrepublik in Der Deutschen Geschichte – Eine Skizze." *Wandlungsprozesse in Westdeutschland. Belastung, Integration, Liberalisierung, 1945 Bis 1980.* Ed. Herbert, Ulrich. Gottingen: Wallstein, 2002. 7–49.

Hesselberger, Dieter. *Das Grundgesetz. Kommentar Fur Die Politische Bildung.* Bonn: Bundeszentrale fur Politische Bildung, 2001.

Hilf, Meinhard. "Die Gemeinsame Grundrechtserklarung Des Europaischen Parlaments, Des Rates Und Der Kommission Vom 5. April 1977." *Europäische Grundrechte Zeitschrift* 4 (1977): 158–61.

"Sekundares Gemeinschaftsrecht Und Deutsche Grundrechte. Zum Beschluss Des Bundesverfassungsgericht Vom 29. Mai 1974." *Zeitschrift für auslåndisches offentliches Recht und Volkerrecht* (1975): 51–66.

Hirschman, Albert. "Exit, Voice, and the Fate of the German Democratic Republic: An Essay in Conceptual History." *World Politics* 45 2 (1993): 173–202.

Hix, Simon. *The Political System of the European Union*. London: MacMillan Palgrave, 1999.

Hoffmann, Stefan-Ludwig. *Human Rights in the Twentieth Century*. Cambridge; New York: Cambridge University Press, 2010.

Humphreys, Peter. *Media and Media Policy in West Germany: The Pess and Broadcasting since 1945*. Leamington Spa: Berg, 1989.

Hyde-Price, Adrian. *Germany and European Order. Enlarging Nato and the Eu* Manchester: Manchester University Press, 2000.

Inglehart, Ronald, and Karlheinz Reif. *Eurobarometer: The Dynamics of European Public Opinion: Essays in Honour of Jacques-René Rabier*. London: Macmillan, 1991.

Institut für Staatslehre und Politik (Mainz Germany). *Der Kampf Um Den Wehrbeitrag*. Veröffentlichungen Des Instituts Für Staatslehre Und Politik in Mainz. 2 vols. München: Isar Verlag, 1952.

Ipsen, Hans Peter. "Bverfg Versus Eugh Re "Grundrechte," Zum Beschuß Des Zweiten Senats Des Bundesverfassungsgerichts Vom 29 Mai 1974 (Bverfge Bd, 37 S, 271)." *Europarecht* 14 3 (1975): 223–38.

———. *Europaisches Gemeinschaftsrecht*. Tubingen: JCB Mohr (Paul Siebeck), 1972.

———. "Verfassungsperspektiven Der Europaischen Gemeinschaften – Vortag Gehalten Am 17 April 1970." Lecture at the *Berliner Juristischen Gesellschaft*. Berlin: Walter de Gruyter, 1970.

Ipsen, Hans Peter, and Gert Nicolaysen. "Haager Kongreß Fur Europarecht Und Bericht Uber Die Aktuelle Entwicklung Des Gemeinschaftsrechts." *Neue Juristische Wochenschrift* 17 1964 (1964a): 339–44.

Jachtenfuchs, Markus. "The Governance Approach to European Integration." *Journal of Common Market Studies* 39 (2001): 245–64.

Jaenicke, Gunther. "Das Verhaltnis Zwischen Gemeinschaftsrecht Und Nationalem Recht in Der Agrarmarktorganisation Der Europaischen Wirtschaftsgemeinschaft." *Zeitschrift fur auslandisches offentliches Recht und Volkerrecht* (1963): 485–535.

John, Anke. "Konzeptionen Fur Eine Eg-Reform: Der Europaische Verfassungsdiskurs in Der Bundesrepublik 1981–1986." *Die Bundesrepublik Deutschland Und Die Europaische Einigung 1949–2000: Politische Akteure, Gesellschaftliche Krafte Und Internationale Erfahrungen: Festschrift Fur Wolf D Gruner Zum 60. Geburtstag*. Eds. Konig, Marieke and Matthias Schulz. Stuttgart: Franz Steiner Verlag, 2004. 559–76.

John, Michael. *Politics and the Law in the Late Nineteenth-Century Germany: The Origins of the Civil Code*. Oxford: Oxford Historical Monographs, 1989.

Kaelble, Paul W. "Europabewusstsein, Gesellschaft Und Geschichte: Forschungsstand Und Forschungschancen." *Europa Im Blick Der Historiker. Europaische Integration Im 20. Jarhundert: Bewusstsein Und Institutionen*. Eds. Hundemann, Rainer, Hartmut Kaelble and Klaus Schwabe. Munich: R Piper & Co Verlag, 1995. 1–29.

Kahn, Paul W. *The Cultural Study of Law: Reconstructing Legal Scholarship*. Chicago: University of Chicago Press, 1999.

Kaiser, Joseph, and Peter Badura. "Bewahrung and Veränderung Demokratischer Und Rechstaatlicher Verfassungsstruktur in Den Internationalen Gemeinschaften." *Veroffentlichungen der Vereinigung der Deutschen Staatsrechtslehrer* 23 (1964): 147–287.

Kaiser, Wolfram. *Christian Democracy and the Origins of European Union.* New Studies in European History. Cambridge; New York: Cambridge University Press, 2007.

"Institutionelle Ordnung Und Strategische Interessen: Die Christdemokraten Und 'Europa' Nach 1945." *Das Europaische Projekt Zu Beginn Des 21. Jahrhunderts.* Ed. Loth, Wilfried. Opladen: Leske & Budrich, 2001. 81–98.

Kaiser, Wolfram, Brigitte Leucht, and Morten Rasmussen. *The History of the European Union: Origins of a Trans- and Supranational Polity 1950–72.* Routledge/Uaces Contemporary European Studies Series 7. New York: Routledge, 2009.

Katzenstein, Peter J. *Policy and Politics in West Germany: The Growth of a Semi-Sovereign State.* Philadelphia: Temple University Press, 1987.

Tamed Power: Germany in Europe. Ithaca, N.Y.: Cornell University Press, 1997.

Kauders, Anthony. "Democratisation as Cultural History, Or: When Is (West) German Democracy Fulfilled?" *German History* 25 2 (2007): 240–57.

Keller, Helen, and Alec Stone-Sweet. *A Europe of Rights: The Impact of the Echr on National Legal Systems.* Oxford; New York: Oxford University Press, 2008.

Kennedy, Duncan. *The Rise and Fall of Classical Legal Thought.* Washington, DC: Beard Books, 1975.

"Toward an Historical Understanding of Legal Consciousness: The Case of Classical Legal Thought in America, 1850–1940." *Research in Law and Society* 3 (1980): 3–24.

"Two Globalizations of Law and Legal Thought: 1850–1968." *Suffolk University Law Review* 36 3 (2003): 631–79.

Kettenacker, Lothar. *Germany since 1945.* Oxford: Oxford University Press, 1997.

Kiefer, Marcus. *Auf Der Suche Nach Nationaler Identitaat Und Wegen Zur Deutschen Einheit: Die Deutsche Frage in Der Uberregionalen Tages-Und Wochenpresse Der Bundesrepublik 1949–1955.* 2nd ed. Frankfurt am Main: Peter Lang, 1993.

Kirchheimer, Otto. *Political Justice; the Use of Legal Procedure for Political Ends.* Princeton, N.J.: Princeton University Press, 1961.

Klein, Eckart. "Stellungnahme Aus Der Sicht Des Deutschen Verfassungsrechts." *Zeitschrift fur auslandisches offentliches Recht un Volkerrecht* 1975 (1975): 67–78.

Kleßmann, Christoph. *Die Doppelte Staatsgrundung. Deutsche Geschichte 1945–1955.* 5th ed. Gottingen: Vandenhoek & Roprecht, 1991.

Knoch, Habbo. *Bürgersinn Mit Weltgefühl. Politische Moral Und Solidarischer Protest in Den Sechziger Und Siebziger Jahren: Politische Kultur Und Solidarischer Protest in Den Sechziger Und Siebziger Jahren.* Goettingen: Wallstein Verlag, 2007.

Kokott, Julianne. "German Constitutional Jurisprudence and European Legal Integration: Part 1." *European Public Law* 2 2 (1996a): 237–69.

"German Constitutional Jurisprudence and European Legal Integration: Part Ii." *European Public Law* 2 3 (1996b): 413–36.

"Report on Germany." *The European Courts and National Courts – Doctrine and Jurisprudence: Legal Change in Its Social Context.* Eds. Slaughter, Anne-Marie, Alex Stone-Sweet and JHH Weiler. Oxford: Hart Publishing, 1998. 77–132.

Kolinsky, Eva. "The Euro-Germans: National Identity and European Integration in Germany." *Europeans on Europe: Transnational Visions of a New Continent.* Eds. Maclean, Mairi and Jolyon Howorth. London: MacMillan, 1992. 160–83.

Kommers, Donald P. "The Federal Constitutional Court in the German Political System." *Comparative Political Studies* 26 4 (1994): 470–92.
  Judicial Politics in West Germany: A Study of the Federal Constitutional Court. Beverly Hills, Calif.; London: Sage Publishing, 1976.
Lindseth, Peter L. *Power and Legitimacy: Reconciling Europe and the Nation-State.* Oxford; New York: Oxford University Press, 2010.
Lipgens, Walter. *A History of European Integration.* Vol. 1. The Formation of the European Unity Movement 1945–50. Oxford: Clarendon Press, 1982.
Löffler, Bernhard. *Soziale Markwirtschaft Und Administrative Praxis, Das Bundeswirtschafts-ministerium Unter Ludwig Erhard.* Stuttgart: Franz Steiner Verlag, 2002.
Loth, Wilfried. "Konrad Adenauer and Die Europäische Einigung." *Die Bundesrepublik Deutschland Und Die Europäische Einigung 1949–2000: Politische Akteure, Gesellschaftliche Kräfte Un Internationale Erfahrungen: Festschrift Für Wolf D Gruner Zum 60. Geburtstag.* Eds. Konig, Marieke and Matthias Schulz. Stuttgart: Franz Steiner Verlag, 2004. 39–60.
Madsen, Michael Risk. "From Cold War Instrument to Supreme European Court: The European Court at the Crossroads of International and National Law and Politics." *Law and Social Inquiry* 1 (2007): 137–59.
Majone, Giandomenico. *Evidence, Argument and the Persuasion in the Policy Process.* New Haven, Conn.; London: Yale Univesity Press, 1989.
Mann, Clarence J. *The Function of Judicial Decision in European Economic Integration.* The Hague: Martinus Nijhoff Publishers, 1972.
Mann, Golo. *Deutsche Geschichte Des 19, Und 20, Jahrhunderts.* Frankfurt am Main: Fischer Verlag, 2004.
Mattli, Walter, and Anne-Marie Slaughter. "Law and Politics in the European Union: A Reply to Garrett." *International Organisation* 49 1 (1995): 183–90.
  "Revisiting the European Court of Justice." *International Organisation* 52 1 (1998): 177–209.
  "The Role of National Courts in the Process of European Integration: According for Judicial Preferences and Constraints." *The European Courts and the National Courts – Doctrine and Jurisprudence: Legal Change in Its Social Context.* Eds. Slaughter, Anne-Marie, Alex Stone-Sweet and JHH Weiler. Oxford: Hart Publishing, 1998. 253–76.
Mayer, Franz C, and Jan Palmowski. "European Identities and the Eu – the Ties That Bind the Peoples of Europe." *JCMS: Journal of Common Market Studies* 42 3 (2004): 573–98.
Medrano, Juan Diez. *Framing Europe: Attitudes to Europe Integration in Germany, Spain, and the United Kingdom.* Princeton, N.J.: Princeton University Press, 2003.
Meier, Gert. "Bundesverfassungsgerichtsbeschluß Anmerkung." *Neue Juristische Wochenschrift* 48 (1974): 1704–5.
  "Commentary to European Court of Justice Decision 29/69." *Deutsches Verwaltungsblatt* (1970): 614–15.
Meinecke, Friedrich. *Die Deutsche Katastrophe; Betrachtungen Und Erinnerungen.* Zürich: Aero-verlag, 1946.
Mény, Yves. ""De La Democracie En Europe: Old Concepts and New Challenges." *Journal of Common Market Studies* 41 2003 (2003): 1–13.
Menzel, Eberhard. "Die Auswärtige Gewalt Der Bundesrepublik." *Veroffentlichungen der Vereinigung der Deutschen Staatsrechtslehrer* 12 (1954).
Merkl, Peter. "The German Response to the Challenge of Extremist Parties 1949–1994." *The Postwar Transformation of Germany: Democracy, Prosperity and Nationhood.* Eds. Brady,

John S, Beverly Crawford and Sarah Elise Wiliarty. Ann Arbor: University of Michigan, 1999.

Milward, Alan S. *The Reconstruction of Western Europe, 1945–51*. London: Methuen, 1984.

Moeller, Robert G. *War Stories: The Search for a Usable Past in the Federal Republic of Germany*. London: University of California Press, 2003.

Moravcsik, Andrew. *The Choice for Europe: Social Purpose and the State Power from Messina to Maastricht*. London: UCL Press, 1998.

"In Defence of The "Democratic Deficit": Reassessing Legitimacy in the European Union." *Journal of Common Market Studies* 40 (2002): 603–24.

"Negotiating the Single European Act: National Interests and Conventianal Statecrafft in the European Community." *International Organisation* 45 (1991): 19–54.

Mosler, Hermann. "Begriff Und Gegenstand Des Europarechts." *Zeitschrift fur auslandisches offentliches Recht un Volkerrecht* (1968): 481–502.

"Internationale Organisation Und Staatsverfassung." *Rechtsfragen Der Internationalen Organisation, Festschrift Für Hans Wehberg Zu Seinem 70. Geburtstag.* Eds. Schätzel, Walter and Hans-Jürgen Schlochauer. Frankfurt am Main: Vittorio Klostermann, 1956. 273–300.

"Zur Anwendung Der Grundsatzartikel Des Vertrages Über Die Europâische Gemeinschaft Fûr Kohle Und Stahl." *Zeitschrift für ausländisches öffentliches Recht und Völkerrecht* (1957): 407–27.

Mössner, Jörg Manfred. "Einschränkungen Von Grundrechten Durch Ewg-Recht?" *Aussenwirtschaftsdienst des Betriebs-Beraters* 4 (1971): 610–13.

Müller, Wolfgang. *Die Europapolitischen Vorstellungen Von Kurt Schumacher 1945–1952: Eine Alternative Für Deutschland Und Europa?* Stuttgart: Ibidem Verlag, 2003.

Münch, Fritz. "Internationale Organisationen Mit Hoheitsrechten." *Rechtsfragen Der Internationel Organisation. Festschrift Für Hans Wehberg Zu Seinem 70, Geburtstag.* Eds. Schätzel, Walter and Hans-Jürgen Schlochauer. Frankfurt am Main: Vittorio Klostermann, 1956. 301–23.

Nicholls, AJ. *The Bonn Republic: West Germany Democracy 1945–1990*. London: Longman, 1995.

Noelle-Neumann, Elisabeth. "Phantom Europe: Thirty Years of Survey Research on German Attitudes toward European Integration." *Contemporary Perspective on European Integration: Attitudes, Non-Governmental Behavious, and Collective Decision Making.* Ed. Hurwitz, Leano. London: Aldwych Press, 1980. 53–74.

Ophüls, Carl Friedrich. "Gerichtsbarkeit Und Rechtsprechung Im Schumanplan." *Neue Juristische Wochenschrift* 4 8 (1951a): 693–7.

"Juristische Grundgedanken Des Schumanplans." *Neue Juristische Wochenschrift* 4 8 (1951b): 289–92.

"Quellen Und Aufbau Des Europäischen Gemeinschaftsrechts." *Neue Juristische Wochenschrift* 16 (1963): 1697–701.

"Über Die Auslegung Der Europäischen Gemeinschaftsverträge." *Wirtschaft, Gesellschaft Und Kultur. Festgabe Für Alfred Müller-Armack.* Eds. Greiß, Franz. and Fritz W Meyer. Berlin: Duncker & Humblot, 1961.

Parsons, Craig. "Showing Ideas as Causes: The Origins of the European Union." *International Organisation* 56 1 (2002): 47–84.

Paterson, William E. *The Spd and European Integration*. London: Saxon House/Lexington Books, 1974.

Pendas, Devin O. *The Frankfurt Auschwitz Trial, 1963–1965: Genocide, History, and the Limits of the Law.* Cambridge: Cambridge University Press, 2006.

Pescatore, Pierre. "Aspects of the the Court of Justice of the European Communities of Interest from the Point of View of International Law." *Zeitschrift fur auslandisches offentliches Recht un Volkerrecht* (1972): 239–52.

Peter, Jürgen *Der Historikerstriet Und Die Suche Nach Einer Nationalen Identität Der Achtziger Jahre.* Frankfurt am Main; Berlin; Bern; New York; Paris; Vienna: Peter Lang, 1995.

Phelan, Will. "Why Do Eu Member States Offer a 'Constitutional' Obedience to Eu Obligations? Encompassing Domestic Institutions and Costly International Obligations." *TCD Institute for International Integration Studies* 256 (June 2008).

Pigorsch, Wolfgang. *Die Einordnung Völkerechtlicher Normen in Das Recht Der Bundesrepublik Deutschland. Eine Studie Ze Den Artikeln 25, 59 Und 79 Des Grundgesetzes Für Die Bundesrepublik Vom 23. Mai 1949.* Hamburg: Hansischer Gildenverlag, 1959.

Pulzer, Peter. *German Politics 1945–1995.* Oxford: Oxford University Press, 1995.

Radbruch, Gustav. "Gesetzliches Unrecht Und Übergesetzliches Recht." *Süddeutschen Juristenzeitung* (1946): 105–8.

Rasmussen, Hjalte. *On Law and Policy in the European Court of Justice: A Comparative Study in Judicial Policymaking.* Dordrecht; Boston; Lancaster: Martinus Nijhoff Publishers, 1986.

Rasmussen, Morten. "Constructing and Deconstructing European 'Constitutional' European Law. Some Reflections on How to Study the History of European Law." *Europe: The New Legal Realism.* Ed. Henning Koch, Karsten Hagel-Sørensen, Ulrich Haltern and Joseph Weiler (Eds.). Aarhus: DJØF Publishing, 2010. 639–60.

"Exploring the Secret History of the Legal Service of the European Executives, 1952–1967." *Contemporary European History.* Forthcoming.

Riegel, Reinhard. "Bundesverfassungsgerichtsbeschluß Anmerkung." *Neue Juristische Wochenschrift* 48 (1974a): 2176–7.

"Zum Problem Der Allgemeinem Rechtsgrundsätze Und Grundrechte Im Gemeinschaftsrecht." *Neue Juristische Wochenschrift* 36 (1974b): 1585–90.

"Zum Verhältnis Von Ewg-Recht Und Staatlichem Verfassungsrecht." *Bayerische Verwaltungsblätter* 4 (1973): 96–100.

Riese, Otto. "Über Den Rechtsschutz Von Privatpersonen Und Unternehmen in Der Europäischen Wirtschaftsgemeinschaft." *Probleme Der Europäischen Rechts. Festschift Für Walter Hallstein Zu Seinem 65. Geburtstag.* Eds. Caemmerer, Ernst, Hans-Jürgen Schlochauer and Ernst Steindorff. Frankfurt am Main: Vittorio Klostermann, 1966. 414–30.

Ritter, Gerhard. *Europa Und Die Deutsche Frage; Betrachtungen Über Die Geschichtliche Eigenart Des Deutschen Staatsdenkens.* München: Münchner Verlag, 1948.

Rittstieg, Helmut. "Commentary to European Court of Justice Decision 11/70." *Aussenwirtschaftsdienst des Betriebs-Beraters* 4 (1971): 183–5.

Rogosch, Detlef. "Sozialdemokratie Zwischen Nationaler Orientierung Und Westintegration 1945–1957." *Die Bundesrepublik Deutschland Und Die Europäische Einigung 1949–2000: Politische Akteure, Gesellschaftliche Kräfte Und Internationale Erfahrungen: Festschrift Für Wolf D Gruner Zum 60. Geburtstag.* Eds. Konig, Marieke and Matthias Schulz. Stuttgart: Franz Steiner Verlag, 2004. 287–310.

Rupp, Hans Heinrich. "Die Grundrechte Und Das Europäische Gemeinschaftsrecht." *Neue Juristische Wochenschrift* 9 (1970): 353–9.

Säcker, Horst *Das Bundesverfassungsgericht*. Bonn: Bundeszentrale für politische Bildung, 2003.

Sadurski, Wojciech. ""Solange, Chapter 3": Constitutional Courts in Central Europe – Democracy – European Union." *EUI Working Paper 2006/40* (2006).

Scharpf, Fritz W. "The Joint Decision Trap: Lessons from German Federalism and European Integration." *Public Administration* 66 3 (1988): 239–78.

Scheingold, Stuart. *The Rule of Law in European Integration: The Path of the Schuman Plan*. New Haven, Conn.; London: Yale University Press, 1965.

Scheingold, Stuart, and Leon N Lindberg. *Europe's World-Be Polity: Patterns of Change in the European Community*. Englewood Cliffs, N.J.; Hemel Hempstead: Prentice-Hall, 1970.

Scheuring, Dieter H. "The Approach to European Law in German Jurisprudence." *German Law Journal* 5 6 (2004): 703–19.

Schilmar, Boris. *Der Europadiskurs Im Deutschen Exil 1933–1945*. Munich: Oldenbourg Wissenschaftsverlag, 2004.

Schimmelfennig, Frank. "Competition and Community: Constitutional Courts, Rhetorical Action, and the Institutionalization of Human Rights in the European Union." *Journal of European Public Policy* 13 8 (2006): 1247–64.

Schlochauer, Hans Jürgen. "Das Verhältnis Des Rechts Der Europäischen Wirtschaftsgemeinschaft Zu Den Nationalen Rechtsordnung Der Mitgliedstaaten." *Archiv des Völkerrechts* 11 1 (1963): 1–34.

——— "Der Gerichtshof Der Europäischen Gemeinschaften Als Integrationsfaktor." *Probleme Der Europäischen Rechts. Festschrift Für Walter Hallstein Zu Seinem 65. Geburtstag*. Eds. Caemmerer, Ernst, Hans-Jürgen Schlochauer and Ernst Steindorff. Frankfurt am Main: Vittorio Klostermann, 1966. 431–52.

——— "Der Übernationale Charakter Der Europäischen Gemeinschaft Für Kohle Und Stahl." *Juristen-Zeitung* 10 (1951): 289–90.

——— "Rechtsformen Der Europäischen Ordnung." *Archiv des Völkerrechts* 5 (1955): 40–62.

——— "Zur Frage Der Rechtsnatur Der Europäischen Gemeinschaft Für Kohle Und Stahle." *Rechtsfragen Der Internationalem Organisation, Festschrift Für Hans Wehberg Zum Seinem 70. Geburtstag*. Eds. Schätzel, Walter and Hans-Jürgen Schlochauer. Frankfurt am Main: Vittorio Klostermann, 1956. 361–73.

Schneider, Michael. *Demokratie in Gefahr? Der Konflikt Um Die Notstandsgesetze Sozialdemokratie, Gewerkschaften Und Intellektueller Protest 1958–1968*. Bonn: Neue Gesellschaft, 1986.

Schuppert, Gunnar Folke. "Public Law: Towards a Post-National Model." *Germany, Europe and the Politics of Constraint*. Eds. Dyson, K and KH Goetz. Oxford: Published for the British Academy by Oxford University Press, 2003. 109–25.

Schwarz, Hans-Peter. *Adenauer: Der Staatsman: 1952–1967*. Stuttgart: Deutsche Verlags-Anstalt, 1991.

Scott, James Brown. *James Madison's Notes of Debates in the Federal Convention of 1787 and Their Relation to a More Perfect Society of Nations*. New York: Oxford University Press, American branch, 1918.

Seuffert, Walter. "Grundgesetz Und Gemeinschaftsrecht." *Konkretionen Politischer Theorie Un Praxis*. Eds. Arndt, Adolf, et al. Stuttgart: Ernst Klett Verlag, 1972. 169–87.

Shapiro, Martin M, and Alec Stone-Sweet. *On Law, Politics, and Judicialization*. Oxford; New York: Oxford University Press, 2002.

Slater, Martin. "Political Elites, Popular Indifference and Community Building." *The European Community: Past, Present and Future*. Ed. Tsoukalis, Loukas. Oxford: Blackwell Publishing, 1983. 69–93.

Sontheimer, Kurt. *Die Adenauer-Ära*. Munich: Deutscher Taschenbuch Verlag, 2003.

Sontheimer, Kurt, and Wilhelm Bleek. *Grundzüge Des Politischen Systems Der Bundesrepublik Deutschland*. Bonn: Bundeszentrale für politische Bildung, 2000.

Spiermann, Ole. "The Other Side of the Story: An Unpopular Essay on the Making of the European Community Legal Order." *European Journal of International Law* 10 4 (1999): 763–89.

Stein, Eric. "Lawyers, Judges and the Making of a Transnational Constitution." *American Journal of International Law* 75 1 (1981): 1–27.

"Toward Supremacy of Treaty – Constitution by Judicial Fiat: On the Margin of the Costa Case." *Michigan Law Review* 63 (1964): 491–518.

Sternberger, Dolf. "Verfassungspatriotismus, Aus: Frankfurter Allgemeine Zeitung Vom 23.5.1979." *Verfassungspatriotismus Als Ziel Politischer Bildung?* Eds. Behrmann, Günter C and Siegfried Schiele. Schwalbach: Wochenschau Verlag, 1979. 2–4.

Stirk, Peter MR. *A History of European Integration since 1914*. New York: Pinter, 1996.

Stone-Sweet, Alec. "Constitutional Dialogue in the European Community." *The European Courts and National Courts – Doctrine and Jurisprudence: Legal Change in Its Social Context*. Eds. Slaughter, Anne-Marie, Alex Stone-Sweet and JHH Weiler. Oxford: Hart Publishing, 1998. 305–30.

Governing with Judges: Constitutional Politics in Europe. Oxford: Oxford University Press, 2000.

"Path Dependence, Precedent and Judicial Power." *On Law, Politics, and Judicialization*. Eds. Shapiro, Martin and Alex Stone-Sweet. Oxford: Oxford University Press, 2002.

Stone-Sweet, Alec, and Thomas L Brunell. "The European Court and the National Courts: A Statistical Analysis of Preliminary References 1961–1995." *Journal of European Public Policy* 5 (1998): 66–97.

"The European Court, National Judges, and Legal Integration: A Researcher's Guide to the Data Set on Preliminary References in Ec Law 1958–98." *European Law Journal* 6 2 (2000): 117–27.

Teschner, Julia. "No Longer on Europe's Europhiles? Euroscepticism in Germany in the 1990s." *European Integration* 22 (2000): 59–86.

Thomas, Nick. *Protest Movements in 1960s West Germany: A Social History of Dissent and Democracy*. Oxford; New York: Berg, 2003.

Thränhardt, Dietrich. *Geschichte Der Bundesrepublik Deutschland*. Frankfurt am Main: Suhrkamp Verlag, 1996.

Thym, Daniel. "The European Constitution: Notes on the National Meeting of German Public Law Assistants." *German Law Journal* 6 4 (2005): 793–803.

Tomuschat, Christian. "Alle Guten Dinge Sind Iii? Zur Diskussion Um Die Solange-Rechtsprechung Des Bverfg." *Europarecht* 25 4 (1990): 340–61.

Vanke, Jeffrey. "Consensus for Integration: Public Opinion and European Integration in the Federl Republic, 1945–1966." *Die Bundesrepublik Deutschland Und Die Europäische Einihung 1949–2000: Politische Akteure, Gesellschaftliche Kräfte Und Internationale Erfahrungen: Festschrift Für Wolf D Gruner Zum 60. Geburtstag*. Eds. Konig, Marieke and Matthias Schulz. Stuttgart: Franz Steiner Verlag, 2004. 327–40.

Vauchez, Antoine. "The Transnational Politics of Judicialization. Van Gend En Loos and the Making of Eu Polity." *European Law Journal* 16 1 (2010): 1–28.

Verdroß, Alfred. "Zum Problem Der Völkerrechtlichen Grundnorm." *Rechtsfragen Der Internationalen Organisation, Festschrift Für Hans Wehberg Zu Seinem 70. Geburtstag.* Eds. Schätzel, Walter and Hans-Jürgen Schlochauer. Frankfurt am Main: Vittorio Klostermann, 1956. 385–94.

Vogel, Klaus. *Die Verfassungsentscheidung Des Grundgesetzes Für Eine Internationale Zusammenarbeit: Ein Diskussionsbeitrag Zu Einer Frage Der Staatstheorie Sowie Des Geltenden Deutschen Staatsrechts.* Recht Und Staat in Geschichte Und Gegenwart. Tübingen: Mohr, 1964.

Von Bogdany, Armin. "A Bird's Eye View on the Science of European Law: Structures, Debates and Development Prospects of Basic Research on the Law of the European Union in a German Perspective." *European Law Journal* 6 3 (2000): 30.

von der Groeben, Hans. "Über Das Problem Der Grundrechte in Der Europäischen Gemeinschaft." *Probleme Der Europäischen Rechts: Festschrift Für Walter Hallstein Zu Seinem 65 Geburtstag.* Eds. Caemmerer, Ernst, Hans-Jürgen Schlochauer and Ernst Steindorff. Frankfurt am Main: Vittorio Klosterman, 1966. 226–47.

von Doemming, Klaus-Berto, Rudolf Werner Füsslein, and Werner Matz. "Entstehungsgeschichte Der Artikel Des Grundgesetzes Im Auftrage Der Abwicklungsstelle Des Parlamentarischen Rates Und Des Bundesministers Des Innerns Auf Grund Der Verhandlungen Des Parlamentarischen Rates." *Jahrbuch des Öffentlichen Rechts der Gegenwart* 1 1 (1951): 222–35.

von Meibom, Hans Peter. "Beiträge Zum Europarecht." *Neue Juristische Wochenschrift* 11 (1965): 465–7.

Weatherill, Stephen. *Law and Integration in the European Union.* Clarendon Law Series. Oxford; New York: Clarendon Press; Oxford University Press, 1995.

Weatherill, Stephen, and PR Beaumont. *Eu Law.* 3rd ed. London: Penguin, 1999.

Weber, Max. *Schriften Zur Sozialgeschichte Und Politik.* Stuttgart: Reclam, 1997.

Weiler, JHH. "Community, Member States and European Integration: Is the Law Relevant?" *The European Community: Past, Present and Future.* Ed. Tsoukalis, Loukas. Oxford: Blackwell, 1983. 39–56.

The Constitution of Europe – "Do the New Clothes Have an Emperor?" and Other Essays on European Integration. Cambridge: Cambridge University Press, 1999.

Weiler, JHH, and Ulrich Haltern. "Constitutional or International? The Foundations of the Community Legal Order and the Question of Judicial Kompetenz-Kompetenz." *The European Courts and National Courts – Doctrine and Jurisprudence: Legal Change in Its Social Context.* Eds. Slaughter, Anne-Marie, Alex Stone-Sweet and JHH Weiler. Oxford: Hart Publishing, 1998. 331–64.

Weiler, Joseph. *The Constitution of Europe: "Do the New Clothes Have an Emperor?" and Other Essays on European Integration.* Cambridge; New York: Cambridge University Press, 1999.

Wengler, Wilhelm. "Aus Wissenschaft Und Praxis: Grundrechtsminimum Und Equivalenz Der Grundrechtsschutzsysteme." *Juristen-Zeitung* 10 (1968): 327–9.

Wittmann, Rebecca. *Beyond Justice: The Auschwitz Trial.* Cambridge, Mass.: Harvard University Press, 2005.

Zimmerman, Benedict, and Michael Werner. "Beyond Comparison: Histoire Croisee and the Challenge of Reflexivity." *History and Theory* 45 (2006): 30–50.

Zuleeg, Manfred. "Fundamental Rights and the Law of the European Communities." *Common Market Law Review* 8 (1971): 446–61.

Index

Made in the USA
Middletown, DE
03 November 2016